Galbert of Bruges and the Historiography of Medieval Flanders

GALBERT OF BRUGES AND THE HISTORIOGRAPHY OF MEDIEVAL FLANDERS

Edited by
Jeff Rider and Alan V. Murray

THE CATHOLIC UNIVERSITY OF
AMERICA PRESS • WASHINGTON, D.C.

The paper used in this publication meets the minimum requirements of American National Standards for Information Science—Permanence of Paper for Printed Library Materials, ANSI Z39.48-1984.

∞

LIBRARY OF CONGRESS CATALOGING-IN-PUBLICATION DATA
Galbert of Bruges and the historiography of medieval Flanders /
edited by Jeff Rider and Alan V. Murray.
p. cm.
Includes bibliographical references and index.
ISBN 978-0-8132-1719-2 (pbk. : alk. paper) 1. Galbert, de Bruges, d. 1134. De multro, traditione, et occisione gloriosi Karoli comitis Flandriarum—Congresses. 2. Flanders—Historiography—Congresses. 3. Charles, Count of Flanders, d. 1127—Death and burial—Congresses. I. Rider, Jeff, 1954– II. Murray, Alan V. III. Title.
DH801.F46G35 2009
949.3′101092—dc22 2009013073

CONTENTS

ACKNOWLEDGMENTS

The research and editorial work for this volume was supported by a grant from the Thomas and Catharine McMahon Memorial Fund of the Department of Romance Languages and Literatures of Wesleyan University and by both project and travel grants from the Office of Academic Affairs of that university. The publication of this volume was made possible thanks to a further grant from the Thomas and Catharine McMahon Memorial Fund. We are profoundly grateful for this assistance. We would also like to thank Mariah Klaneski of Wesleyan University's Academic Media Studio for her help in preparing the maps preceding the Introduction to this volume.

ABBREVIATIONS

Actes	*Actes des Comtes de Flandre 1071–1128,* ed. Fernand Vercauteren (Bruxelles, 1938).
CC CM	Corpus Christianorum, Continuatio Mediaeualis
Galbert	Galbertus notarius Brugensis, *De multro, traditione, et occisione gloriosi Karoli comitis Flandriarum,* ed. Jeff Rider, CC CM 131 (Turnhout, 1994).
Herman	"Hermanni liber de restauratione monasterii sancti Martini Tornacensis," ed. Georg Waitz, MGH SS 14 (Hanover, 1883), 274–317.
MGH SS	Monumenta Germaniae Historica, Scriptores
PL	Patrologia Latina
Rider, *God's Scribe*	Jeff Rider, *God's Scribe: The Historiographical Art of Galbert of Bruges* (Washington, DC, 2001).
Suger	Suger, *Vie de Louis VI, Le Gros,* ed. and French trans. Henri Waquet (Paris, 1929).
trans.	*The Murder of Charles the Good, Count of Flanders by Galbert of Bruges,* trans. J. B. Ross, Records of Civilization, Sources and Studies 61 (New York, 1959).
Walter	Walterus Tervanensis, "Vita Karoli comitis Flandrię," in *Walteri archidiaconi Tervanensis Vita Karoli comitis Flandrię et Vita domni Ioannis Morinensis episcopi,* ed. Jeff Rider, CC CM 217 (Turnhout, 2006), 1–79.
Warlop	Ernest Warlop, *The Flemish Nobility before 1300,* trans. J. B. Ross and H. Vandermoere, 2 vols., 4 parts (Kortrijk, 1975–1976).

All biblical citations are from *Biblia sacra iuxta vulgatam versionem,* adiuvantibus Bonifatio Fischer et al., 2nd ed., 2 vols. (Stuttgart, 1975); translations from *The New Oxford Annotated Bible,* ed. Herbert G. May and Bruce M. Metzger (Oxford, 1973).

THE COUNTY OF FLANDERS C.1127

ECCLESIASTICAL

- - - - - - Borders of the Dioceses
——— Rivers
† Episcopal Seats

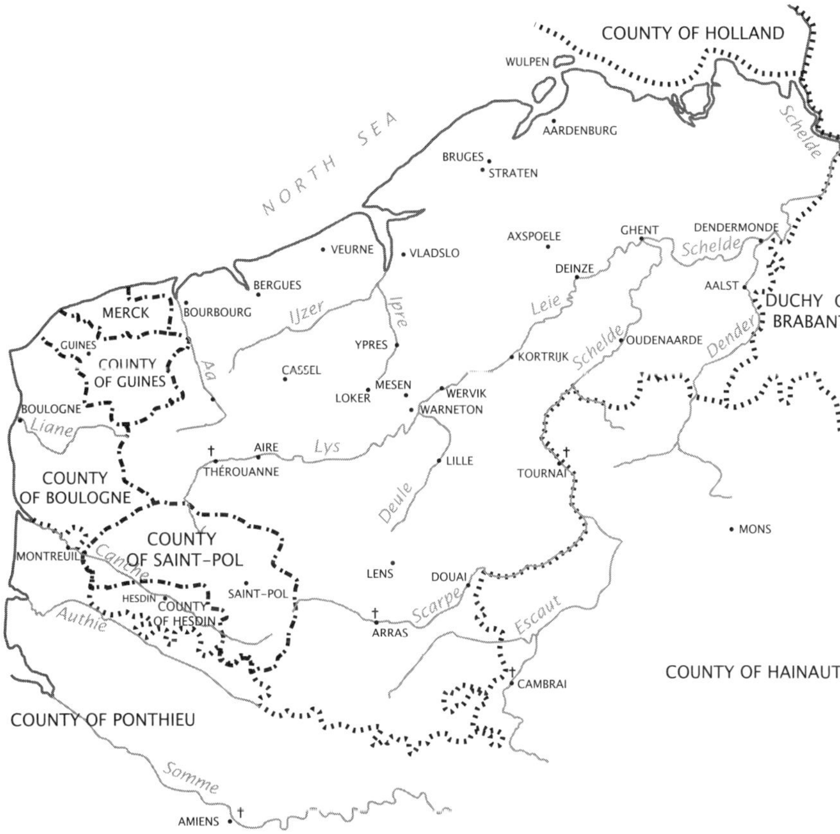

THE COUNTY OF FLANDERS C.1127

POLITICAL

- Borders of Dependent Counties
- Borders of the County of Flanders
- Rivers
- † Episcopal Seats

Galbert of Bruges and the Historiography of Medieval Flanders

Introduction

JEFF RIDER & ALAN V. MURRAY

The *De multro, traditione, et occisione gloriosi Karoli comitis Flandriarum* (The Murder, Betrayal and Killing of the Glorious Charles, Count of Flanders) by Galbert of Bruges is an eyewitness account of the assassination of Charles "the Good," count of Flanders, while he was at prayer in his castral church of Saint Donatian in Bruges on March 2, 1127, and of the turbulent events leading up to the murder and through to the installation of Thierry of Alsace as count of Flanders in summer 1128. Charles's assassination was one of the most stunning events of the early twelfth century, and it affected the balance of power between England, France, and the Empire and the commercial life of the most prosperous regions of Europe. Because Charles had no children and had not named a successor, his death led to a prolonged struggle for the countship between various candidates. The king of France, Louis VI, was initially successful in exercising his rights as overlord of the county of Flanders and chose William Clito, the son of Duke Robert Curthose of Normandy and nephew of Henry I of England, to be the new count, but this success cost him and the new count so much in promises and concessions to the Flemish nobility and bourgeoisie that William's position was precarious from the start. Henry I's enmity toward the new count had a chilling effect on the important commercial relations between the cities of Flanders and England, and the loss of revenues, coupled with a series of unpopular actions taken by William, led to rising discontent with the new count in urban centers such as Lille, Bruges, Saint-Omer, and Ghent. By March 1128, William was no longer in control of the county, and by the end of July, he lay dead from a wound suffered while besieging his rival, Thierry. The favorite of the bourgeoisie, Thierry quickly imposed himself as count, a position he held for forty years, until his death in 1168.

The people and events surrounding Charles's assassination are uniquely well-documented in Galbert's chronicle. He was a functionary in the count's central administration, was well-acquainted with Charles and many of the other actors in this drama, was an eyewitness to many of the events he relates, and was exceptionally well-positioned to gather information about others. Formally bizarre (it is written in the form of a journal, the only one we have from Europe in the twelfth century), and almost equally offensive to all its potential audiences, Galbert's unique and eccentric text slept through the Middle Ages locked, probably, in some chest in Bruges. No medieval copies of it survive, and there is no reason to believe that more than one copy of it ever existed during the period.[1] The chronicle was "discovered," and praised, by the Flemish historian Jacob de Meyer in the middle of the sixteenth century,[2] and it has been a well-known and much-used historical source for the legal, political, social, architectural, and geographical history of Flanders since then. In the last fifty years, it has been one of the most frequently studied and anthologized sources for the history of northern Europe in the early twelfth century. Indeed, it is rare to find a contemporary historian of the Middle Ages who has not read it.

The success of the chronicle over several centuries is probably due, first and foremost, to its "popular" character. The principal audience Galbert had in mind when he wrote the *De multro* seems to have been his fellow townspeople of Bruges rather than the learned, well-read, Latinate, largely ecclesiastical audience for whom histories and saints' lives were normally written at the time. The *De multro* is essentially, primarily, and predominantly the work of a townsman writing for his fellow townspeople—a minimally educated, shallowly read, predominantly Flemish-speaking, largely secular group of people—a great many of whom he knew. When Galbert wrote, that is, he undoubtedly had a clear idea of the people for whom he was writing, could see their faces in his mind, could imagine them reading or hearing what he had written, could imagine their reactions; and the people he imagined were not, or at least not mostly, bishops, abbots, archdeacons, schoolmasters, cathedral clergy, monks, kings, counts, or barons, but notaries and clerks, town knights, and the more important townspeople—

1. See Jeff Rider, "Galbert of Bruges' 'Journal': From Medieval Flop to Modern Bestseller," in *Verhalende Bronnen: Repertoriering, Editie en Commercialisiering,* ed. Ludo Milis, Véronique Lambert, and A. Kelders, Studia Historica Gandensia: Publicaties van de Opleiding Geschiedenis van de Universiteit Gent 283 (Ghent, 1996), 67–93.

2. See Jacob de Meyer (Jacobus Meyerus), *Commentarii sive Annales rerum Flandricarum libri XVII* (Antwerp, 1561), 40r. This work was completed and published after his death by his nephew Antoine de Meyer.

minor officials, employees, and small businesspeople, so to speak, rather than people who directed and managed the major institutions of the day.[3]

When Galbert's contemporary Walter, an archdeacon of Thérouanne in southern Flanders, wrote his lives of Count Charles and Bishop John of Thérouanne, he undoubtedly had an equally clear idea of his immediate audience, could likewise see their faces in his mind, could imagine them reading or hearing what he had written, could imagine their reactions. As he tells us in the prologues to these works, however, the faces he saw when he wrote were those of "John, bishop of the holy church of Thérouanne, . . . Lord Goscelin, the deacon, and our brothers," and of "many of the brothers" of that church.[4] These lives are essentially, primarily, and predominantly the work of a member of a bishop's household writing for the other members of the household, all of whom he knew. Walter was undoubtedly more familiar with the genres and generic conventions of historiography and hagiography than was Galbert; moreover, his "Latin," as Alphonse Wauters noted, "was better,"[5] but the fundamental differences between Walter's lives and Galbert's *De multro* were not due, at least not due mainly, we believe, to Galbert's weaker grasp of Latin or Walter's greater familiarity with literary and rhetorical convention, but were due rather to the different audiences for whom the two authors imagined they were writing. Galbert's audience would have found Walter's lives precious and long-winded; Walter's audience would have found the *De multro* strange and inelegant. It is true that Galbert wrote in Latin, but this was most

3. Professor Van Caenegem has already observed that the public who would have most appreciated Galbert's work was "the common folk, the general public, that long enjoyed the tales of Reinard the Fox and was embodied in Uilenspiegel, the public that laughed up its sleeve when the prince and the notables—count, noble and clerk—were unmasked in all their smallness, avidity, and ambition" (Raoul C. Van Caenegem, *Galbert van Brugge en het Recht,* Mededelingen van de Koninklijke Academie voor Wetenschappen, Letteren en Schone Kunsten van België, Klasse der Letteren 40/1 [Brussels, 1978], 6; cf. idem, in Galbert of Bruges, *Le Meurtre de Charles le Bon,* trans. J. Gengoux, gen. ed. Raoul C. Van Caenegem [Antwerp, 1978], 62; and idem, "Galbert of Bruges on Serfdom, Prosecution of Crime, and Constitutionalism (1127–28)," in *Law, Custom and the Social Fabric in Medieval Europe: Essays in Honor of Bryce Lyon,* ed. Bernard Bachrach and David Nicholas, Studies in Medieval Culture 28 [Kalamazoo, Mich., 1990], 92). All translations are ours unless otherwise noted. We would like to thank Professor Walter Simons of Dartmouth College for his help with this particular translation.

4. "Iohanni, sanctę Teruannensis ęcclesię episcopo, . . . domni Gocelini decani et fratrum nostrorum" (Walter, [1], 3, 20/21); "nonnulli ex fratribus" (Walteri Tervanensis, "Vita Domni Ioannis Morinensis episcopi," [1], 36, in Walteri archidiaconi Tervanensis, *Vita Karoli comitis Flandrię et Vita Domni Ioannis Morinensis Episcopi,* ed. Jeff Rider, CC CM 217 (Turnhout, 2006).

5. Alphonse Wauters, "Gualbert," in *Biographie nationale,* 34 vols. (Brussels, 1866–1968), 8: 393.

probably because the weight of cultural tradition and the apparently complete lack of writing in Flemish at the time made it inconceivable to do otherwise. He also seems to have been reasonably well-educated, and some of the stylistic gambols and flourishes he had been taught in school or found in his occasional readings naturally came back to him as he wrote. Although the faces he saw when he wrote were those of his fellow townspeople, there are signs in the work that indicate that he hoped it would be read beyond Bruges and even beyond Flemish-speaking Flanders; perhaps somewhere in the back of his mind he hoped for some success in even the more sophisticated literary circles that formed the readiest audiences for a work in Latin. But for Galbert, Latin was first and foremost a working language, the language in which one wrote, rather than the vessel of a literary tradition. His work is written in Latin, but it does not belong to the Latinate tradition. It is a secular, popular work, written when one did not yet write in secular, popular languages.

It is this essentially popular character of the *De multro* that is responsible for its success over the following centuries and into the present. Galbert probably felt quite alienated from the other townspeople of Bruges when he finished his initial draft of his record of the events of 1128, and he appears to have put the whole thing away without ever going back and giving it a final revision or "publishing" it, since he felt that the people for whom he had first and foremost written it would not want to hear or read it.[6] When the *De multro* resurfaced in the fifteenth century, however, it was not in the context of a Latin history or a compilation of saints' lives. The earliest surviving evidence of its existence is instead a brief French résumé of Galbert's account of the servile and adulterous origins and ultimate fate of the family behind Charles's assassination, which Roland or Antoine de Baenst, members of one of the most important families of Flanders, with implantations in both Ghent and Bruges, copied into a family record book at the end of the fifteenth century.[7] When the *De multro* first reappeared, that is, it was in precisely the milieu for which it had been written three centuries earlier, that of important townspeople, and the part of the chronicle that one of

6. See Rider, *God's Scribe,* 192–98.

7. This résumé is found on folios 37r–37v of manuscript 442 of the Stadsbibliotheek in Bruges. The manuscript is described by Pierre-Joseph Laude, *Catalogue méthodique, descriptif et analytique des manuscrits de la Bibliothèque publique de Bruges* (Bruges, 1859), 385–86, no. 442, and Alphonse de Poorter, *Catalogue des manuscrits de la Bibliothèque publique de la ville de Bruges,* Catalogue général des manuscrits des bibliothèques de Belgique 2 (Gembloux, 1934), 500–501, no. 442. The résumé is printed in Galbert, Appendix 1, 173–75.

the De Baenst family deemed worth recopying is not the tale of the saintly martyr or its account of the legal and constitutional issues surrounding the choice of the count of Flanders, but the town gossip about the Erembalds and the ironic story of how their social-climbing was punished.

This same "popular" appreciation of Galbert's work may be seen in some of the earlier scholarly encounters with it as well. As was mentioned above, Jacob de Meyer, the first historian to cite the *De multro,* compared it favorably to Walter of Thérouanne's *Vita Karoli,* writing that "a certain monk [!] named Walter wrote about the life and death of this Charles for John, the bishop of Thérouanne; but Galbert of Bruges did so better and in more detail."[8] When De Meyer wrote that Galbert had written "better" than Walter, he was referring presumably not to Galbert's Latin, but to his ability to tell a story, to bring the events he recorded to life. He was, that is, saying that he responded more immediately and directly to Galbert's work than to Walter's, was more easily and quickly caught up in it. The complete text of the *De multro* was first printed in 1668 by the Bollandists Godefroid Henschen and Daniel Van Papenbroeck, who praised Galbert for the "supreme diligence" with which he observed and recorded the events of 1127–28,[9] and in the introduction to his 1776 reedition of the Bollandists' text, the Danish historian Jacob Langebek wrote that he recommended the *De multro* to his readers for its

> accuracy and . . . the richness of its information. . . . Besides the history of Charles' assassination and the events following it up to the restoration of peace in Flanders under Thierry, [Galbert] recounts clearly and pleasantly various interesting things, otherwise unknown, concerning the rites of homage in this period, its forms of punishment and arms, its instruments of war, the ways of besieging and assaulting a town, clothing, and other things. Indeed, Galbert can and should be numbered, not among the hagiographical authors, but among the good, skillful, and accurate historical writers of the twelfth century.[10]

Langebek clearly appreciated the historical value of all the information Galbert's chronicle provides, but he also seems to have just liked it as a work of literature, for Galbert's ability to tell a story "clearly and pleas-

8. De Meyer, *Commentarii,* f. 40r.

9. Godefroid Henschen and Daniel Van Papenbroeck, "De B. Carolo bono, comite Flandriae, martyre," in *Acta Sanctorum,* 1 March (Antwerp, 1668), 153C.

10. Galbert of Bruges, "Historia vitae et passionis S. Caroli Com. Flandr. Auctore Galberto notario," ed. Jacob Langebek, in *Scriptores rerum Danicorum medii aevi* 4 (1776; rpt. Nendeln, 1969), 110–11.

antly," and concludes that Galbert was a "good, skillful" writer as well as an accurate one.

Again in the nineteenth century, in the introduction to his 1856 reedition of the Bollandists' text for the *Monumenta Germaniae Historica,* Rudolf Köpke praised Galbert for an "accuracy . . . almost unmatched" and observed that he "composed a book, even though he was much troubled by hope, fear and sadness, that grips and troubles the reader no less."[11] Köpke, too, was "gripped" by the writing and had an immediate response to it, as well as appreciating its "accuracy." Thirty years later, Alphonse Wauters observed that Galbert's

> work is above all interesting for the lively and original information it provides about the role played by the burghers in Flanders at that time. Far superior to his contemporary, Walter, whose Latin was better, he is as precise but more concise, more lively, more endearing. The "Passion of Count Charles of Flanders," *Passio Karoli comitis Flandriae,* surely constitutes the best historical account of the time. . . . Galbert's vivacious narrative, his exact knowledge of the setting, and his judicious observations make it a precious journal.[12]

Like the other scholars already cited, Wauters simply liked the way Galbert wrote. The story he told was concise, lively, and endearing, as well as exact and well-informed. It was a good read.

The popular character of the *De multro* has been confirmed by its success in translation over the last two centuries. François Guizot published a French translation of it in 1825,[13] which proved popular enough for an abridged version of it to be published in the Bibliothèque des chemins de fer, a series of books intended to be sold to travelers in train stations![14] Another French translation was published in 1830 by Joseph-Octave Delepierre and Jean Perneel, and was successful enough to be reprinted twice.[15] The chronicle's success in translation continued unabated in the twentieth

11. R. Köpke, "Vita Karoli comitis Flandriae," in *Monumenta Germaniae Historica, Scriptores,* 38 vols. (Hannover, 1826–2000), 12:533–34.

12. Wauters, "Gualbert," c. 393.

13. Galbert of Bruges, "Vie de Charles le Bon, Comte de Flandre," trans. François P. G. Guizot, in *Collection des mémoires relatifs à l'histoire de France depuis la fondation de la monarchie française jusqu'au XIIIe siècle,* 8 (Paris, 1825), 237–433.

14. Galbert of Bruges, *La Légende du bienheureux Charles le Bon, Comte de Flandre: Récit du XIIe siècle,* Bibliothèque des chemins de fer, 2 sér.: Histoire et Voyages (Paris, 1853).

15. Galbert of Bruges, *Histoire du règne de Charles le Bon, précédée d'un résumé de l'histoire des Flandres,* trans. Joseph-Octave Delepierre and Jean Perneel (Brussels, 1830; rpt. 1831, 1844). On this translation, see Antoon Viaene, "Galbert van Brugge in eerste moderne vertaling: Een Vlaams initiatief van archivaris Delepierre," *Biekorf* 78 (1978), 193–99.

century, thanks especially to James Bruce Ross's English translation, first published in 1959 and almost continuously in print since that time.[16] A fourth French translation of the chronicle and the first Dutch translation of it were published under the direction of Professor R. C. Van Caenegem in 1978,[17] a new paperback Dutch translation by Bert Demyttenaere appeared in 1999,[18] and a new English translation of the work is currently in preparation.

The basis of the *De multro*'s success thus stems from its being the work of a townsman writing for his fellow townspeople, a work written by a member of the "middle class" for other members of the "middle class," many of whom he knew. Not all members of this group were as talented as Galbert, of course, and one can imagine that many of them would have written absolutely dreadful accounts of the events of 1127–28; but Galbert might also have written a dreadful account of those events had he intended his work for Bishop John of Thérouanne or King Louis VI of France. Even though it is written, and written in Latin, Galbert's work retains something of the vis-à-vis of conversation—it reads as if it were addressed to a roomful of burghers—and an embeddedness in its material context that Walter's *Vita Karoli,* for example—which reads as if it were addressed to a single listener, John—mostly (but not entirely) lacks. Thanks to this quality, which stems from both Galbert's talents as a raconteur and his idea of the audience for whom he was writing, the *De multro* has made sense to most people more or less immediately ever since it was written. Nowadays it usually needs to be translated into a modern language (and was already translated into French in the fifteenth century), and some aspects of twelfth-century culture need to be explained to modern audiences, but once these impediments—which are impediments to the appreciation of any work, popular or elite, produced in a foreign culture, whether ancient or modern—are removed, most people "get it," understand Galbert, right away and see immense similarities, and comprehend the differences, between his world and theirs.

The rise of a widespread approach to all kinds of medieval texts that Nancy Partner associates with "modern scholarship," Gabrielle Spiegel

16. Galbert of Bruges, *The Murder of Charles the Good, Count of Flanders,* trans. James Bruce Ross, Records of Civilization, Sources and Studies 61 (1959; rev. ed., 1967; rpt. Medieval Academy Reprints for Teaching 12, Toronto, 1982; rpt. New York, 2005).

17. *De Moord op Karel de Goede, Dagboek van de gebeurtenissen in de jaren 1127–28,* trans. Bert Demyttenaere, gen. ed. Raoul C. Van Caenegem (Antwerp, 1978); *Le Meurtre de Charles le Bon,* trans. J. Gengoux, gen. ed. Raoul C. Van Caenegem (Antwerp, 1978).

18. *De Moord op Karel de Goede,* trans. Bert Demyttenaere (Louvain, 1999).

with "positivism" and "modernism," and Roger Sherman Loomis—himself one of the leading practitioners of this approach—with "the scientific method"[19] suppressed or at least discouraged this kind of "direct response" to medieval literature, as C. S. Lewis would have put it,[20] this ability "to approach medieval histories naturally and directly," in Partner's words,[21] in many scholars from the late nineteenth to the late twentieth century. This "modern," "positivistic," "scientific" method of reading emerged around the 1870s and probably remained the most common way of reading medieval texts until around 1970.[22] It did not focus on the qualities of the texts themselves; it developed its impressive critical and philological skills not in order to read the texts more sensitively, but in order to discover the "reality" it projected "behind" them. It did not, moreover, see any inherent link between this reality and the texts' witness to it: the link was arbitrary, accidental; the reality was immutable, existed independently of its representation, and could have been transmitted by an infinite number of writers in an infinite number of ways. Hence the complaints about the inattention, inaccuracy, or ineptitude of the medieval historians who were often not up to the task of describing the events of their times or of the medieval authors who "garbled" the oral traditions behind their stories. The scientific method of reading came to texts with the desire to create global schemata, to paint a comprehensive picture of the political, intellectual, or anthropological reality of which each text offered only a local and imperfect glimpse, and it did not hesitate to mine them for the jewels of "fact" they contained concerning the reality behind them.

19. Nancy Partner, *Serious Entertainments: The Writing of History in Twelfth-Century England* (Chicago, 1977), 4; Gabrielle Spiegel, "History as Enlightenment: Suger and the Mos Anagogicus," in *The Past as Text: The Theory and Practice of Medieval Historiography* (Baltimore, Md., 1997), 165; cf. idem, "In the Mirror's Eye: The Writing of Medieval History in North America," in *The Past as Text,* 63; Roger Sherman Loomis, "The Scientific Method in Arthurian Studies," *Studi Medievali* 3 (1930), 288–300. On Loomis, see Jeff Rider, "Roger Sherman Loomis: Medievalism as Anti-Modernism," *Studies in Medievalism* 6 (1994), 143–162.

20. C. S. Lewis, "The Anthropological Approach," in *English and Medieval Studies Presented to J. R. R. Tolkien on the Occasion of his Seventieth Birthday,* ed. Norman Davis and C. L. Wrenn (London, 1962), 226–27.

21. Partner, *Serious Entertainments,* 4.

22. Reporting a remark concerning medieval British history made in 1771, Partner writes: "Some 570 years earlier, William of Newburgh had been of much the same opinion; one hundred years later, such an opinion would be held in utter contempt" (*Serious Entertainments,* 3–4). For Spiegel, the key dates in the installation of this approach to medieval texts are 1877, when Henry Adams was appointed to teach the Middle Ages at Harvard, and 1910, when Charles Homer Haskins was appointed there ("In the Mirror's Eye," 61–63). Loomis arrived at Columbia in 1919, where he stayed until his retirement in 1958.

Thanks to a change in our own *mentalité* and the work of a great many historians and literary scholars over the last thirty-five years, we have begun to relearn how to read medieval stories, fictional and historical, "naturally and directly," to use them as they were meant to be used, to focus on their performative, rhetorical qualities and art, to liberate them from the grip of scientific readings. Indeed, scientific readings now seem like something of a historical aberration, a temporary forgetting of the essentially discursive or rhetorical nature of these texts, which led to an indirect and unnatural reading of them that, in its quest for facts they were only secondarily or indirectly intended to relate, paid scant attention to their abundant prima facie evidence concerning their rhetorical goals and the discursive traditions in which they were written.

The history of the *De multro*'s reception offers an exemplary illustration of the flow and ebb of the modernist approach to medieval histories. As we have seen above, there is substantial evidence that the chronicle's literary qualities have been appreciated continuously by a broad spectrum of European and North American readers since the fifteenth century, that most people over the last five hundred years have responded to it naturally and directly, and that many readers continued to do so even during the reign of the modern, positivistic, scientific method of reading. It became difficult for *scholars* to do so, however, in the wake of Henri Pirenne's modern or positivistic interpretation of the *De multro* in the introduction to his edition of the text in 1891. This introduction had a profound and long-lasting effect on the way the chronicle was read for much of the twentieth century, an effect that was renewed and reinforced in 1959 by James Bruce Ross's introduction to her immensely valuable and successful translation of the text. Pirenne and Ross's image of the *De multro* as a true journal and of Galbert as a simple, honest man of the crowd, who was nonetheless an accurate, natively gifted diarist, was accepted with little dissent or modification for eighty years, and as a result the artistic and intellectual aspects of the chronicle were systematically overlooked or ignored over much of the last century by historians bent on mining it for its "facts." This of course was the fate of many medieval texts, but Galbert's chronicle suffered particularly from this tendency because its journalistic form and its author's style lent it an air of unusual transparency and simplicity. The form of the chronicle permitted historians to believe that the method and circumstances of its composition prevented Galbert from understanding the events he relates in any profound way, making any argument about them, or imposing any form on them. It permitted, even encouraged, them to think that the *De multro* is not yet a history because the material it relates has not yet been reformulated through the kind of intellectual work and reflection associated with historical writing.

The form, subject, and content of Galbert's "journal" made it perhaps *the* darling of the positivistic approach to medieval histories, and it was thus one of the last major, one might even say canonical, medieval histories to be reached by the "new wave" of historiographical studies that began flowing in the 1960s. The foundations of a new appreciation of Galbert had already been laid, however, between 1950 and 1971 in a series of studies by Paul Bonenfant, Jan Dhondt and, especially, Heinrich Sproemberg, and a new understanding of Galbert and his work has been built on those foundations in a series of studies published since the late 1970s.[23] Over the last thirty-five years, as a result, Galbert has gone from being an artless man of the crowd to being a well-trained and subtle writer as well as the first, and one of the most sophisticated, legal and political theorists of the medieval bourgeoisie. The *De multro* is now perceived as a complex and sophisticated—albeit unfinished—example of twelfth-century historiographical art that deserves our closest attention as a work of literature.

The essays collected in this volume unite studies by established scholars who have been largely responsible for radical changes in the understanding of Galbert and his chronicle since the era of Dhondt, Bonenfant, and Sproemberg with those of younger scholars who bring their own perspectives and disciplinary skills to the topic. They have emerged from different forums held over several years: a conference devoted to "Galbert van Brugge en de aanvang van de Nieuwe Tijd in de twaalfde eeuw" (Galbert of Bruges and the Beginning of Modern Times in the Twelfth Century), organized by the Institute for Cultural History of the University of Amsterdam and the university's Onderzoekschool Mediëvistiek (Research Center for Medieval Studies) in October 1999; two sessions at the International Medieval Congress in Leeds, England, in July 2001; and a session at the annual meeting of the Medieval Academy of America in New York in March 2002. With the advantage of focusing on a single, well-known, widely read, and unusually rich text, these essays serve as models of the work presently being done in various domains of medieval history and represent a significant next step in the understanding of the *De multro.*

23. For the history of twentieth-century scholarship on Galbert and his work, see Rider, *God's Scribe,* 1–9.

PART ONE

GALBERT OF BRUGES AT WORK

1

"Wonder with Fresh Wonder"

Galbert the Writer and the Genesis of the *De multro*

JEFF RIDER

Galbert was a resident of the town of Bruges and had served in the comital administration of Flanders for at least thirteen years by the time of the assassination of Count Charles in 1127. He was well-acquainted with Charles and many of the other actors in this drama; he was an eyewitness to many of the events he relates; and he was exceptionally well-positioned to gather information about others. He may have written a great deal before he began work on the *De multro* and he probably organized the chronicle journalistically right from the start because he was used to keeping a fiscal register, in which he made frequent entries recording various transactions and the days on which they occurred, as part of his work for the comital administration, and this seemed to him to be the normal way to organize information.[1] At the end of the long Introduction Galbert added to the *De multro* in the fall of 1127, he wrote: "In this account of his [Charles's] passion, the reader will find the subject divided by days and the events of those days, up to the vengeance, related at the end of this little work."[2] The degree to which Galbert carried out this intention to impose a journalistic order on his chronicle is evident in the surviving manuscripts, but has been obscured by the chapter divisions imposed on the text by its modern editors. When the Bollandists first published the *De multro* in 1658, they divided the text into 23 chapters and 191 paragraphs that bore little relation

Nova admiratione . . . admiretur (Galbert, [Prol.], 37/39; trans. 80, trans. mod.).

1. See Rider, *God's Scribe,* 20–21, 40–41, esp. n45.

2. "In hac passionis subscriptione consequenter inveniet lector distinctiones dierum et gestorum quae in ipsis facta sunt diebus usque ad vindictam subnotatam in fine opusculi" ([14], 19/22; trans. 117).

to the divisions in the manuscripts. When he reprinted the Bollandists' text in the *Monumenta Germaniae Historica* in 1856, Rudolf Köpke redivided the text into 123 chapters and again obscured Galbert's own divisions. In the manuscripts, for example, the brief prologue is followed by a single long chapter made up of the modern editorial chapters [1], 1/[12], 21. This is followed by another introductory manuscript chapter consisting of modern chapters [12], 22/[14], 25, at the end of which Galbert announces the journalistic organization of the rest of the chronicle. The next manuscript chapter is a very long one (modern chapters 15–21) devoted to the events of March 2, 1127, and the remaining manuscript chapters, up to the end of the work, are—with rare exceptions—devoted to a single day (modern chapter 22 to March 3; modern chapter 23 to March 4; modern chapter 24 to March 5; and so on). The journalistic organization of the *De multro* is thus due to a conscious decision on Galbert's part, one which he respected conscientiously throughout his work, and a substantial effort of organization and composition, but it has been obscured by Köpke's chapter divisions, which were taken over by both Pirenne and Ross. These modern editorial divisions of the work have in some cases had an unhappy influence on our understanding of Galbert's thought.

In addition to keeping a fiscal register, Galbert may also have written an occasional document or taken notes at various kinds of proceedings as part of his work.[3] He may well have enjoyed aspects of his official writing, and the pleasure he obviously took in writing his chronicle suggests he did, but he did not choose to write these documents himself, did not determine their nature and extent. He may even have written some things for himself over the years, occasional verses or poems, short literary exercises of the kind that had been required of him in school, but it seems very unlikely that he had ever intended to write and "publish" a substantial work of his own design. As a functionary, he was not supposed to write literature or history, and, had Charles not been assassinated, he would have been nothing more for us than a name in the witness lists of a couple of charters of the counts of Flanders. Nothing he wrote would ever have come down to us, and nothing other than the *De multro* has.

The existence of the *De multro* shows, however, that Galbert was capable of writing literature or history and suggests that—as is the case today—there was a substantial class or group of people (mostly men,

3. See Rider, *God's Scribe,* 27, esp. n88.

one presumes, in the early twelfth century, but probably including some women) who were sufficiently educated to do so, but who did not do so because they were not supposed to, because it was not their place to do so, because they did not have access, or at least did not have the right access, to the social (principally ecclesiastical) networks that enabled "publishing" in the early twelfth century. So why, one wonders, did Galbert decide to write the *De multro?* And why, having written the *De multro,* did he never write anything else like it?

I have argued elsewhere that the *De multro,* as it exists today, is in fact three different works written one on top of another, so to speak, all of them incomplete.[4] During the first stage of his work on the *De multro,* which stretched from about March 9 to about May 22, 1127, Galbert noted what he saw and heard on wax tablets and transferred his notes to parchment sporadically, when he had the opportunity to do so. I believe that he began, at least, to recopy these notes and put them in final form some time after May 22, and it is possible that he finished this recopying and had a final version of modern chapters 15–67 and 72–85 (although these chapters were subsequently revised, and the version of them that has come down to us does not represent the first version of the *De multro*) before the end of 1127, perhaps before September 10, the date of the first entry after the entry dated to May 22. His intention at this point seems to have been to write a chronologically ordered description of the siege, a "description according to the sequence of events . . . that occurred during the siege by common edict, or was done in the fighting, and its cause,"[5] although he eventually extended his description to include other events growing out of the assassination and siege. He seems to have thought that this sequence of events

4. See Rider, *God's Scribe,* 50–53, 142–46, 198–99.

5. "secundum rerum eventum descriptionem . . . quod in obsidione communi edicto et facto ad pugnam et ejus causam congestum est" (Galbert, [35], 39/44; trans. 164; trans. mod.). This intention is glimpsed again in modern chapter 57 (part of the manuscript entry for April 11, 1127), where Galbert interrupts his description of the execution of the traitor Bertulf to remark: "And although I may seem to have a convenient place here to recount his genealogy, nevertheless, it seems to me I should let the work I have undertaken suffice and omit such an account, for I have set out to relate the outcome of the siege and not the adulterous origin of the family of the provost and his kin" (Et quamquam locum genealogiae ejus describendae hic obtinere videar, tamen videor mihi satis operae inceptae labore sufficere et eis descriptionibus supersedere, in qua eventum obsidionis et non adulterinum exordium generationis praepositi et suorum proposui me executurum; Galbert, [57], 50/55; trans. 210). At the beginning of modern chapter 72, Galbert concludes his long digression into the history of the counts of Flanders and the Erembald family by writing that "now we should go back to the narration of events at Oudenaarde" (Revertamur ergo ad describendum in Oldenarda eventum; Galbert, [72], 1/2; trans. 240), which the digression has interrupted.

ended when "on May 22, the holy Sunday of Pentecost, the [new] count [William Clito] and the castellan Gervaise and Walter of Vladslo and the knights of Flanders who were present swore that they would preserve the peace to the best of their ability throughout the whole land of Flanders."[6]

Gallbert's decision to write this *descriptio,* even if it was intended to be nothing more than an account of the assassination, the siege, and its consequences, is remarkable. He does not seem to have written anything like this before, and he was not, as far as we can tell, asked to write it by anyone. It is noteworthy, moreover, that he appears to have been the only person in Bruges who reacted to the assassination in this way (although other accounts may have been written that are lost to us), even though there were a reasonably large number of other people in the town for whom writing was also a habitual activity and who were also capable of taking notes and writing a substantial work in Latin. Taking notes on what was going on around him and then writing them up into an ordered description was an evidently unique, or at least rare, and somewhat curious reaction to the assassination. Given the nature of the *descriptio,* it is possible that Galbert said nothing in it about the circumstances in which he began to take notes or his reasons for doing so, and there is in any case nothing in the surviving *De multro* that gives us any direct information about these things. Galbert does, however, say something about these circumstances and reasons in a couple of passages that were added to the *De multro* during the second stage of its composition.

I believe that Galbert decided to transform his work from a description of the siege to a *passio Karoli,* a description of Charles's life and death and the punishment of his assassins, sometime between May 22, 1127, and the end of that year, probably after he had finished a fair copy of at least most of the *descriptio* (the primitive version of modern chapters 15–67 and 72–85), and probably after mid-September.[7] The largest and most important change Galbert made to the work in connection with this revision was the addition of a long introduction (the modern Prol. and chapters 1–14), in which he tells us:

When I set out to describe the death of such a prince, I did not spend time on eloquent ornaments nor did I seek for just the right rhetorical effects, but only

6. "Undecimo kalendas Junii, dominica sancta Pentecostes, comes et castellanus Gervasius et Walterus ex Florerdeslo et milites Flandriae qui aderant juraverunt pacem sese pro posse suo conservaturos per totam terram Flandriarum" (Galbert, [85], 31/34; trans. 258).

7. See Rider, *God's Scribe,* 50–53, 221–25, 274n78.

the truth of things, and commended the strange outcome of his death in writing to the memory of the faithful, albeit in an arid style. Nor was there a good place or time to write when I turned my mind to this work for our place was then so disturbed by fear and anxiety that all the clergy and the people, without exception, were in immediate danger of losing both their goods and their lives. It was there, surrounded by impediments and in the narrowest confines, that I began to compose my mind, which was tossing as if it had been thrown into Euripus, and subdue it to the mode of writing. While my spirit was being taxed in this way, that little spark of charity, warmed and exercised by its fire, fully enflamed my heart's whole spiritual strength and subsequently gave my inner self, which fear had seized from the outside, enough freedom to write. I don't much care, therefore, if anyone should try to detract from or prattle against this mental study—which, constrained as I was, I have commended to your hearing and that of all the faithful in common—in any way. I am secure in the knowledge that I speak a truth known to all who suffered the same dangers with me, and I commend it to the memory of our posterity.[8]

In an addendum that was probably also added in fall 1127 to the long manuscript entry for March 17, 1127 (modern chapters 35–39), he wrote similarly:

And it should be noted that in such a great tumult of events and the burning of so many houses—set on fire by lighted arrows shot onto the roofs of the town from within the castle, and also by brigands from the outside in the hope of looting—and in the midst of so many dangers by night and so many conflicts by day, though I, Galbert, had no place for writing, I noted down on tablets a summary of events until at some point, in a longed-for moment of peace during the night or day, I could set in order the present description according to the sequence of events. And in this way, constrained as I was, I transcribed for the

8. "Tanti quidem principis mortem descripturus, non elaboravi eloquentiae ornatum seu diversorum colorum distinguere modos sed rerum veritatem solummodo exsequi, et quamquam stilo arido tamen memoriae fidelium scribendo commendavi peregrinum mortis ipsius eventum. Neque equidem locum et temporis oportunitatem, cum animum in hoc opere intenderem, habebam, quandoquidem noster locus eodem tempore sollicitabatur metu et angustia adeo ut, sine alicujus exceptione, tam clerus quam populus indifferenti periclitaretur occasu et rerum suarum et vitae. Ibi inter tot adversa et angustissimos locorum fines, cepi mentem fluctuantem et quasi in Euripo jactatam compescere et juxta scribendi modum cohibere. In qua animi mei exactione illa caritatis scintillula suo igne fota et exercitata omnes virtutes spirituales cordis funditus ignivit et subsequenter hominem meum, quem a foris timor possederat, scribendi quadam libertate donavit. Super hoc igitur mentis studio quod, in tam arto positus, vestro et omnium fidelium auditui in communi commendavi, si quis quidquam obgarrire et detrahere contendat, non multum curo. Securum enim me facit quod veritatem omnibus apertam qui mecum eodem percellebantur periculo loquor, et eam posteris nostris memorandam commendo" ([Prol.], 14/35; trans. 79–80, trans. mod.).

faithful what you see and read. I did not note down individual deeds because they were so numerous and so confused but noted with an intent mind only what occurred during the siege by common edict, or was done in the fighting, and its cause, and I forced myself to do this, as if unwillingly, in order to commend it to writing.[9]

These passages, we must remember, were probably written at least six months after Galbert began taking notes in March 1127 and after he had decided to transform the *descriptio* into something else, but they do suggest several things about the circumstances in which he began to take notes and his reasons for doing so.

When, in fall 1127, Galbert thought back to the circumstances in which he had begun taking notes, one of the things he remembered most clearly was the material obstacles he had faced. He had found himself "in the narrowest confines," "constrained," and had had no place where he could write, no *locum scribendi.* This probably means that he didn't have anywhere to write, but probably also more precisely that his habitual place of writing, which was presumably in the burg, or castle, of Bruges, was inaccessible or of difficult access, as were, probably, his habitual writing implements. All he had, at first, were his wax tablets, which were probably an element of his clothing, worn or carried on his belt.[10] Anyone used to writing in a particular place, such as an office or study, and on a particular computer (and perhaps even during a particular part of the day) can understand Galbert's position by imagining how difficult it would be to start writing something that promised to be long and demanding if one couldn't work in one's office or at a fixed time and had only a pencil and paper—especially with flaming arrows landing on the roofs round about.

Galbert also remembered finding it difficult to write for psychological reasons. He appears to have thought of writing as a mental exercise that required a certain amount of composure and concentration. He could not write while his mind was "tossing as if it had been thrown into Euripus" or

9. "Et notandum, quod in tanto tumultu rerum et tot domorum incendiis—quae per ignitas sagittas nocte tectis suburbiorum injecerant ab intus, et latrunculi exterius ut sibi aliquid furarentur—et inter tot noctium pericula et tot dierum certamina, cum locum scribendi ego Galbertus non haberem, summam rerum in tabulis notavi donec aliquando, noctis vel diei expectata pace, ordinarem secundum rerum eventum descriptionem praesentem. Et sic secundum quod videtis et legitis in arto positus fidelibus transcripsi. Neque quid singuli agerent prae confusione et infinitate notavi sed hoc solum intenta mente notavi quod in obsidione communi edicto et facto ad pugnam et ejus causam congestum est, atque ad hoc quasi me invitum, ut scripturae commendarem, coegi" ([35], 33/45; trans. 164, trans. mod.).

10. On Galbert's wax tablets, see Rider, *God's Scribe,* 30–34.

"taxed." Writing required "freedom" from other concerns. He had first "to compose [his] mind . . . and to subdue it to the mode of writing (scribendi modum)," before he could write. Galbert's use of the word *modum,* or mode, is interesting in this connection. There is obviously a reminiscence here of the "rhetorical effects" or, literally, "the modes of various colors" that he mentions a couple of sentences earlier, and in the next section of the chronicle he likewise refers to the "modes of eloquence" with which Nature itself endowed some uneducated people, to the degree that they were able to win cases in law courts against "those who were trained and skilled in the rhetorical art."[11] Galbert is thus using "mode" here in a learned or technical sense—writing is part of the science of letters—but the word also retains, I think, something of the sense of a mean or a measure: writing requires control, composure, reflection; it requires that one be neither too hot nor too cold, neither too fast nor too slow, neither too lively nor too dull; it requires a certain equilibrium, a certain state of mind.[12]

Both of the above-cited passages also suggest that Galbert did not begin taking notes during the week immediately following the assassination, when Bruges was relatively calm and under the control of its traditional lords, the Erembalds (who also, of course, happened to be at the heart of the assassination), but that he began to do so only after Gervaise of Praet and his forces entered Bruges on March 9 and drove Charles's assassins and their sympathizers into the fortified burg of Bruges, where they besieged them and were soon reinforced by other aristocrats from around Flanders. Writing may thus have been a habitual activity for Galbert, and his impulse to take notes on what was going on around him in early March 1127 and organize them journalistically may have been in part reflexive, but he does not appear to have begun taking notes immediately after Charles's assassination, when it would have been relatively easy to do so, so it was not an immediate reflex. He appears rather to have begun taking notes only

11. "There were many illiterate people, endowed by nature herself with the modes of eloquence and rational methods of inference and argument, whom those who were trained and skilled in the rhetorical art were not able to resist or refute" (Erant enim multi illiterati, quibus ipsa natura eloquentiae modos et rationabiles praestiterat conjecturandi et argumentandi vias, quibus nullatenus illi qui disciplinati erant et docti artem rhetoricam obviare vel avertere poterant; Galbert, [1], 28/31; trans. 84, trans. mod.).

12. I find myself wondering if Galbert is not also here making some distinction, perhaps only unconsciously, between the singular *scribendi modum,* on the one hand, and the plural "diversorum colorum . . . modos" and "eloquentiae modos," on the other. His mode is that of (simple) writing—plain, unadorned writing, which has only one mode (*modum*)—not the many modes (*modos*) of eloquence or of rhetorical coloring.

after the beginning of the siege, when it was materially and psychologically harder for him to do so than it would have been the preceding week. He does not, that is, seem to have taken notes during the week when the Erembald family continued to control Bruges and it seemed like the assassins might get away with their crime, but only when it seemed like they might not. It was something about the siege, rather than something about the assassination—or at least something about the siege coming after the assassination—that motivated him to take notes.

Galbert gives us a further indication of the reasons for which he began to take notes in March 1127 in yet another passage from the introduction he added in the fall:

> If anyone reads this dry style and this little handful of a book, therefore, I ask and admonish that he not make fun of it or condemn it but wonder with fresh wonder at what is written down and what came to pass by the ordinance of God only in our time, and learn not to despise or kill earthly rulers whom we are bound to believe were placed over us by the ordinance of God, as the apostle says: "Let every soul be subject to every power, either to the king as supreme or to governors as sent by God."[13]

The second admonition (that the reader "learn not to despise . . .") is clearly related to the hagiographical intentions motivating Galbert's transformation of the *descriptio* into the *passio,* but the first (that the reader "wonder with fresh wonder at what is written down and came to pass") does give us, I believe, insight into Galbert's initial motives. These terms—*admiratio, admirari*—had a particular resonance in the twelfth century that the modern English terms *wonder* or *marvel* only partially capture and that is conveniently set forth in the first half of Hugh of Saint Victor's *De tribus diebus.*[14]

For Hugh, two conditions are necessary to provoke *admiratio.* First, the subject must be confronted with two realities or levels of reality that are related as cause and effect, creator and created, symbolized and symbol.

13. "Rogo ergo et moneo, si cui haec stili ariditas et hujus opusculi exiguus manipulus ad manus venerit, non derideat et contemnat sed nova admiratione quae scripta sunt et Dei ordinatione congesta nostro solummodo tempore admiretur, et discat potestates terrenas non despicere vel morti tradere, quas credendum est Deo ordinante nobis esse praepositas, unde apostolus: *Omnis anima omni potestati subjecta sit, sive regi tamquam praecellenti sive ducibus tamquam a Deo missis*" (Galbert, [Prol.], 35/43; trans. 80, trans. mod.). The biblical citation is from 1 Pt 2:13–14.

14. For a broad discussion of wonder or *admiratio* in the Middle Ages and the early modern period, see Caroline Walker Bynum, "Wonder," *American Historical Review* 102 (1997), 1–26.

In Hugh's terms, the visible world forms one level of reality and was created precisely to manifest another, invisible, level of reality. He begins the essay by writing that "the good Word and wise Life that created the world can be discerned by contemplating the world. But the Word itself cannot be seen; it created that it might be seen and is seen through that which it created."[15] It is in and through the visible created world, which Hugh terms a "simulacrum," that the human mind may perceive the "three *invisibilia*" of God—His power, His wisdom, and His goodness—which manifest themselves respectively in the immensity, the beauty, and the utility of His creations:

[T]he simulacra of *invisibilia* are themselves called *visibilia,* so that the simulacrum of [God's] invisible power is the immensity of the created universe, the simulacrum of [His] invisible wisdom is the beauty of the created world, and the simulacrum of [His] invisible goodness is the utility of the created world. The more closely each created thing approaches to a likeness of its Creator, the more clearly it declares its Creator. Therefore, the more perfectly a visible simulacrum retains expressed in itself the image of the divine likeness, the better it should exhibit the invisible exemplar.[16]

The second condition that is necessary to provoke *admiratio* is that the symbolized reality must be and remain obscure and incomprehensible to the subject. For Hugh this is necessarily the case, not only because the symbolized reality consists of spiritual *invisibilia,* but because of the incommensurability of the human and the divine. Human beings, who are "mortal and still subject to sin," cannot comprehend the divine power, wisdom, and goodness except in and through the visible world that was created to manifest them: "the human mind cannot be instructed about invisible things except by means of visible and familiar things, which are related to it."[17] The invisible, higher reality thus remains obscure and be-

15. "Verbum bonum et uita sapiens quae mundum fecit contemplato mundo conspicitur. Et Verbum ipsum uideri non potuit, et fecit quod uideri potuit, et uisum est per id quod fecit" (Hugh of Saint Victor, *De tribus diebus* 1.1/3, ed. Dominic Poirel, CC CM 177 [Turnhout, 2002], 3. All translations are mine unless otherwise noted.)

16. "Simulacra autem inuisibilium ipsa uisabilia dicuntur, utpote inuisibilis potentiae simulacrum est creaturarum inmensitas, inuisibilis sapientiae simulacrum est creaturarum decor, inuisibilis benignitatis simulacrum est creaturarum utilitas. Omnis autem creatura, quanto uicinius similitudini creatoris appropinquat, tanto uicinius creatorem suum declarat. Illud ergo uisibile simulacrum inuisible exemplar prius ostendere debet, quod diuinae similitudinis imaginem perfectius in se expressam retinet" (ibid. 16.548/556, p. 34).

17. "mortales, et peccato adhuc obnoxii"; "humanus animus non potest de invisibilibus erudiri, nisi per visibilia et cognita, ac cognata sibi" (Hugh of Saint Victor, *Commentariorum*

yond the mind's grasp, even when it is expressed through the world. The importance of the obscurity and incomprehensibility of the symbolized reality or level of reality in producing this effect is underlined when Hugh urges his readers to try to imagine the immensity of creation: "wonder since you are unable to do so," he writes, "but wonder all the more being unable to do so."[18] When it apprehends the divine power, wisdom, and goodness that are manifested in creation, the mind "wonders," rather than being surprised or delighted shall we say, precisely because it is unable to comprehend them.

Admiratio is brought about, then, when one apprehends—in, through, behind, and beyond a first reality or level of reality—a second reality or level of reality that one cannot comprehend but that appears to be the cause and the reference of the first one: when the human mind apprehends, in and through the works of the Creator, His power, wisdom, and goodness, it "wonders." The elements of the created world are thus properly termed "wonders" and the power, goodness, and wisdom that created them are said to be "wonderful."[19]

Thomas Aquinas refined the concept of *admiratio* in the next century, and, although Galbert's concept was undoubtedly closer to Hugh's than to Thomas's, his writings do help us better understand the idea. For Thomas, André Guindon writes, "astonishment (*admiratio*) arises from the coming together of three conditions. First, one must see an effect, discern a manifest result. Moreover, that which one perceives should be other than it is in reality. But astonishment is produced only there where the third condition is added to these first two: on the side of the object, the cause is hidden or, on the side of the subject, the cause is unknown."[20] *Admiratio* results from the occultation or ignorance of causes.

Aquinas further distinguishes two kinds of occultation resulting in two kinds of *admiratio,* which Guindon terms "subjective" and "objective."[21] In the one case, the occult cause is "natural" and therefore ultimately intelligible; such occultation produces "wonders" (*mira, admirabilia*). In the other

in hierarchiam coelestem s. Dionysii Aeropagitae 2, PL 175, col. 956B, A. Compare *De trib. dieb.* 14.488/494, 15.529/541, pp. 30–31, 33).

18. "Miraris quia deficis, sed melius deficiendo miraris" (*De trib. dieb.* 3.73, p. 8).

19. See, for example, *De trib. dieb.* 4.130/134, p. 11. God is already called "wonderful" or "marvelous" (*admirabilis*) in Is 9:6. On the tradition behind the concept of a "wonderful" God, see André Guindon, "L'émerveillement: Etude du vocabulaire de l'*admiratio* chez Thomas d'Aquin," *Eglise et Théologie* 7 (1976), 86, 89–95.

20. Guindon, "L'émerveillement," 77–78.

21. Ibid., 83–85.

case, the occult cause is supernatural, is God, and is therefore ultimately unintelligible; such occultation produces "miracles" (*miracula*). Subjective *admiratio,* in other words, is the effect produced by wonders, while objective *admiratio* is the effect produced by miracles. "We are astonished [*admiramur*] at a thing," writes Aquinas in his *Summa contra Gentiles,*

> when we see an effect without knowing the cause. And since at times one and the same cause is known to some and unknown to others, it happens that, of several who see an effect, some are astonished and some not. . . . Accordingly, a thing is wonderful absolutely when its cause is hidden absolutely. This is what we mean by a *miracle,* something, namely, that is *wonderful in itself* and not only in respect of this person or that. Now God is the cause which is absolutely hidden from every man. . . . When a finite power produces the proper effect to which it is limited, it is not a miracle although it may be wonderful to one who does not understand that power. . . . Therefore, whatever is done by the power of any creature whatsoever cannot properly be described as a miracle, although it may be wonderful to one who does not understand the power of that creature. But that which is done by the power of God, which, being infinite, is incomprehensible, is truly a miracle.[22]

Superhuman beings—demons, angels, and the like—cannot, in fact, perform miracles, which are due to God's action alone, but they can produce wonders, "natural effects whose secret escapes mortals and [therefore]

22. "*Admiramur* enim aliquid cum, effectum videntes, causam ignoramus. Et quia causa una et eadem a quibusdam interdum est cognita et a quibusdam ignota, inde contigit quod videntium simul aliquem effectum, aliqui mirantur et aliqui non mirantur. . . . Illud ergo simpliciter mirum est quod habet causam simpliciter occultam: et hoc sonat nomen *miraculi,* quod scilicet sit *de se admiration plenum,* non quoad hunc vel illum tantum. Causa autem simpliciter occulta omni homini est Deus. . . . Quando aliqua virtus finita proprium effectum operatur ad quem determinatur, non est miraculum: licet possit esse mirum alicui qui illam virtutem non comprehendit. . . . Quicquid igitur virtute cuiuscumque creaturae fiat, non potest dici miraculum proprium, etsi sit mirum virtutem illius creaturae non comprehendenti. Quod autem fit virtute divina, quae, cum sit infinita, de se incomprehensibilis est, vere miraculum est" (Thomas Aquinas, *Summa contra Gentiles* 3.101, 102 [Rome, 1934], 349–50; trans. Anton C. Pegis, *Basic Writings of Saint Thomas Aquinas,* 2 vols. [New York, 1945], 2:198–99, 199–200). In the *Summa Theologica* Thomas writes similarly that "admiration . . . arises when an effect is manifest, whereas its cause is hidden. . . . Now the cause of a manifest effect may be known to one, but unknown to others. Wherefore a thing is wonderful to one man, and not at all to others. . . . Now a miracle is so called as being full of wonder; as having a cause absolutely hidden from all: and this cause is God" (Admiratio autem consurgit, cum effecti sunt manifesti et causa occulta. . . . Potest autem causa effectus alicuius apparentis alicui esse nota, quae tamen est aliis incognita. Unde aliquid est mirum uni, quod non est mirum aliis. . . . Miraculum autem dicitur quasi admiratione plenum, quod scilicet habet causam simpliciter et omnibus occultam. Haec autem est Deus; *Summa Theologiae* 1a, q. 105, a. 7, 3 vols. [Turin, 1950], 1:500; *Summa Theologica,* trans. by Fathers of the English Dominican Province, 5 vols. [1948; rpt. Westminster, Md., 1981], 1:520).

astonish them," because they have a superior knowledge of the created universe and the laws of nature.[23] A work of human art may produce *admiratio* in a similar way, for, Aquinas notes, "the works of skillful craftsmen seem wonderful to others who do not see how the work is done."[24]

As both Hugh and Aquinas point out, *admiratio* ultimately has a heuristic or pedagogic effect.[25] *"Admiratio,"* Hugh observes in the section of his *De meditatione* devoted to meditation "on created things," "gives rise to a question, the question to investigation, the investigation to discovery," and, as we saw above, he writes that the entire "marvelous" universe was created precisely in order to bring the human mind to an apprehension of its Creator's power, wisdom, and goodness.[26] Aquinas similarly defines *admiratio* as "a certain desire to know which arises in a human being when he or she sees an effect but is ignorant of its cause or when the cause is of such a nature that it surpasses his or her thought or power of apprehension,"[27] and, in a passage that echoes Hugh's thought, he tells us that God performs miracles "to manifest His power . . . to manifest Himself to the minds of men, . . . to bring the intellectual nature to the knowledge of God."[28] For Aquinas, as Guindon observes, *admiratio* produces "a thirst for knowledge, a desire to know causes, an investigation. . . . When the human spirit discerns facts that it cannot explain, a movement begins in it, a *quaestio* which is simultaneously a flight from ignorance and a quest for truth."[29] Miracles,

23. Guindon, "L'émerveillement," 87–89.

24. "Unde et ingeniosorum artificum opera mira redduntur cum ab aliis non percipitur qualiter operantur" (*Summa contra Gentiles* 3.103, p. 353; trans. 2:203). Galbert's use of the terms *miraculum* and *mirum* seems to anticipate and illustrate the distinction Thomas makes here. In chapter 22, for example, Galbert refers to the healing—through "divine mercy (divina misericordia)"—of a lame man lying under the bier holding Charles's body as a "miracle (miraculum"; Galbert, [22], 53/60; trans. 139–40), while he says that the silver vessel Charles purchased at the fair of Ypres shortly before his death "was marvelously made so that the liquid which it held disappeared as one looked at it" (miro opere fabricata, suis spectatoribus potum quem in se continebat furabatur; Galbert, [16], 59/60; trans. 124).

25. Cf. Bynum, "Wonder," 1, 10, 25–26.

26. "Tria sunt genera meditationum: unum in creaturis, unum in scripturis, unum in moribus. . . . In primo admiratio quaestionem generat, quaestio investigationem, investigatio inventionem" (Hugh of Saint Victor, *De meditatione,* in *Six Opuscules Spirituels,* ed. and French trans. Roger Baron [Paris, 1969], 44).

27. "Est autem admiratio desiderium quoddam sciendi, quod in homine contingit ex hoc quod videt effectum et ignorat causam: vel ex hoc quod causa talis effectus excedit cognitionem aut facultatem ipsius" (*Summa Theologiae* 1a 2ae, q. 32, a. 8; 1:156–157; trans. 2:732; my trans.).

28. "Ad suae virtutis manifestationem . . . se mentibus hominum manifestet . . . ad cognitionem de Deo intellectuali naturae praebendam" (*Summa contra Gentiles* 3.99, pp. 348–349; trans. 2:197).

29. Guindon, "L'émerveillement," 78–79.

indeed the whole "wonderful" universe, are signs that are intended to draw the human mind to their occulted Cause.

Galbert, as was noted above, does not seem to have begun taking notes immediately after the assassination, but only once the siege had begun. The assassination troubled him profoundly, but, by itself at least, it was not enough to make him start taking notes. As Galbert himself tells us, taking notes and writing was hard once the siege had begun, harder than it would have been during the preceding week of relative peace between the assassination and the siege. But the siege, or at least the siege in the aftermath of the assassination, did provoke Galbert into taking notes despite the very real material and psychological obstacles he had to overcome to do so, and he appears, moreover, to have been the only person in Bruges who reacted to the siege in this way (insofar as the surviving documentation permits us to judge). There was something about the siege that made Galbert feel he had to do something, and the something he had to do was to take notes rather than run, hide, or grab a sword. There was something about the siege that made Galbert—perhaps alone of all the literate people in Bruges—want a detailed, chronologically organized record of it; he not only didn't want to forget what happened, he wanted to be able to remember it, to review it, in detail and in its temporal order. He was interested not only in first causes and final effects, but in the process by which things moved from one to the other. He evidently felt that something was happening in the course of the siege that could be and deserved to be understood and could only be understood fully as a process, as a manifold of events grasped together in a temporal order.[30] When the siege began, Galbert evidently apprehended a higher reality in, through, behind, and beyond the events unfolding around him. His *admiratio* gave rise to a *quaestio,* and the *quaestio* to an investigation that, for him, took the form of taking chronologically organized notes.

Galbert's unexampled reaction to the siege of the assassins and their accomplices in Bruges thus seems to have been motivated by *admiratio,* by a sense that he apprehended God's providence, "Dei ordinatio," in the *eventum* of the siege going on around him. His description of the beginning of this siege was undoubtedly thoroughly rewritten when he transformed the *descriptio* into the *passio,* but his sense that a divine force was driving the

30. Cf. Louis Mink, "History and Fiction as Modes of Comprehension," in idem, *Historical Understanding,* ed. Brian Fay, Eugene O. Golob, and Richard T. Vann (Ithaca, N.Y., 1987), 42–60.

events is still patent in the surviving text and was perhaps even emphasized in the process of revision. "On March 7, Monday," he writes,

God unsheathed the swords of divine punishment against the enemies of His Church, and He moved the heart of a certain knight Gervaise to undertake vengeance more forcefully and quickly than was thought possible at that time. . . . It would take too long to tell with what sorrow and fear those traitors were afflicted [when Gervaise's first attacks were successful] and, on the other hand, with what joy all the other exulted because now both sides knew that God himself had begun his vengeance impartially. . . . Our burghers, on hearing that God had begun the vengeance so quickly, rejoiced in this knowledge . . . . In their hearts they gave thanks to God who with merciful eyes had deigned to look again upon His faithful in this place of horror and confusion, and was hastening to exterminate the wicked murderers. . . . Now they secretly sent messengers to Gervaise and his men, promising mutual faith and friendship and pledging the most faithful loyalty. In addition they swore to avenge their count and, on the following day, to admit the army of Gervaise inside the town and receive them like brothers within their defenses. I cannot tell you how joyfully Gervaise and his men, on hearing this embassy, received the words of the messengers, and rightly so, knowing that whatever they did in carrying out the vengeance had been ordained by God.[31]

The visible actors here, Gervaise, his men, the burghers of Bruges, are simply the proxies, the *simulacra,* of the true, invisible Actor whose presence Galbert apprehended in these events without comprehending it.[32] If, according to Hugh of Saint Victor, "the simulacrum of [God's] invisible power is the immensity of the created universe, the simulacrum of [His] invisible wis-

31. "Nonas Martii, feria secunda, divinae ultionis gladios evaginavit contra inimicos ecclesiae suae Deus, et commovit cor cujusdam militis Gervasii in exercendam vindictam acrius et celerius quam eo tempore aestimabatur. . . . Quanto ergo timore et dolore laborarent traditores illi, et e contra quanto gaudio exsultarent praeter eosdem omnes alii, supersedere longum erat eo quod pari intentione Deum ipsum incepisse vindictam omni ex parte intellexissent. . . . Burgenses igitur nostri, audito quod Deus vindictam tam cito incepisset, in sola conscientia gaudebant. . . . Seorsim vero gratias Deo referebant, qui misericordiae suae oculis dignabatur revisere fideles suos in loco horroris et confusionis, qui et exterminare festinabat homicidas pessimos. . . . Summiserunt autem secretos internuntios ad Gervasium et suos, componentes se fide et amicitia et fidissima securitate in invicem. Insuper conjuraverunt vindictam comitis sui et ut die subsequenti intromitterent exercitum Gervasii ad se infra suburbium et reciperent eos sicut fratres intra munitiones suas. Audita ergo legatione, Gervasius et sui quam laetiore et justiore animo susceperunt internuntiorum verba, non potero explicare, scientes dispensatum a Deo fuisse quidquid in vindicando agerent" (Galbert, [26], 1/4, 46/50; [27], 7/8, 11/13, 15/23; trans. 147, 149, 150).

32. On the literary effects of this theology of history in which God is the sole author of history, see Rider, *God's Scribe,* 131–33.

dom is the beauty of the created world, and the simulacrum of [His] invisible goodness is the utility of the created world," Galbert seems to have felt that the simulacrum of His invisible providence (*ordinatio, dispensatio*)—or what he in one place calls His "art (ars)"[33]—is the history, the *eventum,* of the created world: "what came to pass (quae . . . sunt . . . congesta)."

This sense of wonder remains the primary, driving force of Galbert's work throughout the rest of 1127 and 1128. It was probably in fall 1127, for example, that Galbert "discovered" that the biblical notion of old sins remembered and punished in the third or fourth subsequent generation could explain the fates of both Charles and the Erembalds and made the second and third additions to the entry for April 17. These additions explain that Charles, the fourth count after Robert I the Frisian, was murdered as punishment for Count Arnold III's betrayal and death in battle against Robert, who had invaded the county and eventually usurped it, despite having sworn an oath not to molest Arnold, and also explain that Hacket, the son of Erembald and brother of the provost Bertulf, was the fourth castellan of Bruges after Boldran, whom Erembald had betrayed, murdered, and replaced, so that the Erembalds, too, were being punished in the "fourth generation" for their ancestor's crimes.[34] Galbert introduces the third addition to the entry for April 17, the one that explains how the biblical notion of old sins remembered and punished in subsequent generations could explain the fates of the Erembalds as well as that of Charles, by writing: "Finally, if it were worth hearing, which it truly isn't, but must

33. Galbert, [89], 25, 27; trans. 262, 263 (translated as "strategem").

34. "In connection with this deed . . . who died for the sake of justice" (Et notandum in hoc facto . . . inter sanctos martyres suscepit; Galbert, [69], 80–[70], 12; trans. 237); and "Finally, in the fourth or third line of descent . . . '. . . those who hate me'" (Tandem si dignum esset auditu . . . ". . . *qui oderunt me"*; Galbert, [70], 27–[71], 36; trans. 238–40). On the composition of this chapter, see Rider, *God's Scribe,* 70–72. It is possible—I myself believe it likely—that Galbert's decision to transform the *descriptio* into the *passio* was at least partially motivated by a reading of Walter of Thérouanne's *Vita Karoli,* and that he was reminded of the biblical passage concerning old sins remembered and punished in subsequent generations in particular by a reading, or rereading, of the first chapter of the *Vita Karoli,* where Walter writes: "For then, when the man upon whom, second only to God, the people's welfare had until then been founded was taken from them, *the iniquities of our fathers were remembered in the sight of the Lord* [Ps 109:14; Vulgate Ps 108:14], as the prophet says, and our old sins were castigated with a new punishment, and the censure of divine judgment, which had formerly lain concealed in God's prescience, was revealed and made public" (Tunc namque secundum prophetam *in memoriam rediit iniquitas patrum nostrorum in conspectu Domini* et antiqua peccata nostra noua ceperunt ultione feriri, ut, in cuius manu post Deum hactenus constitit salus populi, eo de medio sublato, manifeste daretur intelligi, et diuini iam in publicum prodiret censura iudicii, quę prius latuerat in occulto prescientię Dei; Walter, [2], 10/16; my trans.). On Walter's possible influence on Galbert, see Rider, *God's Scribe,* 50–53, 221–25, 274n78.

be written out of wonder alone [*admiratione sola*], in the fourth or third line of descent God subsequently avenged the old treachery in the family of the traitors too by new dangers and a new kind of fall."[35]

This apprehension of God's will at work in the daily events around him and the *admiratio* it provoked are still there at the very end of the work. In the entry for July 27, 1128, Galbert writes: "On July 27, the sixth day after the Transfiguration of the Lord on Mount Tabor, the Lord deigned to bring an end in a certain manner both to what he had foreseen and to what we had suffered in this strife" through the death of William Clito in the siege of Aalst.[36] And he begins the long addendum he added to the work some time after July 29, which forms the penultimate entry of the work, by writing:

> And it should be noted that when the town of Bruges stood in such great peril that the citizens believed there was no remedy possible except through God's aid and therefore appeased God by penitence of heart, He came to their rescue with his customary dispensation. For He slew Count William by the sword of His justice. . . . Meanwhile a messenger came to us at Bruges to announce the death of Count William. On hearing the news the citizens and all of us gave thanks to God for such a great liberation of their persons and their goods. For it was a marvelous dispensation of God which arranged for that prince to die in such a way.[37]

William may have seemed to unknowing men to have died from a wound inflicted by "a footsoldier [who] rushed out from the enemy, and, piercing the palm of the count's right hand with his lance, he drove it through the middle of the arm adjacent to the hand,"[38] but Galbert knew that God

35. "Tandem si dignum esset auditu, quod vere non est, sed admiratione sola scribendum, in quarta vel tertia generis linea Deus vindicavit consequenter in genere traditorum scilicet antiquam traditionem novis periculis, novo genere praecipitationis" (Galbert, [70], 27/30; trans. 238; trans. mod.).

36. "Sexto kalendas Augusti, sexta feria post transmigrationem Domini in monte Thabor, dignabatur Dominus suae praevisionis et nostrae simul persecutionis ponere in hac seditione quadammodo finem" (Galbert, [119], 1/4; trans. 307).

37. "Et notandum, quod cum in tantis periculis Brugensium locus fuisset ut cives nullo consilio sibi posse, nisi a solo Deo, mederi credidissent et ideo cordis sacrificio Deum placassent, dispensatione solita Deus subvenit ipsis. Nam consulem Willelmum gladio sui judicii enecavit. . . . Interea apud Brugas nuncius venit qui mortem denuntiaret Willelmi consulis. Quo audito, cives et omnes nostrates Deo referebant gratias pro tanta liberatione sua et rerum suarum. Igitur mirabilis dispensatio Dei, quae hoc modo principem illum mori dispensavit" (Galbert, [120], 15/19, 28/32; trans. 308–9).

38. "peditum ab hostibus prosiliens, lancea eandem dextram consulis in palma perfigens, medium brachii, quod adjunctum manui coheserat, perfodit" (Galbert, [119], 7/10; trans. 307).

Himself had in fact killed him with the sword of His justice through a "mirabilis dispensatio" of events.[39]

Although a simulacra or an effect may produce *admiratio* in more than one person, *admiratio* is an essentially private, subjective experience (which is why a single effect may, as Aquinas notes, provoke *admiratio* in one person but not another), and the *De multro* is in fact a sort of private journal, a *journal intime,* not because of its form or its spontaneity, but because it is first and foremost a reflection, an investigation that Galbert carried out for himself, to satisfy his own curiosity. In the passage from the introduction to the *passio* that I cited at the beginning of this essay, Galbert refers to his work as a "mental study," a *mentis studium.* He uses the word *studium* only four other times in the *De multro.* In its very first sentence, he tells us that Charles ruled "at a time when the *studium* of winning for themselves the height of glory and praise through knightly deeds was thriving among the princes of whom we knew in the realms around us."[40] The word *studium* is hard to translate here in a single English word. It means "zeal," but it also means "study" in the sense of sustained application, reflection, and discipline. Galbert uses the word again in the next section of the chronicle, where he tells us that during the reign of peace instituted by Charles, his subjects resolved their conflicts in courts rather than with arms, "devising by skill and study every kind of argument for use in the courts, so that when anyone was attacked he could defend himself by the strength and eloquence of rhetoric, or when he was attacking, he might ensnare his enemy, who would be deceived by the wealth of his oratory."[41] *Studium* clearly refers here to a sustained reflection, to mental work, as opposed to the spontaneous discovery of arguments through *ingenium.* Galbert uses the word a third time in chapter 60, writing that when the assassins and their supporters had been driven into the church of Saint Donatian, the king and his men went into the dormitory abutting the church and "studi-

39. For other examples, see n. 53 below. On Galbert's concept of God, see my "The God of History: The Concept of God in the Works of Galbert of Bruges and Walter of Thérouanne (1127–1130)," in *"In Principio erat verbum." Mélanges offerts en homage à Paul Tombeur par des anciens étudiants à l'occasion de son éméritat,* ed. Benoît-Michel Tock, Textes et Etudes du Moyen Age 25 (Turnhout, 2005), 357–78.

40. "Cum inter regnorum principes, quos circa nos cognovimus, summum gloriae ac laudis sibi ascribendi studium per militiae facinora enituisset" (Galbert, [Prol.], 1/3; trans. 79, trans. mod.).

41. "omnia ingeniorum et studiorum argumenta ad placita componentes ut in virtute et eloquentia rhetoricae unusquisque se defensaret cum impetitus fuisset, vel cum hostem impeteret qua colorum varietate oratorie fucatum deciperet" (Galbert, [1], 23/26; trans. 84).

ously investigated and marked the place to pierce the church."[42] Galbert uses the word for the last time in chapter 106, where he tells us that when the citizens of Bruges received a letter from Louis VI on April 10, 1128, in which he asked them to send representatives to him at Arras so that he might negotiate a peaceful resolution to the conflict between Count William and the citizens of the several towns who had rebelled against him, "the citizens at once began to argue and deliberate about sending a reply."[43] The phrase that Ross translates as "began to argue and deliberate," *rationis et consilii studium inierunt,* is again difficult to render in English. More literally, one might translate it as: "went into a study of reason and advice." *Studium* here seems to mean a meeting, a conclave, in which a group of people think and reason together. For Galbert, then, *studium* seems above all to imply reflection, deliberation, applying the mind to something and thinking it through, and he refers to his work, most interestingly, not as a *product* of *studium,* but *as* a *studium.* His work, that is, is not a *product* of thinking things through, it *is* a thinking-things-through. Writing—at least this kind of writing—was a *studium* for Galbert and, as we saw earlier, a *modum:* it required freedom, composure, equilibrium, sustained application, discipline, reflection, and judgment. It amounted to a mental, even spiritual, exercise, and the residue, the written text, was at once a record of the mental and spiritual exercise through which Galbert had gone and a mental and spiritual exercise through which, he thought, listeners or readers might also go as they heard or read it.[44]

Galbert's decision in fall 1127 to transform the *descriptio* into a *passio Karoli* was in fact a decision to "publish" his private mental study so that others might, as he had done, "wonder with fresh wonder at what is written down and what came to pass by the ordinance of God only in our time, and learn not to despise or kill earthly rulers whom we are bound to believe were placed over us by the ordinance of God." Galbert's motives for transforming the *descriptio* into the *passio* and publishing it thus seem to have been what one might term social and charitable. The purpose of

42. "studiosius exquirerent et praesignarent locum pertundendi templum" (Galbert, [60], 28/29; trans. 218, trans. mod.).

43. "Statim cives super remittendis litteris rationis et consilii studium inierunt" (Galbert, [106], 14/15; trans. 284).

44. According to John O. Ward, later in the same century John of Salisbury referred similarly to "the activity of being a historian . . . simply as 'studium'" in his *Historia pontificalis* (John O. Ward, "Some Principles of Rhetorical Historiography in the Twelfth Century," in *Classical Rhetoric and Medieval Historiography,* ed. Ernst Breisach, Studies in Medieval Culture 19 [Kalamazoo, 1985], 107).

the new work is "to describe the death of such a great prince . . . and commend [. . .] the strange outcome of his death in writing to the memory of the faithful," to "commend" "this mental study . . . to your hearing and that of all the faithful in common," to "commend" "a truth known to all who suffered the same dangers with me . . . to the memory of our posterity." To that end, he "transcribed for the faithful what you see and read." He "noted with an intent mind only what occurred during the siege by common edict, or was done in the fighting, and its cause, and I forced myself to do this, as if unwillingly, in order to commend it to writing." The word that came to his mind again and again is "commend" (*commendare*), and it seems that Galbert thought of his work as a handing over of something to someone.

Galbert is a bit less precise about what he is handing over (the strange outcome of Charles's death,[45] his chronicle or "mental study," a truth known to all who suffered the dangers of the siege, what occurred during the siege), but he does seem to have a clear idea of the audience to whom he is handing it over: "the faithful," "you," and "all of the faithful in common," "our posterity." Although it is again not clear exactly who the "you" Galbert had in mind was, I believe that it was, in the first instance, the citizens of Bruges and, more generally, the citizens of Flanders.

There are, however, indications that Galbert also had a wider audience in at least the back of his mind. His detailed description of the scaling ladders constructed by the men of Ghent ([35], 46/54; trans. pp. 164–65), for example, was obviously intended for people who had not seen them, who had not, that is, been in Bruges on March 17–18, or at least not near the burg. This group may have included people from Bruges, but it also seems that Galbert had a more distant and larger audience in mind: all the people who would never have occasion to see scaling ladders. It was perhaps this sense of writing for an audience that was not directly implicated in the events about which he was writing that allowed Galbert to be so ironic on occasion, sharing a good laugh with the members of his distant and future audiences at the expense of the people around him. One finds examples in his account of "the barons"' casuistical justifications for accepting money from the besieged,[46] of "the knights of our place" hunting for the count's treasure, of the priest Eggard, and of the motives of the "young men of our place" when they invaded the church; in his mockery of the provost's

45. Or, in the passage cited just below, a "true and reliable account of his life and death."
46. [29], 42/58; trans. 155–56.

chamberlain, Alger; and in the critical tone in his accounts of the sacking of the castle and the church that involved many residents of Bruges.[47] This mockery of the citizens of Bruges becomes more developed in the chapters written in late spring 1128, when Galbert no longer thought that his audience was principally the citizens of Bruges.

What is perhaps most interesting and most surprising is the size of the eventual audience he seems to envision: the faithful, all the faithful in common, posterity. This is evident again when, in chapter 14, Galbert writes: "And so we, the inhabitants of Flanders, who mourn the death of such a great count and prince, ever mindful of his life, beg, admonish, and beseech you, after hearing the true and reliable account of his life and death (that is, whoever shall have heard it), to pray earnestly for the eternal glory of the life of his soul and his everlasting blessedness with the saints."[48] The "you" whom Galbert addresses here is clearly not the citizens of Bruges or Flanders, but someone living outside of Flanders or at least outside of Galbert's Flanders: other Christians throughout the world, Christians living in future times. In Galbert's mind, at least in fall 1127, his record of Charles's *passio* and its aftermath, inspired, indeed made possible, by charity, was a gift to all Christians, present and future, *in communi,* that would allow them to go through the same process of *admiratio, quaestio, investigatio,* and *inventio*—wonder, questioning, investigation, and discovery—that he had.

When he decided to convert the *descriptio* into a *passio,* then, Galbert was not trying to be original. He in fact appears to be trying to transform the *descriptio* into a conventional hagiographical text, and the aspects of his work that do seem somewhat unconventional can perhaps be attributed to amateurism and unfamiliarity with convention rather than a flouting of it.[49] He was performing "crucial ideological work," as David Van Meter has put it with respect to Walter of Thérouanne's *Vita Karoli,* trying to answer the troubling doubts that the assassination had raised about Charles's

47. [35], 25/29; trans. 163–64; [39], 19/23; trans. 172; [61], 23/28; trans. 219–20; [63], 42/52; trans. 223–24; [41], 64/83; trans. 176–77; [43], 1/7; trans. 178; [45], 7/16; trans. 182–83; [75], 31/47; trans. 244–45.

48. "Nos itaque terrae Flandriarum incolae, qui consulis et magni principis mortem deflemus, vitae ejus memores obsecramus, monemus et rogamus ut, audita vera et certa descriptione et vitae et mortis ipsius, quicumque audiveritis, deposcatis animae ejus vitae aeternae gloriam et beatitudinem cum sanctis perennem" (Galbert, [14], 14/19; trans. 117).

49. Galbert was probably not, however, entirely ignorant of the genre of the saint's life. He appears to have known Hariulf, abbot of Oudenburg (see Galbert, [114], 18; trans. 297), and had perhaps read his life of Saint Arnulf; I also think it likely that he read Walter of Thérouanne's *Vita Karoli* in fall 1127 (see note 35 above). Ross seems to suggest that he may also have known a life of Saint Maximus (trans. 95n8).

abilities as a ruler, the providential nature of history, and the divine ordainment of political authority by both showing that Charles had been a good prince, rather than a tyrant or an ineffectual one, and explaining why God had permitted this good prince to be assassinated.[50] Galbert did this work less well, or at least less professionally and efficiently, than Walter, and had the *passio* been the final version of the *De multro,* it would be little more than a rather curious example of twelfth-century hagiography, an example of what can happen when people who do not have a full grasp of the generic conventions of hagiography try to write it, valued mostly for Galbert's skills as a raconteur and, as Jacob Langebek wrote in 1776, for "the accuracy and richness of its information."[51] We should thus be thankful that several of the more important cities of Flanders rebelled against William Clito in spring 1128, that Galbert, suspecting that God was again stirring the kettle of events, again took up his stylus and began to record these new events, and that the lessons he found in these new events alienated him profoundly from his most immediate audiences, the burghers of Bruges and the citizens of Flanders, so that by the time he finished taking notes in summer 1128, he no longer felt he had an audience for his work and never went back and revised it in its entirety. I have traced the evolution of the work in spring and summer 1128 elsewhere,[52] so all I want to underline here is that the *De multro* both began and ended as an essentially private reflection driven by *admiratio,* even though for a while, in the fall, winter, and early spring of 1127–28, Galbert thought he could share his *mentis studium* with all Christians, present and future, *in communi.*

Having argued for years that the *De multro* is not a journal but a journalistically organized work of history, I would now like to argue that it is ultimately a *journal intime,* not because of its form or because it offers us Galbert's unrevised observations and impressions of what was going on

50. David Van Meter, "Eschatology and the Sanctification of the Prince in Twelfth-Century Flanders: The Case of Walter of Thérouanne's *Vita Karoli comitis Flandriae,*" *Sacris Erudiri* 35 (1995), 131. Cf. Nicolas Huyghebaert, "Galbert de Bruges," *Dictionnaire d'histoire et de géographie ecclésiastiques* 19 (Paris, 1981), 738; Walter Mohr, "Geschichtstheologische Aspekte im Werk Galberts von Brügge," in *Pascua Mediaevalia: Studies voor Prof. Dr. Jozef-Maria De Smet,* ed. R. Lievens, E. Van Mingroot, and W. Verbeke, Medievalia Lovaniensia ser. 1, Studia 10 (Leuven, 1983), 246; J. Marotta, "Teaching Medieval Narrative," in *1983 NEH Institute Resource Book for the Teaching of Medieval Civilization,* ed. Howell Chickering (Amherst, 1984), 23; and Rider, *God's Scribe,* 50–76.

51. "adcuratione et rerum ubertate" (Galbert of Bruges, "Historia vitae et passionis S. Caroli Com. Flandr. Auctore Galberto notario," ed. Jacob Langebek, in *Scriptores rerum Danicorum medii aevi* 4 [1776; rpt. Nendeln, 1969], 110; my trans.).

52. Rider, *God's Scribe,* 142–98.

around him, but because it is, first and last, Galbert's personal *mentis studium,* a text that both was and is a record of his quest to discover God's *ordinatio,* his *dispensatio* in the events he had witnessed in Flanders in 1127–28, a quest motivated, in the first instance at least and throughout, not by a desire to record events, not by a desire to garner prayers or teach a lesson, *sed admiratio sola,* but by wonder alone.[53]

The *De multro* can, of course, be read and studied for many reasons and in many ways, perhaps for even more reasons and in even more ways than most medieval texts. It is in fact difficult to grasp the *De multro* as a whole, as a single text, in part because of its journalistic form and in part because Galbert's sense of what he was writing and why underwent major changes between spring 1127 and summer 1128, and he never went back and thoroughly revised his work. What we have is an incomplete draft of a work in which bits and pieces of earlier versions are still present. I do believe, however, that the work has a certain unity insofar as it is the product of a single, albeit increasingly well-defined and sophisticated, intention and a single, albeit long-drawn-out, process. The *De multro* has a beginning, a middle, and an end, but the story it tells is that of Galbert's discovery of the meaning of the events of 1127–28, and, above all, of his discovery of historiography rather than that of the events in Flanders in 1127–28. Galbert's initial wonder produced a *quaestio* and an investigation that he conducted through the *modum scribendi,* by taking notes, arranging them chronologically, and reflecting on them, and this *studium* eventually led him to the discovery of a divine *ordinatio* in the events he had recorded that could not have been discovered in any way other than through a *studium* carried out in the *modum scribendi.* The *De multro* is held together by a sustained and increasingly sophisticated process of apprehension, study, and discovery that is both conducted through and recorded in writing. We can, of course, note many differences between Gal-

53. On the origin of historical reflection, both medieval and modern, in *admiratio,* see also Bynum, "Wonder," 1–4, 24–26, who writes that "surely what characterizes historians above all else is the capacity to be shocked by the singularity of events in a way that stimulates the search for 'significance' (a word that includes—but is not limited to—cause or explanation)" (3–4). It would be interesting to study Galbert's use of *admiratio* and related terms throughout the *De multro,* but unfortunately I can't do so here. I would, however, recommend to the reader's attention the passage discussed in Robert Stein's essay, ch. 9 in this volume (Galbert, [30], 13/19; trans. 157); and [6], 23; trans. 95; [12], 45; trans. 113; [45], 30; trans. 183; [57], 48/49; trans. 210; [63], 57; trans. 224; [73], 13; trans. 241; [81], 41; trans. 252; [83], 7/8; trans. 253; [96], 5; trans. 271; [113], 60; trans. 296; and [116], 47; trans. 303; in addition to the passages cited elsewhere in this essay.

bert's historiography and our own—most importantly, perhaps, his sense that events already had a meaning that historiography sought to discover as compared to our sense that historiography gives meaning to events. But, in the end, we still do pretty much what he did: we act as if there were a meaning to be discovered and seek to produce meaning through study and writing. For both Galbert and us, historiography renders life intelligible; he was perhaps writing to understand something, while we write to make something understandable, but the ultimate end is, I believe, similar: the production of values by which one can live and act. We may not share the values Galbert "discovered," but we recognize what he was doing and recognize how very much like us he was. The *De multro* is an unfinished draft of a work—indeed three works—of history, but it is also, and above all, the largely finished and largely unintentional autobiography of a remarkable mind and a profoundly original historiographer, and its true hero, the person with whom we identify and who draws us into the work, is not Charles, William, Thierry, God, the burghers of Bruges, or the citizens of Flanders, but Galbert himself.

PART TWO

GALBERT OF BRUGES AND THE DEVELOPMENT OF INSTITUTIONS

2

Galbert of Bruges and "Law Is Politics"

R. C. VAN CAENEGEM

Galbert of Bruges's story of the dramatic events in the county of Flanders during the years 1127 and 1128 is well known to medievalists. It has been studied for many years by, among others, legal historians, who have scanned the data on constitutional and criminal law and the law of persons.[1] In the present contribution I intend to scrutinize Galbert for the relationship between law and politics.

But first, a reminder of some facts about the *notarius* from Bruges and his narrative may not be amiss. On March 2, 1127, Charles the Good, count of Flanders, was murdered at Bruges in the church of his castle by rebellious serfs, whose influence in the country was under threat. As the count was childless, a struggle for the succession broke out among several pretenders, who all belonged to the Flemish dynasty. After various dramatic ups and downs—and the punishment of the conspirators who had the count's death on their consciences—two final pretenders were left. The first was William Clito, a grandson of William the Conqueror (who had married Mathilda, daughter of a count of Flanders) and a son of the Con-

This essay is based on a lecture given in Amsterdam on October 15, 1999, at a colloquium devoted to *Galbert van Brugge en de aanvang van de Nieuwe Tijd in de twaalfde eeuw* (Galbert of Bruges and the Beginning of Modern Times in the Twelfth Century), organized by the Institute for Cultural History of the University of Amsterdam and the Onderzoekschool Mediëvistiek (Research Center for Medieval Studies).

1. See R. C. Van Caenegem, *Galbert van Brugge en het Recht,* Mededelingen van de Koninklijke Academie voor Wetenschappen, Letteren en Schone Kunsten van België, Klasse der Letteren, 40/1 (Brussels, 1978); and R. C. Van Caenegem, "Galbert of Bruges on Serfdom, Prosecution of Crime, and Constitutionalism," in *Law, Custom, and the Social Fabric in Medieval Europe: Essays in Honor of Bryce Lyon,* ed. Bernard S. Bachrach and David Nicholas, Studies in Medieval Culture 28 (Kalamazoo, Mich., 1990), 89–112.

queror's oldest son, Duke Robert Curthose of Normandy. The latter had been ousted in 1106 from his duchy by his younger brother Henry I, king of England, and imprisoned in that country: William Clito's dream was, of course, to liberate his father and restore him to his duchy. Becoming count of Flanders would provide him with an excellent base for action. The king of France, Louis VI, also viewed this possibility with a favorable eye, since he was at loggerheads with the English monarch and saw Flanders as a welcome ally in his struggle. It was therefore understandable that, being the feudal overlord of the county (at least the part west of the Scheldt River), the king intervened in Flanders in order to introduce his candidate, William Clito, as the new count (an endeavor in which, in a first phase, he was successful).

The other important candidate was Thierry of Alsace, a grandson of the Flemish Count Robert I the Frisian (via the latter's daughter Gertrude, who had married Thierry II, duke of Upper Lotharingia). For a variety of reasons, William Clito lost the goodwill of the Flemish towns so that—with English support—Thierry saw his fortunes improve steadily until, in 1128, a real civil war broke out between the followers of William and Thierry. In the summer of that year, the military balance seemed to favor William, but in July 1128, he was wounded by a spear and died soon afterward. So the struggle for the succession was ended, and Thierry of Alsace was accepted and recognized as the new count.

Those are the events that Galbert of Bruges, who was employed in the comital chancery, recorded in a diary, which constitutes a first-rate source for the study of the law. All the more so since he was professionally trained to draft official documents and to observe precisely and put in writing accurately legal situations and transactions.

* * *

The words "law" and "politics" in the title of my paper are derived from a slogan of the School of Critical Legal Studies, which used to enjoy a great success, especially at Harvard in the 1970s and 1980s. The phrase in full ran as follows: "Law is Politics under another guise." The law, in other words, does not stand by itself, severed from politics. The School did not believe in the pretended objectivity that was above political commitment, and it was opposed to the autonomists who believe that the law consists of the observance and refining of eternal principles, which, through exegesis and logical deduction, lead to the great theories. The Critical School believed that the law can best be understood as the fruit of political change.[2] These views of Critical Legal Studies are, of course, not entirely new. The discussion was already raging in Germany in the nineteenth century: I refer to Rudolf Jhering's *Kampf ums Recht* (The Struggle for the Law).[3] Several social groups vie with each other for mastery of the law, because control of the law ensures an enormous influence on society. Hence also the discussion in Germany on the question whether legal history is *Ideengeschichte* or *Machtsgeschichte,* the history of ideas or the history of the exercise of power. Political history or cultural history? This German polemic has had a strong influence in America, as has German legal science in general. Let me refer on this point to Matthias Reimann's 1995 book, *Historische Schule und Common Law: Die deutsche Rechtswissenschaft im 19. Jahrhundert im amerikanischen Rechtsdenken* (Historical School and Common Law: German Jurisprudence in American Legal Thought in the 19th Century).[4]

When one is dealing with the theme of Law and Politics, several elements automatically come to mind. The great European codifications, for example, were the result of profound political change. In the seventeenth century, the Puritans seized power in England, and one of the points on their revolutionary program was the codification of the common law. They created a commission for that purpose, but their regime did not last long enough to realize their ambition, and the common law is still uncodified. It was pure political history.[5] The same can be said for the French codes after the Revolution. The *Ancien régime* disappeared, and so did the *ancien droit* consisting of customary, Roman, and canon law. Everything had to be eliminated, in order to make way for modern codes. The revolutionaries went to work and one project after another was concocted, but as soon as one concept was ready to be promulgated, the political climate changed and it was rejected in favor of another text that suited the new ideas better. Finally, in 1804, the *Code civil* won the day, the fruit of the new, postrevo-

2. J. M. Kelly, *A Short History of Western Legal Theory* (Oxford, 1992), 432–36, with special reference to R. M. Unger, "The Critical Legal Studies Movement," *Harvard Law Review* 96 (1982–83): 561–675.

3. Rudolf Jhering, *Kampf ums Recht* (Vienna, 1872).

4. Matthias Reimann, *Historische Schule und Common Law. Die deutsche Rechswissenschaft im 19. Jahrhundert im Amerikanischen Rechtsdenken* (Berlin, 1993).

5. The ideal was a "pocket-book code in plain man's English," from which readings could be held on Sundays in church. The chairman of the aforementioned commission of 1652 was the very erudite common lawyer Sir Matthew Hale, who dreamt of a *Corpus juris communis.* As is well known, none of these plans was realized. See J. H. Baker, *An Introduction to English Legal History,* 3rd ed. (London, 1990), 244–50.

lutionary, one could almost say counterrevolutionary, regime of Napoleon. His code is consequently a thoroughly conservative law book.[6]

Politics also played a major role in the elaboration of the *Bürgerliches Gesetzbuch* (Civil Law Book), which became operative in Germany in 1900, the last year of the nineteenth century. This BGB was based mainly on Roman law in its German form, that is, that of the *gemeines Recht* (common law) or *Pandektistenrecht* (pandectist law). This was a professorial system and mainly the work of the leading pandectist, Bernhard Windscheid. But when the National Socialist German Workers' Party (NSDAP) came to power in 1933, one of its first aims was to replace the *Bürgerliches Gesetzbuch* (the very term *bürgerlich*—civil/bourgeois—was suspect) by a *Volksgesetzbuch,* or people's law book. We find this desideratum already in the 1923 program of the NSDAP, where the party was given the task of replacing the cosmopolitan materialism of Roman law by a real *deutsches Gemeinrecht* (not the *gemeines Recht,* but a *deutsches Gemeinrecht,* a German community law). In 1933, the Akademie für Deutsches Recht (Academy for German Law) was founded with Hans Frank as director, and the elaboration of the new *Volksgesetzbuch* was started. Several projects were prepared and published, but the Nazi-code itself never became law.[7] After 1945, the political change again had an impact on the law, and Roman law, abominated by the defunct regime, was again given pride of place. I refer, *inter alia,* to Paul Koschaker's 1947 book, *Europa und das römische Recht.*[8] Afterward Helmut Coing, in the Max-Planck-Institut für Europäische Rechtsgeschichte (Max-Planck-Institute for the History of European Law), embarked on the vast enterprise of the *Handbuch der Quellen und Literatur der neueren europäischen Privatrechtsgeschichte* (A Handbook of the Sources and Literature of the New European History of Private Law), where the Roman law plays a preeminent role.[9] Coing also published a textbook of the *gemeines Recht,* as the main common element in the laws of the Euro-

6. See *inter alia,* the recent work by J. L. Halperin, *L'impossible Code civil* (Paris, 1992).

7. H. Hattenhauer, "Das NS-Volksgesetzbuch," in *Festschrift für Rudolf Gmür,* ed. A. Buschmann et al. (Bern, 1983), 255–79. On the role of Hans Frank, see C. Schudnagies, *Hans Frank. Aufstieg und Fall des NS-Juristen und Generalgouverneurs,* Rechtshistorische Reihe 67 (Frankfurt, 1989).

8. Paul Koschaker, *Europa und das römische Recht* (Munich, 1947). I possess a copy of this first edition, on poor paper, and often wonder where in Germany in 1947 the means were found to publish this paean to the role of Roman law in European history.

9. Helmut Coing, ed., *Handbuch der Quellen und Literatur der neueren europäischen Privatrechtsgeschichte,* 3 vols. (Munich, 1976–1988).

pean nations.[10] The name of Franz Wieacher should also be mentioned here. As a young scholar in the thirties, this leading legal historian, Romanist (author of an authoritative textbook on classical Roman law), and historian of modern European law had been sympathetic to the ideas of the Akademie für Deutsches Recht, whose scientific staff he joined, but after the war, in a different political landscape, he discovered the importance of Roman law. His classic *Privatrechtsgeschichte der Neuzeit* starts with an extensive chapter on the discovery and study of Justinian's law book in the later Middle Ages.[11]

Another aspect of the interplay between politics and law is, of course, the fact that legislation is, by definition, made by political leaders, kings, and assemblies, that is, political figures who act according to their own agendas and interests: legislation is by its very nature political. I shall not enter into any details, and limit myself here to mentioning the *lex comitum Flandriae* (law of the counts of Flanders) on the degradation of freemen who married unfree women,[12] and the *lex obsidionis* (law of the siege) promulgated by the leaders of the anti-Erembald camp and objected to by the people of Bruges because it ran contrary to their interests: when a burgher was arrested by one of the castellan's men, the people of Bruges shouted "that they did not intend to suffer the lordship of anyone at all,"[13] meaning they refused to submit to anybody's judgment, as it was in their own competence to punish the crime committed by their fellow citizen.[14]

Leaving aside these matters, I come now to my main theme, the political use of legal rules: the law as servant of politics, not philosophy as *ancilla theologiae* (the handmaiden of theology), but the law as *ancilla dominii* (the handmaiden of power). It often appears that the underlying motive for an appeal to legal norms can be found in a political decision or political necessity and that legal norms are used—in some cases misused—to realize that goal, or at least to give it a juridical coloring. An appeal to

10. *Europäisches Privatrecht 1500 bis 1800,* 2 vols. (Munich, 1985–89).

11. Franz Wieacker, *Privatrechtsgeschichte der Neuzeit* (Göttingen, 1952). In 1996, the Cambridge scholar Tony Weir published an English translation of the second edition (1967) of Wieacker's classic work—with an introduction by R. Zimmerman—under the title *A History of Private Law in Europe* (Oxford, 1996). It was reviewed by James O. Whitman of the Yale Law School in the *Law and History Review* 17 (1999): 400–402, where the reader will find interesting data on Wieacker's career.

12. Galbert, [25], 47/52.

13. "se nunquam velle pati dominium cujusquam" (Galbert, [59], 37; trans., 215).

14. Galbert, [59], 14/53; cf. [88], 11/23.

the law goes down well with public opinion, and it is a concession to the profound yearning for law and justice in the human soul. This political application is an improper use (one could call it manipulation) rather than an abuse of the law. It is clear that not every use of the law for a political aim can be called manipulation: the winner of a lawful election who claims his seat makes totally legitimate use of it. What I am concerned with is an appeal to legal norms, not because of the law itself or merely to safeguard a legal principle, but as a means to an end, as camouflage in order to obtain the real, political aim. When, in other words, somebody has, in a certain political situation, tolerated a particular abuse for several years, and then suddenly, in a changing political constellation, gets all worked up and indignantly demands that the law should be fully and rigorously applied, it should be clear that this concern for the restoration of the law is not caused by a love of legal principle, but that the latter is manipulated in order to achieve a political target.

* * *

I shall now present examples from Galbert's text to illustrate the ways in which feudal law, canon law, the law of evidence, criminal law, and the law concerning freedom and serfdom were all manipulated for political ends in the Flemish crisis of 1127–28. The first examples belong to feudal law, which often appears in Galbert's diary, either in the very words of his dramatis personae or in his personal reflections. However, these references undergo some striking metamorphoses in function of the changing political décor. Let us begin with the crucial question of the succession to Charles the Good. In a first stage, the French king, as feudal overlord, nominated the successor to his vassal in the absence of a direct descendant. This was done in accordance with the rules of feudalism and was accepted by the French and Flemish barons and the other Flemings. Louis VI made use of the law, which in this case suited him very well, but Clito was also politically acceptable to the Flemings. He belonged to the old comital dynasty of the county. He was likewise familiar with Flanders, where he had spent some years as a child, when he was hunted from Normandy by his wicked uncle, and the county was ready to give him a chance.

One year later, the situation had changed. Clito had made himself politically impossible, at least to the urban element and part of the nobility and the knighthood. A series of legal, political, and economic complaints were addressed to the king and to William Clito. The young count had, in particular, displeased the towns in matters of serfdom and freedom, which was a very touchy subject throughout society, but especially in the urban world. In August 1127, Clito had found one of his fugitive villeins in Lille during the yearly fair, had claimed him, and had had him put in fetters. The fugitive serf, according to the law of that time, had to be taken back to the manor where he belonged. Nevertheless, the citizens of Lille had rushed to arms and fighting had broken out. Clito and his small escort had had to withdraw, but the count had come back with a strong knightly army, had subjected the town, and had forced it to pay a fine because it had resisted his exertion of his own good right.

The new count had also displeased the towns as far as tolls and other exactions, which were associated with serfdom, were concerned. This was, for example, the case in Bruges on September 17, 1127, and in Ghent in February 1128.[15] What had happened? Clito had quitclaimed to the citizenry certain tolls that were traditionally the feudal possessions of local barons. The count had granted that revenue to the burghers, but, in so doing, he had given away what was not his to give. The exemption was unlawful, but politically expedient, as Clito needed the support of the towns, which desired nothing more ardently than to be free from tolls and exactions. However, he had violated the legal rights of his vassals, who traditionally held those incomes in fief and derived their living, at least in part, from them also. One could furthermore wonder if the towns had a right to demand this exemption, as they must have known that the count could not dispose arbitrarily of his vassals' fiefs: by abolishing the tolls, he deprived his own men without due process, without enquiry, and without the judgment of their feudal court.[16] It is clear that it was unlawful, but we understand very well the political necessity that had led the new count to do so.[17]

Another example of the manipulation of feudal law: the broken prom-

15. Galbert, [88], 1/11, and [95], 1/23.

16. Galbert speaks of "evil exactions and assaults" (exactiones pravas et infestationes, [95], 12; trans., 268, trans. mod.) committed by the castellan of Ghent, Wenemar II. This can refer to illegal tolls, rents, and annuities and to variants of the tallage, which were associated with serfdom. William Clito had done exactly the same in Bruges in April 1127, when he remitted the rent (*census*) on their houses and tolls to the citizens of Bruges, which naturally displeased the local knights who held the toll in fief. Indeed, it was not in the count's power to remit that toll without the consent of the fiefholders. So the count had to reconsider, and five months after he had remitted the toll, it was levied again. See Dirk Heirbaut, *Over lenen en families: Een studie over de vroegste geschiedenis van het zakelijke leenrecht in het graafschap Vlaanderen (ca. 1000–1305),* Verhandelingen Koninklijke Vlaamse Academie van België voor Wetenschappen en Kunsten, nieuwe reeks 2 (Brussels, 2000), 141n13.

17. On the Ghent revolt, see R. C. Van Caenegem, "The Ghent Revolt of February 1128," in *Law, History, the Low Countries and Europe,* ed. Ludo Milis et al. (London, 1994), 107–12.

ise on the relief (*relevium*).[18] Clito had paid a relief of one thousand marks to the king, in spite of the latter's sworn statement that he required no relief for Clito's recognition and was entitled to none. Flanders, so we read in chapter 121, had been unlawfully sold by the king of France.[19] The citizens of Bruges had wanted to avoid the *relevium,* as they knew full well that this entailed an open recognition of Louis VI's position as suzerain. By his anti-English policy, Clito had damaged Flemish trade with England.

He had also rejected the judicial procedure in the "constitutional court" of Ypres, where judgment might have been expected by the people (the "responsible men among the clergy and the people":[20] an echo of the theme of popular sovereignty) in a peaceful gathering at the beginning of Lent, a sacred period for the Peace of God. Clito, however, had occupied Ypres "with an armed force"[21] for which he had, of course, been reproached.[22]

All these developments had created a different political climate, and in this new light, feudal law suddenly took on a quite different complexion. The king's right to appoint a new count was rejected because, the Flemings maintained, he was not in a position to sell the county, and the Flemish counts had always been elected. Thierry, so it was said, was elevated to the comital dignity according to customary law, that is, by election and not by royal appointment. The famous relief was nothing more than a friendly gesture, a ritual "relief of arms,"[23] and the acceptance of Louis's candidate was just a beau geste toward a kinsman of the Flemish dynasty. It implied no judicial obligation, the anti-Clito camp argued in April 1128, and certainly could not neutralize the ancient tradition.[24]

Who was right in this debate on appointment versus election? In fact, Flanders had traditionally known neither nomination by the king nor election by the people, as there had been a direct line of succession from the beginning of the dynasty in the ninth century down to Baldwin VII, who had died in 1119 and whose successor Charles also belonged to the comital dynasty and could invoke a *designatio* (designation) by his predecessor. In the absence of a descendant of the deceased vassal, the nomination by the

18. Galbert, [106], 15/19; the entry is dated to April 10, 1128, so the relief must have been paid before this.

19. Galbert, [121], 14.

20. "sapientiores in clero et populo" (Galbert, [95], 27; trans., 268).

21. "manu armata" (Galbert, [95], 51; trans., 270).

22. Galbert, [95], 23/61; the "constitutional court" was supposed to be held on March 8, 1128.

23. "armatura" (Galbert, [106], 44; trans., 285).

24. Galbert, [106], 31/53.

feudal overlord in 1127 was admittedly in accordance with the rules of the feudal game, but the motif of an election had also been heard right at the start of the crisis in 1127. In his entry for March 16, 1127, only a fortnight after the murder, Galbert writes: "the countess of Holland . . . was hoping that all the barons of the siege would elect her son as count."[25] In chapter 47, dated March 20–22, 1127, we read that Louis VI convoked the barons to Arras in order to elect a count.[26] In chapter 51, dated March 27, 1127, we read that the people of Bruges and the "Flemings" (i.e., the inhabitants of the Liberty of Bruges in the restricted sense of the word: the area surrounding Bruges that was immediately dependent on it) swore an oath that they would elect a good count.[27] The election mentioned in chapter 47 is different from the election mentioned in chapter 51, for the first case involves a free choice among several candidates, whereas the second refers only to the confirmation or acceptance of a nomination made by a higher authority. On the other hand, Galbert also mentions nomination very early on. We read in chapter 34, dated March 16, 1127, that two knights maintained that the king had given the county to William of Ypres and that those who had made promises to the countess of Holland were worried.[28] Returning from the assembly summoned by Louis VI in Arras, Walter the Butler explained to the citizens of Bruges that the French and Flemish barons had "elected" Clito "on the order and advice of the king,"[29] and, somewhat later, the language is even more apodictic: "I order . . . you to accept Count William, who was recently elected and endowed with the county by the king."[30] It is, however, also made clear that the rejection of an unlawful feudal overlord was legitimate: the feudal *ius resistendi* (right of resistance) is referred to in a speech attributed to Ivan of Aalst in chapter 95, where we also hear echoes of canon law (on the election of a bishop by *populus et clerus* [the people and clergy], see Manegold of Lautenbach and Gregorian representations).[31]

The attitude of Gervase of Praet is fascinating in this context. The

25. "comitissa Hollandensis . . . [s]perabat enim omnes obsidionis principes electuros filium ejus in comitem" (Galbert, [34], 2/5; trans., 161).

26. Galbert, [47], 13/21.

27. Galbert, [51], 1/10.

28. Galbert, [36], 8/13.

29. "jussu et consilio regio, elegerunt" (Galbert, [52], 24/25; trans., 196).

30. "Praecipio . . . ut suscipiatis noviter electum comitem Willelmum et a rege comitatu donatum" (Galbert, [52], 39/42; trans., 197, trans. mod.).

31. Galbert, [95], 10/39. Manegold of Lautenbach was an Alsatian monk, whose *Liber ad Gebehardum* (1082–85) enjoyed widespread circulation because of his ideas on popular sovereignty and the right of the subjects to replace an unlawful ruler (see Van Caenegem, "The Ghent Revolt," 110–11). On this speech, see also Rider, *God's Scribe,* 149–62.

king and the new count had appointed this local notable to be castellan of Bruges on April 2, 1127.[32] After the political rupture between Clito and the people of Bruges had become final, Gervaise continued to be loyal to Clito, to whom he had done homage, and even left Bruges on March 26, 1128, so as not to dishonor himself.[33] But a few days later (April 2), when it appeared that Clito had been condemned by the people as lawless and faithless, Gervase renounced his allegiance to his culpable lord.[34] Feudal principle was sacrificed to political expediency. Gervase was bound politically to Bruges and Thierry, but feudally to Clito, so he faced a conflict of loyalties. When he returned to Bruges on April 2, he declared to Count Thierry, "If God had granted us and the fatherland the favor of your presence right after the death of our lord and your cousin Charles, we would have acknowledged no one but you in the countship," but that was a subterfuge, which Bert Demyttenaere has called a "legitimizing concoction."[35] Indeed, Galbert later tells us that Thierry had almost immediately declared himself a candidate for Charles's succession, in a letter that had arrived in Bruges on March 22, 1127, but that the barons and the people had not acted because the letter was allegedly not authentic and because the king of France was in a hurry.[36] Our conclusion must be that feudal law had many uses and that Mr. Bumble may have been right after all when he said that "the law is a ass."[37]

The situation with respect to canon law was hardly any better, and Galbert has some ironic, even sarcastic, things to say when excommunications started to be bandied about on all sides.[38] He quotes an especially strong example of the manipulation of canon law in chapter 107, where we read that Clito "freely" (*libere*) restored twelve churches to Bishop Simon of Noyon-Tournai "so that he might appear as the advocate and defender of the churches of God in Flanders, with this understanding, that the bishop, by the ban and word of excommunication, should condemn all citizens whatsoever of the land of Flanders who had received Thierry as count."[39]

32. Galbert, [54], 10/21.

33. Galbert, [100], 1/18.

34. Galbert, [104], 1/22.

35. "si Deus hanc gratiam contulisset nobis et patriae ut vos statim post mortem domini nostri et nepotis vestri Karoli praesentem habuimus, neminem in comitatum praeter vos suscepimus" (Galbert, [104], 6/9; trans., 281). Cf. the essay later in this volume by Bert Demyttenaere. On Gervaise's conversion, see also Rider, *God's Scribe,* 169–71.

36. Galbert, [47], 23/39.

37. Charles Dickens, *Oliver Twist* 51, ed. Kathleen Tillotson (Oxford, 1966), 354.

38. See Galbert, [113], 51/61; [114], 84/95; [115], 11/15.

39. "ut advocatus et defensor staret ecclesiarum Dei quae in Flandria sunt, eo tenore,

And what about the law of evidence? So far my examples of political manipulation have been transparent and even glaring, but here things get a bit more subtle, and we will occasionally have to read between the lines. It was generally known that Lambert of Aardenburg had been part of the conspiracy against the good count. Nevertheless, on April 9, 1128, he underwent with success the ordeal of hot iron and by so doing purged himself of the accusation of treason and murder; but, on April 30 of the same year, he was killed near Oostburg in a fight with the people of Oostburg and Aardenburg. Galbert interprets this as divine punishment because Lambert had not truly repented. Indeed, for Galbert, the successful ordeal of April 9 had not in reality been a mode of proof, but a sign of divine mercy toward a repenting sinner, who was given a last chance to mend his ways. To us, this seems an improper use of the ordeal, which strictly speaking ought to provide proof of guilt or innocence, but here appears as a divine measure to give the sinner another chance. According to Galbert, Lambert passed the ordeal of fire successfully and was not condemned and executed because the Lord wished to give him a chance to redeem himself, but he threw it away and thus deserved to be killed in the fight at Oostburg.[40]

Let us have a closer look at this simple and straightforward Galbertian picture, for the description leaves us with some questions. Galbert says that Lambert purged himself in the presence of count Thierry, but adds at the end of the paragraph: "Daniel and Ivan were not present."[41] What does this mean and why is it relevant? An exciting attraction like an ordeal always drew a crowd, but many people were naturally absent as well. So why mention that those two barons specifically were absent at the administration of the ordeal? Is Galbert suggesting that things would have turned out differently if they had in fact been present, that is, that in that case Lambert might well have been found guilty because the two barons would have influenced the procedure to Lambert's detriment (even if they had been justified in doing so, since Lambert was after all manifestly guilty)? So, was Lambert successful thanks to Thierry? Because a deal had been struck between those two? This may well have been the case, for in chapter 108, dated April 30, 1128, we read that Lambert had refused to give up or postpone his attack on Oostburg in spite of "the oath he had sworn to

quatenus episcopus banno et excommunicationis verbo damnaret omnes quicumque Flandrensis terrae cives suscepissent consulem Theodericum" (Galbert, [107], 20, 22/25; trans., 287).

40. Galbert, [105], 1/4; [108], 1/48.

41. "Daniel et Iwan non interfuerunt" (Galbert, [105], 3/4; trans., 282).

Count Thierry not to stir up any discord."[42] In other words, Thierry had seen to it that Lambert would succeed in his ordeal on the condition that he renounce further violence against the burghers of Aardenburg (who were friends of those of Bruges, who were themselves friends of Thierry)—a deal in which Daniel and Ivan did not want to take part. Some readers may wonder how members of the public could influence the result of an ordeal, which was a *sacramentale* (religiously sanctioned oath) administered by the clergy. It should, however, be understood that the ordeal was held in the midst of a vast crowd where all sorts of people, particularly leading local figures, could make their influence felt.[43]

Let us now turn to the manipulation of criminal law. In Galbert's chapter 52 we read that King Louis rewarded the Flemish barons who were willing to elect his candidate with the confiscated possessions of the traitors.[44] This must, no doubt, have been a handsome encouragement, but was it legal? Could the king just give away those lands? Confiscated goods went to the count's treasury, but Charles was dead. Ought those possessions to have remained in the comital treasury until his successor could dispose of them? It is a fact that a fief was administered by the overlord during *Mannfall* (the period between the death of a vassal and the investiture of his successor), so maybe it was legal. In any case, it certainly was politically welcome and rewarding.

I now come to my last and most important example, the manipulation of the law concerning freedom and serfdom, which led to the Erembalds' revolt. In a strictly legal sense and from the point of view of legal positivism, the case against the Erembalds was straightforward and even simple. According to the norms of the time, they were comital serfs. Robert of Crecques likewise became a serf a year after his marriage to one of the unfree "Erembald girls," and this was proclaimed in public in 1126.[45] The

42. "sacramentum jurandi, quod comiti Theoderico fecerat ut nullam . . . seditionem moveret" (Galbert, [108], 35/37; trans., 288).

43. On Lambert's ordeal and death, see also Rider, *God's Scribe*, 175–76. On the influence of the community on the outcome of ordeals, see R. I. Moore, *The Formation of a Persecuting Society*, 2nd ed. (Oxford, 2007), 117–24. In 1997, I had the good fortune to witness a "medieval" ordeal, which, after many years of my knowing ordeals only through old books, was quite an experience. At the Journées d'Histoire du Droit organized by the Institut d'Anthropologie Juridique in Limoges, a French anthropologist showed a film of an ordeal that had taken place in a remote mountainous area of a former French colony in West Africa. The defendant had been accused of theft during the night, for which there naturally were no witnesses, so resort was had to the ordeal of hot water, administered by the local shaman and witnessed by the whole community.

44. Galbert, [52], 35/39.

45. Galbert, [7], 22/35.

lords of Crecques, from the castellany of Saint-Omer, were vassals of the bishop of Thérouanne. Robert had, in the presence of the count, challenged a knight who was "free according to the descent of his family," but the latter refused to enter into judicial combat with a serf.[46] Consequently, the Erembalds, who had suddenly been shown up in a court of law and in public as servile, were claimed by Count Charles according to the *ius comitis* (law of the count).[47] The proud bondmen were cornered; they rebelled and finally did not hesitate to murder their own good lord. However, if we look beyond legal positivism and take into account a sense of justice and humanity, natural law and the "evolving standards of decency,"[48] the matter is not so simple. Legal positivism is in fact hugely problematic. We refer to the anti-semitic Nuremberg Decrees, which technically speaking were the law of the Third Reich according to the ideas of the time. We also remember Pope Innocent III, who annulled the Magna Carta because it was granted to the barons under duress, but had the barons not rightly revolted against their tyrannical king? Did the Erembalds not have some sort of "acquired rights"? Galbert says that they had been considered free people for a long time and had been treated as such.[49] That is how they were perceived by the citizens of Bruges. Was it humane to degrade the family and deprive its members of their honor in the very century of the emancipation of serfs and of expanding urban autonomy? The upward mobility of the Erembalds fitted very well into that context, and some, perhaps many, citizens of Bruges were undoubtedly of servile origin. It is in the course of the twelfth century that the principle was gradually established that nineteenth-century legal historians have expressed in the phrase *Stadtluft macht frei* (town air makes one free) and that may already have played a role in the famous incident of Lille in

46. "secundum suae cognationis propagationem liber erat" (Galbert, [7], 25/26; trans., 99). In chapter 25 Galbert explains it precisely, as follows: "Robert was that knight who was free before he had taken to wife the provost's niece but who, after he had kept her for a year, belonged to the count in servile status according to the law of the counts of Flanders" (erat autem ille Robertus miles liber antequam uxorem accepisset neptem praepositi, sed postquam annuatim illam tenuisset, secundum legem comitum Flandriae, servili conditione ad comitem pertinebat, Galbert, [25], 47/50; trans., 146).

47. The expression *ius comitis* appears in chapter [7], 30, where it is synonymous with the *lex comitum Flandriae* (law of the counts of Flanders) of chapter [25], 49/50, as the two passages deal with the same incident concerning Robert of Crecques.

48. I quote here the words of Justice Brennan of the U.S. Supreme Court, who argued that the death penalty had to be considered a cruel and unusual punishment according to the evolving standards of decency of a modern society, and was therefore unconstitutional. See W. J. Brennan, "Constitutional Adjudication and the Death Penalty: A View from the Court," *Harvard Law Review* 100 (1986–87): 313–31.

49. Galbert, [7], 39/44.

August 1127.[50] It was against this trend that Count Charles reacted, and not only as far as his own serfs were concerned.

So why this sudden onslaught on Bertulf and his kin? Their usurped freedom had been tolerated for a long time by the counts and accepted by many in the land. Bertulf had been provost of Saint Donatian and consequently head of the whole comital administration for more than thirty years. He had held the office since 1091, under Counts Robert I the Frisian, Robert II of Jerusalem, Baldwin VII, and Charles the Good. The servile status of the Erembalds, "forgotten" for so long, was suddenly rediscovered, and the law had to be enforced absolutely and triumphantly. Had Robert of Crecques simply fallen from the sky? The motive cannot have been purely juridical, for in that case measures would have been taken much earlier and things would not have been allowed to get that far. We are, in other words, faced with a political decision, where the law was used for a political aim, that is, to break the power of the Erembalds and, in Galbert's words, "to restore the honor of the realm."[51] We are reminded of the famous words at the conversation of Montmirail between Becket and Henry II in 1169, where the archbishop made various concessions "saving God's honor," or the meeting between the two at Montmartre later in that same year, where the king refused to confirm the agreement that had been negotiated by giving Becket the kiss of peace.[52] Nothing forced Count Charles to proceed against his own chancellor after the "discovery" of the Erembalds' servility. The count was not obliged to treat the Erembalds in the same way as other serfs who were being claimed. He could have freed them in recognition of the services they had rendered to the state. He could have accepted a compromise, as was suggested on February 27–28, 1127, when, as Galbert tells us, "mediators came and appealed to him on behalf of the provost and his nephews, begging the count to turn his wrath from them and to receive them mercifully back into his friendship," but were rebuffed.[53] Galbert himself was amazed by the frontal attack on the Erembalds, where he writes: "If anyone considers the number of his

50. Galbert, [93], 1/6.

51. "revocare honestatem regni" (Galbert, [7], 6/7; trans., 96, trans. mod.).

52. "salvo honore Dei," James Craigie Robertson, ed., *Materials for the History of Thomas Becket,* 7 vols., Rolls Series 67 (London, 1875–85), 6: 517, cited in A. L. Poole, *From Domesday Book to Magna Carta, 1087–1216* (Oxford, 1951), 212.

53. "ascenderunt coram eo intercessors ex parte praepositi et nepotum ipsius, qui exorarent comitem ut idignationem suam ab eis averteret et sub amicitia sua miseratus eos reciperet" (Galbert, [10], 29/32; trans., 106).

[Bertulf's] clan and the greatness of their deeds, the more marvelous seems God's attack on them and the destroying hand He turned against them."[54] It was all in vain, as the count was determined to break the impudent Erembalds, who to him were a mafia, a state within the state. Nor was the count the only one in the county to find them too powerful. Others at the top of the social ladder egged him on because they disliked and feared the social consequences of the rise of such serfs (Walter of Loker and Fromold are named in this context), and we know that Charles always acted in consultation with the magnates.[55]

What was the count's ultimate aim? What scenario did he envision? What would probably have happened if he had not been killed? We are here engaging in an exercise in counterfactual history.[56] If the count had not been murdered, there probably would have been a session of the *curia comitis* (count's court), possibly in Bruges at Easter 1127. There the servile condition of the Erembalds would, according to the count's scenario, have been established, either through the interrogation of aged witnesses or through Bertulf's failure to prove his free status.[57] Afterward, the members of the clan would have been thrown out of their jobs, and their chattels would have gone to their lord.[58] Moreover, various taxes would have been claimed from them, and they would have been forbidden to marry freely or to enter the clergy without the consent of their lord. There might even have been accusations of financial malversation, as Bertulf was the head of the financial administration of the county. All this would have

54. "Si quis velit audire multiplicitatem sui generis et magnitudinem factorum, mirabilem magis pugnam Dei et manum ejus quam contra ipsos destruendos exercuit credere liquet" (Galbert, [57], 47/50; trans., 210).

55. Galbert writes that "he ruled the county according to the judgment of the barons and responsible men" (judicio principum et virorum prudentium comitatum regebat, [12], 42/43; trans., 113).

56. I refer to N. Ferguson, ed., *Virtual History, Alternatives and Counterfactuals* (London, 1998).

57. Compare Glanvill's treatise *De legibus et consuetudinibus Anglie,* from the late twelfth century, where we find a description of the procedure followed in the "hearing concerning status," which takes place "when anyone demotes another from freedom to villeinage" (de questione status placitum, quod est inter aliquos quando scilicet aliquis trahit alium a libertate ad uilenagium; *The Treatise on the Laws and Customs of the Realm of England Commonly Called Glanvill* 5.1, ed. and trans. G. D. G. Hall, 2nd ed. [Oxford, 1993], 53). From France we know the case of Henry of Lorraine, a counselor to Louis VI, who in 1112 was accused of being servile and who established his free status in the *curia Regis* (king's court) by swearing "that like himself, his father and grandfather had been born free and had remained free" (J. B. Ross, trans., 99n10). At that time, this was a formalistic, "dangerous" oath and therefore not without risk.

58. Cf. Glanvill, *The Treatise on the Laws* 5.4, p. 56.

meant something like the *mort civile* (civic death) and a real destruction. It would, moreover, have had social implications for all classes, as it meant turning back the clock on the upward mobility of families and towns, so that we can speak of a retrograde and even reactionary measure. To the Erembalds it meant unbearable degradation, undoing the emancipation and ascension of generations. It also constituted gross ingratitude in their eyes, for they had done a great deal for the county and the comital dynasty. It likewise meant unimaginable shame, and we know how sensitive medieval people were to honor and dishonor. Objectively, the count may have had right on his side, but subjectively, the threatened lineage felt the count's action to be deeply unrighteous.

And what scenario, one might wonder, did Bertulf envision? What would have happened if his conspiracy had succeeded? To start with, Charles and various other enemies would have been eliminated: a night of the long knives! After that, a new count would have had to be found, somebody after Bertulf's heart.[59] His candidate was known: William of Ypres, a bastard of Philip of Lo, who was himself a son of Robert I the Frisian. William of Ypres had already raised his standard in Bruges and had received support from Bertulf and his nephews.[60] It turned out to be an illusion, but the Erembald scenario was by no means crazy or totally unrealistic. One should keep in mind the amazing tranquility that reigned in Bruges from the murder of Charles on March 2 until the arrival of Gervaise of Praet, the leader of the counterrevolution, on March 9. Some barons were sympathetic to the conspirators, maybe because they found Charles, the son of a king, too haughty and severe. There was also a good deal of sympathy in Bruges for Bertulf and aversion to the Straetens, who were enemies of both the Erembalds and the people of Bruges. And as late as March 19, Galbert, speaking for the people of Bruges, refers to the provost and his brothers and nephews as "very powerful and noble men in the county."[61] William of Ypres had a solid power base in West Flanders and there were people who found him acceptable,[62] and in chapter 25 (dated

59. Galbert writes that some of Charles's supporters would have preferred to die than "to see the traitors flourish under the rule of another count" (sub alio praesidente consule . . . traditores florere viderent, [19], 40/41; trans., 131).

60. Galbert, [44], 6/9; [20], 25/31; [25], 1/20; [47], 14/15.

61. "potentiores et nobiliores in comitatu" (Galbert, [45], 39/40; trans., 184).

62. In chapter 34, dated to March 16, Galbert reports the rumor that Louis VI had nominated him to be count ([34], 8/11).

March 6, 1127) Galbert maintains that he would have been count if he had gone to Bruges at once.[63]

I hope that my analysis of some legal themes in Galbert of Bruges has shown that in the twelfth-century county of Flanders, as elsewhere and at other times, law and politics were hard to separate.[64]

63. Galbert, [25], 20/23.

64. I would like to address a special word of thanks to Bert Demyttenaere, whose invitation to lecture at the Galbert-Colloquium at Amsterdam in October 1999 gave me a welcome opportunity to reread Galbert from a different point of view.

3

Not European Feudalism, but Flemish Feudalism

A New Reading of Galbert of Bruges's Data on Feudalism in the Context of Early Twelfth-Century Flanders

DIRK HEIRBAUT

Galbert of Bruges's journal is one of the best sources we have on feudalism in medieval Europe, but its popular success has overshadowed the fact that Galbert did not write about some abstract, textbook medieval feudalism, but about real relationships between lords and vassals in a specific area, Flanders, and at a specific moment in history, 1127–28. If one reads Galbert's account of the murder of Count Charles the Good in its context, it becomes clear that Flemish feudalism in 1127–28, as described by Galbert, is indeed illustrative of Western European feudalism in general, but that it also had some peculiarities of its own, and that these have been disregarded up to now by historians who have used Galbert as a source.

Although Galbert's book was "an utter failure in the Middle Ages,"[1] it has been very popular in recent years with both the general public and scholars, though sometimes for very different reasons. For the former Galbert simply offers a good story. Apart from the fact that it does not do justice to women (but that can also be said about the average Hollywood movie),[2] the journal has everything to catch a modern reader's interest:

I would like to thank Prof. em. Raoul Van Caenegem and his wife, Patricia Carson, Dr. Mike Raley, Dr. Rik Opsommer, Gerard Sinaeve, and Luk Burgelman for their remarks and comments on this essay. Needless to say, any remaining errors are entirely my own.

1. Rider, "Galbert of Bruges' 'Journal,'" 67.

2. Cf. the essay later in this volume by Martina Häcker, "The Language of Misogyny in Galbert of Bruges' Account of the Murder of Charles the Good."

war, murder, treason, and adultery, combined with great speeches, gossip, cynicism, and, at times, a bit of humor. Scholars, of course, (claim to) have been reading Galbert for other reasons than their students. As a journalist, he is among the best. As a notary in the central administration of Flanders in Bruges, he witnessed many events firsthand. Though he was not university trained, he was well-educated (and may have studied at the cathedral school of Laon).[3] He was a legal and administrative professional at a time when such men were rare. Moreover, he must have been exceptional even among his fellow clerics in Bruges, for he had his own views, which he was ready to adapt if changed circumstances forced him to do so. In sum, Galbert is valuable because he saw a lot, understood it, and could go beyond it. Besides that, when he gives the words of oaths, he is very accurate in his translation into Latin of what was said in Dutch or French, and he tries to convey the general sense of longer speeches even if they may not be recorded verbatim.[4]

All of Galbert's qualities are evident when he writes about feudalism, and, therefore, it is not surprising that his text has often been cited. According to Robert Fossier, the famous description of the homage to Count William Clito in Bruges in 1127 has been edited a hundred times.[5] In the same vein, Theodore Evergates states: "Beyond the frequently reprinted descriptions of fealty by Fulcher of Chartres (ca. 1020) and of homage by Galbert of Bruges (1127) . . . few non-literary texts are available."[6] Though both Fossier and Evergates exaggerate, Galbert's text has been a favorite source for feudalism because his qualities as a historian come to the fore when he writes about it. As François-Louis Ganshof wrote about Galbert's description of homage: "Nous ne connaissons cependant pas de texte à la fois aussi explicite et aussi précis que le récit où Galbert de Bruges . . . rapporte comment en 1127 le nouveau comte de Flandre, Guillaume de Normandie accueillit les vassaux de son prédécesseur."[7] Ganshof's enthusi-

3. Van Caenegem, *Galbert van Brugge en het Recht,* 11–12; Bert Demyttenaere, "Mentaliteit in de twaalfde eeuw en de benauwenis van Galbert van Brugge," in *Middeleeuwse cultuur: Verscheidenheid, spanning en verandering,* ed. Marco Mostert, R. E. Künzel, and A. Demyttenaere (Hilversum, 1994), 87–88; Rider, "Galbert of Bruges' 'Journal,'" 70–71.

4. Alan V. Murray, "Voices of Flanders: Orality and Constructed Orality in the Chronicle of Galbert of Bruges," *Handelingen der Maatschappij voor Geschiedenis en Oudheidkunde te Gent* n.s. 48 (1994): 103–19; Rider, "Galbert of Bruges' 'Journal,'" 77.

5. Robert Fossier, *Enfance de l'Europe,* 2 vols. (Paris, 1982), 1:443.

6. Theodore Evergates, *Feudal Society in Medieval France. Documents from the County of Champagne* (Philadelphia, 1993), xiii.

7. François Louis Ganshof, *Qu'est-ce que la féodalité?* (Paris, 1982), 117.

asm might be explained by a certain bias since, like Galbert, he was proud of being from Bruges, but other historians have also praised Galbert's description, such as Paul Hyams, who has called it a "textbook homage."[8] Galbert's representations of other aspects of feudalism have received similar praise. For example, Marc Bloch studies ten cases in his classic article about the procedures for the annulment of the relationship between a lord and his vassal, half of them found in Galbert's text.[9]

This popularity has led to a counterreaction. Recent works on feudalism shy away from Galbert,[10] or judge his account of feudal relationships to be simplistic.[11] Ganshof and his contemporaries liked Galbert precisely because he described feudalism as if he had their students in mind. Now, however, that same quality makes Galbert suspect. The old works of Ganshof, Bloch, Boutruche, or Strayer are now condemned because they used many different sources to compose a picture of a European feudalism that never existed, disregarding the contexts of their sources and lumping them together to arrive at the feudalism they saw as the norm. The new tendency is to put more stress on the context of the cases one studies,[12] and the new favorite has become the *Conventum Hugonis,* a narrative written around 1030 about the conflict between William, duke of Aquitaine, and the castellan Hugh of Lusignan.[13] Galbert's text, because it comes so close to the norm described in the old textbooks, shares their disgrace. Yet, one should not forget that Galbert is still a voice from the past and not a construct of modern historians. Instead of neglecting Galbert, one should read him with

8. Paul Hyams, "Warranty and Good Lordship in Twelfth Century England," *Law and History Review* 5 (1987): 448.

9. Marc Bloch, "Les formes de la rupture de l'hommage dans l'ancien droit féodal," *Revue historique de droit français et étranger* 36 (1912): 141–77. He could, in fact, have found a sixth case in Galbert's work, but Bloch did not see that *hominium reicere* is a synonym of *diffiduciare* (see below): the renunciation by Gervase of Praet of his homage to William Clito (Galbert, [104], 9/13) should thus be added to Bloch's list.

10. For example, the index of the latest (and very impressive) synthesis in French on feudalism (Eric Bournazel and Jean-Pierre Poly, eds., *Les féodalités* [Paris, 1998]), does not even mention Galbert.

11. Evergates, *Feudal Society,* xiii.

12. George T. Beech, "The Lord/Dependant (Vassal) Relationship: A Case Study from Aquitaine c. 1030," *Journal of Medieval History* 24 (1998): 1–30, esp. 1–3; and more generally Susan Reynolds, *Fiefs and Vassals: The Medieval Evidence Reinterpreted* (Oxford, 1994).

13. See Beech, "Lord/Dependant Relationship," 1–30, and the literature quoted there in notes 10–16; Dominique Barthélemy, *L'An Mil et la Paix de Dieu* (Paris, 1999), 332–54, and idem, "Autour d'un récit de pactes («Conventum Hugonis»): La Seigneurie châtelaine et le féodalisme, en France au XIe siècle," in *Il feudalesimo nell'alto medioevo,* 2 vols., *Settimane di studio del Centro italiano di studi sull'alto medioevo* 47 (2000), 1:447–89.

new eyes, in his context, the context of the generally precocious Flemish feudalism in 1127–28, and not as an archetype of European feudalism.[14]

Foreign Influences on Flemish Feudalism in 1127–28?

Before trying to interpret Galbert's data in the Flemish context, one must first answer the question: to what degree was feudalism in Flanders typically Flemish in 1127–28? After all, the two main contenders for power in the county were of foreign origin. Thierry of Alsace was a German[15] and William Clito a Norman. In Thierry's case the Alsatian connection was not very important. The speech of Ivan of Aalst in February 1128, denouncing William Clito's rule, was full of revolutionary ideas, such as the theory that the prince's power came from a contract with his people, and he could thus be dismissed if he no longer fulfilled his part of it. Ivan may have found part of his inspiration in letters from Thierry of Alsace, and maybe those letters referred to the theories of Manegold of Lautenbach, an Alsatian monk, who had developed a contractual theory of power during the Investiture Contest.[16] All this is likely, but not proven, and it is in any case of limited importance since Ivan went much further in his speech than Manegold.[17] Only one change in Flemish feudal law, moreover, may be attributed to Thierry after he came to power in 1128. The *fief de reprise* (a fief created by surrendering one's allod to a lord and receiving it back as a fief) existed in Flanders before 1128,[18] but Thierry began to use it in a new way. Some vassals, who wanted to alienate a fief, had to replace it with one of their allods to get their lord's consent. Thierry may have brought

14. The breakthrough of feudalism in Flanders can be situated around 1000, whereas in most other parts of Europe it appeared only at a later date. See Dirk Heirbaut, "Flanders: A Pioneer of State-Oriented Feudalism? Feudalism as an Instrument of Comital Power in Flanders during the High Middle Ages (1000–1300)," in *Expectations of the Law in the Middle Ages,* ed. Anthony Musson (Woodbridge, Suffolk, 2001), 24–25; and idem, *Over lenen en families,* 46–50.

15. See Dirk Heirbaut, "On and Over the Edge of the Empire: The Counts of Flanders and Hainault and the Election of the Kings of the Romans (1000–1314)," in *Königliche Tochterstämme, Königswähler und Kurfürsten,* ed. Armin Wolf (Frankfurt, 2002), 425–26.

16. Van Caenegem, "Galbert of Bruges on Serfdom," 105–7; idem, "Democratie en rechtsstaat in het twaalfde-eeuwse graafschap Vlaanderen," *Tijdschrift voor Rechtsgeschiedenis/Revue d'histoire du droit/Legal History Review* 61 (1993): 213; and Dirk Heirbaut, "Galbert van Brugge: Een bron voor de Vlaamse feodaliteit in de XIIde eeuw," *Tijdschrift voor Rechtsgeschiedenis/Revue d'histoire du droit/Legal History Review* 60 (1992): 49–62, esp. 60.

17. On Ivan's speech in general, see Rider, *God's Scribe,* 149–64.

18. E.g., *Gesta episcoporum Cameracensium continuata,* ed. Georg Waitz, in MGH SS 14 (Hanover, 1883), 190 (1093).

this system with him from his homeland, but, again, this is not certain.[19]

At least one historian claims that William Clito's Norman origin made a difference in 1127–28. Robert Fossier is convinced that the homage done to William Clito in Bruges reflects Norman practices, because William Clito was a Norman.[20] Fossier is right in wanting to draw more attention to William Clito's Norman origin,[21] which Flemish historians have tended to overlook, but the influence of Norman practices can be discerned in only one of his undertakings, and not even clearly in that one: some of the murderers of Count Charles were thrown from a tower,[22] an uncommon punishment in Flanders, but better known in Normandy.[23] However, this punishment was meant to be cruel and, most of all, unusual.[24] In all other cases, William Clito followed Flemish practices even though he had Norman advisors at his court.[25] Everything happened "according to the customs of the counts of Flanders, his predecessors."[26] This reference to specifically Flemish practices was very unusual in the twelfth century, as there was normally no doubt about the applicable law. The next text to mention the customs of Flanders does not appear until 1204, and it does so then only because Flemish law was applied outside Flanders,[27] but thereafter references to Flemish law become more common.[28] That no Nor-

19. Heirbaut, Over *lenen en families,* 153, esp. n94.

20. Fossier, *Enfance,* 1:474.

21. See, e.g., Sandy Hicks, "The Impact of William Clito upon the Continental Politics of Henry I of England," *Viator* 10 (1979): 1–22; Renée Nip, "The Political Relations between England and Flanders (1066–1128)," in *Anglo-Norman Studies, XXI: Proceedings of the Battle Conference, 1998,* ed. Christopher Harper-Bill (Woodbridge, Suffolk, 1999), 145–67; David Crouch, *The Reign of King Stephen, 1135–1154* (London, 2000), 24–28.

22. Galbert, [81], 13/52.

23. Raoul Van Caenegem, "Public Prosecution of Crime in Twelfth-Century England," in *Church and Government in the Middle Ages: Essays presented to C. R. Cheney,* ed. Christopher Nugent Lawrence Brooke et al. (Cambridge 1976), 49n19. Van Caenegem thought that this punishment was used in Flanders only this one time. However, a common murderer in Aire was executed in a similar fashion in 1179 (William of Andres, *Chronica Andrensis,* ed. Johann Heller, MGH SS 24 [Hanover, 1879], 714), so it is possible that Flemings had known this kind of punishment before 1127.

24. Cf. Galbert, [37], 46/49; [52], 13/16; [113], 41/44. See also Rider, *God's Scribe,* 81–87.

25. Galbert, [93], 1/6; *Actes,* n° 129, pp. 302–3 (1127–28); Orderic Vitalis, *The Ecclesiastical History of Orderic Vitalis,* ed. and trans. Marjorie Chibnall, 6 vols. (Oxford, 1969–1980), 4:376.

26. "secundum omnem modum praedecessorum suorum comitum Flandriae" (Galbert, [52], 34/35; trans., 197). Comparable expressions at [54], 6/10; [55], 26/27.

27. A. C. F. Koch, *Oorkondenboek van Holland en Zeeland tot 1299,* 5 vols. (The Hague, 1970–2005), n° 272, 1:451–52.

28. Dirk Heirbaut, *Over heren, vazallen en graven: Het persoonlijk leenrecht in Vlaanderen, ca. 1000–1305,* Studia, Algemeen Rijksarchief en Rijksarchief in de Provinciën 69 (Brussels, 1997), 35.

man law was used in 1127–28 was to be expected, since the Flemings saw their county as a separate entity, a "fatherland" (*patria*),[29] even a "realm" (*regnum*).[30] In later times too, the arrival of a foreign ruler never led to a change of laws.[31] Besides, one wonders how much William Clito himself really knew about Norman feudalism. He had had to leave the duchy at an early age and had received most of his education in Flanders.[32] In short, there was almost no foreign influence on Flemish practices in 1127–28. In fact, only at the end of the thirteenth century, and then only in some regions, did neighboring principalities start to have a limited impact on Flemish feudalism.[33]

Aspects of Feudalism in Galbert of Bruges

Those who know Galbert's text only through a few passages included in one of their textbooks will perhaps be surprised to learn that his journal is not first and foremost about feudalism. Flanders, even in 1127–28, was anything but a feudal society.[34] Flanders was a creation of its count, and he was the central element of life there. However, a new power, the cities, was rising. Galbert, who was a cleric, reflects their views (he may even have been writing at the behest of some of the citizens of Bruges).[35] Anything he writes about feudalism is incidental to his story. Therefore, certain aspects of feudalism are neglected in his journal: *fiefs-rentes, fiefs de reprise,* inheritance, matrimonial property, and transactions of fiefs.[36] In short,

29. Galbert, [Prol.], 49; [1], 3; [4], 25, 34; [5], 11; [11], 32; [13], 4, 23; et passim.

30. Galbert, [1], 10, 12, 17; [2], 2; [7], 7, 8, 37; [8], 2; [9], 30, 31; [13], 27; et passim. For the use of similar terminology by other Flemish authors, see Walter Mohr, *Die Entwicklung des flämischen Eigenständigkeitsgefühls bis zum Beginn des 13. Jahrhunderts* (Saarbrücken, 1977), 27–31, 41–50.

31. Cf. Dirk Heirbaut, "*Les lois, enquêtes et jugements des pairs du castel de Lille:* Een unieke getuige van het Vlaamse recht rond 1300," in *De rechtspraktijk in beeld. Van Justinianus tot de Duitse bezetting,* ed. B. C. M. Jacobs (Tilburg, 1997), 18.

32. Galbert, [52], 27/28; Walter, [6], 11/26.

33. Heirbaut, *Over lenen en families,* 209.

34. Heirbaut, *Over heren,* 310–14; Heirbaut, "Flanders," 23–34; cf. Thomas Bisson, "Lordship and Tenurial Dependence in Flanders, Provence and Occitania (1050–1200)," in *Il feudalesimo nell'alto medioevo,* 2 vols., *Settimane di studio del Centro italiano di studi sull'alto medioevo* 47 (2000), 1:393.

35. Stephanie Coué, "Der Mord an Karl dem Guten (1127) und die Werke Galberts von Brügge und Walters von Thérouanne," in *Pragmatische Schriftlichkeit im Mittelalter. Erscheinungsformen und Entwicklungsstufen,* ed. Hagen Keller, Klaus Grubmüller, and Nikolaus Staubach, Münstersche Mittelalter-Schriften 65 (Munich, 1992), 108–29. Cf. Rider, *God's Scribe,* 74–76, 192–98.

36. On all these, see Heirbaut, *Over lenen en families.*

the material element of feudalism, the fief, is lacking in his story. Galbert concentrates on the personal element of feudalism since the personal relationship between a lord and his man was still important at this time. Indeed, there were still vassals without a fief in Flanders till the end of the twelfth century.[37] Yet, Galbert gives the impression that all comital vassals received a fief in Bruges,[38] and already at the end of the eleventh century the fief was considered to be necessary for a feudal relationship.[39] Even so, Galbert concentrates on the personal aspect of feudalism: the formalities establishing the bond between man and lord, the vassal's obligations, the Peers of Flanders, the breach of the feudal contract and its sanctions, and the influence of feudal concepts on the relationship between the count and his subjects.

The Formalities Establishing the Bond between Man and Lord

Galbert is best known for his description of the ceremonies of homage, fealty, and investiture by Flemish vassals to their new count, William Clito, on April 7, 1127.[40] As the region around Bruges, the Carolingian *pagus Flandrensis,* was the oldest possession of the counts of Flanders, their position there was very strong and there were thus a great number of comital vassals in this part of Flanders.[41] Consequently, it took the count three days to receive homage and fealty from them and to invest them with their fiefs.[42] Galbert would thus have been able to witness these feudal rituals firsthand over and over, and it is not surprising that his account of them sounds like a "textbook homage." Unlike other clerics, he must have known all too well what he was writing about.

37. Lambert of Ardres, *Historia comitum Ghisnensium* 96, ed. Johann Heller, MGH SS 24 (Hanover 1879), 607.

38. "Then the count, with a wand which he held in his hand, gave investiture to *all* those who by this compact had promised loyalty and done homage and likewise had taken an oath" (Deinde virgula, quam manu consul tenebat, investituras donavit eis *omnibus* qui hoc pacto securitatem et hominium simulque juramentum fecerant; Galbert, [56], 10/12; trans., 207; my emphasis). Cf. Galbert, [55], 43/46; [104], 21/24.

39. William of Andres, *Chronica Andrensis* 35, p. 698 (1097).

40. On this passage, see also Rider, *God's Scribe,* 88–93.

41. Renée Doehaerd, "*Flandrenses* dans la *Passio Karoli* de Galbert de Bruges (1127)," *Belgisch tijdschrift voor filologie en geschiedenis* 71 (1993): 841–49.

42. Galbert, [55], 7/[56], 21.

Homage

The first act of the Bruges ceremonies was the homage by the vassal: "First they did homage in this way. The count asked each one if he wished to become wholly his man, and the latter replied, 'I so wish,' and with his hands clasped and enclosed by those of the count, they were bound together by a kiss."[43] This homage was a complex act, consisting of three elements: a declaration of intention, a hand gesture, and a kiss. The declaration was very simple. The count, the lord, asks the other party whether he is willing to become his vassal. The other replies that he is, in this case by saying: "I so wish" (*volo*). Elsewhere the formula is somewhat longer: "'I wish . . . to do homage and pledge my faith to you.'"[44] This combination of question and answer is reminiscent of the procedure in feudal courts with its ritual of questions by the lord, or his representative, and answers by the vassals.[45] Outside Flanders one can also find comparable declarations of the intent to become a vassal.[46]

That is less true for the next element of the 1127 homage in Flanders: the hand gesture. It was typical for Flanders and neighboring regions, but was absent in many other parts of Europe.[47] This second element of the homage is usually called the "mixing of hands" (*immixtio manuum,*[48] a term that does not appear in Flemish sources): the vassal placed his clasped hands between the hands of his lord, who closed his own hands over them.

The final element of the homage in 1127 was the kiss, which has led to the wildest interpretations. First of all, one should stress that there was nothing unusual in the fact that lord and man kissed each other on this occasion. After all, they had just concluded a contract, and the kiss was a common formality for doing so.[49] However, Galbert is the only one to

43. "Primum hominia fecerunt ita: comes requisivit si integre vellet homo suus fieri et ille respondit: 'Volo,' et junctis manibus, amplexatus a manibus comitis, osculo confederati sunt" (Galbert, [56], 3/6; trans., 206).

44. "Volo . . . hominium et fidem vobis facere" (Galbert, [104], 15/16; trans., 281).

45. Dirk Heirbaut, "De procedure tot overdracht van onroerende goederen in het oud-Vlaamse recht: enkele feodale voorbeelden uit de dertiende eeuw," *Handelingen der maatschappij voor geschiedenis en oudheidkunde te Gent* 51 (1997): 41–42.

46. Ganshof, *Féodalité,* 119.

47. Heirbaut, *Over heren,* 65n32; Rik Opsommer, *"Omme dat leengoed es thoochste dinc van der weerelt." Het leenrecht in Vlaanderen in de 14de en 15de eeuw,* 2 vols. (Brussels, 1995), 2:647n331.

48. Ganshof, *Féodalité,* 119.

49. Yannick Carré, *Le baiser sur la bouche au moyen âge. Rites, symboles, mentalités à travers les textes et les images, XIe–XVe siècles* (Paris, 1992), esp. 187–215.

mention this kiss. Other Flemish sources of this period neglect it, but their reports of homage are spare.[50] Later sources do refer to a custom of kissing when doing homage,[51] but there is no evidence that these allusions are more than theoretical.[52] It may be that our sources are incomplete, but it is more likely that not every homage was accompanied by a kiss, which seems to have been popular mainly in French feudalism,[53] and Flanders was on the edge of the kingdom of France.

According to Jacques Le Goff, the kiss had a specific symbolism in the ritual of homage. The *immixtio manuum* expressed the subjection of the vassal, because he was kneeling when he offered his hands to his lord. It created an unequal relationship. The fealty, however, restored the equality between man and lord, and that was expressed in the kiss.[54] One cannot deny that the *immixtio manuum* and the kiss had an important symbolic role, and that Le Goff's theory fits in well with other studies stressing mechanisms of subjection and saving face in a single complex ceremony.[55] Unfortunately, Le Goff bases his theory on Galbert's text, which contradicts the conclusions he draws from it.[56] For Le Goff the kiss is part of the ritual of fealty and not of homage, but Galbert leaves absolutely no doubt about the kiss as an element of homage. The kiss is mentioned before the "secondly" (*secundo loco*) that introduces Galbert's description of fealty. Le Goff furthermore assumes that the kiss stands for equality and the *immixtio manuum* for inequality. The first is in all likelihood true, the second may be disputed. Neither Galbert nor any other Flemish document mentions that the vassal was kneeling during the *immixtio manuum,* and later Flemish sources stress that, although the vassal should come to his lord without weapons and with head, throat, and arms bared, he should not kneel.[57]

50. E.g., *L'histoire-polyptique de l'abbaye de Marchiennes (1116–1121)* 30, ed. Bernard Delmaire (Louvain-la-Neuve, 1985), 87–88 (c. 1120).

51. E.g., Leopold August Warnkönig, *Flandrische Staats- und Rechtsgeschichte,* 3 vols. in 5 parts (Tübingen, 1835–42), 3.2, n° 91, pp. 156–57 (1266/1267).

52. Cf. Opsommer, *"Omme dat leengoed,"* 2:649–50.

53. Ganshof, *Féodalité,* 126–27.

54. Jacques Le Goff, "Les gestes symboliques dans la vie sociale. Les gestes de la vassalité," in *Simboli e simbologia nell'alto Medioevo,* 2 vols., *Settimane di studio del Centro italiano di studi sull'alto Medioevo* 23 (Spoleto, 1976), 2:706–7.

55. See, for examples, the studies by Gerd Althoff in his *Spielregeln der Politik im Mittelalter: Kommunikation in Frieden und Fehde* (Darmstadt, 1997).

56. For another criticism of Le Goff's interpretation of Galbert's text, though on other grounds, see Susan Reynolds, "Afterthoughts on *Fiefs and Vassals,*" *Haskins Society Journal* 9 (1997): 7–12.

57. "sonder knielen" (without kneeling; *Leenrechten van Vlaanderen,* art. 106, in Louis Gil-

The complex of a declaration of intention, a hand gesture, and a kiss was called "homage" (*hominium*) by Galbert. In the eleventh century, Flemish sources did not use a specific word for homage, but described only the *immixtio manuum.*[58] The term *hominium* appears for the first time in 1103,[59] and remained the most popular Latin term for homage in Flanders throughout the twelfth century, though some other terms were also used, such as *homagium,* which would become dominant in Flanders in the thirteenth century.[60] That *hominium* was still a recent term in Flanders in 1127, and that writers did not agree on its use, does not mean that Flemish feudalism was still in its infancy. Rather, it shows the inadequacy of Latin to express feudal concepts in Flanders. There is a contrast between the vernacular, where only one, precise word was used for homage (Dutch: *manscepe,* French: *houmage*),[61] and the variety of Latin terms and expressions. This indicates that the terminology in the vernacular came first, and that the Latin terms and expressions were only later translations, about which there was not complete agreement.[62]

Fealty

In 1127 homage was followed by fealty: "Secondly, he who had done homage pledged his faith to the count's spokesman in these words: 'I promise on my faith that I will henceforth be faithful to Count William and that I will maintain my homage toward him completely against everyone, in good faith and without guile.' And in the third place he swore an oath to this effect on the relics of the saints."[63] Like homage, fealty was

liodts–Van Severen, ed., *Coutume du Bourg de Bruges,* 3 vols., Coutumes du pays et comté de Flandre, Quartier de Bruges [Brussels, 1883–85], 3:258).

58. Cf. Benjamin Guérard, ed., *Cartulaire de l'abbaye de Saint-Bertin* (Paris, 1840), n° 28, pp. 202–3 (1087).

59. Lambert of Arras, *Epistolae,* ed. Michel-Jean-Joseph Brial, *Recueil des historiens des Gaules et de la France* 15 (Paris, 1808), 196.

60. E.g., Thérèse de Hemptinne and Adriaan Verhulst, eds., *De oorkonden der graven van Vlaanderen (Juli 1128–1191),* II.1, *Regering van Diederik van de Elzas (Juli 1128–17 Januari 1168)* (Brussels, 1988), n° 95, pp. 155–57 (1146).

61. Noël Didier, *Le droit des fiefs dans la coutume de Hainaut au moyen âge* (Paris, 1945), 28.

62. Cf. for city charters J. W. J. Burgers, "Het ontstaan van de twaalfde-eeuwse Vlaamse stadskeuren," in *Van vader- naar moedertaal: Latijn, Frans en Nederlands in de dertiende-eeuwse Nederlanden,* ed. Rita Beyers (Brussels, 2000), 94. On the influence of the vernacular on Latin in Flanders more generally, see Emily Kadens, "De invoering van de volkstaal in ambtelijke teksten in Vlaanderen: een status quaestionis," *Millennium, tijdschrift voor middeleeuwse geschiedenis* 14 (2000): 27–28.

63. "Secundo loco fidem dedit is qui hominium fecerat prolocutori comitis in iis verbis:

a complex act. Its constituent parts were a promise to be faithful and an oath. By the twelfth century, a promise was still a part of fealty only in Flanders and neighboring Hainaut. Elsewhere, the oath was sufficient, and in the thirteenth century that would also be the case in Flanders.[64] The words of the promise (and the oath), as Galbert reports them, contain a reference only to a general norm: to "maintain . . . homage . . . completely against everyone, in good faith and without guile." Later oaths are sometimes more elaborate,[65] but that may simply be because more documents have been preserved.

The presence of the *prolocutor,* the "spokesman,"[66] in 1127 is intriguing. In this period, in Flanders and elsewhere, the relationship between man and lord was still personal, at least in the sense that both parties had to be present in person for the rituals establishing the bond between them.[67] Yet, the promise and the oath of fealty are addressed not to the count, but to his spokesman. This figure is neglected in most studies of Galbert. Ganshof suggested that the spokesman was necessary because the Bruges vassals spoke Dutch, while William Clito, a Norman, did not and would thus not have understood the technical language of the oath-formula.[68] But, in a letter to the citizens of Bruges, the French king points out to them that William grew up among them.[69] It would have been strange if he had not learned enough Dutch in all those years to understand his vassals. Moreover, if the *prolocutor* acted as an interpreter, why then is he not mentioned from the start? Why does the count himself, without the help of the *prolocutor,* ask the vassal if he wants to be his man? During the act of fealty, furthermore, the count listens without speaking. In 1127, William Clito listened to these oaths for three days. Even if he did not speak the language, he would undoubtedly have come to understand the formulas that were repeated continuously over such a period of time. Therefore, the *prolocutor* was present not to help the count, but to help the vassal. For the

'Spondeo in fide mea me fidelem fore amodo comiti Willelmo et sibi hominium integraliter contra omnes observaturum fide bona et sine dolo.' Idemque super reliquias sanctorum tertio loco juravit" (Galbert, [56], 6/10; trans., 206–7).

64. Heirbaut, *Over heren,* 63.

65. E.g., Archives départementales du Nord (Lille), Series B, 498/4213 (1299).

66. About the *prolocutor,* see Raoul Van Caenegem, *Geschiedenis van het strafprocesrecht in Vlaanderen van de XIe tot de XIVe eeuw,* Verhandelingen van de Koninklijke Vlaamse Academie voor Wetenschappen, Letteren en Schone Kunsten van België, Klasse der Letteren, 24 (Brussels, 1956), 152, 280–82, and Heirbaut, *Over heren,* 198–203.

67. Heirbaut, *Over heren,* 70–73.

68. Ganshof, *Féodalité,* 117n5.

69. Galbert, [52], 24/28.

latter the oath to his new count was a momentous occasion, but he did not necessarily know its wording, and it would have been useless to give him a piece of parchment with the oath formula. Hence the *prolocutor,* who was a specialist in the words and phrases of the law. He spoke the necessary formula first and the vassal simply repeated after him. It is testimony to Galbert's eye for detail that he does not gloss over the *prolocutor,* as do all other Flemish texts.[70]

In 1127, homage began with the count's asking the vassal to serve him "wholly" (*integre*), and the fealty consisted of a promise and an oath to serve the count "completely against everyone" (*integraliter contra omnes*). The count's vassal was clearly a liege vassal, a vassal who will serve his lord before all others, in 1127. The term "liege" itself does not appear in Flanders until 1111,[71] though the word was probably already known in the middle of the eleventh century.[72] From Galbert's account, one can derive that in Flanders a comital vassal was in general a liege vassal,[73] but the importance of liege vassality in Flanders was limited. In Galbert's time, there were still prominent vassals whose only lord was the count.[74] Later in the twelfth century, one could become the liege vassal of more than one lord,[75] but liege had a different meaning then in Flanders. The count's monopoly on legitimate violence had become so absolute by 1164 that one could no longer fight for any other Flemish lord. Thus, liegeancy in the old sense had become obsolete. A liege vassal became the holder of a liege fief, that is, a fief with the maximum relief of ten pounds.[76]

Galbert's terminology with respect to fealty is very interesting. Like his contemporaries, he still uses both the terms *fides* and *fidelitas.*[77] Only in the thirteenth century would the general European tendency prevail in

70. There is not much information about the *prolocutor*'s role even for oaths in criminal cases (cf. Van Caenegem, *Strafprocesrecht,* 152).

71. Vereauteren, *Actes,* n° 52, pp. 131–33.

72. Dirk Heirbaut, "The Fief-Rente: A New Evaluation, Based on Flemish Sources," *Tijdschrift voor Rechtsgeschiedenis/Revue d'Histoire du Droit/The Legal History Review* 67 (1999): 30n216.

73. The same was true for the vassals of neighboring princes in Hainaut, Normandy and England. See Walther Kienast, *Untertaneneid und Treuvorbehalt in Frankreich und England. Studien zur vergleichenden Verfassungsgeschichte des Mittelalters* (Weimar, 1952), 93–130, 260–76; Didier, *Le droit des fiefs,* 33.

74. Galbert, [100], 7/10.

75. Many examples can be found in the survey of the possessions of the Abbey of Saint Vaast of Arras, edited by Eugène-François Van Drival, *Cartulaire de l'abbaye de Saint-Vaast d'Arras rédigé au XIIe siècle par Guimann* (Arras, 1875), e.g., 241, 243, 331.

76. Heirbaut, *Over heren,* 105–6; Heirbaut, *Flanders,* 25–28.

77. E.g., Galbert, [103], 6; [104], 10, 15.

Flanders to use *fidelitas* in a feudal context and *fides* in other cases.[78] Galbert (like Gislebert of Mons in Hainaut) also uses a dichotomy of *fides* or *fidelitas* and *securitas.*[79] According to Ganshof, the former is then used for the positive obligations of the vassal (the services he owes his lord), the latter for the negative ones (the duty not to act against the lord's interests).[80] This is true, but Galbert uses *securitas* mostly (though not exclusively) when he describes the recognition of a new count by ordinary subjects, not by vassals,[81] and it is in the latter context that *securitas* also surfaces in other sources.[82] There was a distinction not only between *fidelitas* and *securitas* in 1127, but also between homage and fealty, which remained distinct acts in Flanders until the end of the thirteenth century.[83]

Investiture

After the vassals had done homage and fealty, they were invested with their fief: "Then the count, with a wand which he held in his hand, gave investiture to all those who by this compact had promised loyalty and done homage and likewise had taken an oath."[84] Information on investiture is very rare in Flanders before 1200. Galbert is an exception, but even his information is rather meager. He is the only one to use the word "investiture,"[85] and he tells us that a rod was used to symbolize the act of the investiture (but was not handed over to the vassal, as it served to invest all vassals).[86] Symbols representing the object vested, such as cornstalks,

78. Olga Weijers, "Some notes on 'fides' and related words in medieval Latin," *Bulletin Du Cange: Archivum Latinitatis medii aevi* 40 (1977): 94–96.

79. Galbert, [38] [52], 33; [54], 8/9; [55], 43/46; [56], 1/3; [59], 48; [98], 14/17; [101], 22/25; [104], 10/11; [119], 27/30; Gislebert of Mons, *Chronicon Hanoniense* 43, 82, ed. Léon Vanderkindere (Brussels, 1904), 75, 121.

80. Ganshof, *Féodalité,* 138–39.

81. E.g., Galbert, [20], 25/30; [55], 43/46.

82. Even as late as 1273 (Archives départementales du Nord [Lille], Series B, 398/1789).

83. Archives départementales du Nord (Lille), Series B, 4047/3121 (1290). In the fourteenth century they had already become one (*Leenrechten van Vlaanderen,* art. 107, 3:257–58; Raymond Monier, ed., *Les lois, enquêtes et jugements des pairs du castel de Lille: Recueil des coutumes, conseils et jugements du tribunal de la Salle de Lille, 1283–1406* [Lille, 1937], n° 129, pp. 84–85).

84. "Deinde virgula, quam manu consul tenebat, investituras donavit eis omnibus qui hoc pacto securitatem et hominium simulque juramentum fecerant" (Galbert, [56], 10/12; trans., 207).

85. See also Galbert, [122], 9. However, other texts may use forms of the verb *investire* (e.g., De Hemptinne and Verhulst, *Oorkonden* 2.1, n° 202, pp. 314–15 [1150–62]).

86. Reynolds thinks this rod may have been a symbol of the count's authority rather than the act of investiture, but this is based upon the idea that everyone, not just fiefholders, was

were also used, as Galbert relates that these were returned when the vassal severed his ties to his lord.[87] Neither Galbert nor any other Flemish source of his time informs us about the words the count spoke when he gave investiture to his vassal. Thus, we can only guess what conditions of heritability, warranty, and so on were imposed. Our "textbook homage" is very incomplete with respect to this aspect of the ceremony. In the scene at Bruges, the classic order[88] of homage, fealty, and investiture was followed. It all happened in this order, with investiture as the final act of the ceremony. Other descriptions were not so precise,[89] but Galbert was right. Only in the later Middle Ages could one in Flanders have received a fief before homage.[90]

The Vassal's Obligations

Galbert's journal contains some data about the obligations of lords and vassals, but in most cases there is little that cannot be found more extensively in other sources.[91] There is one exception: the duty of the vassal to stand surety for his lord. This was a very common obligation of the vassal in Western Europe,[92] but it has generally been neglected by historians. In Galbert's story it explains the famous speech by Ivan of Aalst on February 16, 1128. It is in all likelihood the second-best-known passage of Galbert's text, after the description of the homage in Bruges in 1127. In this complaint against Count William Clito, Ivan acted as the *prolocutor* of the citizens of Ghent. He rebuked the count for not respecting the privileges he had given the burghers of Ghent and other cities and proposed that a special court composed of the Peers of Flanders and representatives of the clergy and the people (some kind of extended comital *curia*) should convene in Ypres to judge the count. If it found him to be unworthy of his

invested with his lands (Reynolds, "Afterthoughts," 9–11), whereas only the *feodati* were in fact so invested (see discussion below). It is not clear whether the staff was the count's own, as the *prolocutor* was also holding a staff (in the vernacular he was called a *staver* [man with a staff]; Van Caenegem, *Strafprocesrecht,* 152), which he may have held out to the count.

87. Galbert, [38], 51/54.

88. Bernhard Diestelkamp, *Das Lehnrecht der Grafschaft Katzenelnbogen (13. Jahrhundert bis 1479)* (Aalen, 1969), 135–36.

89. For examples, see Heirbaut, *Over heren,* 65n33.

90. Opsommer, *Leengoed,* 2:643.

91. For a detailed study, see Heirbaut, *Over heren,* 149–255.

92. Heinrich Mitteis, *Lehnrecht und Staatsgewalt. Untersuchungen zur mittelalterlichen Verfassungsgeschichte* (Weimar, 1933), 616–18.

dignity, he would have to give it up. Thus, in a nutshell Ivan formulated ideas about constitutionalism and parliamentarism, almost a century before Magna Carta,[93] and it may not be an exaggeration to call Ivan's speech Flanders's greatest contribution to the development of modern law.[94] Galbert's account of this speech is not verbatim (he was not present himself, as it happened in Ghent, not in Bruges), but there is no doubt that he has recorded it faithfully.[95] Yet, one mystery remains: why did Ivan act as *prolocutor* for the citizens of Ghent? True, it was not unusual for highly placed people to act as *prolocutores,*[96] but one wonders why Ivan, of all people, was chosen. After all, his speech is about the rule of law and popular sovereignty, and he should have been the last to cherish these notions. He was a Peer of Flanders (whose special status will be studied in the next paragraph), indeed the first of the Peers.[97] His power was so great that he was sometimes called a count.[98] One can hardly imagine anyone less sympathetic to the plight of citizens. Moreover, his conduct showed, if anything, that his own activities were not subject to rule of law and popular sovereignty. He deprived his niece of her rich inheritance in 1128[99] and was killed for it some decades later.[100] His family, the lords of Aalst, was successful in their efforts to preserve and expand serfdom.[101] In fact, Aalst was the only region of Flanders where serfdom survived until the end of the Ancien Régime.[102] Ivan's defending freedom is like the devil preach-

93. Heirbaut, "Galbert," 60–62; Raoul Van Caenegem, "Mediaeval Flanders and the Seeds of Modern Democracy," in *Foundations of Democracy in the European Union: From the Genesis of Parliamentary Democracy to the European Parliament,* ed. John Pinder (New York, 1999), 4–17.

94. Dirk Heirbaut, "The Belgian Legal Tradition: Does It Exist?" in *Introduction to Belgian Law,* ed. Hubert Bocken and Walter de Bondt (Brussels, 2001), 20–21; Raoul Van Caenegem, "Reflexions on the Place of the Low Countries in European Legal History," in *Europäisches Rechtsdenken in Geschichte und Gegenwart: Festschrift für Helmut Coing zum 70. Geburtstag,* ed. Helmut Coing et al., 2 vols. (Munich, 1982), 1:16–17.

95. Murray, "Voices of Flanders," 118.

96. Cf. Hariulf of Oudenburg, *Vita Arnulfi episcopi Suessionensis* 4, ed. Oswald Holder-Egger, MGH SS 15.2 (Hanover, 1888), 880.

97. He had succeeded his brother, who had been the *"par parium Flandrie"* (Galbert, [91], 2/3).

98. "comes Alostanus" ("Chronicon Trunchiniense," in *Recueil des Chroniques de Flandre / Corpus Chronicorum Flandriae,* ed. Joseph Jean De Smet, 4 vols. [Brussels, 1837–65], 1:603).

99. Lambert of Ardres, *Historia* 122, p. 620 (she received only a few allods).

100. Warlop, 1.1:224–28. See also Karel Gerard Van Acker, "Een jachtpartij met rivalen: intriges en gevolgen (1140)," *Appeltjes van het Meetjesland* 40 (1989): 193–97.

101. Lambert of Ardres relates some stories about how Ivan's aunt, Gertrude, who was married to a lord of Ardres, used her power to reduce free people to serfdom (Lambert of Ardres, *Historia* 129, p. 625).

102. Eric Thoen, *Landbouwekonomie en bevolking in Vlaanderen gedurende de late mid-*

ing good works. Something rings false, and one must look for his ulterior motives.

In part, he was motivated by self-interest. He was in the pay of the king of England and others who did not want William Clito to succeed in Flanders since he was the son of Robert Curthose, a pretender to the English throne.[103] The civil war, of which his speech was the start, gave him ample occasion for disinheriting his niece, and he would eventually go on to become the son-in-law of the new count, Thierry of Alsace.[104] But there is more. Ivan and his fellow Peer of Flanders, Daniel of Dendermonde, had stood surety for William Clito in 1127, when the new count had been recognized by the city of Ghent in return for granting the citizens certain rights and freedoms: "the oaths that we swore in your name concerning the remission of the toll, the maintenance of peace and the other rights." They had sworn together with the count: "we took this oath together with you." They were the "guarantors" he had given to the city of Ghent to ensure that he would keep his word.[105] No document recording these oaths has been preserved, but there is a charter from William Clito for the city of Saint-Omer that mentions the oaths of the king of France and the Flemish nobles.[106] One year later, the victor in the Flemish civil war, Thierry of Alsace, confirmed Saint-Omer's charter, and this time more details are given about the nobles' oath: "The aforementioned barons further swear that if the count tries to dispossess the burghers of Saint-Omer of their customs and deal with them without the judgement of the aldermen, they [the barons] will abandon the count and ally themselves with them [the burghers] until the count restores their customs in their entirety and permits them to be judged by the aldermen."[107]

When he made his speech, then, Ivan acted as he should. His obliga-

deleeuwen en het begin van de moderne tijden. Testregio: de kasselrijen van Oudenaarde en Aalst (eind 13de–eerste helft 16de eeuw), 2 vols. (Ghent, 1988) 1:421–45.

103. See the references in note 21 above.

104. "Cartulaire de l'abbaye de Tronchiennes," n° 7 (1139), in *Recueil des Chroniques de Flandre / Corpus Chronicorum Flandriae,* ed. Joseph Jean De Smet, 4 vols. (Brussels 1837–65), 1:708.

105. "sacramenta quae pro vobis juravimus de condonato teloneo, de confirmanda pace et de ceteris justitiis . . . in idipsum vobiscum conjuravimus . . . fidejussores" (Galbert, [95], 14/16, 19, 35/36; trans., 268).

106. Georges Espinas, "Le privilège de Saint-Omer de 1127," *Revue du Nord* 29 (1947): 43–48.

107. "Prefati barones insuper iuraverunt quod si comes burgenses Sancti Audomari extra consuetudines suas eicere et sine iudicio scabinorum tractare vellet, se a comite discessuros et cum eis remansuros, donec comes eis suas constitutiones integre restitueret et iudicium scabinorum eos subire permitteret" (De Hemptinne and Verhulst, *Oorkonden* 2.1, n° 2, pp. 14–17).

tion as a guarantor of the count's promises was not to execute the count's duties in his stead, but to ensure that the count kept his word. He did not have to act in place of the count; he had to make the count act. He was a so-called influence surety.[108] He was chosen as spokesman by the citizens of Ghent because he was the most influential noble from their region, lord of the neighboring seigniories of Aalst, Waas, and Drongen and advocate of Saint Peter's abbey in Ghent.[109] He and his family were so powerful in the Ghent region that they were sometimes called "of Ghent."[110] For example, Gilbert of Gant (Ghent), who received Folkingham from William the Conqueror, was a younger son of the house of Aalst.[111] As sureties for the count, Ivan and his fellow peer Daniel of Dendermonde first had to try to make their lord see reason. Therefore, they "called the count to a reckoning."[112] If they failed to convince the count, Ivan and Daniel had to leave the count's side and stand by the citizens until their conflict with the count had been resolved in a satisfactory manner, but Ivan went beyond that. He called for the count's resignation: if the latter was judged to be foresworn, he would have to leave the county. William, of course, did not agree,[113] but in the end he lost the county and his life.

It would thus seem that the Flemish cities had found an effective solution to an essential problem. Princes might confer privileges under duress, but they were likely to rescind them when circumstances changed to their advantage. Most cities were not able to institute a mechanism to guarantee that their lord would keep his word. In this case, they did, and, consequently, when Thierry of Alsace won the Flemish civil war in 1128, he had to let his city charters be guaranteed by his most prominent nobles.[114] The success of this mechanism proved to be its own downfall, for the count could not fail to resist this threat to his authority. After 1128, vassals no longer guaranteed that the count would respect city charters, with one exception: Saint-Omer.[115] There, the count failed to push through his new policy.

108. For more information, see Philippe Godding, "Les sûretés personnelles dans les Pays-Bas méridionaux du XIe au XVIIIe siècle," in *Les sûretés personnelles,* 3 vols., *Recueils de la société Jean Bodin pour l'histoire comparative des institutions* 28–30 (1969–74), 2:263–364.

109. Warlop, n° 1.16, 2.1:589, 591.

110. *Actes,* n° 107, 245–47 (1127); n° 127, 293–99 (1127).

111. Warlop, n° 1.6, 2.1:588, 592.

112. "posuerunt comitem ad rationem" (Galbert, [95], 8; trans., 267).

113. Galbert, [95], 39/43.

114. De Hemptinne and Verhulst, *Oorkonden* 2.1, n° 2, pp. 14–17; Galbert, [103], 3/6.

115. De Hemptinne and Verhulst, *Oorkonden* 2.1, n° 233, pp. 365–70 (1164; charter for the commune, but no vassals' sureties are mentioned in the contemporary charter for the comital

The role of the vassal as a guarantor of a city charter in Flanders was limited to 1127–28. It did not exist before those years and disappeared thereafter. Yet, Flemish vassals did stand surety for their lord in the context of international treaties. They guaranteed the execution of the treaty of Dover with the English king in 1101,[116] and from 1191 on they are sureties for the count's faithful behavior as the French king's vassal.[117] Ghent would revive this system in the fifteenth century, however, when it recognized Maximilian of Austria, the husband of Charles the Bold's heiress, as count of Flanders, and this led later to the revolt of one of the sureties, Philip of Cleves.[118]

Privileged Vassals: The Peers of Flanders

As the count's reaction to Ivan's speech showed, Ivan belonged to a very special group of comital vassals. The count wanted to reject the homage Ivan had done to him so that Ivan would become his equal and they could fight a duel: "'I wish, then, to make myself your equal by rejecting the homage you have done to me, and to challenge you without delay to combat, because as count I have thus far acted rightly and reasonably in every way.'"[119] Ivan was a Peer of Flanders, a *par, par terrae, regni par, par patriae* or *par Flandriae.*[120] The Peers of Flanders were comital vassals with a special status.[121] They were the lords of seigniories on the edge of the county, and their fortresses were a key element of its defense. The Peers' lands had come under the count's control, sometimes as late as the end of the eleventh century,[122] but they continued to enjoy greater autonomy and prestige than other vassals. They were not counts themselves, like some

aldermen: n° 231, pp. 360–63; see also Alain Derville, *Saint-Omer des origines au début du XIVe siècle* [Lille, 1995], 105–9).

116. *Actes,* n° 30, art. 17, pp. 88–95 (1101; about the date, see François-Louis Ganshof, Raoul Van Caenegem, and Adriaan Verhulst, "Note sur le premier traité anglo-flamand de Douvres," *Revue du Nord* 40 [1958], 245–57).

117. Heirbaut, *Over heren,* 229–31.

118. A. De Fouw, *Philips van Kleef: Een bijdrage tot de kennis van zijn leven en karakter* (Groningen, 1937), 139–275.

119. "Volo ergo, rejecto hominio quod mihi fecisti, parem me tibi facere et sine dilatione bello comprobare in te quia bene et rationabiliter adhuc per omnia in comitatu egerim" (Galbert, [95], 40/43; trans., 269).

120. See Galbert, 214, s.v. "Pares Flandriae," and Lambert of Ardres, *Historia* 119, p. 619.

121. Heirbaut, *Over heren,* 164–71. About other peers in Flanders, see Jean-François Nieus, "Pairie et «estage» dans le comté de Saint-Pol au XIIIe siècle," *Revue du Nord* 81 (1999): 21–40.

122. Lambert of Ardres, *Historia* 119, p. 619 (refers to 1086–91).

very great and very autonomous vassals in the south of the county,[123] but they occupied a like place in the feudal hierarchy, as they too were second (only) to the count.[124] The only difference between them and the count was that they had done homage to him. One should not overestimate this statement. A Peer of Flanders was not necessarily the vassal of only the count—he could also be the vassal of a foreign prince[125] or of a church within or without Flanders[126]—but he was never the vassal of another Flemish layman.

The Peers of Flanders form an element in an elaborate feudal hierarchy in Flanders. At its top stood the count. He could be a vassal outside Flanders, but only of consecrated princes (kings and bishops).[127] Inside Flanders, he was no one's vassal; he could only be a lord. He was not the only feudal lord in the county, but, unlike other lords, he had no lord in Flanders, only vassals.[128] In Flanders he was always on top. The Peers of Flanders formed the next tier of the feudal hierarchy. The count could have foreign lords but no Flemish ones, whereas the Peers of Flanders could have Flemish lords, but they could only be the count and churches. One finds other vassals under them—barons, knights, and vavasors (*vavassores*)—but it is not clear what distinguished these categories from one another.[129] The barons seem to have had about thirty to forty knightly vassals,[130] whereas knighthood probably separated the knights from the vavasors.[131] This seems to indicate a feudal hierarchy of one count, twelve Peers,[132] about at least fifty other barons,[133]

123. About these, the older literature can no longer be consulted. See Jean-François Nieus, "Aux marges de la principauté: les 'comtés vassaux' de la Flandre, fin X^e^–fin XIIe siècle," *VIe Congrès de l'association des Cercles francophones d'histoire et d'archéologie de Belgique* (Mons, 2002), 309–32; and for more detailed discussions Jean-François Nieus, *Un pouvoir comtal entre Flandre et France: Saint-Pol, 1000–1300* (Brussels, 2005), and Heather J. Tanner, *Families, Friends and Allies: Boulogne and Politics in Northern France and England, c. 879–1160* (Leiden, 2004) (unfortunately, this work ignores the literature in Dutch).

124. "alter a comite" (Galbert, [89], 29).

125. E.g., Lambert of Ardres, *Historia* 121, p. 620.

126. E.g., *Actes,* n° 106, pp. 240–43 (1122).

127. *Chronique de Baudouin d'Avesnes,* in *Istore et croniques de Flandres,* ed. J. Kervyn de Lettenhove, 2 vols. (Brussels, 1879–80), 2:613.

128. Heirbaut, *Over heren,* 110–11.

129. William of Andres, *Chronica Andrensis* 99, p. 720.

130. Warlop, 1.1:99.

131. We still need a study—like that of Jean Yver, "'Vavassor.' Note sur les premiers emplois du terme," *Annales de Normandie* 40 (1990): 31–48—about the precise meaning of this term in Flanders.

132. For this number, see discussion below.

133. John Baldwin, *Les registres de Philippe Auguste* 1 (Paris, 1992), n° III/G, 308–24, esp. 314–17, mentions sixty barons for Flanders and Artois (which in 1127–28 was still part of Flan-

about two thousand knights,[134] and an unknown number of vavasors. Flanders was exceptional in that it already had clear ideas of feudal hierarchy in Galbert's day. Elsewhere in Europe, such clear distinctions appeared only late in the twelfth century, and sometimes, maybe, under Flemish influence.[135] It is not by chance that, when the princes of the Empire and the Peers of France emerge around 1180, the count of Flanders is very prominent in both of these most exclusive clubs of vassals.[136] The old ideas of hierarchy disappeared in the thirteenth century. The term "baron" tends to be reserved for the Peers of Flanders,[137] but those had become extinct, and references to vavasors almost disappear.[138] However, the fundamental principle of the count's unique position remained. The fact that all others under him became more equal could only strengthen his place at the top.

Galbert does not give the number of Peers of Flanders, but Lambert of Ardres later says there were twelve.[139] Warlop has tried to find out who these twelve were. To complete their number he had to consider both Ivan and his older brother as Peers in 1127.[140] This may seem farfetched, but research has since shown that it was not unusual for two Peers to come from one family.[141] On other points, one can no longer agree with Warlop and other Flemish historians who have studied the Peers of Flanders who thought that the Peers' high status and relative autonomy in their territories gave them other privileges, such as the right to elect a new count, to judge the count, and to refuse to continue to acknowledge him.[142] At first

ders), but the Peers were included in that number. In all likelihood there were more barons in 1127–28.

134. This is the number commonly given for the Flemish knights in this period. See Jan Frans Verbruggen, *Het leger en de vloot van de graven van Vlaanderen vanaf het ontstaan tot in 1305* (Brussels, 1960), 73.

135. For France, e.g., see Reynolds, *Fiefs,* 270–319.

136. Heirbaut, "Flanders," 33–34 (apart from the Flemish example, the Carolingian legend of twelve peers also played a role in France; see Jean François Nieus, "Du donjon au tribunal. Les deux âges de la paire châtellaine en France du Nord, Flandres et Lotharingie (fin XIe–XIIIe s.) (1re partie)," *Le Moyen Age* 112 [2006]: 37–39). This double importance may also have been visible in other ways. The then count of Flanders, Philip of Alsace, was godfather to the French king and possibly also, though this is disputed, to the youngest son of the German emperor, both of whom were named Philip (cf. Erwin Assmann, "Friedrich Barbarossas Kinder," *Deutsches Archiv für Erforschung des Mittelalters* 33 [1977]: 463–64).

137. Heirbaut, *Over heren,* 165.

138. An exception may be found in Thierry De Limburg-Stirum, ed., *Coutumes de la ville d'Audenarde,* n° 17 (c. 1300), 2 vols., Coutumes du pays et comté de Flandre, Quartier de Gand 4–5 (Brussels, 1882–86), 2:26–27.

139. Lambert of Ardres, *Historia* 119, p. 619 (1086–91).

140. Warlop, 1.1:141.

141. Heirbaut, *Over heren,* 166n192.

142. Warlop, 1.1:150–51.

glance, this all seems plausible. The count of Flanders was almost entirely autonomous from the king of France until the end of the twelfth century, so there may indeed have been a need for a body who could elect a new count or censure a ruling one, and who would have been better placed to do so than those who were second only to him, that is, the first under him? In reality, however, the Peers never elected a new count. Normally, a reigning count would designate his own successor;[143] the Peers might have provided counsel, but had no other power.[144] In 1127, however, the murdered Charles the Good had designated no successor. Therefore the French king, in an unprecedented and not to be repeated move, chose the new candidate, and the actual election by the Flemish nobles in Arras took place "on the order and advice of the king."[145] Their decision simply confirmed a royal order. Only in 1128 would some Peers (Ivan and Daniel) claim the right to elect a new count, but even then they claimed the right to do so together with the cities.[146] At that time they were already rebelling against William Clito, and their claim that they had the right to choose a new count was nothing more than a justification after the fact.[147]

The right to judge the count did not exist either. True, Gervase of Praet refers to a judgment against the count by the Peers of Flanders and the whole people,[148] which may be a reference to a real procedure. In his speech at Ghent, after all, Ivan had called for a court of Peers and representatives of the people and the clergy to judge the count, but there is no indication that this court was ever held.[149] Besides, Ivan's speech had called only for a moral condemnation. If the proposed court found that the count had been "'lawless and faithless, a deceiver and perjurer,'" then the count should, of his own volition, act accordingly: "Give up the countship! relinquish it to us."[150] What Ivan proposed here was in line with the normal mode of operation in the comital court in nonfeudal complaints against the count. In those cases the count could choose to summon his

143. Cf., e.g., "of our son Baldwin, already designated as count" (filii nostri Balduini jam in comitem designati; De Hemptinne and Verhulst, *Oorkonden* 2.1, n° 111, pp. 179–82 [1148]).

144. Galbert, [69]; Gislebert of Mons, *Chronicon Hanoniense* 82, p. 121; Herman, 12, p. 280.

145. "jussu et consilio regio" (Galbert, [52], 24/25; trans., 196).

146. Galbert, [106], 36/42.

147. See also the preceding article by R. C. Van Caenegem.

148. Galbert, [104], 11/13.

149. Heirbaut, *Over heren,* 169; Raoul Van Caenegem, "Law and Power in Twelfth-Century Flanders," in *Cultures of Power: Lordship, Status, and Process in Twelfth-Century Europe,* ed. Thomas N. Bisson (Philadelphia, 1995), 152; Rider, *God's Scribe,* 159–62.

150. "exlex, sine fide, dolosus, perjurus, discedite a comitatu et eum nobis relinquite" (Galbert, [95], 31/32; trans., 268).

court[151] and ask its advice, but the final decision still lay with him.[152] The Peers could not judge the count. There is not even proof that they formed a separate court in Galbert's time.[153] In the thirteenth century, the Peers did form, not a court of their own, but a separate section of the comital court, competent in cases concerning their peerages.[154] But by 1305 only four of them were left, and their court had lost its exclusive character,[155] so that in the later Middle Ages their existence had become the subject of myths.[156]

The Breach of the Feudal Contract and Its Sanctions: Sanctions against the Vassal

Galbert does not go into the details of what constitutes a breach of the feudal contract. In general, the vassal had to serve his lord "in good faith and without guile," and anything violating that principle was a fault on the part of the vassal. This may sound vague, but such a general clause had its advantages. By imposing a general duty of good faith upon the vassal, feudal law did not have to foresee every particular case,[157] and it would be useless to sum up everything that could be seen as a breach of the feudal contract.[158] Galbert is more interested in the sanctions that followed on such a breach: the renunciation of the feudal relationship by the lord and criminal punishments.

The renunciation of the feudal relationship by the lord is mentioned only once by Galbert.[159] After Ivan's speech in Ghent, Count William was so infuriated that he would have broken his feudal bond with Ivan so that

151. "Let your court, *if you please,* be summoned" (Ponatur curia vestra, *si placet;* Galbert, [95], 25; trans., 268; my emphasis).

152. Cf. *Actes,* n° 19, pp. 60–62 (1096).

153. See, however, Warlop, 1.1:141. The text to which he refers, however, mentions a court of barons, not peers, since three of its members are not Peers of Flanders. The same holds for Daniel Lambrecht and Jan Van Rompaey, "De staatsinstellingen in het Zuiden van de 11de tot de 14de eeuw," in *Algemene geschiedenis der Nederlanden* 3 (Haarlem, 1982), 81.

154. E.g., Ghent, State Archives, Charters of the counts of Flanders, collection de Saint-Genois, n° 12 (1218).

155. Heirbaut, *Over heren,* 170–71.

156. The so-called four Beers of Flanders (*beers, bers* is the nominative of *baron* in Old French, and "baron of Flanders" had replaced the term "Peer of Flanders" in the thirteenth century).

157. Heirbaut, *Over heren,* 263.

158. Those who want a list can find one for Flanders in Opsommer, *Leengoed,* 2:767–75.

159. The terminology is the same as for a renunciation by the vassal, and will be dealt with in the next paragraph.

they could fight a duel as equals, if he had been less afraid of the crowd of citizens.[160] In this case there clearly would have been no judgment by peers, but Galbert does not indicate what would have happened to Ivan's fief (the issue probably being moot, anyway, in the case of a duel to the death since Ivan was heirless). Walter of Thérouanne, however, relates that William of Ypres, one of the claimants for the throne in 1127, renounced the homage to him by his vassal Alard of Warneton, and thereafter took back the fief he had given him, because Alard had hidden Bertulf, the leader of the plot against Charles the Good.[161] Again, there was no judgment by peers, yet this renunciation of the feudal relationship by the lord without a trial by one's fellow vassals was unusual. There are no traces of it either before or after 1127–28. The normal sanction was the loss of the fief,[162] for which a judgment by peers seems to have been necessary,[163] even in the first half of the eleventh century.[164] This seems early but was perhaps not unusual, as there are indications that the judgment by peers may have been known elsewhere in France in the eleventh century.[165] Consequently, one wonders why it was absent in 1127–28, but Galbert's story suggests that William Clito could not have renounced Ivan's homage without the latter's consent.[166] In contrast, William of Ypres acted against a vassal who had helped Bertulf, the leader of the count's murderers. At the time, the frenzy against Bertulf and his followers was so great that even those who had only spoken to them during the siege of the tower, into which they had retreated, could expect punishment.[167] Given those circumstances, William of Ypres's vassal got off lightly. The situation in 1127–28 was exceptional and thus cannot be seen as representative of normal practice.

Like the participants in the earlier conspiracy against Robert the Frisian, which Galbert also mentions, the count's murderers generally received criminal punishments in 1127: they were executed, exiled, or outlawed.[168]

160. Galbert, [95], 39/43.

161. Walter, [38], 17/34; cf. Walter, [53], 13/18.

162. Cf. *Actes,* n° 30, art. 7, pp. 88–95 (1101).

163. De Hemptinne and Verhulst, *Oorkonden* 2.1, n° 269, art. 13, pp. 424–27 (1167); cf. *Actes,* n° 30, art. 10, pp. 88–95 (1101).

164. Cf. Michèle Courtois, *Chartes originales antérieures à 1121 conservées dans le département du Nord* (Nancy, 1982) (unpublished mémoire de maîtrise, Nancy II), 62–63 (1038).

165. See, however, Reynolds, *Fiefs and Vassals,* 132.

166. "'I wish, then, to make myself your equal by rejecting the homage you have done to me. . . .' But Ivan refused" ("Volo ergo, rejecto hominio quod mihi fecisti, parem me tibi facere. . . ." At Iwan renuit; Galbert, [95], 40/43; trans., 269).

167. Galbert, [59], 14/34.

168. Galbert, [29], 5/27; [37], 20/38], 54; [48]; [52], 13/16, 35/39; [57]/[58]; [75], 15/26; [80],

If they were vassals, then they were guilty of treason against the count. In Flemish law, every hostile deed against a person to whom one owed fealty qualified as treason.[169] In the feudal relationship, this meant that a Flemish vassal was guilty of treason against his lord only if he committed an act that was a crime under common (i.e., nonfeudal) law, and its victim was his lord. This could happen in two circumstances: a crime against the person of the lord or an attack upon the count's authority. In case of treason, the lord could demand that the vassal lose his life and his goods, but by the thirteenth century at the latest, the ordinary criminal court was competent, not the lord's court. If the vassal lost his goods, his fiefs returned to his feudal lord, not to the lord who had high jurisdiction and received the nonfeudal goods.[170] Thus, the vassal was punished more harshly than a common criminal, with a mixture of feudal and criminal elements, which Heinrich Mitteis has labeled *Lehnsstrafrecht,*[171] or feudal criminal law. For example, whereas a person who had beaten another without blood-letting was only fined, a vassal could be executed simply for beating his lord,[172] and unlike a common criminal, a banished vassal lost all his goods.[173]

This different treatment of vassals is also evident in 1127–28. During the inquest into the murder of count Charles the Good, a jury of indictment named several persons as accomplices.[174] At first, William Clito wanted to execute them all, but when the accused protested, the comital court distinguished the vassals from the others. The former were outlawed without any trial, but the latter were treated more leniently. Some were

1/6; [87]/[88]; [102], 15/20; cf. [70], 25/26. See also Hariulf of Oudenburg, *Vita Arnulfi* 13, p. 887; Lisiardus of Soissons, *Vita Arnulfi episcopi Suessionensis* 35, ed. Renée Nip, in *Arnulfus van Oudenburg, bisschop van Soisssons (†1087), mens en model. Een bronnenstudie* (Groningen, 1995) (doctoral thesis, RU Groningen; <http://dissertations.ub.rug.nl/FILES/faculties/arts/1995/r.i.a.nip/bijlagen.pdf>), 272.

169. Raoul Van Caenegem, *Geschiedenis van het strafrecht in Vlaanderen van de XIe to de XIVe eeuw,* Verhandelingen van de Koninklijke Vlaamse Academie voor Wetenschappen, Letteren en Schone Kunsten van België, Klasse der Letteren 19 (Brussels, 1954), 82.

170. Heirbaut, *Over heren,* 268–71.

171. Mitteis, *Lehnrecht,* 681–85.

172. Monier, ed., *Les lois, enquêtes et jugements des pairs du castel de Lille,* n° 298, pp. 198–99 (1296); cf. *Leenrechten van Vlaanderen,* art. 22, 3:214–15.

173. Hariulf of Oudenburg, *Vita Arnulfi* 13, p. 887; Lisiardus of Soissons, *Vita Arnulfi* 35, p. 272 (1082); Walter, [10], 39/45 (1120); William of Andres, *Chronica Andrensis* 130, p. 728 (1201).

174. See Alan V. Murray, "The Judicial Inquest into the Death of Count Charles of Flanders (1127): Location and Chronology," *Tijdschrift voor Rechtsgeschiedenis/Revue d'histoire du droit/Legal History Review* 68 (2000): 47–61; the text of the inquest is published in "Enqueste et jugement de chiaus qui le Conte Charlon avoient ochis," ed. J. Rider, in *Walteri Archidiaconi Teruanensis Vita Karoli comitis Flandrię et Vita domni Ioannis Morinensis episcopi,* ed. J. Rider, CC CM 217 (Turnhout, 2006), 199–209.

given a chance to prove their innocence, and a few were even pardoned.[175] This feudal criminal law that treated criminal vassals more severely was to survive in Flanders till the first half of the fourteenth century,[176] though it was already coming under criticism at the end of the previous century.[177] It has been less studied outside Flanders, though it was very prominent in Anglo-Norman feudalism.[178] In 1124, King Henry I was rebuked by Count Charles the Good for ordering three rebels to be blinded. Two of the three posed no problem since they were the king's liege vassals. The third, the king confessed, "never did homage to me," and under normal circumstances, might have expected a lesser punishment, but the king had taken offense at some derisive songs that this person had sung about him.[179]

The imprisonment of a vassal by his lord was related to this criminal feudal law. It also derived from the lord's power over the person of his vassal, and was already known in Carolingian times.[180] It was a temporary disciplinary measure, which was very popular in dealing with the most prominent vassals, whom the lord could not execute outright, but who were too dangerous to be given free rein.[181] Thus in 1127–28 William Clito imprisoned his cousin, William of Ypres, a bastard of the comital house, for almost a year.[182]

Sanctions against the Lord

Like his vassal, the lord could commit felony.[183] The most common way for the lord to do so was to act wrongfully against the vassal himself. In 1128, for example, Ivan of Aalst and Daniel of Dendermonde claimed that the count had planned to fight them "craftily" when he should have met them in peace "without evil intent."[184] Another way for the lord to

175. Galbert, [88], 21/41.

176. *Leenrechten van Vlaanderen,* art. 22, 3:214–15.

177. Monier, ed., *Les lois, enquêtes et jugements des pairs du castel de Lille,* n° 298, pp. 198–99 (1296).

178. Cf. Mitteis, *Lehnrecht,* 681–85.

179. "homagium michi nunquam fecit" (Orderic Vitalis, *Ecclesiastical History,* 6:352–54).

180. Cf. Walther Kienast, *Die fränkische Vasallität. Von den Hausmeiern bis zu Ludwig dem Kind und Karl dem Einfältigen* (Frankfurt, 1990), 123–24.

181. Ferrand of Portugal, count of Flanders, for example, was imprisoned for twelve years after the battle of Bouvines.

182. Galbert, [79], 11/12; [86], 1/11; [90], 1/3; [102], 9/11.

183. The term "felony" is used here only for the sake of convenience. The word was unknown in Flemish feudalism.

184. "dolose," "sine dolo" (Galbert, [95], 58, 56; trans., 270, trans. modified).

commit felony was to act against an agreement for which he had given his vassal as a surety. Ivan's speech against William, discussed above, provides a case in point. There was also a third way for the lord to commit felony. If he acted against a higher norm, he also acted unfaithfully, and his vassal was henceforth discharged from his obligations. In Flanders, the supreme principle was fealty toward the prince, the count of Flanders.[185] In a conflict between the count and another lord, a Fleming had no option but to support his count. The principle "the man of my man is not my man" was not accepted; instead it was rather "the man of my man is my subject." The vassals of the Erembalds followed this rule when they renounced their homage to these "most impious traitors" who had "betrayed the prince of this land."[186] Galbert notes with approval that the Flemish barons considered themselves to be absolved of their oaths to the traitors.[187] The Flemings were unwavering in this. Until the end of the thirteenth century, even after excommunications by bishops and papal legates and threats from the French and German kings (the count's suzerains), they remained staunchly loyal to their count.[188] In itself this is not surprising, but it is remarkable that this "national" sentiment was present at such an early date and directed toward a count, not a king.[189]

Whenever a lord acted wrongly, his vassal had several options. First, he could seek satisfaction from his lord. The lord could then spontaneously do his vassal justice, or he might instead lay their dispute before his court. Ivan made a travesty of this process with all his posturing and seditious talk when he gave his speech in Ghent, but apart from its lack of moderation, the speech was not unusual. If the lord was not willing to bring the dispute before his court, or if this would no longer serve any purpose, the vassal had to react in another way. In the Flanders of Galbert's time, the vassals never called in the help of their lord's suzerain. Comital vassals did not complain about the count at the court of the French or German king because the

185. E.g., *Actes,* n° 81, pp. 180–84 (1116).

186. "impiissimi traditores . . . principem terrae hujus . . . tradidistis" (Galbert, [38], 42, 47/48; trans., 171).

187. Galbert, [29], 44/51.

188. Heirbaut, *Over heren,* 116–27; Heirbaut, "On and Over the Edge of the Empire," 433–46.

189. Walter Mohr, *Entwicklung.* See also Véronique Lambert, *Middeleeuwse historiografie en nationale identiteit. Een vergelijking van het graafschap Vlaanderen en het hertogdom Normandië,* 2 vols. (unpublished doctoral thesis, University of Ghent, 2000); Véronique Lambert, "Methodologische beschouwingen bij het onderzoek naar de concepten 'natie', 'nationalisme' en 'nationale identiteit' in de Middeleeuwen," *Jaarboek voor middeleeuwse geschiedenis* 4 (2001): 66–85.

count never allowed his overlords to interfere in the internal workings of the county. The French king's intervention in 1127 was an exception because the count was dead and the succession was unsure.[190] The wronged vassal had only one real recourse: to renounce his homage and fealty to his lord (i.e., the so-called *diffiduciatio*). Galbert, unlike Walter of Thérouanne, never uses the word *diffiduciare*[191] (the substantive *diffiduciatio* being completely unknown in Flanders, then and later), but instead uses a parallel expression, *hominium reicere,*[192] and in other Flemish texts like expressions can be found.[193]

Like homage, *diffiduciatio* needed a certain ritual. The vassals of the Erembalds in 1127, and Gervase of Praat one year later, first set out their grievances against their lord in a speech inspired by the circumstances, so it may be that it was not a necessary part of the ritual.[194] Thereafter, the vassal threw away a stalk, which Galbert called *exfestucare.*[195] Bloch thinks that it is likely that the stalk was broken before the vassal discarded it.[196] However, there are many descriptions of this ritual in Flanders, because it was also used when a fief was sold, and none of them mentions that the stalk was broken.[197] There are some indications that the vassal was supposed to renounce his homage in the presence of his lord, but only the vassals of the Erembalds did so in 1127, and in their case, their lords were shut up in a tower they were besieging. In 1128, the rebels against William Clito sent either messengers[198] or a letter.[199] William could hardly have blamed them for this lack of courage. A month earlier, after all, he had himself refrained from dismissing Ivan from his homage after the speech

190. See Dirk Heirbaut, "Le cadre juridique. Institutions et droit en Flandre vers 1302," in *1302, le désastre de Courtrai: Mythe et réalité de la bataille des Éperons d'or,* ed. Raoul Van Caenegem (Antwerp, 2002), 124–29.

191. Walter, [53], 18.

192. Galbert, [95], 41; [104], 10/11.

193. E.g., also in the twelfth century: "homagium remandare" (Lambert of Wattrelos, *Annales Cameracenses,* ed. Georg Heinrich Pertz, MGH SS 16 [Hanover, 1859], 530–31).

194. Galbert, [38], 37/51; [104], 5/21.

195. Galbert, [38], 50, 53; [95], 39, 60/61; [98], 5; [101], 31.

196. Bloch, "Les formes de la rupture," 165–66.

197. Cf. Heirbaut, "Procedure," 47–48, for which all Flemish charters from 1000 to 1300 have been consulted.

198. Galbert, [95], 54, 61.

199. Galbert, [101], 29/32. This is the real meaning of "those knights from Oostkerke, with their names inscribed on parchment, sent a message on behalf of themselves and many others, to Count William in Ypres" (illi milites ex Ostkerca ex nomine inscriptos parchameno sese et plures alios transmiserunt consuli Willelmo in Ipra; Galbert, [101], 29/31; trans., 278), and not that their names were given earlier by Galbert (they were not; only Hugo Snaggaerd was mentioned), as Bloch thinks (Bloch, "Les formes de la rupture," 145).

in Ghent because he feared the anger of the crowd. The use of messengers and letters was very rare in Galbert's time, when feudalism was still a very personal affair (even in the thirteenth century only two very august vassals were allowed to send a representative for their homage),[200] but it was warranted by the circumstances.

The renunciation of homage had grave consequences. The vassal could now fight against his lord since he no longer was bound to be faithful to him. This was why William Clito had to renounce Ivan's homage to him before he could fight a duel with him. A fight was inevitable when homage was renounced because the vassal renounced only his homage (or more elaborately his "homage, fealty, and security"),[201] not his fief. He therefore had to take up arms if he wanted to keep it, and this was the weak point of defying the lord. Non-comital (i.e., lesser) vassals could never do so. The count, guardian of the peace, did not allow the order of his county to be disturbed by fights between them and their lords.[202] There was one exception, but, ironically, it too confirmed this rule. The vassals of the Erembalds renounced their homage and fought their lords, but in doing so, they were taking revenge for the count's murder, thus restoring, not disturbing, the peace.

In theory, comital vassals could also defy their lord, but in reality most of them were powerless to do so. The knights from Oostkerke had to experience this firsthand. In the general enthusiasm of the revolt against William Clito, they went over to Ivan's party and renounced their homage to William,[203] but later, as the tide was turning against the rebels, they switched sides again. On that same day, however, William Clito was killed, so that they ended up on the wrong side once more.[204] Clearly, they were anything but masters of their fate. Only the most powerful comital vassals, like Ivan, could really exercise their right to defy the count when wrongfully treated. This right to resist the count disappeared even for them after 1164, when Philip of Alsace's power gave Flanders an unheard-of peace.[205]

200. Eleonore of Castile, queen of England (Olivarius Vredius, *Genealogia comitum Flandriae,* 2 vols. [Bruges, 1642–43], 2:100–101), and Philip of Courtenay, titular emperor of Constantinople (cf. J. Bovesse, "Notes sur Harelbeke et Biervliet dans le cadre de l'histoire des Maisons de Namur et de France," *Handelingen van de koninklijke commissie voor geschiedenis* 150.3 [1984], 469–70).

201. E.g., "hominium, fidem et securitatem" (Galbert, [38], 53/54; trans., 171).

202. Heirbaut, *Over heren,* 205–8; Heirbaut, *Flanders,* 26–27.

203. Galbert, [98], 21/26; [101], 29/32.

204. Galbert, [120], 25/28.

205. Lambert of Wattrelos, *Annales Cameracenses,* 536.

Some Flemish nobles tried to fight their count after 1164, and their right of resistance was even recognized (exceptionally) by the count,[206] yet no vassal rebelled without the support of a foreign prince. It is true that a Flemish vassal could try to pursue the count in the court of the king of France from the reign of Philip August on, but that happened only once, and the complaining vassal was also a very important vassal of the French king.[207] In short, the right of the vassal to defy his lord was virtually nonexistent; almost the only time it had any real significance was in 1127–28. The same held true elsewhere in Europe. Vassals who, following the niceties, renounced their homage and then fought their lords were rare.[208]

The Influence of Feudal Ideas

At first sight, one can find arguments in Galbert's journal that support the thesis that Flanders was a feudal society in his time. For example, when William Clito went to Saint-Omer, he was met by the young men of the city, who asked him to confirm as "a kind of 'fief'" the right to hunt small game in the surrounding woods.[209] *Feodum,* this time, does not mean fief. It is just a favor, a *beneficium.* This nontechnical use of *feodum* is highly exceptional,[210] and cannot be seen as an indication of the influence of feudalism. It is different for the homage and fealty done to a count (or, at least, a contender for the comital title) by ordinary citizens, non-vassals, in 1127–28[211]

206. Warnkönig, *Rechtsgeschichte,* 3.2, n° 132, pp. 210–11 (1229).

207. Heirbaut, *Over heren,* 119. Moreover, the vassal concerned wanted to sell his Flemish holdings, and the French lawsuit was mainly a mechanism for raising the price the then countess of Flanders had to pay.

208. Cf. Donald J. Kagay, "The Iberian *diffidamentum:* From Vassalic Defiance to the *Code duello,*" in *The Final Argument: The Imprint of Violence on Society in Medieval and Early Modern Europe,* ed. Donald J. Kagay and L. J. Andrew Villalon (Woodbridge, 1998), 73–82, where references to actual diffiduciations in a feudal context are conspicuously lacking.

209. "quatenus feodum" (Galbert, [66], 10/11; trans., 228). See also Raoul C. Van Caenegem, "Notes on Galbert of Bruges and his Translators," in *Peasants and Townsmen in Medieval Europe. Studia in honorem Adriaan Verhulst,* ed. Jean-Marie Duvosquel and Erik Thoen (Ghent, 1995), 625; and the essay by R. C. Van Caenegem, "Galbert of Bruges and 'Law Is Politics,'" discussed above.

210. I know of only one other example for Flanders: Archives départementales du Nord (Lille), Series 1 H, n° 631/3137 (1115–31). Elsewhere, church benefices were sometimes called *feodum* (e.g., Arnoud-Jan Bijsterveld, "*Dusela villa Taxandrie:* Een drietal onopgemerkte oorkonden betreffende Duizel uit de elfde en de dertiende eeuw," *Noord-Brabants historisch jaarboek* 13 [1996]: 180–81). On the term *feodum* in Flanders, see Heirbaut, *Over lenen en families,* 19–21.

211. Galbert, [20], 25/30; [25], 33/37; [55], 43/46; [66], 36/37; [94], 6/9; [101], 22/25; [102], 3/6; [103], 6/7; [122], 1/5.

(sometimes through their representatives).[212] They appear to have considered themselves to be quasi-vassals. As subjects they had no rights, only duties toward their count; when they had done homage, however, their situation was more like that of a vassal. Their relationship with the count was no longer one-way, but had become reciprocal. Instead of subjects, they had become contract-partners, with obligations and rights. This also meant that if the count did not respect his part of their bargain, they were discharged from their duties and could fight him. Thus, the influence of feudalism contributed to the development of the idea that subjects have certain rights that the ruler should respect, because his power is based on a contract with his people.[213] This also happened outside Flanders.[214] In fact, in other parts of Europe, the influence of feudalism was so strong that cities had vassals of their own.[215] However, in Flanders, the influence of feudalism on the contractual view of the relationship between ruler and ruled and that view itself were less prominent in 1127–28 than is generally thought.

Galbert gives the impression that it was standard practice for Flemish citizens to do homage and fealty to a new count,[216] but neither before nor after 1127–28 did ordinary Flemings do so (if they had, the distinction between those of the count's murderers who had done homage to him and those who had not would have been pointless and impossible),[217] though one might think so if one is unaware of the context. In Flanders, homage and fealty were done by the vassals; ordinary people swore only an oath of fealty,[218] in a tradition that went back to Carolingian times.[219] What happened in 1127–28 was exceptional, and even Galbert indicates that homage was normally reserved for those holding a fief, the *feodati*.[220] One may even wonder whether Galbert has written down the truth, as Walter of

212. Galbert, [54], 6/10.

213. Heirbaut, "Galbert," 58–62.

214. See, in general, Joseph Canning, *A History of Medieval Political Thought 300–1450* (London, 1996), 163–64.

215. Bryce Lyon, "What Role Did Communes Have in the Feudal System?" *Belgisch tijdschrift voor filologie en geschiedenis* 72 (1994): 241–53.

216. Galbert, [54], 9/10; [55], 43/46.

217. Galbert, [88], 36/41.

218. Gislebert of Mons, *Chronicon Hanoniense* 5–6, p. 8; Thierry De Limburg-Stirum, *Codex diplomaticus Flandriae. Inde ab anno 1296 ad usque 1325,* n° 105 (1299), 2 vols. (Bruges, 1879–89), 1:273–74.

219. Matthias Becher, *Eid und Herrschaft. Untersuchungen zum Herrscherethos Karls des Gro(en* (Sigmaringen, 1993), 78–194.

220. Galbert, [55], 82/85; [104], 22/24.

Thérouanne is silent about the homage by the citizens.[221] Yet, Walter does not pay much attention to all these ceremonies, whereas Galbert mentions this homage many times (because he was, unlike Walter, really interested in what happened to the citizens)[222] and is generally so reliable that it would be hard to imagine him distorting the truth in this matter.

Even if one believes Galbert, the events of 1127–28 cannot always be seen as evidence of the influence of feudalism on the development of contractual ideas about the prince's power. In fact, the first homage by ordinary citizens mentioned is the homage and fealty by the Flemish merchants at the Ypres fair to William of Ypres, but they would not have seen this as a contract, because they had not been given any choice. Recalcitrant merchants were even imprisoned, and they were freed only after they had done homage and fealty[223] (which goes to show that William was already a hard and rash man before he gave Flemings a bad name in England as the captain of Stephen of Blois's mercenaries). It is hard to see anything in this extortion but the opposite of the respect for inviolable rights, which is typical of contractual ideas about power. William had been advised to seek this recognition by Bertulf, the head of the conspiracy against Charles the Good. Bertulf, chancellor of Flanders, had probably thought that vassals would do homage to William while others would swear fealty. That everyone, even foreigners, had to do homage was William's innovation. It was imitated by William Clito,[224] who, in all likelihood, wanted thus to counter William's claims. That other pretenders also imitated the practice was to be expected,[225] as was the citizens' tendency to begin to see the granting and confirming of privileges by a new count as a payment for their recognition of his accession to power. These privileges are "the price of their election and acceptance of the person of the new count."[226] Although their homage, unlike that of the vassals, was collective and not individual,[227] and they did not receive fiefs,[228] the citizens had, at least, moved one step closer to being vassals.

221. Walter, [46], 19/23; [49], 15/20.

222. Coué, "Geschichtsschreibung," 108–29.

223. Galbert, [20], 25/31; [25], 15/20.

224. Galbert, [54], 6/10; [55], 43/46; [66], 36/37.

225. Galbert, [94], 6/9; [101], 22/25; [102], 3/6; [103], 6/7; [122], 1/5.

226. "quatenus pro pretio electionis et susceptionis personae novi consulis" (Galbert, [55], 30/31; trans., 203).

227. It took but a moment for the citizens to do homage, whereas three days were needed for the vassals' homage (Galbert, [55], 43/45; [56], 1/21).

228. Only the *feodati* did (Galbert, [55], 82/85; [104], 22/24).

Nevertheless, the cities did not immediately take the next logical step: they did not renounce their relationship by the ritual of the *effestucatio* and challenge the count as a vassal who had a contract with the count would have done if the latter had failed to respect it. The first, and in fact only, city to do so was Ghent, the city that asked Ivan of Aalst to denounce the count's perjury.[229] The citizens of Bruges did not do so, even though they played a prominent role in the rebellion, were urged by the citizens of Ghent to follow their example,[230] and could wax even more rhetorical about popular sovereignty than Ivan.[231] Ideas of a contractual relationship between the Flemings and their prince, influenced by feudalism, were mainly a Ghent phenomenon. Consequently, it was, most of all, in Ghent that they survived. The new count, Thierry of Alsace, had to bow for his cities, but his son, Philip, could impose his will. At least for as long as he lived. As soon as they had heard of his death, the citizens of Ghent wrangled a new charter from his widow in 1191. Its first article stated that they had to remain faithful to the count only for as long as the count was willing to treat them in a just and reasonable way.[232] Thereafter, Ghent would always be an unruly city for the counts, so that *In Defence of a Rebellious City* is the very apt title for a recent book describing its history.[233] The city of Ghent may have been inspired by feudal examples in 1128, but it was about the only one.

Conclusion

Galbert of Bruges can no longer be seen as the prime source for the description of some kind of ideal Western European feudalism. Though Flemish practices in 1127–28 reflect general European patterns at times, they are in many cases specifically Flemish, and the development of feudalism in Flanders in 1127–28 was ahead of the development of feudalism in most of the rest of Europe. Galbert's journal is not about European feudalism, but about Flemish feudalism at a specific moment in time. The events Galbert described, moreover, were exceptional and shocking even for that time, most of all for the community of lords and vassals. It is significant

229. Galbert, [95], 1/39.

230. Galbert, [98], 1/8.

231. Galbert, [106], 14/53.

232. Walter Prevenier, *De oorkonden der graven van Vlaanderen (1191–aanvang 1206),* 3 vols. (Brussels, 1964–71), n° 1, 1:1–16.

233. Johan Decavele, ed., *Ghent: In Defence of a Rebellious City* (Antwerp, 1989).

and appropriate that Warlop uses 1127–28 as a watershed in his book about the history of the Flemish nobility.[234] It was THE crisis. As a result, few events in 1127–28 followed normal patterns, feudal or otherwise. In short, Galbert should not be considered a general authority on feudalism. He described not ordinary feudalism, but extraordinary feudalism. He is anything but the textbook author on feudalism Ganshof and others took him to be, and what they write about him should be read with caution. This does not, however, mean that we should now disown him, as the new authorities on feudalism seem to do. As long as one takes the context into account, Galbert's journal is still a very valuable (and enjoyable) source for the study of feudalism, even though Flemish feudalism was exceptional in many ways: it was earlier, more controlled, more family-orientated, and less influenced by foreign practices than almost any other feudalism in Europe.[235] Add to that the murder of the count and a civil war and it is clear that Galbert shows feudalism at its worst (and, sometimes, its best). Flemish feudalism in 1127–28 was not "normal," but only when feudalism was under the most extreme stress can one really see its strengths and weaknesses, and for that Galbert's journal still deserves to be on the must-read list of any specialist of feudalism.

234. Warlop, esp. c. 4: "The crisis."

235. Heirbaut, *Over heren,* 309–20; Heirbaut, *Over lenen en families,* 207–17.

4

Galbert of Bruges and the Urban Experience of Siege

STEVEN ISAAC

More than four centuries after Galbert of Bruges recorded the tumultuous events of 1127–28, William Shakespeare set himself the task of imagining and recreating the conditions of a medieval siege, in this case, that of Harfleur by Henry V. After costly assaults that doubtless embittered his surviving troops, the English king threatened Harfleur's inhabitants (who were also its defenders) with quite a graphic litany of atrocities that his soldiers would perpetrate upon them, their wives, and children should the besiegers finally enter the city by force. He ended the roll call of likely outrages by demanding: "What say you? Will you yield, and this avoid? Or, guilty in defense, be thus destroyed?"[1] In the Bard's version of events, the vivid imminence of what Henry threatened cowed the city's governor into surrender. In the actual event, the city's leaders maintained a vigorous defense, one that gave little hope of a quick capitulation. Further assaults and countermeasures ensued before Harfleur's defenders requested of King Henry the formulaic waiting period (four days in this case) to request a relief force from their French overlord. When that aid was not forthcoming, they were able to stave off the city's sack by a negotiated surrender.[2]

Shakespeare may be forgiven a bit of literary license in his need to move his play onward, but this scene should still give the military historian reason to pause. The forces that typically worked upon medieval burghers defending their communities did not lead them to roll over at the first sign of

1. William Shakespeare, *The Life of King Henry the Fifth,* III.3.43–44, ed. Claire McEachern (Harmondsworth, 1999), 49.

2. Anne Curry, *Agincourt: A New History* (Stroud, 2006), 96–98.

trouble. Going back at least to the twelfth century, medieval cities repeatedly and successfully showed themselves able to fend off besiegers. Nonetheless, they were often the prey of kings and magnates, of marauders, and of rival cities. These two elements, power and vulnerability, combined to create a peculiar military culture in medieval cities, especially those of the twelfth century. Thus, the paradox in our sources: the almost simultaneous images of townspeople as fearful and bellicose.[3] As the image of cities as nonfeudal islands in a feudal sea recedes, the martial components of urban life grow more apparent. The role of the urban environment as a breeding (and proving) ground for foot soldiers, the ones loathed and dreaded for their effectiveness, becomes all the more understandable. Once considered oddities, those aspects can now be seen as normative, and nowhere is this perhaps more evident than in the record left us by Galbert of Bruges.[4] In his account, we see the very process that shortly thereafter yielded the type of professional soldiers that traumatized the social elites of the latter 1100s.

Galbert's entries have an immediacy, a wealth of detail, and that very vividness that military historians so rarely find in medieval sources—all of which begs the question: why have we not turned more often to him? The road from Shakespeare's after-the-fact imagination to Galbert's almost daily journal is not all that far. The laws of war that Fluellen took for granted at both Harfleur and Agincourt immediately recall the "laws of the siege" developed at Bruges in the spring of 1127.[5] Still, few historians have traveled this road fully.[6] Because of the wealth of evidence available, the four-

3. The picture is all the more apparent in the latter part of Galbert's history, as the people of Bruges suffer the vicissitudes of Thierry's campaign for the comital title (Galbert, [107]/[118]). See also Guibert of Nogent's description of how the burghers of Laon strove to hide the trappings of their wealth so as not to attract the rapacious attention of nearby nobles (*Autobiographie* 3.11, ed. Edmond-René Labande [Paris, 1981], 366).

4. Ross's notes (trans.) betray repeated astonishment or puzzlement over the close relations between townsmen and their lords, including intermarriage, general socializing, and habitual negotiation of "feudal" customs.

5. An interesting analysis of Shakespeare's reliance upon, and twisting of, historical traditions may be found in Theodor Meron, *Henry's Wars and Shakespeare's Laws* (Oxford, 1993). The conventions of siege warfare were well-established by Galbert's day, with roots stretching back into both Greek and Roman traditions as well as Old Testament injunctions (see especially Dt 20:10–15). One of the best treatments of this topic, detailing both customary practice and exceptions, is Matthew Strickland, *War and Chivalry* (Cambridge, 1996), 212–24.

6. One exception is Laurence Marvin, "'. . . Men famous in combat and battle . . .': Common Soldiers and the Siege of Bruges, 1127," *Journal of Medieval History* 24 (1998): 243–58. Marvin traces the martial qualities of the civic militias and adventurers that responded to the siege of the assassins in spring 1127. I agree with most of his conclusions, but I am interested here in looking at how townspeople responded when the events were not so clearly in their favor.

teenth century in general and the Hundred Years War in particular have become something of a scenic overlook: urban levies dominated the course of battles such as Courtrai and Mons-en-Pévèle; conversely, townsfolk suffered dramatically as targets in the Hundred Years War.[7] Galbert's record of the crises of 1127 and 1128 shows, though, that the seeds of urban military prowess were in the ground long before. Moreover, his account has that eyewitness quality more common in later wars but so rare in twelfth-century narratives.[8] If we leaven his account with the evidence of other similarly involved witnesses who knew well their own urban milieus, the situation of the Flemish cities in the first third of the twelfth century appears precocious, but hardly peculiar.[9]

One of the few studies of urban populations in their twelfth-century military context has been James Powers's analysis of the towns of the Luso-Hispanic frontier. Powers filled the absence of urban narratives by gleaning from Muslim chroniclers occasional hints of how Christian townspeople weathered campaigns; more fruitful, however, was his analysis of the *fueros,* the lengthy, itemized charters that detailed the liberties and responsibilities of urban inhabitants. From the emphasis on patrol duties, speedy musters, penalties for dereliction of duty, and concern for treachery, Powers concluded unsurprisingly that the lives of townspeople on the frontier were "stressful." They enjoyed unusual freedoms, true, but at the cost of being a frontline defense, which often had to hold out in isolation during

7. Most recently, James Tracy, ed., *City Walls: The Urban Enceinte in Global Perspective* (Cambridge, 2000), dedicated two historical analyses to medieval topics: one focused on the late thirteenth century, the other on French cities during the Hundred Years War. See also Ivy A. Corfis and Michael Wolfe, eds., *The Medieval City under Siege* (Woodbridge, 1995), where all the chapters concentrating on pre-twelfth century sieges deal almost wholly with Christendom's frontiers, not its internal conflicts. Finally, Christopher Allmand, "War and the Non-Combatant in the Middle Ages," in *Medieval Warfare: A History,* ed. Maurice Keen (Oxford, 1999), 253–72.

8. For this reason, J. F. Verbruggen rightly stressed the value of vernacular sources over Latin alternatives, whenever such sources are available. See *The Art of Warfare in Western Europe during the Middle Ages from the eighth century to 1340,* 2nd ed., trans. Sumner Wilard and Mrs. R. W. Southern (Woodbury, 1997), 14–15, 94, and especially 188–89, where he weaves historical and fictional accounts together seamlessly. His injunctions have been followed and repeated by John Gillingham, "Richard I and the Science of War in the Middle Ages," in *War and Government in the Middle Ages: Essays in Honour of J. O. Prestwich,* ed. John Gillingham and J. C. Holt (Woodbridge, 1984), 79, where he promotes the "belief that vernacular brings us closer than Latin to the thoughts and actions of soldiers."

9. Because of my specific interest here in ordinary townsmen, I will pay only glancing attention to the vivid portrayal of the Erembalds while besieged. My assumption, which is ready-made for exceptions, is that as men apprenticed to warfare, they differed in their actions under stress from urban men and women, as well as from most of the professional religious.

Muslim offensives. When not being besieged or raided, they stayed busy anticipating these threats.[10]

One might easily argue that such exposed settlements were a peculiar case. All the towns of western Christendom held a similar frontier status, however; they were rarely so interior to any polity as to ignore the possibility of being captured or coerced by external foes. Moreover, the easy fracturing of feudal conglomerations led often enough to formerly internal, even allied, forces becoming a threat. In Galbert's pages the inhabitants of Bruges pass from simple burghers to militia and back again with alacrity and no disjunction; the transformation (or was it one?) should remind us of Christopher Allmand's point that the term "civilian" had little currency before the eighteenth and nineteenth centuries.[11]

On an obvious frontier or not, towns had a military value that medieval princes—and some historians of the twentieth century[12]—clearly recognized. More importantly, the urban inhabitants knew it themselves. "It is time to discard the antiquated notion of burghers huddled behind their walls," wrote David Nicholas in his survey of medieval cities.[13] He was referring to the physical layout of cities, but his comment could well apply to a number of further attributes: the involvement of burghers in the feudal relations of secular and ecclesiastical magnates as well as the assumed antipathy (and ineptitude) of townspeople in military matters. Their precocity in such matters was originally pointed out over fifty years ago by Charles Petit-Dutaillis in his work on the French communes. For the majority of the towns that obtained the status of commune, Petit-Dutaillis found virtually no change in their day-to-day administration or privileges save for the oath (*conjuratio*) by which they swore their loyalty to the granting power and, perhaps most importantly, each other. The ability to associate openly initiated, if it did not confirm, the burghers' confidence in their ability to impose their will upon local circumstances. "It was an aggressive lordship which, in the early thirteenth century, waged

10. James F. Powers, "Life on the Cutting Edge: The Besieged Town on the Luso-Hispanic Frontier in the Twelfth Century," in *The Medieval City under Siege,* ed. Corfis and Wolfe, 17–34.

11. Allmand, "War and the Non-Combatant," 253.

12. See F. M. Powicke, *The Loss of Normandy,* 2nd ed. (Manchester, 1960), 210–12; Achille Luchaire, *Social France at the Time of Philip Augustus,* trans. Edward Krehbiel (New York, 1967), 412–17; Georges Duby, *Le Dimanche de Bouvines* (Paris, 1973), 90–92; and Charles Petit-Dutaillis, *The French Communes in the Middle Ages,* trans. Joan Vickers (New York, 1978), passim.

13. David Nicholas, *The Growth of the Medieval City: From Antiquity to the Early Fourteenth Century* (New York, 1997), 93.

wars and concluded peace treaties with the neighboring barons."[14] What French communes were accomplishing by the thirteenth century, however, the Flemish towns were clearly doing already in the unsettled conditions after Charles the Good's assassination.

Given the transformation and interplay of so many dynamics in the twelfth century, the physical space of cities could hardly be static, nor was it always clearly delineated. The economic revival of the period saw the growth of new civic nuclei outside the constraints of older, smaller enceintes. These suburbs, better described by the appellation *faubourgs,* tended to arise along those axes that led to profit: thoroughfares, riverbanks, and notably often, the environs of new monastic establishments.[15] This growth in turn led to new parish churches and the endowments necessary for them. These new settlements were not the homes of the timid; they lay exposed, often for decades, without their own defenses. They were the creations of the new merchants who dared the expanses between settlements or of the desperate peasants and artisans who could find opportunity nowhere else and yet might still be members of a commune.[16] Centralizing authorities had a clear interest in promoting these developments as well. Adriaan Verhulst has amply demonstrated the role of the Flemish counts in spurring a renewed growth among the Flemish cities in the tenth and eleventh centuries. Where the counts built new fortifications, such as at Ghent, Bruges, and Saint-Omer, their political and economic programs attracted weapons makers and leather workers, artisans naturally affiliated with military life.[17] The count's involvement, however, scarcely gave any guarantee of peace or security, either from external foes or from internal threats. The intense interest in stability and order displayed by urban chroniclers such as Galbert resulted from the violent latencies in the medieval city. Sworn associations, be they communes, guilds, or even more militant efforts such as the Peace Brethren (*paciferi*) of the later 1100s, had

14. Petit-Dutaillis, *The French Communes,* 67.

15. André Chédeville, J. LeGoff, and J. Roussiaud, *La Ville en France au Moyen Age* (Paris, 1980), 55–83.

16. Even if his overall thesis has been displaced by recent scholarship, Henri Pirenne's description of the revival of inter-city trade is still worth recalling here, especially his picture of "merchant troops" on the road with the period's other less-savory populations (*Medieval Cities: Their Origins and the Revival of Trade* [Princeton, 1952], 120–21). See also Petit-Dutaillis, *The French Communes,* 62.

17. Adriaan Verhulst, *The Rise of Cities in North-West Europe* (Cambridge, 1999), 90–91; and "The Origins of Towns in the Low Countries and the Pirenne Thesis," *Past and Present* 122 (February 1989): 3–35.

as their aim the quelling of unrest, which could spring from any number of frictions: rival lordships, economic exploitation, unchecked brigandage, old feuds (which could often spread from individuals to involve whole neighborhoods or various networks). The desire to avoid tumult and risk also led to one of the paradoxical aspects of urban military culture: more than a few towns gained charters exempting them from military service in return for significant financial contributions to the grantor.[18]

Towns were thus thoroughly enmeshed in feudal obligations. The ecclesiastical presence in towns alone represented one form of lordship, and secular lords seeking advantages in the new economy of the twelfth century also had interests in towns. The resistance of many ecclesiastical authorities to communes derived from a perception—likely accurate—that the burghers were creating an association that in most cases would curtail the privileges of local churchmen. In the same vein, towns might garner a charter from a king or count to counter the exactions of a local secular lord. Historians may still debate whether such grants were truly feudal in nature, but the language of the documents makes clear the inroads of feudal thinking into new arenas. Many towns swore loyalty, if not homage per se, to their lord "against all comers" along with pledges of troops.[19] In the south, the distinction between bourgeois and feudal was even more blurred. John Mundy found the mingling of these elements reached the margins of society in Toulouse: "Even in the thirteenth century the most important butchers and meat markets in the City were held as fiefs of the count and submitted to his regulation." In a similar vein, tanners and boatmen on the Garonne testified that they owed the count service on his siege weapons when called upon.[20] Geoffrey of Vigeois relates one remarkable case from the early 1140s in which a magnate of Puy Saint-Front swore homage to one of his peasants to forestall a feud. The prior of Vigeois's tone makes it clear how exceptional he found this incident, but the example shows us how elastic these forms could be to the actual practitioners.[21] Such cases frustrated the sensibilities of northern lords when they

18. See the example of Dijon in Petit-Dutaillis, *The French Communes,* 64.

19. Petit-Dutaillis, *The French Communes,* 67–71.

20. John Hine Mundy, *Liberty and Political Power in Toulouse 1050–1230* (New York, 1954), 31; *Layettes du Trésor,* I, nos. 149, 413. The weapons in question were *petrariae* and *frondevolis.* The latter, if related to *fundibalus,* would refer to slingers, but potentially even to operators of trebuchets (*fundibalarium*).

21. Geoffrey of Vigeois, *Chronica,* in Philippe Labbe, *Nova Bibliotheca Manuscriptorum Librorum,* 2 vols. (Paris, 1657), 2:302.

came upon these arrangements; one wonders, though, if the merchants of northern towns viewed them in envy.

All these issues and more filled the week immediately following the assassination of Charles the Good. First and foremost, the burghers found themselves as entangled in multiple loyalties as any "vassal" of the time. The first parts of Galbert's record demonstrate a clear appreciation of the peace and commercial prosperity Charles had brought to Flanders. At the same time, the contradictions within Galbert's record, especially his awkward explanations of the citizens' participation in the counsels of "their lords,"[22] betray a vestigial Brugeois loyalty to the Erembalds as the family of their castellan. Professor Dhondt's conclusions on the solidarities within Flemish society are all to the point here: the comital office was a convenient, communal focal point whose stability encouraged competing groups to coalesce. When that position was thrown into wide-open competition in 1127, the tensions just under the surface in Flanders quickly emerged. The people of Bruges formed one solidarity (but an easily riven one), which vacillated at first between the Erembalds, the count of Holland, and the incoming "barons of the siege." Even so, the burghers acted with confidence after the initial shock. A year later, consensus again had to be established as to whether to join Ghent in preferring Thierry of Alsace over William Clito. As Jeff Rider has pointed out in his recent study of Galbert, that consensus was much harder to establish because of the sense (Galbert's sense, at least) that the pledge to Clito remained binding, and to reject him was to rebel against a divine appointment as well as a worldly one.[23] For Galbert, spiritual tactics were a part of any *realpolitik;* was this assumption, however, a part of Galbert's conditioning as a townsman or a result of his training in the Church? Galbert's bitter tone in his final chapters betrays the pressures exerted among the burghers themselves to maintain and justify a new consensus in the face of apparent condemnation by God on the battlefield.[24] True, the Flemish cities were exercising, even enunciating, remarkable ideas of their own liberty, but these claims

22. "Now for the first time the townsmen of our place openly entered into the councils of their lords" (Adhuc suburbani nostri loci aperte introierunt ad consilia dominorum illorum; Galbert, [25], 26/27; trans., 144).

23. See Rider, *God's Scribe,* 89–92, and 137, for a compelling picture of how Galbert probably reworked the events and common ideologies of his surroundings into a coherent picture that was not quite as democratic as may first appear.

24. Jan Dhondt, "Les 'Solidarités' médiévales. Une société en transition: La Flandre en 1127–28," *Annales E.S.C.* 12 (1957): 529–60; Rider, *God's Scribe,* 174–78, 192–98.

still sought to operate within traditional framework and hierarchies (i.e., comital and ecclesiastical).

The situation at Bruges was actually rather uncomplicated when compared to that of Limoges a scant fifty years later. A long-running rivalry between the viscount of the city, the abbot of St. Martial's, and the resident bishop grew even more complicated once Richard Plantagenet had been accepted, by virtue of his office as Count of Poitou, as overlord of the city. He was at first acclaimed wildly, primarily because the burghers disliked his father, Henry, duke of Aquitaine, king of England, and the next lord up in the hierarchy of authorities. When Richard's brother, the young Henry, allied himself with Viscount Ademar in a plot to oust Richard, the folk of Limoges were squarely between the proverbial hammer and anvil. At one point, the young Henry and the viscount had forcibly occupied the *bourg* while King Henry, newly reconciled with Bishop Sébrand, encamped his forces in the old city. Taunts and projectiles flew back and forth between the contending forces, with the townsmen caught in the middle. And all the while, Richard was reducing outlying strongholds and ravaging the countryside, activities doubtless visible from both sets of walls.[25]

Gilbert of Mons provides an unintentionally comical portrait of similar forces at play in the next decade. Estranged from his wife and without heirs, Henry of Namur appointed Baldwin of Hainaut as his heir. To demonstrate that he was in earnest, he assembled the townsmen before himself and Baldwin, read out his will, and had them swear homage to Baldwin. Less than a year later, he was induced by the duke of Louvain to reconcile with his wife. Accordingly, he reassembled his burghers and had them swear perpetual loyalty to his new allies. When Baldwin responded by reducing the city's outer defenses to rubble, Henry repented of his "misjudgment," and the townsmen had to come together once more and profess their allegiance to their "rightful" lord.[26] Are we then to wonder whence came urban self-reliance? Should we wonder if familiarity in this case did breed contempt?

Despite the overall dismantling of his arguments about the revival of urban trade, Pirenne gave us a picture that we should not let fade of the new bourgeoisie as adventurous yet disciplined entrepreneurs. "Maritime or land trade was possible only by the grace of the mutual assurance an

25. Geoffrey of Vigeois, *Chronica,* 308, 310, 318–19, 334–35.

26. Gilbert of Mons, *La Chronique de Gislebert de Mons* 122, 129, 139, 142–43, ed. Léon Vanderkindere (Brussels, 1904), 190–91, 195–96, 207–9, 215–22.

association inspired in its members, of the discipline which it imposed on them. . . . Security existed for them only if guaranteed by force, and force was an attribute of collectivity."[27] This attribute, however, was notably absent in the English translation of *The Murder of Charles the Good* that has benefited so many collegiate courses. The notes that make Ross's edition so accessible present, instead, a stereotype at odds with Galbert's own images. She notes on several occasions a "burgher hatred of war."[28] Admittedly, Galbert's opening praises of Charles include the fact that the count outlawed the very presence of weapons in markets and towns. If Galbert can be believed, the instinct for peace was so well nurtured that bows, arrows, and other weapons were laid aside all over the country.[29] With Charles dead, however, a less pacific impulse appears. On the first nightfall after the crime, even though Bruges lay in quiet shock, the murderers prepared the church of Saint Donatian for a possible raid, and their fears soon proved well-grounded. With the first emergency clamor of the church bells, the citizens came running, with swords that apparently had not been laid too far aside.[30] Afterward, they turned immediately to reinforcing, perhaps extending, Bruges's defenses. We can probably assume the involvement of the whole populace in this effort, although Galbert gives little indication throughout his chronicle of when women or youths participated in events. The parade of youths who came out with bows and arrows in companies to greet William Clito at Saint Omer shows the future merchants and artisans receiving another necessary apprenticeship.[31] During the storming of

27. Pirenne, *Medieval Cities,* 119. The emphasis on consensus in Galbert has not escaped his latest editor, either: concerning the oath of the magnates who selected William Clito, Rider commented: "Galbert's description of the circumstances in which this oath was taken also emphasizes the importance of collective consultation, agreement, and action, of, in a word, consensus (note especially the uses of *simul, omnes* and of words beginning with the prefix *con-*)" (*God's Scribe,* 188–89).

28. Ross, trans., 74, and 160n5; elsewhere she notes that the occasional emphasis on burgher military prowess comes from Galbert's pride in his fellow townsmen.

29. Galbert, [1], 6/22.

30. The inhabitants of Laon responded similarly with an impressive array of weaponry once the commune was publicly declared: "bearing swords, double axes, bows, lances, and pikes" (cum ensibus, bipennibus, arcubus et securibus, clavas lanceasque ferentes; Guibert of Nogent, *Autobiographie* 3.8, p. 336; *A Monk's Confession: The Memoirs of Guibert of Nogent,* trans. Paul J. Archambault [University Park, Pa., 1996], 154). By 1181, Henry II of England would issue his Assize of Arms, which expected every freeman of England to have ready an appropriate set of arms. Even those at the bottom of his scale were required to have a gambeson for defense, and either a sword and spear or a bow with arrows. Moreover, these weapons had to be passed down to one's descendants (Roger of Hoveden, *Chronica magistri Rogeri de Houedene,* ed. William Stubbs, 4 vols., Rolls Series 51 [London, 1868–71], 2:253).

31. Galbert, [66], 1/22.

the castle, some women apparently dared to approach the walls in order to bear away the corpse of a fallen knight.[32] From other sources, though, we know that women often took an active role in the defense of their towns. During the siege of Amiens in 1115, a group of eighty women operated two catapults with precision, destroying the two siege towers opposite their position. A century later the death of Simon of Montfort came famously during the siege of Toulouse when female defenders hit him with a stone from a catapult.[33]

Galbert continues throughout his chronicle to present his fellow townsmen as able to respond quickly to threats. The most striking instance came when the chamberlain Gervaise arrived to avenge the count. Although only a few burghers arranged his entry into town, the rest, summoned in alarm from their suppers, took virtually no time to support his cause. Gervaise and his partisans had laid the groundwork for this implausibly quick revolution in loyalties. He had begun his campaign by catching Erembald supporters unprepared in the otherwise formidable stronghold of Raverschoot. Not only did he acquire a great deal of plunder and the momentum of quick success, Gervaise also sent rumor flying into the city along with the captives he released. He followed this maneuver with a bit of calculated arson, burning down within sight of the city walls the house of Wulfric Cnop, one of the chief conspirators. Galbert speaks at this point of a subdued, but rising, current of hope among "our citizens" that they would have help in avenging the count. Whether this particular anticipation was real or not, it is hard not to see the citizenry actively trying to guess which side to support as the probable victor. Their concern for the security of their possessions was, after all, second only to their concern for their lives, and the smoke rising from Cnop's home was as much an omen to avoid as a beacon to follow.[34]

This collective concern had already shown itself in the rush to ready the city's fortifications. Through either duplicitous cunning or the impulse of fear, the inhabitants worked initially with the Erembalds in preparing ditches and a complex palisade. Potential social divides were patched over by necessity: Galbert speaks of the unity of clergy and laity; one senses a

32. Galbert, [41], 36/42.

33. Guibert of Nogent, *Autobiographie* 3.14, p. 414; *La Chanson de la Croisade Albigeoise,* ed. Eugène Martin-Chabot, 3 vols. (Paris, 1973), 3:204–8.

34. Galbert, [26]/[28]; for another example of the citizens' quick response to a threat, see [22], 50/53.

totality of effort by all ages and professions, by men and women alike.[35] Later, as they abandoned the Erembalds and became prosecutors themselves of a siege, the burghers continued to seek security. Their defenses sufficed to give them bargaining power with the arriving barons. Thus, they compelled the magnates to swear to respect the "area and property" of the citizens before letting those lords and their hosts have access through the *faubourg* to the castle.[36] This pledge was one of the kernels in the "law of the siege" that would direct the combined operations of civic militias, feudal levies, and the armed parasites who arrived to feed off the disorder.[37] Even though the Brugeois had chosen to swim with the prevailing tide, they clearly remained alert to threats. Their allies, especially the crowds that had come from Ghent, were barely contained by the law of the siege.[38] For over a month, they also endured the very real risk to themselves of missile weapons, especially from attempts by the besieged Erembalds to burn down structures near the castle, and later the church, in which they were trapped. Nor could the inhabitants focus solely and inwardly on the castle; the opportunists kept outside the city's defenses occasionally lobbed fiery objects into the town in hopes of creating a chance for entry.[39] Such actions were hardly a vain effort: the *fueros* of Castile stipulated that citizens were not to fight fires, whatever their instinctive impulse, until they had confirmed that the gates were still defended. In the case of the siege of Namur, Baldwin of Hainaut demonstrated a relative mercy, or so his chronicler would have us believe. Although the count's mangonels battered both the walls and the city itself, he reputedly kept the destruction to the necessary minimum, and even prevented an overall sack once his forces entered the town. Namur's own count, trapped rather like Erembalds within a fortress inside an occupied town, had no such compunctions, and he spent the night burning down the houses of his own subjects.[40]

The final chapters of Galbert's account provide the best insights yet into how the burgher endured sieges (or not). On March 16, 1128, Bruges made its disaffection with the new count, William Clito, rather clear by

35. Galbert, [25], 56/71.
36. "loca et posessiones" (Galbert, [31], 10; trans., 158); see [31], 7/18 for the negotiations with the barons.
37. On the "law of the siege" (lex obsidionis), see Galbert, [59], 23/26; [88], 11/23.
38. Galbert, [33], 17/26; [43], 1/33.
39. Galbert, [32], 6/18; [35], 33/37; [42], 14/24; [43], 43/60.
40. Powers, "Life on the Cutting Edge," 31; Gilbert of Mons, *La Chronique* 143, p. 219.

denying him entry to the city—and his home within.[41] As anyone who reads these passages immediately realizes, Galbert was torn between his loyalty to the count and his loyalty to his fellow citizens. At first his tone indicates support for his hometown's decision to back Thierry of Alsace as the new count, but this changed as attacks against the town and Clito's victory at Axspoele eroded his earlier certitude. In the interim, he reveals especially the mental vicissitudes of the threatened. Some of the pattern associated with campaigning in heavily fortified districts also reappears. The nephews of Thancmar tested the will of the city quickly with a raid so small it could hardly have hoped to do more.[42] Still, the citizens returned to work on the defenses, finishing the ditch begun over a year before.[43] In a ploy similar to one Powers found used by Iberian cities, the burghers dispatched watches and ambushes. As garrisons in strongholds or patrols of both countryside and roadway, these groups were to locate the city's foe, harass him, perhaps even deflect him, before he could menace the city directly. Of course, nearly every city and landed magnate was doing the same, so that the county was covered with armed bands.[44] It led Galbert to state the urban inhabitant's complaint at its clearest: "Now in truth the whole land was so torn by dangers, by ravaging, arson, treachery, and deceit that no honest man could live in security."[45]

Two months after defying Clito, Bruges nearly experienced what it most feared: the struggling count launched a quick assault from nearby Oostkamp, where resistance was seemingly keeping him busy. His speed nearly brought him success. The fighting was sharp as Clito's forces broke inside the barrier of the ditch and were barely held off at the gates.[46] Notably, it was the only time Bruges was directly menaced. The fear and expectation of a repeated assault nonetheless dominated the burghers, who swung wildly between despair and hope. They knew full well how little the conventions of war applied to them. All too often, as had happened a year earlier when the castle held out against them while they resisted external interlopers, or as happened in the above-mentioned case of Namur, it was their homes and lives that were exposed to the most danger during a siege. Typically, the citadel within a town had professional soldiers for a garrison,

41. Galbert, [97], 4/7; cf. [98], 9/14.

42. Galbert, [107], 1/6.

43. Galbert, [110], 41/43.

44. Galbert, [107]/[113].

45. "Tota vero terra in periculis agitabatur, in rapinis, incendiis, traditionibus, dolis, ita ut nemo discretus viveret securus" (Galbert, [110], 15/16; trans., 291).

46. Galbert, [112], 6/10.

who could expect to negotiate (after a show of some resistance, of course, which often enough came at the expense of the city's infrastructure) an honorable surrender. The townsfolk, however, were "guilty in defense"; their resistance was an offense *ipso facto.* Nor, as Rider has pointed out with respect to Galbert's developing political thought, were there extenuating circumstances.[47] A strong biblical tide ran against Thierry's supporters. Clito may have proved himself tyrannical, but he might very well still be "the Lord's anointed." David had warned his kinsman not to destroy Saul, "'for who can put forth his hand against the Lord's anointed, and be guiltless?"[48] Once the disturbances of 1115 in Laon had subsided enough for the cathedral to be reconsecrated, the archbishop of Rheims lectured his hearers that the harshness of a ruler excused nothing. According to 1 Peter 2:18, they were to be obedient to their masters.[49] If they could not, through victory, prove that God supported their cause, they might well expect the count to apply Old Testament provisions to them: no mercy for the men, the women and children to be treated as spoils of war, and all property to be forfeit.[50]

These fears were doubtless fed by the refugees who fled into the city as the isolated refuges in the countryside drew the attention of the contending counts. In early 1128, Flanders experienced warfare of the type that had already marked much of Louis VI's reign in France and would soon come to England in the unending siege and counter-siege of the Anarchy. The fighting turned on the "fortified homes" (*domos defensabiles/defensales*).[51] The focus on these small places derived from a trio of reasons: they were by their very size more easily taken; as homes to magnates, their loss or retention affected alliances; and the major cities were alternately exposed or protected as these places exchanged hands. It was a sign of the growing strength of the cities. It was the recognition of such strength that led both

47. Rider, *God's Scribe,* 166–67, 173–76.

48. "quis enim extendit manum suam in christum Domini et innocens erit" (1 Sm 26:9). For an exploration of these themes, see Matthew Strickland, "Against the Lord's Anointed: Aspects of Warfare and Baronial Rebellion in England and Normandy, 1075–1265," in *Law and Government in Medieval England and Normandy: Essays in Honour of Sir James Holt,* ed. George Garnett and John Hudson (Cambridge, 1994), 56–79.

49. Guibert of Nogent, *Autobiographie* 3.10, p. 360, where not even "harsh" (*discolis*) masters are exempted (*A Monk's Confession,* 164).

50. Dt 20:10–14.

51. Galbert, [107], 14/16; [113], 5/18; [114], 1/7; [116], 1/36. Suger; *Gesta Stephani,* ed. and trans. K. R. Potter (Oxford, 1976). In addition, the strategy mirrors that outlined by Powers for the area around Toledo ("Life on the Cutting Edge," 28–29).

Plantagenet and Capetian rivals to grant communal charters to cities in key strategic sites, and fear of such strength led Henry II to raze the walls of Limoges at the first sign of dissent from the inhabitants. Thus enfeebled, the citizens still resisted many impositions, but met with little success throughout most of Geoffrey of Vigeois's chronicle. The concentration on minor fortresses also appears throughout the Limousin's wars. The up-and-coming Richard the Lionheart was renowned for capturing "impregnable" places; often as not he took them by speed and surprise rather than assault. He bent the local lords to his will by whittling away their smaller, but essential, fortifications. The numbers are most telling with the count of Hainaut, who had some of Richard's speed, but who also kept a powerful siege train constantly nearby; in the campaigns of 1183, Baldwin took from his kinsman the count of Flanders one city and sixty-five castles.[52]

I do not want to overstate the relative power of cities, though, especially since the fear of their inhabitants indicates how fragile their sense was of their own strength and capability. Again, Galbert's final chapters are most instructive as we see his fellow townsmen grappling with the potential repercussions of having backed—perhaps too quickly—Thierry of Alsace. Since Thierry enjoyed a succession of small victories and was recognized as count by multiple cities, there were initially no doubts about the audacious switch of allegiance, and, as noted above, Galbert's rhetoric initially reflected acceptance of the town's action. As the struggle dragged on and casualties mounted, however, doubts began to surface concerning God's favor. Galbert explains that these misgivings led in turn to defeats, first during a sortie against Oostkamp, then worst of all at Axspoele.[53] The cycle could only intensify since the defeats served as a barometer of divine displeasure, and an interdict was now hanging over the city: several weeks earlier, Clito had persuaded Simon, the bishop of Noyon-Tournai, to anathematize anyone who opposed his claims.[54]

Indeed, the spiritual aspects of enduring a siege certainly deserve more attention. As noted above, medieval revolts involved spiritual consequences alongside the physical ones. Blessings and curses often flew as thick as physical missiles in these frays. Under the onus of corporate excommunication, the folk of Ghent sought to put their house in order by disem-

52. Geoffrey of Vigeois, *Chronica,* 308, 317, 320, 330–31, 332; see, e.g., John Gillingham, *Richard the Lionheart* (New York, 1978), 71–99, 240–77; Gilbert of Mons, *La Chronique* 101, 145.

53. Galbert, [108], 48/57; [111], 5/19; [114], 1/74.

54. Galbert, [107], 19/28. It is difficult not to see this tactic as a form of "spiritual carpet-bombing."

boweling a witch and parading her entrails around the city.[55] The people of Bruges countered the maledictions of the bishop, as well as those of several other clergy in William Clito's camp, by having their own holy men launch anathemas at the count.[56] When word came that before his victory at Axspoele, Clito had done penance by cutting his hair and shunning extravagant garments, Thierry and his urban supporters did likewise.[57] In this spiritual arms race, of course, the townspeople tried not merely to match Clito's performance, but to outstrip his piety. In a show of ecclesiastical solidarity, the clergy of Bruges led relic-laden processions through the town and capped them with other pronouncements of excommunication against William Clito.[58] Galbert himself reported this behavior scornfully, mockingly commenting that "it is marvelous that a priest can cast a spell on God in such a way that, whether God wishes it or not, William may be thrown out of the countship!"[59] A month later, thoroughly at a loss as to which side deserved God's (and his own) approval, Galbert reasoned that the importunities of the burghers were actually serving only to annoy the deity.[60] Two weeks later, with the unexpected death of Clito from a seemingly slight wound, Galbert's final word on the spiritual maneuvers of the burghers was that, somehow, in retrospect, they had actually been penitent enough to appease God.[61] Galbert's taciturn summary is eloquent: part shoulder-shrug and part sigh of relief, it claims all the minimum success that it can, and more importantly, shows the townsman's attention already moving on to the future.

Galbert's vacillations actually demonstrate the remarkable solidarity of the town's clergy with the townspeople. From the start of the crisis, when clergy joined the wall-building effort, they gave physical and spiritual aid to their parishioners. They were rewarded, of course, by Thierry, with gifts for the churches, but their effort often went beyond the minimum one might expect of such "hired" help. If Galbert's complaints can be trusted, they even joined the fighting at some points.[62] Similar spiritual buttressing was demonstrated at Evreux during the captivity of Richard the Lion-

55. Galbert, [112], 3/5; cf. Galbert, [110], 29/37. Given the words of 1 Sm 15:23, that "rebellion is as the sin of divination" (quasi peccatum ariolandi est repugnare), one can hardly avoid seeing a political element in this action.

56. Galbert, [113], 51/61.

57. Galbert, [114], 16/24, 68/74.

58. Galbert, [114], 74/95.

59. "Et mirum est quod sacerdos ita Deum incantare possit ut, velit nolit Deus, Willelmus a comitatu ejiciatur" (Galbert, [113], 60/61; trans., 296).

60. Galbert, [118], 17/38.

61. Galbert, [120], 15/18.

62. Galbert, [116], 64/65.

heart. In the path of Philip's 1194 invasion, the citizenry formed a commune and hurried to prepare some sort of defense. Working on a Sunday, they proceeded to excavate a ditch right across the bishop's territories, even as an archdeacon absolved them for the deed.[63] Further evidence of mutual aid appeared later in the century at Limoges, this time from the secular end. Faced with Henry II's probable anger, and thus a siege, the townsfolk rushed to rebuild their walls, and they quarried the needed stone from the major ecclesiastical sites within town (although the complicity of the clergy in this form of "mining" is uncertain). At some point soon thereafter—and one wonders if there was not a touch of guilt in this—the women of the city put together a cord of tow, which encircled all the walls. Once that circuit had been completed, the cord was donated for candles in all the towns' major sanctuaries.[64] For Geoffrey of Vigeois, the inclement weather that caused most of the besieging army to return home probably needed no further explanation.

The military potential of urban centers was thus well understood by both secular and ecclesiastical leaders, as well as by the populations thereof. It has become a commonplace of recent medieval military history to emphasize how talented the commanders of the Middle Ages were in avoiding the risks of decisive battles.[65] A great deal of seemingly wanton raiding went on, but in many cases, it had the strategic goal of bringing an opponent to negotiations. The other major component of medieval warfare was the innumerable sieges. Such a dynamic, even if we did not have the examples cited above, would indicate that medieval townspeople knew well what sieges involved. Galbert's litany of the perils involved—"apprehension, long vigils, wounds, attacks, and everything that comes with a endless siege"—shows a familiarity with the business even if Galbert himself was frightened by the tumult.[66] Being on the receiving end often enough, some burghers, like those of Ghent, learned the techniques of siegecraft well.[67] But this portrait is full of contradiction. While there can be no doubt that towns in their own fashion were breeding grounds

63. Powicke, *Loss of Normandy*, 98.

64. Geoffrey of Vigeois, *Chronica*, 335.

65. R. C. Smail opened this line of thinking with *Crusading Warfare (1097–1193)* (Cambridge, 1956); Gillingham, "Richard I," 78–91, has provided one of the more convincing reapplications of this thesis to Europe's internal conflicts.

66. "metus, vigilias, vulnera, aggressus, et omnia quae in obsidione perpeti solent adversa" (Galbert, [29], 53/54; trans., 156, my translation).

67. Galbert, [33], 9/10.

of martial behavior, the desire for security and peaceful conditions created a counter-current that struck contemporaries as passive or timid. Galbert notes a careful maintenance of normality, the quiet sitting down to dinner of his fellow citizens, for up to a week following the murders.[68]

This impulse to maintain the forms of normalcy despite the circumstances brings up two other elements that are integral to any understanding of military culture among medieval townsfolk. Firstly, one need only recall that, despite the vivid accounts of activity within Galbert's narrative, the vast majority of the time during a siege was spent in routine. Part of this may well have been busy-work, ongoing rounds of preparatory measures meant to keep people's minds distracted from the potential violence of an actual assault. Such drudgery, however, was the normal state of the conflict: two sides eyeing one another constantly, all the while inching their way toward some advantage by digging trenches, erecting impromptu defenses, looking for the next innovative breakthrough. One of a town's greatest resources in this part of a military contest was the numbers it could field, supplemented as they were by the participation of women and the young. In a time when a rumored army of three hundred knights was considered sufficient to tip the balance of power irrevocably,[69] towns could marshal significantly higher numbers, if not for actual combat, then at least for all other ancillary efforts. Of course, this was also the municipalities' Achilles' heel. A besieging force was at a distance from its most precious noncombatants, whereas the besieged townsfolk, whatever their own martial proclivities, could scarcely avoid thinking about the potential risks to their families. Such considerations could produce wildly divergent results. Some years before at Amiens, the townspeople seemed to die like penned cattle, unable to understand the violence falling upon them. Guibert of Nogent's memoir also showed, in the almost total evacuation of Laon, what might occur because the people understood the violence all too well.[70]

Galbert's journal gives a rare wealth of detail on these conditions and the expectations of urban populations, especially when under the telling

68. Galbert, [28], 27/29.

69. Galbert, [49], 1/4, trans., 190, when it appeared that William of Ypres, benefiting possibly from English monetary aid, was going to prove unstoppable in pressing his claims to the countship. Such numbers were indeed notable, since the count owed only 42 knights as his feudal service to the king of France. See Ross, trans., 190n2, and Verbruggen, *The Art of Warfare,* 5–9, where knightly forces from northwest Europe's great counties rarely approached 1,000, often hovering around 500 or less.

70. Guibert of Nogent, *Autobiographie* 3.11, p. 366; cf. 3.14, p. 408.

strain of a siege or even the threat of one. Did they have a persecution complex? Yes . . . but only because everyone *was* after them. Caught between conflicting claims, towns—which were rich not only in material but also in personnel—could typically fall back on only their own resources. It was an exposed position to be in, and the search for allies and justification (moral, spiritual, political) coincided with actual physical resistance. The most striking aspect of the urban mentality during the pressure of a siege, and perhaps more critically during the dread and anticipation of one, was the nurturing or outright enforcement of corporate will. It was an ad hoc discipline that had to be effective for all the town's disparate members, and such a will was built on a foundation into which no defeatism was allowed to seep. After the debacle at Oostkamp, Galbert complained throughout July 1128 that no one was allowed to speak the truth about the losses. Victory was the only topic permitted.[71] In a story from the Bible that surely went the rounds during sieges, the prophet Elisha found himself besieged at Dothan by a Syrian army. As his servant panicked, Elisha prayed for the man to see as he did. When the request was granted, the servant saw a fiery host filling the hills and encircling the unsuspecting besiegers. Needless to say, his confidence was restored.[72] Like many besieged populations, the Brugeois of 1128 sought their own Elisha in the pronouncements of the clergy, in the parades of relics, in the purging of unholy elements. Twelfth-century townspeople were indeed powerful, but only insofar as their fickle confidence carried them. When they believed that their cause had divine support, as the Brugeois did in 1127, they shaped their own history. If they doubted, however, a sense of guilt could easily immobilize them, as it nearly did in 1128.

71. Galbert, [116], 43/64; [118], 5/17.

72. Kgs 6:8–23. A remarkable parallel was reported at the 1147 siege of Lisbon. As the Flemings and English drew near the city, the narrator tells how many saw an omen of the coming siege in the clouds. White clouds on the crusaders' side engaged like an army with black clouds coming from the direction of the city. When the black clouds were eventually chased from the sky, the watching soldiers were convinced they had just witnessed a demonstration of God's will (*De expugnatione Lyxbonensi/The Conquest of Lisbon,* ed. and trans. Charles Wendell David [1936; rpt. New York, 2001], 88–91).

PART THREE

GALBERT OF BRUGES AND THE POLITICS OF GENDER

5

Galbert's Hidden Women

Social Presence and Narrative Concealment

NANCY F. PARTNER

The prose narrative known to all teachers of basic university level courses in medieval history as *The Murder of Charles the Good* from its beloved translation by James Bruce Ross in 1959 is, according to Jeff Rider, its most recent editor, "the only journalistic history we have from Europe in the twelfth century . . . a contemporary eyewitness account of the assassination of Charles the Good, Count of Flanders," who was murdered at prayer in the castle church at Bruges on March 2, 1127.[1] The near-present-time account written under difficult conditions and under pressure of strong emotion by Galbert, a notary and bureaucrat at the administrative court of Flanders, covers events from the accession of Count Charles through his murder and the social and political chaos in Flanders for the next sixteen months, until Thierry of Alsace secured the countship in the summer of 1128. The events are dramatic: a strong and intelligent ruler of a feudal state (Charles is presented in idealized form combining every chivalric, Christian, and compassionate virtue) imposes a high standard of law and order on his state, and attempts to reduce the encroaching power of an upstart family (the so-called Erembald clan, headed by Bertulf the provost) by means of a legal demonstration of their servile lineage, and thereby provokes them to treason on a wild gamble with political assassination. The conspirators, mostly younger relations of Bertulf, slaughter Charles in full view of many witnesses, then escape to wait out the aftermath. They hope the deed will

1. Rider, *God's Scribe,* 1. This sophisticated and nuanced study of Galbert as a writer is a model of balanced historical context with literary critical penetration; Galbert emerges from Rider's sensitive interpretation as a man of feeling, intellect, and moral struggle.

meet with general public approval, or at least acquiescence, and the appointment of a weaker, friendlier count from among their own allies. It almost worked. Charles's supporters were shocked and frightened; a few were murdered immediately as examples; no one knew whom to trust, and it took some time before the forces seeking vengeance and a legitimate succession got themselves organized. In the meantime, for month after month in the most urbanized feudal state in northwestern Europe, there was effectively no government, no law, and no functioning economy. We are told all this in a book constructed from the diary-like notes of Galbert the notary, an educated man, Latin-literate and pious, but urban in his practical experience, a cleric in the technical and professional sense, but close to a layman in outlook, a modern man, at least compared with most medieval historian authors, who look at politics and secular life through monastic eyes.[2]

This narrative record is a history that still astonishes us for what it includes. Much of it takes place in the towns of a feudal state where the author knew many people, people close to the center of commercial and political life. We have a book with scenes of mixed crowds of townspeople and feudatories looking on as a knight performs the formal ritual for breaking homage within the city walls; urban merchants doing improvised acts of collective non-noble homage; the king of France making deals over rents and tolls. We are told the names of dozens of people. Ecclesiastics and laity mix together unselfconsciously; leading townsmen are treated as the important persons they were in this society. This is a book that for once seems connected to the total undisguised reality of medieval urban life—a reality uncensored by ideological or social constraints. So much is startlingly just "there" in matter-of-fact uproarious combination that it is almost easy to overlook what should be there, *had* to be there, and is not: women.

That absence does make this topic of the women in Galbert of Bruges's narrative of the murder of Charles the Good one of those rare tidy research tasks whose scope and dimensions fit neatly within the confines of a single essay. There is a finite text, some 233 pages in the useful Ross translation, less in Jeff Rider's *Corpus Christianorum* edition. One can comb through it line by line, making careful notes of all females detectable in any way in the text, and then organize one's findings into a few useful categories

2. Rider, *God's Scribe,* 16–28, argues convincingly for Galbert's clerical status and also for its not defining or limiting his perceptions: "Galbert's view was not limited, physically or morally, to what he could see from his office."

(women with a name, or a rank, women cited only by relation to a man, anonymous women doing anything at all)—and there you have it: virtually nothing. This is not entirely a Bad Thing. It certainly encourages clear focus and offers ample discursive space for one's findings.

Plenty, certainly, to list the five women whose names are recorded (Richilda, Gertrude, another Gertrude, Adela, and Dedda) and to note that the count's wife is not among them, and the three cited by their own rank (one countess, two abbesses).[3] If one felt like imposing a strict standard of narrative significance, and eliminated the women who were not even alive during the events narrated, that brief list would shrink from a total of eight to two—the countess of Holland and the abbess of Origny—both lacking proper names. If we move right on to the next conventional category, comprising women mentioned only through their relation to one man: as wife (or daughter, sister, or mother of) of Some Named Man and add the women whose natal family *plus* their marriage links *two* men in some significant relationship to one another, as sister of Man X married to Man Y, or Someone's niece or daughter married to Someone else—(and this includes even the nameless wife of Count Charles, who is mentioned only to explain the relation of her brother, the bishop of Noyon, to her husband)—the list grows to something over twenty (complicated by some vague plural nouns). None of these women *do* anything in the narrative, however, beyond connecting men in personal and political alliances.

There is some female-initiated action in this story, behavior that penetrated the silence and invisibility that typifies female non-presence in medieval narrative. A few women try to care for the dead and dying; one woman trades a dead baby for a live one; one meddles in politics; one founds an evil dynasty. I am going to discuss those in some detail, but exactly how? And to what point? There is no pure recording, for us (secular, feminist, postmodern as we mostly are) anymore than for a twelfth-century notary (religious, patriarchal, premodern as he mostly was). We are not uninvolved and free from determining presuppositions. We are historically "situated" even in ways we cannot reach to define, and our ability to say that does not make it any less true. Like Galbert, we need intelligible form in order to make sense. What I made were a number of lists from my Galbert reading notes,

3. Galbert, [17], 27/31 (the abbess of Origny); [34], 1/8 (the countess of Holland); [68], 4/[69], 28 (Richilda, countess of Mons; Gertrude, countess of Holland; the abbess of Messines; Gertrude, the duchess of Alsace; Adela, queen of Denmark and later duchess of Apulia); [71], 1/25 (the châtelaine Dedda).

but an essay, a discourse, can't be a list. Even without story form, it needs perspective, a point of view, a logic.

If I were doing this project in the 1970s, I might have counted up all the women, been struck by how few and how powerless they were, and perhaps concluded that the exclusion of women from political life and institutions at every level of medieval society is reflected in their virtual absence from a narrative of feudal and urban power politics. Without public presence, they couldn't have narrative presence.[4] Would I have known how to say "patriarchal"? I'm not sure. I'm not sure if, in fact, I would have been able to see even that much. The big fact of social exclusion might easily have rationalized narrative exclusion for me, as for nearly everyone else.

By the 1980s the heavy pervasive hand of patriarchal suppression would have been quite evident, but also quite depressing, too defeatist just to acknowledge as if it were some universal law of human society, merely an anthropological observation. The few unnamed townswomen who broke through the narrative barrier when they offered decent care and gestures of comfort to the dead and dying might have looked braver, more self-confident in the important ritual tasks, life-cycle tasks, entrusted to them. The new word, "gender," would have come to mind, suggesting, perhaps, something about separate spheres and a whole realm of necessary, skilled, competent female work on which men like Galbert depended, whole towns depended. The one noble woman who asserted herself into the chaos of political power brokering, and thus into a few lines of text, would have looked bigger, more important; her aggressive way of deploying lineage-based claims might have suggested new dimensions to gender stereotypes.

By the 1990s, I, long immersed in "linguistic turn" critical analysis, would finally have seen that Galbert, whatever his religious or misogynist habits of mind, was above all else a writer, a writer of narrative, using the literary templates he knew but lacking any models for a narrative of urban life, trying to control a headlong avalanche of reality into a story he could tell. The artificiality of history through its emplotment, the fictionality of nonfiction in any age, would have been strikingly present to me. For Galbert, a literate but not a literary man, making narrative choices, the ones legible on the page, meant massive suppressions and exclusions that had left their shadows and could be traced. Women stood in those shadows.

4. The medieval ideology underlying much of this narrative absence is set out succinctly by Georges Duby, "Women and Power," in *Cultures of Power: Lordship, Status and Process in Twelfth-Century Europe,* ed. Thomas N. Bisson (Philadelphia, 1995), 69–85.

What I see most acutely now in Galbert is a would-be writer almost overwhelmed, a strong and reality-connected mind struggling to control a world gone out of control, despairing and unstrung by the hideousness of events. An order-loving man, a writer of documents and keeper of records, Galbert loathed the fragmented preview-postmodernity of his protomodern world. He didn't want the shattering of hierarchies, or institutions of respect and submission. If anything were left of the conventional order of his society, especially something so basic and unquestioned as male dominance, Galbert would hardly be inclined to disturb it when the daily threat to life, and to narrative, was fragmentation and chaos. So the routine conventions of a patriarchal society, some misogynist stereotypes, areas of moral blindness and uninspected prejudices—all are still there in the writer I read, but are not the whole picture, or not all of it all of the time. With the tidy habits of the bureaucrat that he was, he did what he could to achieve formal control—the same for him as moral control—and a certain surprise emerges for the reader, sensitized to this narrativist optic. In terms of narrative-creation, in terms of literary control, of hermeneutic control, women turn out to play a deeply significant part—not always a flattering part, but perhaps we don't mind that so much now.

How do I get there, to that reading, from five deceased women with names and a couple dozen others with bit parts and no lines?

Galbert's world had, or was supposed to have, a moral order, a social order, and (though he would not have recognized this vocabulary) a narrative order: ideally, all three aligned in harmonious conformity. He expresses some of this in the pathos of his mid-book explanation, where he tells us his own name—Ego, Galbertus—and how without any proper place to write, he struggled for moments of calm in the midst of street violence and house fires accidentally and deliberately set. He made a summary of events on tablets and, obviously later on, set them in order, searched for some order. "I have not set down every single event because they were so many and so confused but noted carefully what was decreed and done by common action throughout the siege, and the reasons for it."[5]

Although he does not keep strictly to this program of selection, Galbert did try to control the accelerating mayhem engulfing Flanders by trying to distinguish the ephemera from the larger actions that would lead his

5. "Neque quid singuli agerent prae confusione et infinitate notavi sed hoc solum intenta mente notavi quod in obsidione communi edicto et facto ad pugnam et ejus causam congestum est" (Galbert, [35], 42/44; trans., 164, trans. mod.).

homeland and his book to some finite conclusion. His guiding principle was to follow the consensus acts of his society's natural leaders, those who were lords by some traditional standard, and those who had distinguished themselves in urban life. Even with this quite mundane rule, he found it nearly impossible to keep his narrative to any coherent direction. The fighting of the siege (the siege of a castle within town precincts where some of the conspirators were holding out against a quasi-military force also inside the town walls) showed little tactical discipline: people were shooting flaming arrows onto the roofs of houses from several directions, and for different bad reasons. And morality was, if anything, even less help: people unrelated to the treasonous Erembalds and uninvolved in the murder conspiracy were inexplicably going *into* the castle to join the besieged men, the known assassins, out of sympathy or, it seems, as opportunistic mercenaries.[6]

An example meeting Galbert's requirements for proper decision making, leading to a legitimate and reasonable action worthy of narration (something "decreed and done by common action"—with *causae*—reasons) is the quarrelling between the citizens of Bruges and those of Ghent when the latter tried to appropriate the count's body: the various townsmen squabble more and more bitterly until "the more sensible men" (*sapientiores*) calm them with advice (and words indubitably Galbert's). "'Do not fight over this! Let us wait rather until God has bestowed on us and the realm a good and legitimate count. Then a decision about the body will be reached by his counsel and that of the barons of the realm and our bishop and all the clergy.'"[7] Implausibly, he reports that invoking this combination of divine assistance and Robert's Rules of Order satisfied everyone. Hard to know, but it is certainly Galbert's preferred standard: proper channels of authority, clear jurisdiction, calm reasoning and cooperation, preferably in committee. Women would never have been included in these consultative bodies, formal or impromptu, representing the loci of social authority, which excluded them also from Galbert's "default" principle of narrative selection. Unthinking misogyny pervaded this world, quite clearly, but that he clung to his bureaucratic ideals in the midst of carnage, looting, and venal opportunism, is, in my opinion, the most civilized thing we know about Galbert.

6. Galbert, [36], 4/8.

7. "'Nolite contendere, sed potius simul expectemus quoad usque Deus nobis et regno contradiderit comitem bonum et legitimum cujus et principum regni et episcopi nostri et totius cleri consiliis de corpore fiat dispensatio'" (Galbert, [43], 28/32; trans., 179).

"We, the inhabitants of the land of Flanders," Galbert says memorably and inclusively, and once only, referring to everyone affected by the murder of the count.[8] "We" are quickly differentiated into levels of authority, degrees of agency, and some objects of particular suffering. Here, looking across Galbert's social landscape, gender theory insistently reminds us of who is not there. Galbert's vocabulary of authority suggests a taken-for-granted social scaffolding of hereditary feudal authority, lordship, based on noble lineage and territorial domination, grounded and justified by basic distinctions of free birth and ineradicable servility. "Those serfs" is his favorite personal insult for the extended powerful family of Bertulf the provost, chief conspirator, allegedly of servile origin, a stain of almost untraceable origin but still socially visible—"those foul dogs, full of the demon, those serfs, murdered their lord."[9] A countryside insult, a peasant insult, turned into a sort of obscenity by a townsman.

Galbert tells us that "a great crowd of citizens and all the people" of Bruges waited in the church at Bruges with King Louis VI for the procession removing the body of Charles.[10] These many people surely mingled shoulder to shoulder in crowded physical reality, but they are always given separate category terms. The citizens, often "our citizens" (*burgenses nostri, cives nostri*), men of Bruges, self-consciously first among urban commoners, are repeatedly singled out by Galbert.[11] And their natural leaders, "the leading men," distinguished by their success, experience, and social dignity with improvised titles lifted from the language of guildhall and urban courts: these *sapientiores* (wiser men), *fortiores et meliores* (stronger and better sort), *seniores et prudentiores* (senior and well-judging men) are the men who talk, mainly to one another, and listen to letters read aloud, make agreements, and decide what is best for the county, the towns, for men like themselves.[12]

To this point there is nothing original in Galbert's mental world and, more to the point here, no hook to bring into sight the females sunk beneath the generic surface of "all the people" in the church, the women among "those who frequented markets or dwelt in towns,"[13] and the brew-

8. "Nos itaque terrae Flandriarum incolae" (Galbert, [14], 14/15; trans., 117).

9. "canes immundi, demonio pleni, servi dominum suum jugulaverunt" (Galbert, [6], 18/19; trans., 95).

10. "collecta civium et universorum multitudine" (Galbert, [77], trans., 246).

11. See, e.g., Galbert [27], 7, 27.

12. See, e.g., Galbert [27], 28; [51], 15; [53], 4.

13. "aut in foro aut infra castra manerent et conversarentur" (Galbert, [1], 18/19; trans., 83).

ers of beer in countryside and town[14]—all collective terms that, we know, had to include as many females as males. Galbert's book is not a chivalric chronicle where the settings of camp and battlefield would justify a single-sex cast of characters; his castle is inside a town, and the open spaces for fighting and consultation were a short walk from town; men and women mingled indoors and out, doing and talking. That is how people lived in the medieval West, unequally but together. The generic poor, another hold-all category, were necessary for the performances of ritual charity: the paupers in Bruges taking pennies from Charles's hand at the very hour of his murder, the sick and crippled who gathered close to the count's corpse inviting a miracle, the poor admitted to the church to receive ritual pennies at the final burial rites.[15] Women would be among the paupers, but those who play their narrative parts as the official poor have neither sex nor age, no quality but their poverty.

Only once does a woman act on her own like a lord, using her noble rank and resources as campaign manager for her preferred candidate to replace Charles. This is the countess of Holland, sufficiently named by her rank alone, a widow and regent for her young son, Thierry. The countess (Gertrude) arrived at the siege in Bruges, bringing a big retinue and her son, at the invitation of a party of citizens and nobles who favored the election of Thierry as count. The countess encouraged them: "she worked hard to secure the friendship of all the important men, bestowing many gifts and making many promises."[16] When this plan didn't work out, she switched her support to her brother, also named Thierry, with whom she sent a joint letter to those leading men filled with campaign promises.[17] Galbert reports the countess's activities matter-of-factly along with those of other power brokers trying to push the chances of whomever they wanted as count. Gender-inflected social history has alerted us to that special locus of potential power for some women: widowhood, which meant adult female status "uncovered" by male guardianship, if combined with sufficient social status and control of enough wealth, especially if augmented by control over a minor male heir, and deployed by a woman with the right personal drive, could equal surprising "masculine-equivalent" author-

14. See Galbert [3], 18/20.
15. Galbert, [15], 7/10; [22], 53/60; [23], 7/11.
16. Galbert, [34], 7/8; trans., 162, trans. mod.
17. Galbert, [99], 1/12.

ity, the kind that carried the countess of Holland right into the foreground of Galbert's narrative.

The reported acts of a few men do reveal that women were not as forgotten in life as they were in narrative; the last thoughts and messages of men near death turn to the women closest to them. Walter, castellan of Bourbourg, dying of his wounds, gives a ring to the abbess of Origny (itself an act of signal trust) to take to his wife along with his final message and wishes. The notary, Fromold, certain he is about to die, likewise takes a gold ring from his finger and sends it to his daughter, certainly accompanied by words we are not told. The castellan Hacket flees to the house of his married daughter for refuge.[18]

Women stepped forward, anonymously but boldly, when "only women" held mourners' vigil around the corpse of Count Charles and openly expressed their sorrow.[19] During the siege in Bruges "some women" dragged the body of a knight, who fell to the street trying to escape the castle, into a house to prepare the corpse decently;[20] at the mass execution when prisoners were thrown from the castle walls, "some women" rushed forward to touch and comfort a dying man.[21] The instances here are few but striking—all of them record the deep connection of women with the rituals surrounding death. These were not merely gender-specific tasks or obligations. These small episodes where Galbert indifferently records the acts of non-noble females, specified by neither names nor number, just "some" or "a few" women of the sort who would be there in town where the important things were taking place, are where gender theory does its work. Gender theory sensitizes us to the difference between narrative absence and social absence, and reminds us that the literal level of a narrative is not a complete or naively "uninterpreted" record of reality. As a hermeneutic catalyst, gender acts as heat on invisible ink, bringing up the narratively rejected to view. Some women, unspecified townswomen, feel their responsibility for preserving the solemn dignity of death so deeply that they openly keep vigil by the corpse of a man with many enemies when his vassals and political friends keep a fearful distance. The risk was of course greater for the men; women mourners were sub-political; their

18. Galbert, [17], 27/31; [18], 39/41; [54], 1/4.
19. "mulieres solae" (Galbert, [21], 13/15; trans., 135).
20. "mulierculae" (Galbert, [41], 36/42; trans., 175).
21. "mulieres" (Galbert, [81], 43/45; trans., 252).

political nonexistence let them do with impunity what Charles's friends did not dare.[22] They were "only women," remarked upon to emphasize the absence of men, but carrying out a duty solemn enough for narrative.

The females who dragged the corpse of a knight into a house and attempted to arrange the body decently are called *mulierculae,* which should be translated as "girls," the servant girls who made up the ordinary class of household help in medieval towns. These few whom Galbert notices and records (and exactly how many did it take to drag a man indoors?) are few in number only in the text, not in the street. Their daring appearance here tells us that girl servants were at the windows, in the doorways, out in the streets watching the fighting in Bruges. Some of them decided on their own, or perhaps at the direction of their mistress, not to leave a body in the street. They were interrupted by men who commandeered the corpse for ritual abuse and degradation. Much later in the book, the women who tried to comfort the dying man who had been thrown off the battlements were also interrupted by a knight who threw a big rock down among them. Their bit part in the execution scene also must be read as a trope, a metonymy, for the many unrecorded females in all Galbert's crowd scenes. We have to repopulate all the crowd scenes in Galbert's book.

There are a few things to be observed here. The first is that Galbert *sees* these women. He obviously approves the women openly mourning his hero Charles, but I also read his brief records of the female impulse toward decency and ritual propriety, extended even to strangers and condemned criminals, as a mark of his respect and approbation. He has words to bestow on them. They govern active verbs, an important writer's distinction when compared, for example, with the whore (*scortum*) kept by the besieged men with them in the castle church: she is only the passive trope for the defilement of the church.

This person, indubitably female and passively carrying a burden of symbolic degradation on her anonymous self, is bluntly identified as *scortum,* "whore," by Galbert. Her full semantic frame involves several more degrading things brought into the defiled church of Saint Donatian by a party of the conspirators who were besieged inside: "So the church of Saint Donatian stood alone and deserted, left to the traitors who had a whore

22. The ways in which women might surface as paradigm types, not individuals, into the historical text is explored subtly by Karl Morrison, "The Hermeneutic Role of Women: A Silence of Comprehension," in *History as a Visual Art in the Twelfth-Century Renaissance* (Princeton, N.J., 1990), 154–95.

there, and chamber pots and cooking vessels and stoves and those unclean people did every unclean thing."[23] The woman stands in syntactical series with the appliances serving bodily needs, defecating and eating, violating the ritual purity of the church; and she stands in functional connection with them as well since she was obviously there as the labor needed to make the pots and cooking appliances and chamber pots serve their purposes. All morally unclean together, the traitors and their foul bodily functions, the probably destitute woman (for who else could not turn down this employment?) is textually overdetermined to the conventional state of female defilement: a "whore."

An example of how the moralized text elides into a gendered text is sharply defined by the extremely odd narrative built around the death of Walter of Vladslo, "one of the peers of the land," which occupies its own chapter, which Ross entitled: "God's punishment of Walter of Vladslo."[24] This nobleman of high rank and social prominence in the court of Count Charles had contrived to position himself to emerge safely at the top no matter which side won control of Flanders. As a trusted ally of the conspirator-assassins, with whom he was allied by marriage, he helped the leaders to escape, while he also stood out as a leader of the forces for vengeance and legitimacy, organizing the siege of the castle in Bruges where the remnants of the conspiracy were holding out. Galbert held these *realpolitik* maneuvers in great contempt and kept careful track of them throughout the book. When Walter died after a fall from his horse, Galbert opened his mortuary chapter by announcing this accident as "the severe and horrible judgment of God" for having been "accessory to the betrayal of his lord," and closed the chapter repeating this charge of "accessory to the treachery," for which he, Walter, "a peer of the land, and next after the count," deserved God's punishment of "a lingering death" when people who knew his guilt didn't dare accuse him because of his power.[25]

These moral denunciations of Walter are rhetorical bookends encasing

23. "Stabat igitur ecclesia sancti Donatiani sola et deserta tandem relicta traditoribus, qui in ea scortum haberent et cloacaria sua et coquinas et furnos et omnia immunda immundi agerent." Galbert, [35], 14/16; trans., 163, tans. mod. One imagines this woman engaged more in cooking and serving food, cleaning and caring for clothing and bedding, than in sexual services during the siege, but her sole narrative function is female (sexual) defilement of a sacred space.

24. "unus parium terrae" (Galbert, [89], 2; trans., 262).

25. "Dei districto et horribili examine," "illum conscium fuisse traditionis domini sui," "traditionis conscius fuisse," "par terrae illius alter a comite," "morte languida" (Galbert, [89], 1, 5, 28/30; trans., 262–63).

a little narrative that turns entirely about the actions, past and present, of his wife, a woman without a personal name but with plenty of enterprise, self-interest, and sheer nerve. Galbert reports that after Walter's death, his widow "announced publicly" that the adult son, long assumed to be Walter's child and her own, was an adopted child and "not his real son."[26] By her own assertion, it was revealed that Walter's first son had died at birth and his mother had traded the dead child for the living newborn male child of the wife of a cobbler, who had been paid money to conceal the deception, with, presumably, the promise of having her own son raised as a nobleman. Both the men, Walter of Vladslo and the cobbler, were totally deceived. Walter had married his son into the immediate family of the provost, Bertulf, at the height of his career, and long before Bertulf organized the murder of Count Charles. Now, in the aftermath of Walter's death and the failure of the conspiracy, Walter's widow stepped forward with this astonishing revelation.

Galbert finds this deeply gratifying narrative material, in several ways, and he credits God with the deep purpose of all this trickery. "And so God's stratagem," he concludes, pulled the social-climbing rug out from under the provost Bertulf, who was always so anxious to marry his kin into noble families. What a joke—he married his niece to the son of a cobbler!—"deceived by the stratagem of God!"[27] And the double-dealing Walter had lived out every nobleman's lineage nightmare, accepting a lowborn child as his own. In Galbert's compressed account, all the moral focus concentrates on the men who matter: the murderer Bertulf, the semitraitor Walter, and a rather startlingly tricky God. The passive men—the deceived cobbler who lost his child and the adopted son who now learns from his mother that he is lowborn—are merely narrative pawns.

It is quite easy to read this sensational piece of journalism through Galbert's eyes, and completely forget that the real active players all through were not the men, but the women. The original child-swap was organized by the noblewoman and the cobbler's wife (neither of whom merits a proper name)—the one so that she could secure the male heir so necessary for every landed family, and the other, one supposes, so that she could smuggle her child into high rank and wealth. Galbert, so anxious to reveal the secret motives of the important actors (he is always telling us what various men believe, desire, secretly think), never pauses to comment on

26. "profitebatur publice," "non . . . verum filium suum" (Galbert, [89], 22/23; trans., 262).
27. "Sicque arte Dei," "Dei arte deceptus" (Galbert, [89], 25, 27; trans., 262–63).

why Walter's wife would now make these revelations. Plausible speculation comes easily: (1) Walter of Vladslo died surrounded by dangerous suspicions in a volatile political climate; (2) he had left his wife connected to the criminal and disgraced family of Bertulf through her "son," and (3) this "son" was his father's heir, but might well go down in the general disgrace of his wife's kin. None of this was advantageous for the widow. So it looks like she decided to cut her losses, publicly disavow her blood tie to the "son" married into the Bertulf clan, and disinherit him at the same time.

This makes sense, of a cold-blooded sort, to me, but I can't prove any of this because Galbert paid no attention whatever to this astonishing woman who ought, one would think, to have been such a promising field for moral indignation and divine retribution. Yet Walter's wife, and the cobbler's wife, these ambitious, tough-minded, daring women, are treated as mere textual functions whose purpose is to set the men up for edifying falls. The bizarre situation, conceived and executed entirely by women to further their own aims, is rendered by Galbert as a protracted political negotiation among men only—with a morally ironic outcome. And that is the interesting point—the way the author's moral sensitivity fades out where the active narrative agents are invisible or insignificant to him, are female and thus narratively submerged.

But the exceptional presence of these few women in Galbert's narrative alerts us (through the optic of gender theory) to the unexceptional if unremarked presence of women, working women and servants, market women, wives and daughters of citizens, the full female complement of urban society, who were there at all the events of Galbert's history. In an urban world of small rooms and few public indoor spaces, nearly all the significant actions he records happened outside, or spilled over from inside, and the women who attained narrative significance by their compassionate attentions to the dying and dead were there in the first place for entertainment, part of the crowd excited by the spectacle of fighting, looting, executions, gossip, celebrity spotting. Some few of them step impulsively out of the crowd and into Galbert's narrative when they act with a meaning he sees and respects. But we should also see them, rhetorically speaking, as metonomies, the offhand "some women" standing for the many women who filled the streets, milled with the crowds, had political opinions, maybe joined in looting the castle when the besiegers broke in.[28] The visible few,

28. An instructive discussion of the prescriptive regime urged on urban women, who were supposed to resist the attractions of the streets outside their doors, behave with self-restraint

the few who act and govern verbs, are visible to Galbert because they have entered the moral order that was the deepest principle of his narrative.

As a self-consciously Christian recorder of a world in which legitimate governance and rational behavior had deteriorated into lawless and selfish brutalities, endlessly repeated, Galbert is remarkably candid about the depth of his disappointment. His morality was not one of religious submission to the mysteries of divine intention, and his insistently moralizing vocabulary does not often match up with any satisfactory meaning expressed by events. Just as the actions of the better sort of men were supposed to have *causae*—intelligible reasons—so God's mind, as imagined by Galbert, had to be rational and, of course, just. This is a book that ends with Galbert scrutinizing events to decipher *qua justitia*—what sort of justice—let God award the victory to what seemed to be the wrong man, the man who seized it by force?[29] And he tortures an answer out of the snakepit of events. If there were to be any discernable meaning in his narrative, a very few events had to be worked very hard as paradigm exemplars—to which most of reality utterly refused to conform. The central exemplar Galbert "discovered" by reflection, using the rhetorical process of "invention," by which "inventoried" information was retrieved from memory for appropriate new use (here I'm gratefully using the inventory idea taught me by Mary Carruther's book, *The Craft of Thought*), was the story of the rise of the Erembald lineage to prominence, the origin of its name.[30]

Here in the first lines of chapter 71 we learn of a onetime castellan of Bruges named Boldran, "whose wife was named Dedda or Duva."[31] This nothing little phrase is perfectly remarkable all by itself; no other "wife of" in the entire book is "named" by her own name (outside a genealogy), much less the fussy scruple of two possible variants, worrying over getting it right—the information being sixty years old. Dedda (or Duva) is a very bad woman. She had often committed adulterous acts with her husband's vassal, Erembald, and "had promised" her adulterous lover that he would

---

and modesty, and whose persistent transgressions against this bourgeois ideal produced a didactic literature is Felicity Riddy's "Mother Knows Best: Reading Social Change in a Courtesy Text," *Speculum* 71 (1996): 66–86.

29. Galbert, [121], 5.

30. Mary Carruthers, *The Craft of Thought: Meditation, Rhetoric, and the Making of Images, 400–1200* (Cambridge, 1998). This book has become indispensable to our understanding of the pragmatic relations between memory and original thought in memory-trained medieval minds; one sees the processes Carruthers explicates in Galbert's "readings" of the hidden tendencies beneath superficial reality.

31. "cujus uxor erat nomine Dedda vel Duva" (Galbert, [71], 3; trans., 239).

have her husband's position as castellan, "if by chance her husband should die soon."[32] Erembald killed his lord by pushing him overboard at night as Boldran, dressed in armor, urinated over the side of his ship.[33] Dedda kept her promises—she and Erembald married; he became castellan, and the marriage produced that nest of vipers: Bertulf the provost, instigator of the count's murder; Hacket; Wulfric; Robert; the vicious Lambert; three others Galbert doesn't name—and their numerous progeny spread through the upper ranks of Flemish society.[34] "Those serfs," Galbert sneers at the lot of them, "foul dogs, . . . those serfs, murdered their lord."

So Dedda is another of those women who connect two men in a special relationship to one another: wife of one, adulteress with the other, instigator of murder between them, felonious murder of a lord by his own man—deep foreshadowing of things to come. And when she incites the murder, it is with promises conditional on prompt action: if her husband "should die soon," artfully hinting that this offer might expire, with perhaps other candidates waiting for their chance. Something about Dedda inspired Galbert's fictional imagination, except that he never offers a clue as to why Dedda hated her husband so implacably. She is presented as all action—sexual and murderous—but no reasons, no *causae.* The murder was Dedda's plan because she "promised" the big rewards to Erembald for being her hit man: she governs a transitive verb all her own, and a masculine surrogate.

At the end of this exemplum, Galbert reverts to masculine authority for the moral, quoting (or misquoting) Exodus about God visiting the iniquities of the fathers on the sons, even to the third and fourth generation (Dedda's grandchildren). The repeated motif of death by "precipitation," Boldran pushed off the side of the ship ("the earlier precipitation"), Charles's killers pushed off the battlements of the castle ("this new precipitation"), reinforces that idea neatly.[35] And I think this episode is usually read chiefly around Galbert's reliance on the idea of the vengeful God and the long reach of retribution over unwitting generations. Even Count Charles's death is portrayed as in some sense payment for earlier sins of his lineage.

But the ostensible "moral" of a story is not always what a story is about

32. "promiserat adultero suo vicecomitatum si forte vir ejus cito moreretur" (Galbert, [71], 13/14; trans., 239).

33. Galbert, [71], 15/18.

34. Galbert, [71], 21/28.

35. "antiqua praecipitatio . . . nova ista praecipitatione" (Galbert, [71], 29/30; trans., 240).

when read in its own narrative terms. The dramatic story elements center on Dedda, her adultery, her betrayal, her conspiracy, her promises, and their fulfillment. She is the moral cause, willful instigator, and physical begetter of all the evils that would befall Count Charles and all Flanders—acting through men with her sexual powers of seduction and procreation. She is the mother of the conspiracy: treason, betrayal, murder, theft, and the contaminating spread of servile bloodlines through noble families.

Dedda's female descendents, females in the third and fourth generations of this family, are the "nieces" so often mentioned by Galbert as the linkages in the extensive network of Erembald influence and power, used cannily by Bertulf to connect his kin with older feudal families. These women spread the contagion of servile lineage, almost as a sexually transmitted blight, through marriage into hitherto unblemished free lineages. Not one of them is named by her own name, but their presence and the dire consequences of marriage with them are mentioned over and over. In this way the female descendents in the third and fourth generations of Erembalds after Dedda and Erembald continue Dedda's strange career. Indeed, one of these women who carried the taint of hereditary servility into a free family became the immediate source of "that most ruinous conflict over servitude and liberty between the pious count Charles and the provost and his kinsmen."[36] Dedda herself is never identified as servile by birth, however evil her nature; and Galbert never explains why she would choose a man of servile family for her husband. But disaster and ruin are transmitted sexually through the female line.

Here, in this chapter, the moral order converges with narrative order for Galbert to produce this gem of historically meaningful fiction. I think he composed this episode, whose formal structure of synecdoche invites close exegesis, with great care and satisfaction because, unlike present reality, the half-legendary past conforms with less resistance to exegetical history. It is also true that the moral order and the narrative order converge nicely here with common misogyny at a rather less elevated level—a narrative convenience that, in Galbert's eyes, just reinforced basic plausibility.

But misogyny alone is not the key to total understanding of this text, although gender theory invites us in that direction. We should remember the countess of Holland, a major player in the high-stakes game of replacing the dead count of Flanders. With the freedom of a high-ranking

36. "conflictus inter comitem Karolum pium et praepositum et suos de servitute et libertate exortus est pernitiosissimus" (Galbert, [25], 51/52; trans., 146).

widow and the power of regency over a minor son, she appeared on the scene at Bruges—the only other woman in the book, besides Dedda, to manipulate men with promises of favors. She turned up "on the night of Saint Gertrude," perhaps Galbert's complimentary way of indirectly announcing the countess's name, which was Gertrude, and like Dedda, her verbs are active: she labored to win over men to her candidate, giving and promising many things.[37] No hint of disapproval colors Galbert's account of this aggressive woman, whose actions are legitimated by rank, lineage, and wealth. We should note that the countess's aggressive maneuvering for power, using males as placeholders and pawns, deploying the seduction of promises, favors, gifts, is quite similar to Dedda's strategy. But Galbert seems to accept the countess's actions as a natural outcome of her position in the world, licit enough under the circumstances, and he records her open ambitions without judgment. The crucial difference seems to be legitimacy: the multiple "adultery" of Dedda brings her dangerous femininity to the foreground. The countess, widowed and continent, secure in her position in the feudal hierarchy, linked to the valid claims of her son and brother, is gender-neutralized and permitted to advance as a legitimate player in the power struggles of post-Charles Flanders.

There is no particular summation that properly encompasses the haphazard and gender-blinkered presence or absence of women in Galbert's book, along with their paradigmatic centrality. Gender theory, applied to Galbert's book as a social document, alerts us to female absence. Narrative theory, searching for formal keys to meaningful order, leads us to female presence. Women are particularly "there" or strikingly "not there" depending on one's mood when one picks up the book; maybe that is how they seemed in Galbert's world. When the citizens of Bruges proclaim (in an extended communal speech composed by Galbert) that they now wanted as count, the "more rightful heir, the son of the *sister* of Count Charles's *mother*," they weren't revealing some startling new ideology of matriarchal succession.[38] They were bolstering their self-interested defiance of King Louis with every little argument they could collect, but female lineage was part of it, or part of it when it was convenient, or when men calculated the full extent of their enemies. And then "some women" are there.

37. "in nocte sanctae Gertrudis . . . laborabat omnium procerum animos convertere in amicitiam sui dando et promittendo multa" (Galbert, [34], 2, 7/8; trans., 161–62).

38. "justiorem terrae heredem . . . filium *sororis matris* Karoli consulis" (Galbert, [106], 32/33; trans., 284, my emphasis).

6

The Language of Misogyny in Galbert of Bruges's Account of the Murder of Charles the Good

MARTINA HÄCKER

The Middle Ages have been both criticized for widespread misogyny and defended against claims that misogyny was paramount. These opposing views are based less on the gender of the scholars—although women seem to be more sensitive to misogyny—than on the type of text studied by them. Texts addressed exclusively to clerics show a greater tendency toward misogyny than texts addressed to a wider audience. Schnell found that misogyny is comparatively widespread in Latin texts, while it is rare in vernacular texts, and argued that "if misogynous passages in Latin texts were translated into the vernacular and thus left their original locus of communication, those who adapted them to the vernacular always felt obliged to apologize for misogynous utterances by saying that they referred only to bad women."[1] It seems worthwhile, therefore, to study the treatment of women in texts that are not directed at clerics but that are nevertheless in Latin, since very few women were able to read Latin in the Middle Ages, and an author writing in Latin would therefore feel no need to tone down any misogynous views he might hold for the sake of a female audience.

1. "Wenn aber lateinische Texte mit misogynen Passagen in die Volkssprache übersetzt wurden und somit ihren ursprünglichen Kommunikationsort verließen, dann fühlten sich die volkssprachlichen Bearbeiter stets bemüßigt, die misogynen Äußerungen abzuschwächen, indem sie betonten, damit seien ja nur die schlechten Frauen angesprochen" (Rüdiger Schnell, *Frauendiskurs, Männerdiskurs, Ehediskurs: Textsorten und Geschlechterkonzepte in Mittelalter und Früher Neuzeit* [Frankfurt am Main, 1998], 13). It ought to be pointed out that German *ansprechen* has a wide range of meanings, including "refer to," "apply to," and "address." On this point in general, see ibid., 11–21.

Galbert of Bruges's account of the murder of Charles the Good, count of Flanders, falls into this category, and it will be the main focus of my essay, although it will also be compared to other contemporary accounts of the assassination.[2]

According to several sources, the conflict between Charles and the relatives of the provost Bertulf arose from an old law concerning marriage between free people and serfs that was revived by Count Charles.[3] This law threatened the status of one of the most powerful families in Flanders, which is generally referred to in modern scholarship as the Erembalds, after the first member of the family to rise to power. Women thus played a major role in the conflict between Count Charles and the Erembalds, and this essay will focus on their treatment in Galbert's chronicle.[4]

The woman whose life was most affected by the events of the years 1127 and 1128 must have been Charles's own wife, Marguerite of Clermont. She did not, however, take an active role in the events following her husband's murder. This raises the question as to whether she was unable or unwilling to do so. Marguerite's inactivity contrasts sharply with the determined behavior of earlier countesses such as Richilda, wife of Count Baldwin VI (1067–70), Clemence of Burgundy, wife of Count Robert II (1093–1111), and Gertrude of Holland, wife of Florent II, count of Holland, who all tried to influence the succession after their husbands' deaths.[5] The fact that Marguerite is hardly mentioned in contemporary sources led Ross to assume that she may never have lived with Count Charles.[6] Nicholas suggests that her noteworthy absence from the political scene may have been due to the continuing power of Clemence of Burgundy and the fact that "her [Marguerite's] husband was a 'stranger and foreigner' to many Flemings, which made it almost impossible for her to overcome that status herself."[7] The second argument requires some modification. Charles's mother was Adela, daughter of Robert the Frisian, who was count of Flanders

2. Other contemporary sources are Walter, Herman, Suger, and the "Passio Karoli comitis auctore anonymo," ed. Rudolf Köpke, MGH SS 12, 619–623. The translations of passages from these texts are my own.

3. Galbert, [7], 25; Herman, 28, p. 285; Suger, 30, p. 242; Walter, [16].

4. For a study of women as a source of information for medieval Flemish authors, see Renée Nip, "Gendered Memories from Flanders," in *Medieval Memories: Men, Women and the Past, 700–1300,* ed. Elisabeth van Houts (Harlow, 2001), 113–31.

5. Karen Nicholas, "Countesses as Rulers in Flanders," in *Aristocratic Women in Medieval France,* ed. Theodore Evergates (Philadelphia, 1999), 115–21.

6. James Bruce Ross, trans., 19. There is, however, no evidence to corroborate this hypothesis.

7. Nicholas, "Countesses," 120.

from 1071 to 1093, and Charles himself had grown up in his grandfather's and uncle's households in Flanders.[8] Marguerite herself, moreover, was no more a stranger to the Flemings than Clemence of Burgundy had been when she became countess. This suggests that if Marguerite lived with her husband up to his death, the difference between her behavior and that of the other countesses must be due to either a difference in personality or an inability to compete with Clemence of Burgundy's power. According to Nicholas, however, Clemence's power had waned by 1121, when she retired to southwestern Flanders after losing her fight—and several of her dower towns—to Charles, who had succeeded her son Baldwin VII in 1119 as count of Flanders.[9]

While neither Marguerite nor Clemence is mentioned by Galbert—he refers to Marguerite only indirectly when he speaks of Bishop Simon of Noyon "who was the brother of Count Charles's wife"[10]—Walter of Thérouanne mentions Marguerite in the context of Charles's designation by his predecessor, Count Baldwin VII: "He [Baldwin VII] himself made Charles, whose honesty and diligence he had already often tested in many ways, his heir and entrusted him with the full power of government. He had also already married him to Marguerite, the daughter of Rainaud II, count of Clermont, and had given him the county of Amiens with the castle of Encre."[11] This donation took place in 1115, which would suggest the same year for Charles's marriage.[12] The information on Marguerite's life is sparse. Her name appears together with her husband's on three charters issued at Veurne on March 18, 1121, at Bergues on September 15, 1121, and at an unknown place on May 6, 1124.[13] As we have seven charters by Charles before her name first appears (which is long after they were married) and eight after she is last mentioned, the absence of her name on charters after

8. Galbert, xi; Walter, vii. See also the genealogical table in Nicholas, "Countesses," 114.

9. Nicholas, "Countesses," 119.

10. "qui frater erat uxoris comitis Karoli" (Galbert, [21], 44; trans., 136, trans. mod.).

11. "Karolum, cuius probitatem prius et industriam in multis sepe probauerat, heredem sibi ipse instituerat eique rerum omnium summam regendam ac disponendam tradiderat. Cui etiam prius nobilem puellam Margaretam, Rainaldi comitis Clarmontensis filiam, matrimonio copulauerat et comitatum Ambianensem cum castello Incrensi donauerat" (Walter, [8], 7/13). Suger, whose account of the events is much shorter, does not mention Marguerite either.

12. See Walter, ix–x n6. Ross suggests 1118 for Charles's marriage (trans., 14–15). This is based on Léon Vanderkindere, who claims that Amiens was Marguerite's dowry from her mother (the house of Vermandois) into whose possession it passed only in 1117 (*La formation territoriale des principautés belges au moyen âge,* 2 vols. [Brussels, 1902], 1:152–53). However, she gives 1115 as the date of the donation of Encre by Baldwin.

13. *Actes,* n° 100, p. 230; n° 103, p. 234; and n° 116, p. 267. See trans., 19 and Walter, xx–xxii.

1124 might well be coincidence and does not suggest that she was not part of the count's household at the time of his death. After his death, Marguerite married, first, Hugh III, count of Saint-Pol, who died in 1144 or 1145, and then Baldwin of Encre.[14] From the little evidence we have, it seems impossible to draw any conclusions about the relationship between Count Charles and his wife.

Galbert's silence on the subject of Charles's wife raises the question as to whether this omission is due simply to the bias of a medieval male author[15] or whether there is some specific reason for it. One motivation may have been a conscious effort on Galbert's part to play down the fact that Count Charles had died without an heir, which would necessarily entail avoiding any mention of his marriage and his wife. Galbert's uneasiness regarding Charles's childlessness can be seen in the fact that he feels obliged to mention two other childless rulers in his prologue, where he compares Charles favorably with the Emperor Henry V, "who after reigning for many years died without heirs," and Henry I, king of England, "who was ruling without heirs in his kingdom."[16] In the case of Henry I, Galbert's statement is clearly not true. Although out of seventeen children he had only one legitimate son, William, who died in 1120, Henry's daughter Mathilda was designated as his heir in 1126.[17]

The dynastic code obliged a nobleman to give an heir to his family and vassals. The failure to provide an heir, that is, childlessness, was in medieval times almost invariably blamed on the woman. As a consequence, many noblewomen were repudiated by their husbands if an expected heir was not born within a certain period of time.[18] Due to the absence of a direct heir at Charles the Good's death, five claimants to the countship of

14. See *De genere comitum Flandrensium notae Parisienses,* ed. G. Waitz, MGH SS 13, 257; Dominique Barthélemy, *Les Deux âges de la seigneurie banale. Pouvoir et Société dans la terre des Sires de Coucy (milieu XIe–milieu XIIIe siècle)* (Paris, 1984), 56–57; Nieus, *Un pouvoir comtal,* 142–50, 268.

15. This would seem to be the argument of Nicholas, who states that "the early twelfth-century chroniclers . . . present history as the acts of powerful men who exercised power primarily by the sword, and consequently had little to say about the countesses" ("Countesses," 111).

16. "qui, cum annos plures sedisset, sine herede diem obiit. . . . sine liberis degebat" (Galbert, [Prol.], 5/7; trans., 79).

17. Ross mentions William's death in 1120, but fails to mention the designation of Mathilda (trans., 79n3).

18. See Georges Duby, *Medieval Marriage,* trans. Elborg Forster (Baltimore, 1978), 7, and Pauline Stafford, *Queens, Concubines, and Dowagers: The King's Wife in the Early Middle Ages* (London, 1983), 81.

Flanders presented themselves in the course of the year 1127 and one more in February 1128.[19] Charles had not taken any measures to avoid conflict in case of a sudden death, that is, by designating one out of the number of his potential successors as his heir. One could therefore argue that he was to a certain extent responsible for the civil war following his murder.[20]

Galbert, who honored Count Charles for his justice and his generosity toward the poor, emphasized his saintly qualities. Charles's murder in a church, during prayer, in the holy time of Lent allows him to appear as a martyr,[21] and the actions of martyrs are beyond criticism. Moreover, the moral code for clerics (and saints) is different from that for secular lords: they are expected to be chaste. In depicting Charles as a saint, Galbert could turn childlessness, a shortcoming according to the dynastic moral code, into chastity, a virtue according to the ecclesiastical moral code.[22]

While Galbert may have had tactical reasons for not mentioning Marguerite, his treatment of other women may tell us more about how he perceived women. Two other countesses are mentioned in the chronicle: Richilda of Hainaut, wife of Baldwin VI, count of Flanders, and Gertrude of Holland, widow of Florent II, count of Holland. Gertrude appears with her son at the besieged town of Bruges on March 16, 1127, and uses bribery to persuade the nobles to elect as count her son, who has rather weak hereditary claims, being related to Charles only through his paternal grandmother: "and she tried hard to secure the friendship of all the barons, bestowing gifts and making many promises."[23] On March 25, 1128, she supports her brother, Thierry of Alsace, who, as a second cousin, has better hereditary claims to succeed Charles as count of Flanders than her son Thierry of Holland.[24]

19. William of Ypres on March 6, 1127 (Galbert [25], 1/47); Thierry of Alsace on March 20, 1127 (Galbert, [47], 23/39) (both were first cousins of Charles); William Clito of Normandy on March 30, 1127 (Galbert, [52], 21/47); Baldwin IV, count of Hainaut, on April 17, 1127 (Galbert, [67], 12/16) (both second cousins of Charles); Thierry of Holland on March 16, 1127 (Galbert, [34], 1/8), related to Charles only through the second marriage of his paternal grandmother; and Arnold, Charles's nephew, in February 1128 (Galbert, [94], 6/9). Cf. Walter, [45].

20. Cf. Claudia Opitz, *Evatöchter und Bräute Christi: Weiblicher Lebenszusammenhang und Frauenkultur im Mittelalter* (Weinheim, 1990), 58–60.

21. See Richard Kieckhefer, "Imitators of Christ: Sainthood in the Christian Tradition," in *Sainthood: Its Manifestations in World Religions,* ed. Richard Kieckhefer and George D. Bond (Berkeley, 1988), 3.

22. Hans-Werner Goetz, *Leben im Mittelalter vom 7. bis zum 13. Jahrhundert* (Munich, 1986), 101–4.

23. "et laborabat omnium procerum animos convertere in amicitiam sui dando et promittendo multa" (Galbert, [34], 7/8; trans., 162).

24. Galbert, [99], 3/12.

Whereas Gertrude uses doubtful means to advance her son's candidacy, Richilda, wife of Baldwin VI of Flanders and Hainaut, fails to secure the countship for her sons during an episode concerning the succession to the county of Flanders, which takes place over fifty years before the murder of Charles. After her husband's death, Richilda leaves Flanders and retires to her mother's home in Mons, leaving the heir to the countship, her adolescent son Arnold, on his own in the Bruges area. According to Galbert, this enables Robert I "the Frisian," count of Holland (Baldwin VI's brother), to win over the majority of the barons, and the inexperienced Arnold, to whom Galbert always refers as the "boy" (*puer*), is killed in the ensuing battle. This episode is recounted in one of Galbert's genealogical digressions. It dates back to 1070–71, which means that Galbert was not a witness to these events, but depended on reports or records. However, even in Galbert's time there existed different versions of these events. Why, then, did he include the episode in his work? Writing from a religious background, where the history of the world is seen as the working of God, Galbert had to find an explanation for the murder of so pious a man as Count Charles. Such an explanation is provided by the genealogy of the counts of Flanders: Charles the Good was Robert the Frisian's grandson. If Robert the Frisian had secured the countship for himself by murdering the legitimate heir, then the murder of his grandson could be explained as the working of God, as a just punishment for the earlier injustice.

Richilda, widow of Count Baldwin VI, is assigned an important role in Galbert's account of Robert the Frisian's treachery, however; instead of remaining at the center of power, she returns to her mother's home, thus giving her brother-in-law the opportunity to usurp power for himself:

> Now when Baldwin, the husband of Richilda, had died in Bruges, his son Arnold, to whom the fatherland belonged, stayed near Kassel and Saint Omer and in those parts after his mother returned to Mons and the proximity of her mother. . . . Now Robert, count of Holland, had heard that the fatherland had been left to his nephews, still of tender years, and that their mother had withdrawn from the region around Bruges; and so he had a favorable moment for treachery, and an opportunity for beginning it.[25]

25. "Igitur cum Balduinus vir Richildis in Brugis obiisset, filius ejus Arnoldus, cui patria pertinebat, cum mater versus Montes et viciniam matris rediit, circa Casletum et Sanctum Audomarum et illas partes conversabatur. . . . Audierat namque Robertus comes Hollandensis patriam relictam nepotibus suis adhuc parvulis aetate, et matrem puerorum simul se a confinio circa Bruggas jacente subtraxisse. Habuit occasionem per hoc et principium oportunitatemque traditionis" (Galbert, [69], 24/33; trans., 234).

Galbert gives a detailed description of how Baldwin VI, in obvious distrust of his brother Robert, had previously tried to secure his sons' succession and thus contrasts the father's provident care with the mother's lack of it. A comparison with the other contemporary sources reveals that Walter of Thérouanne in his *Vita Karoli* and Suger of Saint-Denis in his *Vita Ludovici VI Grossi regis* do not go as far back in the genealogy of the counts of Flanders and that Herman of Tournai in his *Liber de restauratione S. Martini Tornacensis* gives a version that differs at the crucial point: "At that time Baldwin was count of Mons . . . , who, as has been mentioned above, had married Richilda, the countess of Mons, and thus held both counties, namely Flanders and Mons, to whom two sons were born by the same Richilda, Arnold, who, succeeding his father, was slain by his uncle Robert at Kassel, and Baldwin, who together with his mother held the county of Mons."[26] It is worth noting that Herman does not link Richilda's being at Mons to the death of her son. This is not surprising, as medieval widows frequently returned to their own families.[27] It thus seems that Galbert interprets what was normal behavior for a medieval widow as neglect of her parental duties.

Marriages play an important role in Galbert's chronicle. Indeed, according to Galbert, the conflict between the Erembalds and Count Charles of Flanders arises from a law regarding mixed marriages between free men and women of servile origin. After having fallen into oblivion, this law was

26. "Erat tunc quidam Balduinus comes Montensis . . . qui, ut supra dictum est, Richeldem comitissam Montensem coniugem ducens, utrumque comitatum tenuerat, Flandrensem scilicet et Montensem, quique eadem Richelde duos filios genuit, Ernulfum, qui patri succedens a patruo suo Roberto Casleti est occisus, et Balduinum, qui cum matre sua Montensem comitatum tenuit" (Herman, 33, p. 286). Walter Mohr, "Richilde vom Hennegau und Robert der Friese. Thesen zu einer Neubewertung der Quellen," *Revue belge de philologie et d'histoire* 58 (1980): 777–96, and "Richilde vom Hennegau und Robert der Friese. Thesen zu einer Neubewertung der Quellen (2. Teil)," *Revue belge de philologie et d'histoire* 59 (1981): 265–91, discusses the different versions of this story current in historical works of the eleventh and twelfth centuries. They vary with respect to: (1) the genealogy: in some versions, Robert is the elder brother of Baldwin VI count of Flanders, which would justify his claim on the countship, while in others he is the younger son or an illegitimate son, which would give his brother a better claim irrespective of the question of majority; (2) the person who is killed in the course of the events: Robert the Frisian's brother or his nephew; (3) Robert the Frisian's responsibility for the death; (4) the occurrence of an oath in the story; (5) the person to whom the oath is given; (6) the conditions under which the oath is given, i.e., whether Robert receives money or presents or nothing in return for the oath, and whether the oath is sworn on relics or not; and (7) Richilda's role. The great variation shows that the story has been used again and again to justify claims to the countship on genealogical grounds, and it certainly throws some doubt on Galbert's version.

27. See Opitz, *Evatöchter*, 25.

revived and applied by Count Charles. As Galbert tells us, it stated that a free man who married a serf himself became a serf a year and a day after the marriage.[28] Why was this law so well suited to reduce the power of the Erembald clan? In medieval society, women were one of the means by which men tried to increase their influence and prestige.[29] In the case of the free nobles who married the nieces of Bertulf the provost, the attraction lay in the riches and the influential position of the Erembald family in Flemish society, whereas Bertulf and his kin hoped to lose the stigma of servile status by marrying into free families, or so we are made to believe.

One of the nieces of the provost Bertulf is married to Robert of Crecques, and it is when Robert challenges another knight to a duel—and the other knight refuses to fight a duel with him on the grounds of Robert's servile status—that the whole question of the Erembald family's status is raised.[30] None of the other contemporary sources emphasize the legal consequences of the marriages of Bertulf's nieces as Galbert does. Suger and Herman of Tournai mention only that the Erembalds murder Charles because they would not accept that they were of servile status.[31] Walter, who also tells the episode of the refused duel, restricts his account to one sentence.[32] Galbert not only elaborates the story in chapter 7, but also repeats it in chapter 25, and he seems to put the blame on the woman, who has let her husband down: "And so that knight mourned who had lost his liberty on account of his wife, through whom he had believed he could become freer [that is more noble] when he married her."[33] A second niece of the provost Bertulf is married to Fromold Junior, notary and, according to Galbert, a favorite with Count Charles.[34] This becomes evident in chapter 18, when Fromold begs Isaac for his life, saying that if he killed him he would deprive his own nephews [i.e., the sons of Isaac's sister] of their fa-

28. Galbert, [7], 30/32; [25], 47/50.

29. See Duby, *Medieval Marriage,* 99, 108.

30. Galbert, [7], 22/39; [25], 44/52.

31. Suger, 30, p. 242; Herman, 28, p. 285.

32. "It happened that a certain noble knight charged another nobleman with a breach of the peace in the count's court, and the latter reproached him with the stigma of a servile condition, because he had married a female relative of the provost, who was said to be a serf of the count, and refused to answer him as if he were a free man" (Accidit autem ut quidam miles nobilis aduersus alium nobilem in curia comitis de treugarum infractione placitaret et ille, nota ei seruilis conditionis obiecta, eo quod consanguineam illius praepositi, quę comitis ancilla esse diceretur, uxorem duxisset, respondere ut libero refutaret; Walter, [16], 2/6).

33. "Indoluit ergo miles ille qui propter uxorem suam libertatem amiserat, per quam liberiorem se fore crediderat cum eam accepisset" (Galbert, [7], 33/35; trans., 100).

34. "Yet it was true that no one in the court was so intimate with the count in his lifetime, or so dear to him as this Fromold" (Verum tamen fuit quod nullus de curia comiti ita familiaris esset, cum viveret, neque ita carus sicut praefatus Fromoldus; Galbert, [19], 24/26; trans., 131).

ther.[35] It is worth noting that Galbert does not mention the servile status of Fromold, to whom ought to apply the same law that Galbert elaborates in so much detail with respect to Robert of Crecques.

A third of the provost's nieces is the wife of Walter, lord of Vladslo and Eine, one of the peers of Flanders.[36] According to Galbert, Walter of Vladslo's wife substituted a cobbler's son for her own stillborn son, bribing the cobbler's wife with money to say that her, that is, the cobbler's, son had died. After Walter of Vladslo's death, his wife publicly confesses that their son is not their real son, but an adopted son whom, she says, Walter left in the care of a burgher for three hundred pounds. Galbert uses this story as an exemplum of how God's artfulness triumphs over that of the provost, who had tried to gain influence by marrying one of his nieces to the son of Walter of Vladslo, one of the most powerful men in Flanders. Walter of Vladslo's wife in this story not only deceives her own husband, but also shifts the blame onto him as soon as he is dead.

But the child she had borne had died at once at birth. Therefore she substituted the cobbler's son, who had been born about the same time, and secretly sent the dead child, whom she had borne, to the wife of the cobbler, giving her money so that she would claim to have given birth to the dead child and conceal what she had done from her husband. And when that stolen and "adopted" son had grown up, and everyone actually believed him to be Walter's son, the provost went and gave in marriage his niece, the daughter of the son of his brother, to that false son so that they would stand together firmly under all circumstances by reason of that marriage, and would become bolder, stronger, and more powerful.

Now, after the death of Walter, his wife announced publicly that the boy was not his real son, but an adopted son,[37] whom Walter had put away in the home of a certain burgher in pledge for three hundred pounds. And so God's stratagem foiled the stratagem of the provost, who, when he wanted to exalt his family proudly and arrogantly by that marriage, joined it to the son of a cobbler, deceived by the stratagem of God![38]

35. Galbert, [18], 29/35.

36. Galbert mentions two of Bertulf's other nieces: one was married to Walter Crommelin of Lissewege (Galbert, [54], 1/4), one to Guy of Steenvoorde (Galbert, [58], 1/4).

37. I have emended Ross's translation, who translated "non esse verum filium suum sed adoptivum" by "was an adopted son and not his real son," thus changing the order and making it more difficult to see that the antecedent of the following relative pronoun is the adopted son.

38. "At infans, quem pepererat, statim in ipso partu obierat. Supposuit ergo filium sutoris, qui circa idem tempus genitus fuerat, et emortuum quem pepererat uxori sutoris clanculo submisit, dans ei pecuniam ut fateretur se peperisse illum emortuum et viro suo quod factum erat celaret. Cum crevisset ille furatus et adoptivus filius et omnes crediderant vere filium fuisse

The story, as it is told by Galbert, does not seem credible. Why should this woman admit to having deceived her late husband without any apparent reason for such a postmortem confession? Seen in the context of the legal conflict regarding mixed marriages between female serfs and free men, this story may have been circulated by relatives of Walter of Vladslo in order to preserve his inheritance for the family.[39] If Walter's son was a serf, according to the law, Walter's inheritance would fall to the count of Flanders and thus be lost to the family. Walter's brother Cono II of Eine, however, was a free man. It was he who actually inherited Walter's estates.[40] This would not have been possible had Walter's son been considered his father's legitimate heir. It is not implausible that bribery had played a role in this story, but it is more likely to have taken place when Walter of Vladslo's family needed the cobbler's wife to confirm an implausible story, which served to save Walter's estates for his family. The question is why Galbert includes the story in the first place and why he chose to believe this unlikely version. At least a partial answer is provided by the closing sentence. The story served as an example of "God's stratagem deceiving that of the provost." The story contains, however, a linguistic detail that points to an additional motivation: by describing the son as *furatus* and *furtivus,* that is "stolen," rather than "bought," which would be *emptus* or *empticus,* Galbert evokes associations with 1 Kings 3:16–28, the famous story of the judgment of Solomon, and thus makes the woman's crime appear even worse.[41] Galbert thus transfers traits of a well-known biblical exemplum to a woman he describes in his chronicle.

illius Walter, venit praepositus et dedit neptem suam, filiam filii fratris sui, illi furtivo filio uxorem ut firmiter ad omnem fortunam simul per illud conjugium consisterent, audaciores, fortiores ac potentiores forent. Igitur post mortem ipsius Walteri profitebatur publice uxor ejus, puerum illum non esse verum filium suum sed adoptivum, quem idem Walterus apud burgensem quendam posuerat in vadimonium pro trecentis libris. Sicque arte Dei delusa est ars praepositi qui cum vellet superbe et gloriose per illud conjugium cognationem suam extollere, filio sutoris, Dei arte deceptus, eam copulavit" (Galbert, [89], 11/27; trans., 262–63).

39. It is, of course, also possible that the reason for the late admittance of the substitution was remorse, as an anonymous reviewer suggested, but this would still leave us with the question of why the woman should admit the substitution at this point in time and why she should then shift the blame onto her deceased husband. Genuine remorse is hardly compatible with shifting the blame for the act onto someone else rather than openly taking responsibility for it. The fact that the woman blamed her dead husband for the substitution strongly suggests that we are not dealing with belated but true remorse, but rather with a swift action to preserve the family inheritance.

40. Warlop, 1:229.

41. The topic of the stolen child is a common one in the Middle Ages. See Ellen E. Kittell, "Toward a Perspective on Women, Sex, and Witches in the Later Middle Ages," in *Von Menschen und ihren Zeichen: Sozialhistorische Untersuchungen zum Spätmittelalter und zur Neuzeit,* ed. Ingrid Matschinegg, Brigitte Rath, and Brigitte Schuch (Bielefeld, 1990), 15n5.

It is, however, not one of the Provost Bertulf's nieces but his mother who comes off worst: Dedda or Duva, to whom Galbert devotes most of chapter 71. His uncertainty as to the precise form of her name is worth noting, as it points to the doubtfulness of the whole story. This Dedda, according to Galbert, seduces her lover, the eponymous ancestor of the Erembald clan, into murdering her husband, Boldran, by promising him the latter's office of castellan of Bruges if her husband should die suddenly. With Boldran's money, Erembald then buys this office. It is impossible to ascertain whether there is any truth in this story. What is important for our purpose is how Galbert tells the story, which he knows from hearsay, that is *sicut aiunt.* According to Galbert, it is the woman who takes the lead: she "had promised her adulterer the office of castellan, if by chance her husband should die soon." The word *cito* seems telling in the context, as it contains the barely concealed suggestion of murder. "By this wife he [Erembald] begot the provost, Bertulf, and Hacket, Wulfric Cnop, Lambert Nappin, the father of Borsiard, and also Robert, castellan after him in the second place."[42] With these words Galbert closes the episode and continues to link the fall of the Erembalds, which is also a fall in the literal sense of the word, to their origins. Boldran's precipitation by Erembald from a ship is avenged by God when members of the Erembald family are punished for the murder of Charles by precipitation from the tower, proving that God visits the evil of the fathers, or rather the mother and father, in the fourth generation: "In this fourth degree, therefore, the earlier precipitation of Boldran was punished in the persons of Erembald's successors by this new precipitation, which was accomplished from the battlements of the count's house in Bruges. And so, you might say, by the dispensation of God they were punished for the sins of their parents, as it is read in Exodus."[43]

This story of Dedda or Duva is questionable on several grounds: Galbert knows it only from hearsay (*ut aiunt*); it appears that two different

42. "promiserat adultero suo vececomitatum si forte vir ejus cito moreretur. . . . De qua uxore genuit praepositum Bertulfum, Haket, Wulfricum Cnop, Lambertum Nappin, patrem Borsiardi, Robertum quoque castellanum post ipsum secundo loco" (Galbert, [71], 13/14, 22/25; trans., 239). Cf. Rider, *God's Scribe,* 132.

43. "In hoc ergo gradu quarto punita est in successores suos antiqua praecipitatio Boldranni nova ista praecipitatione quae facta est ab propugnaculis camerae comitis in Brugis, et forsitan dispensante Deo, punitum est in eis peccatum parentum, sicut in Exodo legitur" (Galbert, [71], 28/32; trans., 240). To be able to apply the quotation from Ex 20:5 to the Erembalds, Galbert has recourse to counting castellans rather than generations of Erembalds.

versions of the woman's name were used by Galbert's sources; and the story itself existed in at least two versions, as in the anonymous "Passio Karoli comitis," Dedda's or Duva's husband, who in this version is called Holdrannus, is not pushed from a ship, but stabbed and pushed from a bridge:

> At the time of Count Robert the Elder, the Frisian, who was also called the Bearded, and who had a son Count Robert the Younger, there was in Bruges a certain castellan by the name of Holdran, who had a steward by the name of Erembald, a man well versed in his job, but unfaithful to his master, who even soiled the marriage-bed of his master. This Erembald had become so depraved that, when his own master fought on a certain bridge in Bruges with the people, he stabbed him in the crowd with his sword and threw the stabbed man in the tumult off to his death. However the wife of this Holdran married her adulterous lover, the betrayer of her husband, from which fact it became obvious that Erembald committed such a great sin on the unfaithful wife's advice.[44]

Galbert's version of this story, with its link to contemporary history, shows an obvious thematic parallel to that of the story of the wife of Robert of Crecques: it demonstrates God's superior power over those who try to exalt themselves.[45] This is no coincidence. Galbert does not simply record the events of 1127 and 1128, but tries to present history as the working of God. This proved to be an increasingly difficult task, and Galbert himself must have found it hard to perceive the working of God in the killing and destruction that followed the murder of Count Charles the Good, as well as in the rapid succession of Counts William Clito and Thierry of Alsace. Galbert was forced again and again to find explanations for sudden, unexpected changes in the events, and his search for explanations appears to have been guided by two principles: his belief that God punishes present and earlier sins and his perception of women as a source of evil.[46]

44. "Tempore Roberti Fresonis comitis seniori, qui et Robertus barbatus dictus est, habens filium Robertum comitem iuniorem, fuit Bruggis quidam pretor nomine Holdrannus, habens dapiferum nomine Ereboldum, virum quidem officui gnarum, sed infidelium in dominum et ipsius domini maculantem thorum. Qui Eremboldus in tantum perversitatis deiectus est, ut ipsum dominum suum, in quodam ponte Bruggis cum populo dimicantem, inter ceteros mucrone confoderet, et perfossum inter tumultum in mortem precipitaret. Uxor vero Holdranni adulterum suum, mariti proditorem, accepit in maritum, unde innotuit, quod consilio perfidae coniugis Eremboldus tam grande piaculum subiit" ("Passio Karoli comitis," 620).

45. Cf. Ez 21:26, Jb 22:29, and Mt 23:12.

46. As the story of Erembald and Holdran in the "Passio Karoli comitis" shows, Galbert is not alone in blaming the woman. However, while the author of the "Passio Karoli comitis," establishes the woman's guilt through the conclusion he draws from the fact that she later married her husband's murderer, Galbert pretends to know as if from an eyewitness that she promised Erembald her husband's post if he murdered her husband. That this is pure fiction

The women that appear in Galbert's digressions are adulterous (Dedda/Duva), they use bribery (Gertrude of Holland and Walter of Vladslo's wife), they desert their children (Richilda of Hainaut and Walter of Vladslo's wife), they lie or make false claims (Walter of Vladslo's wife and Robert of Creques's wife) and they instigate murder (Dedda/Duva). While Bertulf and his kin are characterized by the worst of the seven deadly sins, *superbia,* the women appear to violate the Ten Commandments. It is, however, worth noting that in all these digressions, there is a man who profits at least temporarily from the respective woman's action (even if this is unintended, as in the case of Richilda): Erembald becomes castellan of Bruges, Thierry becomes count of Flanders, Robert the Frisian becomes count of Flanders, and Robert of Creques and Walter of Vladslo achieve higher status through their marriages and profit from this until the time when Count Charles decides to revive the law concerning the marriage of serfs with nobles.

There are, however, two women whose alleged crimes seem to be evil for the sake of being evil. These are the two alleged witches who are mentioned by Galbert in chapters 110 and 112. These two alleged witches, who lost their lives in Lille and Ghent in May 1128, are not cited in any of the major studies of witchcraft.[47] In chapter 110 Galbert reports that a witch or sorceress (*incantatrix*) sprinkles water on Count Thierry as he crosses a bridge in Lille, with the result that Count Thierry falls ill and refuses food and drink. The woman is seized by his vassals and burnt to death:

And it is worth remembering that when Count Thierry first went to Lille, a certain sorceress ran toward him, going into that body of water which the count was about to cross over by the bridge close by the soothsayer, and she sprinkled the count with water. Then, they say, Count Thierry sickened in heart and bowels so that he loathed food and drink. And when his vassals grew anxious about

invented by Galbert is obvious, as no one apart from the woman and man involved would know about such a promise—if it had existed—and they would have had every reason to keep this knowledge to themselves.

47. The studies that do not mention them include Joseph Hansen, *Zauberwahn, Inquisition und Hexenprozeß im Mittelalter* (1900; rpt. Aalen, 1964); Henry Charles Lea, *The History of the Inquisition of the Middle Ages,* 3 vols. (1885; rpt. New York, 1955); Jeffrey Burton Russell, *Witchcraft in the Middle Ages* (Ithaca, 1972); Andreas Blauert, "Die Erforschung der Anfänge der europäischen Hexenverfolgungen," in *Ketzer, Zauberer, Hexen: Die Anfänge der europäischen Hexenverfolgungen,* ed. Andreas Blauert (Frankfurt am Main, 1990), 11–42. They are, however, mentioned in Willem de Blécourt and Hans de Waardt, "Das Vordringen der Zaubereiverfolgungen in die Niederlande, Rhein Maas Schelde entlang," in *Ketzer, Zauberer, Hexen,* ed. Blauert, 206n16; the woman who was killed in Ghent is also mentioned in Norman Cohn, *Europe's Inner Demons: An Enquiry Inspired by the Great Witch-Hunt* (London, 1975), 154.

him they seized the sorceress, and binding her hands and feet, placed her on a pile of burning straw and hay and burnt her up.[48]

It is worth noting that Galbert knows this only from hearsay, as is apparent from his use of *ut aiunt.* However, he does not seem to have any doubts about the truth of what he is told, as he chooses *et memorandum* (it is worth noting) rather than *et mirum* (it is surprising) as his introductory phrase. Another alleged witch, of whose crime Galbert tells us nothing, is eviscerated by the men of Ghent, and her entrails are carried around the town: "On May 21, Monday, the news reached us from Lens that the king of France had fled from Lille where he had besieged our Count Thierry for four days. At the same time the men of Ghent eviscerated a certain sorceress and carried her entrails around their town."[49] These actions occur at the height of the civil war between Thierry of Alsace and William Clito, the two main contenders for the countship after the murder of Charles. The women seem to be scapegoats, whose deaths serve the purpose of lessening tension and working off frustration. In the following chapters, a competition of casting spells on the opposite party takes place between two priests supporting Thierry and William, respectively. Galbert comments on this practice: "And it is marvelous that a priest can cast a spell on God in such a way that, whether God wishes it or not, William may be thrown out of the countship! . . . Again our priests had the stupidity to say that the priest from Aartrijke and the priest from Koekelare and the cleric Odfrid had put Count Thierry and his men to flight in the battle by incantations, when in fact it is God who disposes and ordains all things!"[50] Jan Dhondt sees in these comments a reflection of Galbert's changing attitude toward this practice, a struggle between "the superstitious Galbert and the rationalistic Galbert," and interprets the latter

48. "Et memorandum quod cum jam primo comes Theodoricus in Insulas conscendisset, quaedam incantatrix occurrit illi, descendens in aquam illam quam comes transiturus erat per pontem juxta incarminatricem. At illa conspersit consulem aquis. Igitur, ut aiunt, comes Theodoricus languebat in corde et visceribus, ita ut comestionem et potum fastidiret. Cumque milites ejus indoluissent super eo, ceperunt incantatricem et ligatis manibus et pedibus, stipulis et straminibus succensis impositam combusserunt" (Galbert, [110], 29/37; trans., 291–92).

49. "Duodecimo kalendas Junii, feria secunda, fama retulit ex Lens regem Franciae fugisse ab Insulis, ubi comitem nostrum Theodericum obsederat per quatuor dies. Eadem tempestate Gendenses evisceraverant quamdam incantatricem et stomachum ejus cicumferebant circa villam suam" (Galbert, [112], 1/5; trans., 293).

50. "Et mirum est quod sacerdos ita Deum incantare possit ut, velit nolit Deus, Willelmus a comitatu ejiciatur. . . . Iterum nostri sacerdotes idiotae dicebant presbyterum ex Artrica et presbyterum ex Cnislara et Odfridum clericum per incantationes fugasse in bello consulem Theodoricum et suos, cum Deus omnia disponat et ordinet" (Galbert, [113], 60/61; [115], 11/15; trans., 296, 301).

statement as Galbert's reaction to the fact that he no longer believes that sorcery can change the outcome of the civil war.[51] It could, however, be argued that Galbert's first statement is already an ironic comment on this strange competition, and that he shows from the beginning a critical distance toward this superstition.[52]

In chapters 110–115 no linguistic distinction is made between sorcery or magic occurring inside and outside the church: the witches are referred to as *incantatrices* and the spells of the priests are called *incantationes.*[53] However, whereas the alleged spells of the witches could not be more severely punished, the priests' spells are not punished at all, and although Galbert loses his belief in the effectiveness of the priests' spells or has never believed in them (depending on one's interpretation of the passage in chapter 113), he never feels any doubts about the witches' spells.

The belief in spells has a long tradition in Germanic societies. Inexplicable misfortunes were often attributed to sorcery, and the punishment for casting spells ranged from fines to the death penalty, depending on the severity of the crime. If the loss of a life was blamed on the spell of an alleged sorcerer or sorceress, he or she was likely to lose his or her life as a result.[54] Several documents dating from Charlemagne's reign attest that the belief in magic must have continued to be strong, but that the actions against those performing magic did not include the death penalty.[55] In 800 the diocese of Salzburg took the following decision on the treatment of magicians:

With respect to incantations, augury or divination and those people who make storms or do other evil deeds, it pleased the holy council to decree that wherever

51. Jan Dhondt, "Une mentalité du douzième siècle: Galbert de Bruges," *Revue du Nord* 39 (1957): 104, 106.

52. Mohr, "Geschichtstheologische Aspekte im Werk Galberts von Brügge," in *Pascua Mediaevalia: Studies voor Prof. Dr. Jozef-Maria De Smet,* ed. R. Lievens, E. Van Mingroot, and W. Verbeke, Medievalia Lovaniensia, ser. 1, Studia 10 (Louvain, 1983), 261n77. Cf. Rider, *God's Scribe,* 192–98.

53. Mohr discusses the use of *incantare* in the sense of "to excommunicate" and argues that Galbert uses it to indicate that there is no legal basis for individual priests to carry out excommunications ("Geschichtstheologische Aspekte," 260). However, at the beginning of the twelfth century, priests appear to have had the power to do so (Jean Gaudemet, *Le gouvernement de l'église à l'époque classique,* part 2: *Le gouvernement local,* Histoire du droit et des institutions de l'Église en Occident 8.2 [Paris, 1979], 259). I am grateful to an anonymous reviewer for pointing out this source to me.

54. Cohn, *Europe's Inner Demons,* 148–55.

55. Hubert Mordek and Michael Glatthaar, "Von Wahrsagerinnen und Zauberern: Ein Beitrag zur Religionspolitik Karls des Großen," *Archiv für Kulturgeschichte* 75 (1993): 33–64.

they are caught, the archbishop of that diocese should see to it that they are retained and put through a most careful examination in order that they would perhaps confess the deeds they performed. But this punishment is to be carried out with such restraint, that they do not lose their lives, but that those who are thrown in jail may be saved so that with the help of God they mend their sinful ways.[56]

According to Cohn, the position of the post-Carolingian church was likewise to discourage the belief in pagan magic and to induce repentance in those who adhered to such magic.[57]

Galbert has an unusually critical mind for his time, and yet he includes in his chronicle the most unlikely stories as long as the culprit is female. This holds not only in the case of the alleged witches, but also in the stories about the countesses Richilda and Gertrude and about the women connected with the Erembald family (Dedda/Duva, Robert of Creques's and Walter of Vladso's wives). How can this be explained? I would argue that it results from the effect of strong indoctrination through misogynous didactic literature, to which, in his time, ecclesiastics especially were exposed in the course of their education; both Galbert's position and the account itself suggest such a background.[58] The purpose behind this indoctrination was, as Schmidt points out, to warn clerics of the female sex as early as possible: "The young student who has already acquired a large repertoire of misogynous proverbs would, it was hoped, as an adult succumb less easily to the sweet venom."[59]

There was a stock of biblical and classical women characters that exemplified women's vices and that was used in medieval literature.[60] Thus

56. "De incantationibus, auguriis vel divinationibus et de his, qui tempestates vel alia maleficia faciunt, placuit sancto concilio, ut, ubicumque deprehensi fuerint, videat archipresbiter diocesis illius, ut diligentissima examinatione constringantur, si forte confiteantur malorum, quae gesserunt. Sed sub tali moderatione fiat eadem districtio, ne vitam perdant, sed ut salventur in carcere adflicti, usque dum Deo inspirante spondeant emendationem peccatorum" ("Concilia Rispacense, Frisingense, Salisburgense, 800 inde ab Ian 20," ed. Albert Werninghoff, MGH *Legum sectio III, Concilia* 2, 2 vols. [Hannover, 1906–8], 1:209). For details on the date and origin of the extract, see the discussion in Mordek and Glatthaar, "Von Wahrsagerinnen," 41–43, esp. n41.

57. Cohn, *Europe's Inner Demons*, 156–60.

58. Cf. Rider, *God's Scribe*, 21–24.

59. Paul Gerhard Schmidt, "Der Rangstreit zwischen Mann und Frau im lateinischen Mittelalter. Mit einer Edition der Altercatio inter virum et mulierum," in *Dispute Poems and Dialogues in the Ancient and Medieval Near East: Forms and Types of Literary Debates in Semitic and Related Literatures*, ed. Gerrit J. Reinink and Herman L. J. Vanstiphout (Louvain, 1991), 215.

60. For biblical references see: Gn 3:1–6 (Eve); Gn 19:31–36 (Lot's daughters); Gn 38:12–19 (Tamar); Gn 39:7–20 (Potiphar's wife); Jgs 16:4–21 (Delilah); 2 Sm 11 (Bathsheba); 1 Kgs 11 (Solo-

we have the fickle woman (Helen of Troy or Dido, queen of Carthage, stereotyped in the famous quote from the *Aeneid* 4.569–570),[61] the garrulous woman (Solomon's wives, who persuade him to build altars for their heathen gods), the greedy woman (Eve, who eats the forbidden fruit), the deceptive woman (Lot's daughters, who make their father drunk and have sexual intercourse with him while he is asleep, and Tamar, who disguises herself as a whore to have sexual intercourse with her father-in-law), and the adulterous woman (Helen and Potiphar's wife, who tries to seduce Joseph). Helen, Eve, Delilah, Herodias, and Jezebel are favorites, followed closely by Tamar, Potiphar's wife, and Lot's daughters. In the anonymous epigram "De perversa muliere" even Bathsheba is made responsible for seducing David and causing her husband Uriah's death, and the woman who recognizes Peter in the court of the high priest's house is made responsible for causing Peter's denial of Jesus:

> A woman steals Paradise from the first living man,
> Locks Joseph in prison,
> Deceives Juda with her apparel,
> Shaves the hair of a strong man,
> Kills Uriah,
> Seduces David into adultery,
> Deprives Solomon of religion,
> Reveals Peter with a diabolical voice,
> Possesses, takes you for your last penny.[62]

---

mon's wives); 1 Kgs 18:4,13, 1 Kgs 21 (Jezebel). The most comprehensive study of misogyny in medieval literature is still August Wulff, *Die frauenfeindlichen Dichtungen in den romanischen Literaturen des Mittelalters bis zum Ende des XIII. Jahrhunderts,* Romanistische Arbeiten 4 (Halle, 1914). An English translation of an anthology of misogynous texts is provided by Alcuin Blamires, ed., *Woman Defamed and Woman Defended: An Anthology of Medieval Texts* (Oxford, 1992).

61. "Varium et mutabile semper femina" (Virgil, *Enéide* 4.569–570, ed. Henri Goelzer and René Durand, trans. André Bellessort, 2 vols., Collection des universities de France [Paris, 1960–61], 1:120).

62.
> Aufert, includit, fallit, nudat, dat, adurit
> Privat, monstrat, habet, exspoliat mulier
> Primo viventi Paradisum, carcere Joseph,
> Ornatu Judam, crine virum validum,
> Uriae mortem, moechando David, Salomonem
> Religione, Petrum voce diabolica.

("Ven. Hildeberti Carmina miscellanae, tam sacra quam moralia. Sive libellus qui dicitur Ploridus aspectus," ed. J. P. Migne, PL 171, 1428). The "diabolical voice" is that of the woman who recognizes Peter as one of Jesus's disciples and thus, as the medieval author of the poem would argue, causes him to deny Jesus (Mt 26:69–72, Mk 14:66–70, Lk 22:55–57).

The same stereotypical views on the character of a woman are found in Albertus Magnus's philosophical works: "[W]oman is less inclined to moral behavior than man . . . therefore women are inconstant and always seeking new things . . . they are not faithful. . . . For it is generally said both proverbially and by the people that women are more mendacious and fickle, timorous, untruthful, deceptive in their speech, and in short woman is nothing but the devil cast in human shape."[63] The interpretation of women's behavior in Galbert's digressions resembles those given in the anonymous epigram and in the *Quaestiones super De animalibus.* While Albertus Magnus does not explicitly mention "adulterous" in his list of characterizing adjectives (although it is probably implied), adultery and deception are certainly the predominant vices in both the epigram and Galbert's digressions. Both are combined in Dedda/Duva's behavior, which shows noticeable similarities to that of Bathsheba in the epigram's misogynic interpretation of the biblical text.

The witches in Galbert's account differ from his other women in that they do not occur in digressions and are given less space. Galbert's report does not contain any comment that suggests that the killing of the two women in Lille and Ghent is the working of God, but neither does it contain any criticism of the events. The Bible provides justification for the killing of sorcerers and witches in Exodus 22:18 ("You shall not permit a sorcerer to live"), but it does not force people to apply this to their contemporaries or suggest that such evildoers are always female.[64]

While it may be seen as the duty of a chronicler to faithfully report such killings, he has the freedom to criticize the events he reports. In this respect, Galbert differs from other chroniclers who report similar events. According to Cohn, the chronicler who reports the death of a woman who is "hurled to her death from the town walls" in 1074 in Cologne because "she was suspected of having driven men mad by means of *maleficia*" ob-

63. "quod femina minus habilis ad mores quam mas . . . ideo mulieres sint inconstantes et nova semper petentes . . . nulla fides est in muliere. . . . Dicitur enim communiter et proverbialiter et vulgariter, quod mulieres sunt magis mendaces et fragiles, diffidentes, inverecundae, eloquentes deceptorie, et breviter mulier nihil aliud est quam diabolus specie humana effigiatus" (Albertus Magnus, *Quaestiones super De animalibus* 15, ed. Ephrem Filtaut, [Münster, 1955], 265).

64. "Maleficos non patieris vivere." It is worth noting that the evildoers in Exodus were not exclusively women, as *maleficos* is used rather than *maleficas.* The term *malefica* is one of several terms used to denote witches. The term *cantatrix* did not originally imply any evildoing, but referred to someone using spells; as its use by Galbert shows, the distinction has already become blurred in his time, as the implication in [110] is clearly that of an evil spell.

serves that "this was done without any regard for the due process of law." The burning of three women in 1090 who were suspected of being "'poisoners' and 'destroyers of people's crops'" is similarly criticized by the author of the story. As Cohn states, "the monk who tells the story speaks of the injustice of the accusations, the 'devilish fury' of the mob, the 'martyrdom' of the victims." The situation in both cases was one of civil unrest, which must have caused fears and feelings of insecurity. At the time of the killing in Cologne the burghers rebelled against the archbishop, while Freising had no bishop at the time of the killing, as there were then two rival candidates for the bishopric.[65] This strongly resembles the situation at the time of the killing of the alleged witches in Flanders, where William Clito and Thierry of Alsace were struggling for the countship in 1128.

Is it fair to speak of misogyny, or is Galbert no more misogynistic than other medieval writers? In his reports of events he did not witness, Galbert, unlike contemporary authors such as Walter of Thérouanne, prefers the versions that show women in an unfavorable light. He lacks the objectivity that, according to Nip, also characterizes Herman of Tournai.[66] In telling the stories of Dedda/Duva and the wife of Walter of Vladslo, he abuses women to demonstrate God's omnipotence. Misogyny is known in didactic literature from the early Church Fathers, but with Galbert it transcends traditional literary boundaries and enters historiography. It also shifts its focus from generalized exempla to individual women, transferring the negative traits of the stereotypical exempla to historical women. This shift is significant, as it coincides with the first killing of alleged witches. From about this time, persecution of witches accompanied periods of crisis, such as civil wars, epidemics, and famines.[67] This suggests that the misogyny that characterizes the depiction of women in Galbert's chronicle may reflect not only his own attitude to women, but a trend in contemporary society.

65. Cohn, *Europe's Inner Demons,* 154–55.

66. Nip states that "Herman was a critical listener to stories told by both men and women, whose narratives he evaluated not according to their gender, but according to their content" ("Gendered Memories," 122).

67. See Blauert, "Die Erforschung," 14–15. This is not to say that women were the only scapegoats of medieval society; Jews of both sexes were, for example, largely made responsible for the plague.

7

The Tears of Fromold

The Murder of Charles the Good, Homoeroticism, and the Ruin of the Erembalds

BERT DEMYTTENAERE

Although he was a keen and critical observer of his society, Galbert of Bruges's eyes were focused on men and largely indifferent to the affairs of women. This is not really surprising, for Galbert was part of a predominantly male world. If one looks attentively at this world, then the murder of Charles the Good and the ruin of the Erembalds appear in a somewhat uncommon light. A strong suspicion emerges that these disastrous events were closely connected with the intimate love between two men: Charles the Good and Fromold the Younger.

Absent Women

That Galbert's mind, however vivid and many-sided it may have been, was tuned to a male world is clearly illustrated by his description of William Clito's joyous entrance into Saint-Omer in the year 1127, in the middle of April. As the count approached, the boys of the city were the first to move into action. Bearing bows and arrows, they marched out to meet the count. Galbert writes: "Agile and swift they advanced in bands, pretending they were going to resist in a battle, girded, with bows ready and strings bent, as if to attack the count and his men at a convenient moment with their arrows." Then, on behalf of the count and his men, messengers asked the boys what they wanted. They loudly demanded the reconfirmation of

I am very grateful to Jeff Rider and especially to Claire Weeda, who patiently and gently polished my English.

their privilege "to wander freely about the woodland glades on feast days and in summer time, to catch small birds, to shoot arrows at squirrels and foxes, and to occupy themselves with such recreational activities pertaining to the youth." After a mock fight and with feigned reluctance, Count William granted their demand. Meanwhile "the citizens had approached, their weapons in hand," and were watching the scene. From a distance they saw the count "amidst applause and peaceful veneration" coming in their direction, and they began to sing his praises, breaking into the resounding dance tones. When the people and the count had come together, the clergy, bearing incense and candles, advanced solemnly in procession. "Filling the air with jubilant voices and harmonious songs, they received the count while all the citizens were clapping their hands and led him solemnly into the church amid the same sweet melodies." Finally, after a prayer service for the count and for peace and safety in the county, homage was done and loyalty pledged to the count.[1]

This splendid description of the successive *rites de passage* will delight every historian or anthropologist. And yet, where are the women? Were there no girls watching the performance? Were they completely indifferent to the warlike boys? And these boys, were they not slightly proud of and excited by a female interest in their appearance? And besides: what were the boys hunting for in the woodland glades? Just small birds, squirrels, and foxes? And what about the married women? Were they twiddling their thumbs at home? Were they cooking, weaving, or working in the garden?

Women in the Background

In Galbert's narrative individual women scarcely enter the scene. In general they appear as silent extras, nameless, looming up as misty figures, rapidly passing before our eyes. Description of their activities is absent or minimal, and when they are mentioned, it is mostly in connection with the actions of men standing in the limelight. Nevertheless, Galbert was

1. "agiles et velociores turmatim procedentes quasi per pugnam resistere simulantes, succincti et praeparati arcubus intensis et nervis quibus, si expediret, sagittando invaderent comitem et suos. '. . . circa nemorum saltus in festis sanctorum et aestatis tempore licenter vagari, aviculas capere, spiriolos et vulpes sagittare et hujusmodi puerilia recreando satagere. . . .' . . . cives obviam armata manu processerant . . . cum plausu et pacis veneratione . . . . Vocum jubilatione et melodum consonantiis personantes, omnibus civibus applaudentibus, susceperunt et usque infra ecclesiam eadem melodiarum suavitate sollemniter perduxerunt" (Galbert, [66], 5/32). All translations are mine.

not blind to women's central role in forging and confirming social bonds, status, power, and wealth through marriage and childbearing. In fact, this role is an almost omnipresent background motif without which his narrative would lose much of its dramatic sense. This becomes tragically obvious when Galbert tells how Bertulf married off his grandniece to a man who was believed to be the son of Walter, peer of Flanders, but who, according to a fairylike and slanderous tale, was a changeling who was later revealed to be the son of a cobbler. Galbert writes: "[T]he provost [Bertulf] came and married off his niece, the daughter of his brother's son, to that surreptitious son, so that thanks to that marriage they would stand together firmly come what may, and would become bolder, stronger, and more powerful."[2] When, after Walter's death, his wife "confessed" that his own son had died at birth and that his professed son was in fact the son of a cobbler, Galbert, apparently delighted, exclaimed: "And so the move of the provost was foiled by God's countermove. When the provost wanted proudly and gloriously to exalt his family by that marriage, he was outwitted by God's move and he coupled his niece to the son of a cobbler!"[3]

Women were married off as a means to promote the family interests and as potential mothers whose children would serve the preservation or enhancement of the status, power, and fortune the family had acquired. A childless marriage therefore could have far-reaching social consequences and easily become a cause of frustration and blame, something of which Galbert was undoubtedly aware. The political troubles he described were rooted largely in the childlessness of Charles's marriage, which he sought to gloss over at the very beginning of his work. Extolling his hero, Charles, he compared him to the princes of the surrounding kingdoms. Each, he wrote, "strove with an uncommon zeal to win glory and praise by knightly exploits, and sought with equal ardor to rule well," and yet the power and the fame of "the emperor of the Romans Henry [V], who . . . died without an heir," and of "the king of the English [Henry I, who was] living in

2. "venit praepositus et dedit neptem suam, filiam filii fratris sui, illi furtivo filio uxorem ut firmiter ad omnem fortunam simul per illud conjugium consisterent, audaciores, fortiores ac potentiores forent" (Galbert, [89], 18/21).

3. "Sicque arte Dei delusa est ars praepositi qui cum vellet superbe et gloriose per illud conjugium cognationem suam extollere, filio sutoris, Dei arte deceptus, eam copulavit" (Galbert, [89], 25/27). As Ernest Warlop suggested, this tale was probably concocted in the milieu of Cono, Walter's brother. If the presumed son and heir of Walter was not in fact his real son, Walter's inheritance would go to his brother, Cono, as indeed happened (see Warlop, 1:229). Cf. the preceding essay in this volume by Martina Häcker.

his realm without children," were less than those of Count Charles, who also died "without an heir, in the cause of justice."[4] Charles's childlessness, which he had in common with other mighty rulers, did not therefore cast a slur on his otherwise glorious reputation.

Galbert tells us about childless male rulers, but says nothing about their wives, nothing about the disgrace or repudiation that could easily be the fate of childless women, nothing about the "anxiety of the barren" and the "sadness of infertility" that were mentioned in the liturgical prayers of the "Mass for the barrenness of women" (*Missa pro sterilitate mulierum*).[5] Henry I's "childlessness" is perhaps all the more striking given that he was blessed with numerous offspring. Only two of them, however, were legitimate. His only legitimate son was drowned on the night of November 25, 1120, in the notorious "White Ship" disaster. At the beginning of 1127, the magnates and prelates present at Henry's court at Windsor swore to accept his remaining legitimate child, his daughter Mathilda, as heir to England and Normandy after his death, and yet Galbert speaks of the "childless," that is, heirless, Henry.[6] Had Galbert not been informed about the events at Windsor, or was he convinced that a fickle woman could not be suited for kingly power?

Galbert's Presumed Misogyny

Was Galbert a woman-hater? Was he indoctrinated by the misogynous literature to which the clergy in his time was exposed?[7] At first glance, it would appear so. Certainly the story he tells about Dedda or "Duva" (i.e., *Dove*), one of the few women in his narrative with some personal impact on the course of events, seems to offer an eloquent illustration of misogyny.[8]

The story of Dove is part of a slanderous tale, sprung mostly from malicious imaginings and obviously borrowed from the oral gossip columns. Dove was, Galbert recounts, married to a certain Boldran, castellan of Bru-

4. "summum gloriae ac laudis sibi ascribendi studium per militiae facinora enituisset et eisdem affectus consimilis ad bene regendum inesset . . . imperator Romanorum Henricus qui . . . sine herede [!] diem obiit, . . . rex Anglorum sine liberis [!] degebat in regno, . . . sine herede [!] . . . pro justitia" (Galbert, [Prol.], 2/13).

5. See Eduard van Hartingsveldt, "De schande van onvruchtbaarheid," in *Vrouw, familie en macht,* ed. M. Mostert et al. (Hilversum, 1990), 72–74 (orationes 6 and 8).

6. See Marjorie Chibnall, *The Empress Matilda: Queen Consort, Queen Mother and Lady of the English,* 2nd ed. (Oxford, 1992), 51–52.

7. See the preceding essays in this volume of Nancy Partner and Häcker, especially Häcker.

8. See Häcker.

ges. However, she also had a lover, one of Boldran's knights and his most trusted man, the disreputable Erembald. The adulterous Dove, so people told Galbert, promised both her hand and the office of castellan to Erembald "if by chance her husband should die in the near future."[9] That was food for thought, and Erembald began plotting the death of his lord, waiting for the right moment. It came during a military expedition, when Boldran and Erembald were both on board a ship on the Scheldt River. The ship had dropped anchor in the middle of the river to await the coming day, and in the silence of the night Boldran went to the edge of the ship to urinate. Suddenly, Erembald rushed up from behind and pushed his lord far from the ship, into the swirling depths. The poor man drowned while the other fighters slept; only Erembald knew the details of his lord's death. The murder accomplished, he married Dove, became castellan of Bruges, and had many children with her.[10]

Was it not natural for a Christian writer to interpret the machinations of Dove, whose name, moreover, was homophonous with Eve's (*Duva, Eva*), within the context of original sin and the fall of mankind, and to see in Dove a new Eve?

Could the mechanism of vindictive justice by which God punishes the whole human race for the sin of its first parents also be applied, on a more limited scale, to a family? Could children be punished for the sins of their fathers to the third or fourth generation? It was a theological issue in those days. Some maintained it was the case; others denied it; and still others, calling on the authority of Augustine, said: "It is not to be asserted, but feared. For humble ignorance is better than arrogant knowledge."[11]

9. "si forte vir ejus cito moreretur" (Galbert, [71], 13/14).

10. Galbert, [71], 1/25.

11. See "Sententiae Anselmi" in *Anselms von Laon Systematische Sentenzen, Beiträge zur Geschichte der Philosophie des Mittelalters. Texte und Untersuchungen,* ed. Franz Pl. Bliemetzrieder, Band 18, Heft 2–3 (Münster, 1919), 74: "Another question is whether the father's actual sins are not original sins for his children. Some say it is the case, others deny it" (Quaeritur etiam, si actualia peccata patrum filiis sint originalia. Quod quidam asserunt; alii autem contradicunt); 76: "In view of all this, we should consider what Augustine says: It is not to be asserted, but feared. For humble ignorance is better than arrogant knowledge" (Inter hec omnia attendendum est, quod dicit Augustinus: Non est asserendum, sed verendum. Melius est enim humiliter ignorare, quam arroganter sapere). A reader may suspect, and not without reason, that the "Sententiae Anselmi" have not been chosen arbitrarily, since at the time of Galbert some students from Bruges were studying at the cathedral school of Laon (Galbert, [12], 49/51). It is even possible that Galbert himself studied at Laon while the learned and famous Anselm (†1117) taught there. But the reader must be warned: the title "Sententiae Anselmi" comes from the editor himself, Bliemetzrieder, who assigned this collection of sentences erroneously to Anselm. However, we can assume that part of these sentences is related, directly or indirectly,

Galbert used this concept of vindictive justice, albeit with some hesitation, as a means of combining a number of apparently disparate events into a meaningful pattern. It enabled him to link the murder of Count Charles to the treacherous politics of his grandfather, Robert I the Frisian (1071–93), who was responsible for the murder of his nephew, the young Arnold III (†1071): the murder of Arnold was punished through Charles's murder. It likewise enabled Galbert to link Erembald's "precipitation" of his urinating lord to the "precipitation" of Erembald's successors from the comital house.[12] Combining facts, gossip, and biblical pericopes, Galbert interprets the course of events within a theological framework in which notions such as original sin, hereditary guilt, and the vindictive justice of God occupy an important place.

Strikingly, however, Galbert is totally silent about any role women may have had in the transmission of hereditary guilt. Dove is not portrayed as the person responsible for the fall of the Erembalds or as a new Eve. The gossip about Dove offered a splendid opportunity for a hardcore misogynist to inveigh against the pernicious nature of the tempting Eve, but Galbert, who knew very well how to rail against somebody, did not seize this opportunity. He speaks of her only as an adulterous woman, just as he calls Erembald an adulterous man. Nowhere does he burst into a tirade against women, and, in striking contrast with some authors of his time, he is completely silent about the woman who, as the main culprit for the fall of mankind, should deserve the severest punishment.[13] In general, Galbert hardly mentions women, neither praising nor blaming them. He was not revealing a marked misogyny; he simply had a blind spot when it came to women.

---

to Anselm's teachings. (See J. De Gellinck, *Le mouvement théologique du XIIe siècle* [Bruges, 1948], 140–42.) We therefore may conclude that Galbert knew of the problem concerning the "original character of actual sins" and that his knowledge on this point probably in some way or another came from the teachings of Anselm of Laon.

12. Galbert, [71], 28/36.

13. See "Sententiae divine pagine" in *Anselms . . . Sentenzen,* 27: "A further question is which of them sins more, the man or the woman. Indeed the woman sins more. . . . And since she sins more, she should be more humble and weaker in church, with her head covered, and she should even be silent in church, as the Apostle says. Her punishment for the sin is greater than the man's since she suffers the pain of menstruation" (Queritur iterum, quis eorum magis peccaverit, vir scilicet an mulier. Mulier quidem magis peccavit. . . . Et quia magis peccavit, debet esse humilior et infirmior in ecclesia capite velato, debet etiam tacere in ecclesia, ut dicit apostolus. Penam etiam majorem habet peccati, quam vir, quia in dolore patitur menstrua). As was the case with the "Sententiae Anselmi" (see note 11), Bliemetzrieder was too ready to attribute the "Sententiae divine pagine" to Anselm, but we may assume that Galbert was acquainted with such misogynic ideas, whether they were inspired by Anselm of Laon or not.

Galbert's Interest in Men and His Male Universe

Nowhere does Galbert show any affection for a woman or any susceptibility to female beauty. His heart and mind were captivated by men instead. I will go further into this matter elsewhere, but here the striking example of Galbert's love for Robert the Boy may suffice. This Robert was the son of the late Robert, brother of Bertulf. He was, as Galbert says, still an *ephebus,* a man between eighteen and twenty years of age, in 1127.[14] He was also one of the leaders of the treacherous conspiracy and resisted until the very end with the besieged in Bruges. Galbert extols the young Robert repeatedly and unashamedly, describing the exceptional popularity that he enjoyed among the people of Bruges, and throughout the land!

Robert the Boy may indeed have been the idol of the people of Bruges. He certainly was the idol of Galbert, who tells us a nicely written and well-composed, but glaringly doubtful, tale in Robert's defense. Written as if he had witnessed everything himself, Galbert's report clearly serves one purpose: to disguise Robert's guilt. According to Galbert, Robert was dragged into the conspiracy without knowing that its objective was to murder Charles the Good. The conspirators "urged him to give them his right hand as a sign that he would do together with them the same thing they, too, were going to do, for which they, too, had mutually joined their right hands." Giving the right hand was an efficacious sign, simultaneously meaning and creating solidarity and mutual duties. That's why Robert the Boy, unaware of any malice, and hence in all innocence, involved himself in the plot: "the young man . . . gave his right hand, not knowing indeed what he was supposed to do with them."[15]

Galbert was preoccupied with men, but this is quite understandable since he lived in a social world in which men did the talking and played the prominent roles. Working in the comital administration at Bruges, the count's principal residence, Galbert was surrounded daily by men, old and young, who lived and worked together and nursed mutual sympathies and antipathies. We can obtain some idea of the male universe in which Galbert was involved by examining three principal characters in his narrative: Count Charles, Bertulf, and Fromold the Younger.

14. Galbert, [74], 25.

15. "convenientes illum ut ipsis daret dextram id idem simul cum ipsis peracturus quod et ipsi peractum irent, pro quo et dextras in invicem contradidissent . . . juvenis . . . dedit . . . dextram, ignorans quidem quid cum illis acturus foret" (Galbert, [11], 14/25).

Charles, the Hero

The hero of Galbert's male universe was Count Charles, son of King Cnut IV of Denmark (1080–1086) and Adela, daughter of Count Robert I the Frisian. Cnut married Adela around 1080 and was assassinated on July 10, 1086. The couple had three children: Ingherta, Cecilia, and Charles. We do not know in which order they were born. After her husband's assassination, Adela, leaving her two daughters in Denmark, returned to her parents in Flanders with "her little boy,"[16] who was, we may guess, about three years old. And so Charles grew up in Flanders "from boyhood to manly strength of body and mind."[17]

After five years Charles was separated from his mother when she was sent to Apulia to marry Duke Roger (†1111), son of Robert Guiscard, at the beginning of 1092. Charles may have received his intellectual education in the chapter of the canons at Bruges, for when an attempt was made to transfer the count's body to the abbey of Saint Peter of Ghent, the furious canons, refusing to be robbed of such a precious relic, exclaimed: "there is no reason at all why he should be taken away *from us, among whom* for the most part he grew up and lived."[18] Since Ghent was part of Flanders, the "us" cannot refer to the people of the county. It is likely that this "us" is to be understood as "we canons of the castral church of Bruges." Charles was trained in military skills with other boys and was inducted into the knightly order, probably at the age of sixteen. He "fought with distinction against his enemies and gained a fine reputation and glorious name among the rulers of the earth."[19] In the early years of the twelfth century, maybe in 1107–8, he went to Jerusalem as a pilgrim-warrior, returning to Flanders a few months before the death of his uncle, Count Robert II (†1111).[20] In 1119, he ascended the Flemish throne.

Charles was married to Marguerite of Clermont through the agency of his cousin and predecessor Baldwin VII (1111–19).[21] She was the only child

16. "filio suo paruulo" (Walter, [3 (2)], 7/8). In my references to the "Vita Karoli comitis Flandrię," I will first give a reference to the chapter of Rider's edition, followed by a reference in parentheses to the MGH edition.

17. "a puero . . . altus est usque in virile robur corporis et animi" (Galbert, [1], 3/4).

18. "Nulla ergo ratio est quare debeat *a nobis* auferri, *inter quos* maxime et nutritus et conversatus est" (Galbert, [22], 37/38, my emphasis).

19. "egregium facinus in hostes arripuit, famam bonam et gloriam sui nominis penes regnorum potentes obtinuit" (Galbert, [1], 5/6).

20. Galbert, [12], 29/35. See Ross, trans., 113n8.

21. Walter, [8], 10/12.

of Count Rainaud II of Clermont and Adela of Vermandois, the widow of Hugh of Vermandois, also called Hugh the Great, the brother of King Philip I (1060–1108).[22] When did Charles marry Marguerite? It is not clear. Walter of Thérouanne says that count Baldwin "had appointed Charles as his heir and had entrusted him with the highest position in the government and administration of everything. Earlier he had also joined him in marriage to the noble girl Marguerite, the daughter of Rainaud, count of Clermont, and had given him the county of Amiens with the castle of Encre."[23] In 1115, the castle of Encre ("Albert" since 1620), some thirty kilometers northeast of Amiens, was seized by Baldwin from his vassal Hugh II, count of Saint Pol, but Baldwin's possession of the castle was not ensured until a peace treaty was arranged between Baldwin and Hugh in 1117.[24] What about the county of Amiens? According to some historians the county of Amiens was brought to Charles by Marguerite as dower from her mother, Adela of Vermandois.[25] This is not what Walter says, and Amiens was in the hands of the house of Coucy, and not the house of Vermandois, in 1115; Amiens was not taken from Thomas of Marles, lord of Coucy, by King Louis VI (1108–37) until the beginning of 1117.[26] Perhaps King Louis gave Amiens to Baldwin VII in that year; so Baldwin could indeed have given "the county of Amiens with the castle of Encre" to Charles in 1117 or 1118. Presumably, then, Charles's marriage took place after the year 1117, and it is possible that Amiens and Encre were given by Charles to Marguerite as her widow's dower.[27]

How old was "the noble girl Marguerite" when she married Charles? Hugh of Vermandois, her mother's first husband, died in Tarsus on October 18, 1101, from a wound he received during the minor crusade (1101–2)

22. *De genere comitum Flandrensium notae Parisienses,* ed. Georges Waitz, MGH SS 13 (Hannover, 1881), 257; *Genealogiae scriptoris Fusniacensis* 15, ed. Georges Waitz, MGH SS 13, 255; Herman of Laon, *De miraculis S. Mariae Laudunensis libri tres* 1.2, PL 156, col. 966.

23. "Karolum . . . heredem sibi ipse instituerat eique rerum omnium summam regendam ac disponendam tradiderat. Cui etiam prius nobilem puellam Margaretam, Rainaldi comitis Clarmontensis filiam, matrimonio copulauerat, et comitatum Ambianesem cum castello Incrensi donauerat" (Walter, [8], 7/13).

24. *Sigeberti continuatio Valcellensis* ad annos 1115 and 1117, ed. L. C. Bethmann, MGH SS 6 (Hannover, 1844), 459.

25. Léon Vanderkindere, *La formation territoriale des principautés belges au Moyen Age,* 2 vols. (Brussels, 1902), 1:152–53.

26. Suger, 11, p. 178; see Achille Luchaire, *Louis VI le Gros. Annales de sa vie et de son règne (1081–1137)* (Paris, 1890), n° 190, p. 96; n° 220, p. 108.

27. The relation of the Flemish count with Amiens and Encre, Marguerite's marriage with Charles, and her marriages after his death require a more profound study. A sensible exposé, although with vague references to the sources, may be found in A. Duclos, *De geschiedenis van den zaligen Karel den Goede, graaf van Vlaanderen, Martelaar* (Bruges, 1884), 42–49.

after the capture of Jerusalem in 1099.[28] His widow's marriage to Rainaud, count of Clermont, could not, therefore, have taken place much earlier than the year 1102. If Marguerite married Charles in 1118, she could not have been older than sixteen. She could of course have been several years younger; one might reasonably guess, taking into account the traditional marriage policy, that she was about twelve. Her marriage to Charles remained childless, but she was not, if we may believe our sources, infertile. After Charles's death, she married Hugh III Camp d'Avène, count of Saint Pol, the son of the above-mentioned Hugh II, by whom she had two sons. After the death of Hugh III, she married Baldwin, lord of Encre, by whom she had at least one daughter.[29]

What kind of relationship did Charles and Marguerite have? Based on the evidence of the charters, Marguerite does not seem to have been very much involved in her husband's public life. Two charters of the year 1121, one issued at Veurne on March 18 and the other at Bergues on September 15, suggest that she was present at the juridical procedure as she is named in the notification.[30] The two other charters in which she is mentioned seem to imply that she was absent. In 1123 she is mentioned namelessly and indirectly in a charter, issued at Veurne, to which Salomon, the "chaplain of the countess," is one of the witnesses.[31] This Salomon appears again as "chaplain of the countess" in the list of witnesses to a charter of 1124 in which Charles makes donations to the church of Saint Martin at Ypres for "the salvation of my soul and those of my wife Marguerite and of Baldwin my cousin, and of my parents."[32]

In view of the childlessness of the marriage some suspicion may arise concerning the sexual relations between Marguerite and Charles.[33] This

28. Guibert of Nogent, *Dei Gesta per Francos* 7.23, ed. R. B. C. Huygens, CC CM 127A (Turnhout, 1996), 313; *Fulcheri Carnotensis Historia Hierosolymitana,* Liber II, XVI, 7, ed. Heinrich Hagenmeyer (Heidelberg, 1913), 433n6.

29. *Genealogiae scriptoris Fusniacensis* 15, p. 255; *De genere comitum Flandrensium,* 257. Concerning the years of birth and death of Hugh II (1070–c. 1118) and Hugh III (1118?–1141?), see Pierre Feuchère, "Regestes des comtes de Saint Pol (1023–1205). 1e partie (1023–1145)," *Revue du Nord* 29 (1957): 44–45.

30. *Actes,* n° 100, p. 230: "Notum sit . . . quod ego et uxor mea, Margaretha"; n° 103, p. 234: "Notum sit . . . quod ego . . . annuente uxore mea Margaretha."

31. *Actes,* n° 114, p. 262.

32. "ob salutem anime mee et uxoris mee Margarete ac Baldewini nepotis mei, parentumque meorum" (*Actes,* n° 116, p. 267). This Salomon appears again as the "chaplain of the countess" in a very dubious charter of 1123 (*Actes,* n° 115, p. 265).

33. See J. M. De Smet, "Charles le Bon," in *Dictionnaire d'histoire et de géographie ecclésiastiques* 12 (Paris, 1953), 485.

barrenness may have been due to some organic deficiency on Charles's part or to some biological incompatibility. It could also have been the result of a spiritual wish to live chastely in a "Saint Joseph's marriage," or of homosexual inclinations (which do not, of course, exclude such a wish). Did Marguerite live with Charles? Did she reside permanently in the county? Where was she and what was she doing on the day of her husband's murder? What did she do the following days? Galbert, who tells us about the presence of the abbess of Origny on the day of the murder and about the visit to Bruges by Petronilla, countess of Holland, two weeks later, does not say a word about the presence of Marguerite. No source reveals her reaction, not even the smallest sigh or sob, to her husband's murder.

The night before the murder, Charles slept in the comital house in Bruges, apparently without Marguerite, but in all probability in the presence of his chaplains, for they were later able to tell Galbert about Charles's troubled sleep. They knew that during the night he had restlessly turned from one side to the other, had from time to time sat up in bed, and had felt quite exhausted at dawn. He went to the castral church that morning in the devout company of his chaplains, and, "he prayed, in his customary way, reading as if he were saying the office and out loud."[34] He, of course, lived not only as a devout man in the world of the clergymen, but also as a distinguished ruler and a valiant warrior in the world of barons and knights. In both worlds he was, according to his devotees, exemplary.

Galbert attempted to present Charles as an eminent figure in whom the religious and earthly virtues were united.[35] Nevertheless, he does not succeed in harmonizing perfectly both sides of Charles's character. He was, Galbert wrote, "generous towards the poor, courteous and honorable among his most distinguished men, cruel and wary towards his enemies."[36] These last qualifications evoke a chivalrous ideal rather than a pursuit of sainthood.[37] Charles's "pilgrimage" to the Holy Land, and the then modern

34. Galbert, [12], 1/14; "more suo officiose et aperte legendo orabat" (Galbert, [15], 14/15). *Officiose* means "as if he were saying the office," although Charles was following his own program of devotion—reading in his prayer-book the seven penitential psalms—while the clergy was simultaneously reciting Prime and Terce (see Walter, [26 (25)], 25-33).

35. Galbert, [Prol.], 47/51.

36. "erga pauperes largus, inter proceres suos jocundus ac honestus, adversus hostes crudelis et cautus" (Galbert, [Prol.], 11/12).

37. See, e.g., *The Medieval French Roman d'Alexandre,* 7 vols., Elliott Monographs in the Romance Languages and Literatures 36–42 (Princeton and Paris, 1937–76), vol. 2: *Version of Alexandre de Paris, Text* 1.1.1–8, ed. E. C. Armstrong et al., 1: "Whoever wants to hear and listen to verses of rich history, / to have a good example of how to cultivate prowess, / to know why

way to salvation by shedding the blood of gentiles, could not conceal that Charles was indeed a man of weapons, someone with blood-stained hands. He was perhaps involved in some "holy" battles against gentiles during his pilgrimage, but he was certainly involved in earthly battles against his fellow Christians in Europe. In this context Galbert writes: "Whatever he did wrong by this guilty rashness, he redeemed with the Lord by repeated almsgiving."[38] Separated from his mother and his two sisters since his early boyhood, and probably seldom accompanied by his young wife, the childless Charles—about forty in 1127—was surrounded mainly by men, men of prayers and men of arms, friends and enemies.

Charles's Enemies and Friends

Charles, of course, had enemies, and we can imagine that he harbored some feelings of hostility toward them. According to Walter of Thérouanne, he was "as lenient with the humble as he was severe toward the arrogant,"[39] which sounds a bit more friendly than "cruel towards his enemies." One of the "arrogant" was the young and brazen Borsiard, "a very haughty and, in his own eyes, great man."[40] Involved in a private war with

to love and to hate, / to keep and cherish one's friends, / to oppress one's enemies so that they may never increase, / to avenge insults and reward good deeds, / to make haste when one can and endure to the end, / listen then at your leisure to the first part of this tale" (Qui vers de riche istoire veut entendre et oïr, / Pour prendre bon example de prouece acueillir, / De connoistre reison d'amer et de haïr, / De ses amis garder et chierement tenir, / Des anemis grever, c'on n'en puisse eslargir, / Des ledures vengier et des biens fes merir, / De haster quant leus est et a terme soffrir / Oëz dont le premier bonnement a loisir).

38. "Quidquid ergo levitatis hujus culpa deliquit, eleemosynarum multiplici redemptione apud Dominum emendavit" (Galbert, [4], 45/47). Galbert tells us just before this that Charles "fought *tornationes*" (tornationes exercuit [4], 44) with his knights, which perhaps suggests that his "guilty rashness" involved an infringement of a ban on tournaments. This is open to question, since Galbert uses the word *tornatio* elsewhere in the sense of a real knightly fight (Galbert, [79], 1/5; [116], 26/27), and the first known condemnation of tournaments dates from 1130. This condemnation was, in any case, part of a new ideology of war. Traditional warfare was, according to many ecclesiastical authorities, something sinful or at least something polluting: soldiers stain their hands with blood. But the armed pilgrimage, the war in the name of God against the infidels outside Christendom, offered a modern, good, and purifying kind of warfare, leading to salvation (see e.g. Guibert of Nogent, *Dei Gesta per Francos* 1, 65/70, p. 87, and Galbert, [5], 1/10). The promulgation of this new warfare was accompanied by a stronger emphasis on peace within Christendom and on the avoidance of spilling Christian blood, and it was in this context that the first condemnations of tournaments soon appeared. On November 18, 1130, a council at Clermont, under the presidency of Pope Innocent II, prohibited tournaments "because they are often manslaughters" (Charles Joseph Hefele, *Histoire des conciles d'après les documents originaux,* trans. H. Lecelercq, 11 vols. [Paris, 1907–52], c. 9, 5.1: 688).

39. "sicut humilibus mansuetus, sic superbis apparebat seuerus" (Walter, [13 (12)], 4/5).

40. "homo nimis elatus et in oculis suis magnus" (Walter, [17 (16)], 9/10).

Thancmar of Straten, Borsiard became the victim of a punitive expedition by Charles, who burned down a stronghold of his that was situated near the domains of the family of Straten. According to Walter of Thérouanne, the intercessors, pleading for reconciliation between Charles and Borsiard, said to the count:

> It should suffice for you, magnanimous lord, to have satisfied your fury up to now by punishing and humiliating Borsiard. It should suffice for you to have burned down his shelter thus injuring him and his whole family. . . . Moreover, restrain the impulses of your hate and anger against his family, and at least now placate those whom you have deeply offended, be it with a late satisfaction.[41]

Walter of Thérouanne is obviously showing off his own rhetorical skill here, putting the invective in the mouth of the intercessors, but certainly not everybody was convinced of Charles's equanimity, impartiality, and holy innocence. At least some members of the Erembald clan believed that Charles bore ill will toward them. According to Galbert, Bertulf, the mighty godfather of the Erembalds, often disparaged the count in the following way:

> If I had so wished, that Charles of Denmark would never have ascended to the dignity of the countship. But now that he has become count thanks to me, he does not remember the good things I did for him. On the contrary, he endeavors to force me and my whole family entirely into servitude, persistently asking the older men whether we are his serfs. But he may ask as much as he likes, we will always be and are free, and no man on earth can make us into serfs!

"Vain grandiloquence," Galbert exclaimed, "for the count, on his guard, had noticed that the provost and his family were slandering him and had learned of both their deceit and treachery"![42]

Charles had many "friends," among whom one could undoubtedly have found many flatterers busily buzzing around the man of power like

41. "Sufficiat, . . . domine, magnanimitati uestrę Burchardi pena et ignominia iram uestram uos actenus exsaturasse; sufficiat uobis receptaculum eius ad ipsius et totius generis sui iniuriam uos incendisse. . . . Sed et circa genus ipsius odii uestri et irę impetus refrenate, et quos grauiter offendistis uel nunc sera satisfactione placate" (Walter, [23 (22)], 8/19).

42. "'Iste Karolus de Datia numquam ad comitatum conscendisset, si ego voluissem. Nunc ergo, cum per me sit comes effectus, non recordatur quod bene sibi fecerim, immo laborat prorsus me cum toto genere meo retorquere in servum, perquirens a senioribus utrum simus ejus servi. Sed querat quantum velit, nos semper erimus et sumus liberi, et non est homo super terram qui possit nos constituere servos.' Frustra tamen jactanter loquebatur, nam consul praecautus detractionem praepositi et suorum intellexerat, et fraudem simul et traditionem audierat" (Galbert, [8], 7/16).

bees around honey. On the day of the murder in Saint Donatian, "those who in former days, that means during the count's life, had shared his friendship" tried to flee from the castle or to hide themselves within the church. The murderous traitors looked for them, particularly for those whom they had marked for death.[43] Some of Charles's reputed devotees were indeed killed, some escaped, others were captured.

Charles had a few favorites among his friends. John, who escaped from the hands of the murderers, was one of them. He was a comital servant who guarded the count's treasury and who, unlike the holder of an honorary office like a "chamberlain," was involved daily in the comital household. Apparently he was often in contact with Charles. Of all his domestic staff the count loved him the most.[44] Charles's most intimate friend, Fromold the Younger, was one of the officials involved in the comital administration. On the day of the murder, Fromold, together with others, fled to the church. He hid himself under bundles of palm branches in a "choir" that served as a depository for the liturgical equipment. He was soon discovered, but fortunately he was not killed on the spot. Some of the traitors wanted to spare his life for the time being because they thought he could give them access to the count's treasure. He was placed in the provost's custody with the other captives, and on the evening of that same day, the traitors extorted the keys of the count's treasure from him. After a few days, on March 5, they finally let him go on the condition that he would either be reconciled with them within eight days or go into perpetual exile, renouncing his fatherland. Fromold went to his beautiful and comfortable house in Bruges, which by the way was a little gift from his friend Charles, for a last supper. For him the decision was easily made: he would sooner renounce his fatherland than reconcile with the traitors who had betrayed his lord, one who had loved him above all others, and whom he had loved almost more than himself.[45]

Bertulf, the Grand Old Man

Bertulf was a son of Dove and Erembald, whose children had acquired important positions in the county, and had become provost of the chapter

43. "Qui vero in comitis amicitia prius, scilicet dum viveret, constiterant" (Galbert, [16], 42/43); Galbert, [18], 1/3; Walter, [29 (28)], 6/11.

44. Galbert, [16], 49/53.

45. Galbert, [18], 6/41; [19], 1/30; [20], 31/36; [24], 1/28.

of secular canons attached to Saint Donatian. In 1127 he had, according to Galbert, been provost for thirty-six years. If Galbert is right, Bertulf's provostship started in 1091. Somewhere around that date a deacon was put in charge of the spiritual guidance of the canons at Saint Donatian, while the chapter's material welfare remained in the provost's care. This division of responsibilities is understandable, since at that time the provost of Saint Donation also became, by virtue of his office, the head of the comital chaplains and officers, and ultimately responsible for the comital revenues.[46] Walter of Thérouanne calls Bertulf the "arch-chaplain and chancellor of the whole court of Flanders."[47]

As head of his family, Bertulf took care of the important family affairs. He saw to it that his nephews were girded with the sword of knighthood,[48] and he pursued the promotion of his family, marrying his nieces to men of power and prestige. He acquired an enormous fortune, using or misusing his central position and receiving large grants from the counts, including Count Charles.[49] Apparently, the counts were highly pleased with Bertulf's contribution to the establishment of an effective central administration. When Charles became count of Flanders, Bertulf had already served, as provost and chancellor, three previous counts: Robert I the Frisian (†1093), Robert II of Jerusalem (†1111) and Baldwin VII (†1119). He was the grand old man of his family, the chapter, Bruges, the comital court, and Flanders. As mentioned above, according to Galbert, Bertulf repeatedly said that "that Charles of Denmark" had ascended the comital throne thanks to his efforts; this "grandiloquence" must have contained some truth. It is very likely that this "éminence grise" played a part in Charles's election as an influential string puller.

Bertulf was of course a clergyman, and he was probably a priest.[50] He was married, but no one criticized him for that. In his time, a married priest was still generally accepted; a clergyman in minor orders could lawfully marry, although in principle he could rise to the "holy orders" only if he abstained from sexual intercourse and did not live with his wife.

46. See Georges Declercq, "De dekens van het Sint-Donaaskapittel in Brugge voor 1200," *Handelingen van het Genootschap voor Geschiedenis Gesticht onder de Benaming "Société d'émulation" te Brugge* 125 (1988): 41–45.

47. "archicapellanus et cancellarius totius Flandrensis curię" (Walter, [15], 3/4).

48. Galbert, [13], 22.

49. Walter, [15], 5/7.

50. See Georges Declercq, "Bertulf, kanselier van Vlaanderen," *Nationaal Biografisch Woordenboek* 13 (Brussels, 1990), col. 73.

Bertulf's wife lived in Veurne, separately, it seems, from her husband.[51] On this point, then, there was no reason to be shocked. However, Galbert makes different allegations against him in his description of Bertulf's agony in the marketplace at Ypres. If the crowd there, eager for a lynching, had let Bertulf live any longer, then, Galbert writes, he could have called to mind everything he had done. "He could indeed have remembered, if need be, how, after he had been pushed violently forward and put unjustly in the place of the provost Ledbert, who was still alive (the honest man who bore everything for the sake of God)," he had trafficked in prebends and "used the revenues of the church to arm his nephews for all kinds of evil deeds."[52] As trafficking in prebends, although commonly denounced, was commonly practiced, we may believe Galbert on this point. Moreover, other documents show that Bertulf, like many other provosts, did not always make a clear-cut distinction between his own property and that of the chapter.[53] And what about Bertulf's "intrusion"? If Ledbert had indeed been removed unjustly to make way for him, it had been on the count's insistence. How could anyone have obtained such a central position in Flanders at any time without the full approval of the count?[54]

Before the treacherous murder Bertulf and his kin enjoyed great popularity among the townspeople of Bruges. "Before the treachery," according to Galbert, the citizens said that "the provost and his kin were religious men, who were on friendly terms with them and who treated everyone who lived in our town and in the realm honorably."[55] The citizens were proud of the Erembalds, their lords and friends, and could not easily accept their guilt! The main responsibility for the murder and its gruesome consequences, so they felt, lay with the Erembalds' enemies, Thancmar of Straten and his family, "who by deceit, strife, and payment had prejudiced the count against their lords, the provost, his brothers and his nephews, the most powerful and most noble men in the county!"[56] In any case, the

51. Galbert, [46], 4/6.

52. "Poterat quidem reminisci, si debuit, quomodo violenter intrusus et viventi praeposito Ledberto, viro honesto et propter Deum omnia patienti, superpositus injuste . . . nepotes suos stipendiis ecclesiae in omne facinus armasset" (Galbert, [57], 32/37).

53. Warlop, 1:191; Declercq, "Bertulf," cols. 75–76.

54. See Warlop, 1:192.

55. "praepositus et sui ante tempus traditionis viri essent religiosi, amicabiliter se habentes erga eos et cum honore omnes tractassent in loco nostro et in regno commanentes" (Galbert, [45], 4/7).

56. "qui dominos suos, praepositum et fratres simulque ejus nepotes, potentiores et nobiliores in comitatu, fraude, seditione, coemptione facta, apud comitem deposuissent" (Galbert, [45], 38/41).

reputation of the Erembalds was now seriously injured, and the number of their allies and friends decreased as things looked increasingly bad for them.

Human beings, who long for discernable contours and a clear image of themselves and their environment, are averse to chaos, confusion, and uncertainty. People often tend, therefore, to reduce a disturbing variety of facts and values to a dualistic, more or less Manichaean, division between two opposed and irreducible domains: that of the absolute good and that of the absolute evil. The predominant interpretation of the facts undoubtedly took such a dualistic turn after the murder of Charles—the deeds of the good Charles versus the deeds of the wicked Erembalds—but we should not accept the dualistic perspective of Charles's devotees without question. As they boosted their hero as the champion of justice and the eminent protector of the poor, they tended to abase his antagonists as diabolic authors of injustice and vile exploiters of the needy, and to sow in this manner the seeds of a long-lasting demonization of the Erembald clan.

It is not easy to determine what Galbert's attitude was toward the Erembalds and Bertulf before the murder. Did he indeed see them as "religious men" who treated everyone in the town and land honorably? After the murder, Galbert tried unmistakably to arrange the facts within a dualistic frame. He extols Charles "imbued with the spirit of piety, wisdom and strength," in glaring contrast with the vile traitors, "imbued with the diabolic spirit," "murderers, drunkards, whoremongers and the serfs of all vices in our land."[57] Obviously, however, and fortunately, he did not succeed in creating a perfectly black-and-white story, as is well illustrated by his strong and lasting sympathy for Robert the Boy.

Galbert did not, however, find it hard to say bad things about his boss, Bertulf. He had probably never liked him. He almost always portrays him in a bad light, even if other, favorable interpretations are possible. When someone came to see the provost, Galbert says, Bertulf ignored him with an air of superiority, even if he knew his visitor perfectly well, and disdainfully asked those sitting near him who it was. He deigned to greet the visitor only after he had been told who it was, at least if it pleased him to do so.[58] It is of course perfectly possible that the old man was nearsighted and,

57. "plenum spiritu pietatis et consilii et fortitudinis"; "pleni demonio" (Galbert, [5], 13/14); "homicidae et potatores et scortatores et omnium vitiorum servi nostrae terrae" (Galbert, [Prol.], 46/47).

58. Galbert, [13], 7/10.

lacking spectacles (which had not yet been invented to help failing eyes), could not immediately recognize his visitor.[59] When Fromold the Elder asked Bertulf to go to his nephews and plead with them for the release of Fromold the Younger, Galbert writes, the provost "went, not quickly, but at an extremely slow pace, like a man who did not care very much about Fromold, whom he held in great suspicion."[60] As if the slow pace might not be due to Bertulf's old legs![61]

Galbert heard that Bertulf had gone barefoot on his flight from Veurne to Warneton, "suffering that punishment voluntarily for his sins in the hope that God would forgive such a great sinner." "This was plausible," Galbert comments, judging from the state of Bertulf's feet after he was captured, but he does not seem very impressed by Bertulf's repentance. He is preoccupied rather by the abasement and loneliness of the once-powerful lord. With malicious pleasure, perhaps mixed with a modicum of compassion, he exclaims: "How terribly that man suffered, he who formerly commanded everyone, prevailed in wealth and earthly honors and, while he was living in the lap of luxury, would have feared the prick of a flea as much as a pike! Behold! He wandered alone, a lonely exile within the boundaries of his own region!"[62] Galbert apparently took a morbid delight in depicting the defamation, humiliation, and gruesome torture of the dying Bertulf, "once glorious and now ignominious, once revered and now disgraced," and only reluctantly mentions that in his last hour, Bertulf, "unless I am mistaken, was invoking . . . God."[63] Later on, Galbert explicitly details the repentance of several traitors, but concerning Bertulf he says: "We have heard about his punishment and nothing about his repentance."[64] This is not entirely in accordance with what he had written earlier, and Walter of Thérouanne had certainly heard about it.[65]

59. Cf. Ross, trans., 115n2.

60. "Et ibat quidem non celeri gressu, sed nimis tardo, utpote ille qui parum de illo curaret, quem valde suspectum habebat" (Galbert, [19], 12/14).

61. Cf. Ross, trans., 130n4.

62. "penam peccatorum suorum sponte perpessus ibat ut tanto peccatori Deus indulgeret . . . . Satisque probabile fuit. . . . Et vere gravissime vir ille dolebat, qui pridem omnibus imperitabat, divitiis et honore seculi pollebat, et cum in voluptate floreret, punctum pulicis ut jaculum formidaret. Ecce! solus et infra terminos suos exul solus pererrabat" (Galbert, [46], 9/17).

63. "olim gloriosus nunc ignominiosus, olim venerabilis nunc turpis . . . nisi fallor, Deum . . . invocabat" (Galbert, [57], 55/58).

64. "De ipsius vero pena et non de penitentia quidquam audivimus" (Galbert, [84], 57/58).

65. "[There the provost] asked that a priest be sent to him and, repenting of his sins, he confessed in the presence of everyone to God and the priest, and, lying prostrate on the floor and striking his chest with his fists, the suppliant asked the Lord for forgiveness" (Vbi [preposi-

Fromold the Younger, Charles's Bosom Friend

Fromold the Younger was the nephew of Fromold the Elder, a venerable man, priest and canon of Saint Donatian and provost of the secular canons attached to the church of Saint Walburgis at Veurne. Fromold the Younger was allied by marriage to the Erembald clan. His wife, a granddaughter of Erembald and Dove, was the sister of Didier and of Isaac, whom Galbert calls "the head of the conspiracy."[66] Fromold had a daughter and sons. On the day of the murder, he gave a golden ring to a priest to pass on to his daughter. Why not to his wife? Was she still alive? Fromold lived in Bruges, where he had a house whose fences and timber were used for the enclosure of the town on March 6, 1127. Outside Bruges, at Beernem, Fromold had another house, which the men of Straten burned down on April 23, 1128.[67] Fromold's father-in-law, whose name we do not know, may have lived in Bruges as well.[68] There is no indication that his children and his wife, if she was still alive, were living with him at Bruges.

On March 5, 1127, after having supper with his friends and servants in his house at Bruges, "he bid farewell to everyone individually, [and] distributed grain, cheese and meat to his servants to support them for the time being" until his fortunes improved.[69] With his two houses and his substantial household, Fromold was clearly a man of comfortable means. Furthermore, he was a considerate man, bidding farewell individually to each of his friends—perhaps Galbert himself was among them—and his servants of whom he took care. He was highly esteemed by his friends: when he and his father-in-law left Bruges, "his friends followed him as far as they could, commending him to God with lamentation and tears."[70]

Fromold was a comital notary. He also guarded the keys to the count's

tus] et presbiterum ad se uocari postulauit, et, peccatorum suorum penitentiam agens, confessionem Deo et illi in conspectu omnium fecit, et, solo prostratus et pectus pugnis percutiens, indulgentiam sibi a Domino tribui supplex postulauit; Walter, [39 (38)], 11/16).

66. "caput traditionis" (Galbert, [28], 16).

67. Galbert, [18], 30/41; [25], 61/66; [107], 13/16.

68. "And accompanied by his father-in-law, he left the castle and the town in which he had lived up until then" (Et abscessit cum socero suo extra castrum et extra suburbium in quo hactenus habitaverat; Galbert, [24], 24/26). If we read *habitaverant* (with manuscripts *A* and *P*) instead of *habitaverat,* his father-in-law also lived in Bruges.

69. "licentia a singulis accepta, frumentum, caseos et carnes servientibus distribuit ad se sustentandos per tempus" (Galbert, [24], 20/22). *Licentia* here does not mean "permission" or "agreement," but "farewell" (cf. the old Dutch *oorlof,* which means "permission," but also "permission to leave," "farewell").

70. "quem quidem amici ejus et planctu et lachrimis Deo commendatum quantum liceret prosequebantur" (Galbert, [24], 25/28).

treasure, as well as the keys to the shrines and the chests in the comital house,[71] and he probably supervised the provisioning of the comital cellars, as he did for Charles's successor.[72] He was a clergyman (since he was a notary), but we do not know if he was a canon. As a notary, he must have been literate. Perhaps he received part of his education at Laon, where at least some students from Bruges were sent to study in Galbert's days.[73] Galbert emphasizes repeatedly the exceptional friendship between Charles and Fromold, who was "more intimate with Count Charles than others of the comital court and for that reason more suspect in the eyes of the provost and his nephews"; "no one in the court was so intimate with the count in his lifetime, or so dear to him as this Fromold"; Fromold was closely attached to the count, who "loved him above all others, and whom he loved almost more than himself."[74] It makes one think of the relationship between Jesus and John, "the disciple whom Jesus loved."[75]

He cherished his bosom friend, Charles, with heart and soul. This appears clearly, or is at least portrayed clearly by Galbert, in his entry for April 14, 1127, the day the count's tomb was liberated. Driving their enemies into the church tower, the besiegers took the gallery where Charles's tomb stood. According to Galbert, the besiegers "filled the inside of the church, as well as the whole castle and its vicinity, with shouts and cries, with the rumbling and the clanging of running men and tumbling arms." Then Galbert jumps suddenly, in the same sentence, from the clamor of war to the besiegers praising God, and from "the inside" to a strange "outside," as if he clumsily added a clause later on by the conjunction "just as" (*sicut*): "just as outside, they praised God and blessed Him for the victory by which God had honored his victors, elevated the king and his men, glorified his majestic name above all others, cleansed his church in part from the defilers, and granted that now for the first time his glorious martyr and count could be mourned, surrounded and supported by the pious veneration and the prayers of his faithful."[76] It is reasonable to think that this

71. Galbert, [20], 31/36.

72. Galbert, [97], 1/4.

73. Galbert, [12], 49/51.

74. "ceteris de curia familiarior comiti Karolo, et idcirco magis suspectus erat praeposito et suis nepotibus" (Galbert, [18], 8/9); "nullus de curia comiti ita familiaris esset, cum viveret, neque ita carus sicut praefatus Fromoldus" (Galbert, [19], 25/26); "prae ceteris se diligentem et quem ipse prae se ipso fere diligebat" (Galbert, [24], 15).

75. "illum discipulum quem diligebat Iesus" (Jn 21:20).

76. "vocibus et clamoribus atque cursuum et ruinae armorumque stridore et fragore non solum templum sed omne castrum et viciniam ejus replentes introrsum, *sicut exterius* Deum

clause was added hastily to introduce the appearance of one of the faithful: Fromold the Younger. For Galbert zooms in on him immediately in a passage that undoubtedly was written not on that day, but presumably some weeks later:

And what he could not do before, Fromold the Younger could now at last do according to his long desire and ardent heart: pour forth a libation of prayers to God for the salvation of his lord, the count, offer a sacrifice of tears and contrition of heart, and rejoice joyously at the sight of the place where his buried lord was resting in peace. At last then for the first time he prepared a memorial service for his lord whom, buried already for so many days, that is, forty-four days, he had not been able to see!

On the day the tomb was liberated, Galbert stood amidst the faithful near the buried count. Perhaps he saw Fromold there, tears welling in his eyes. As if he knew what his colleague was thinking and could hear his prayer, Galbert writes:

No, he could not see his body but only the tomb from the outside! Yet he wished and implored, in a prayer of both lips and heart, that on the day of the common resurrection God would finally permit him to see his lord and prince Charles—raised to double glory in the midst of the faithful rulers and highest princes of his present church—and to stay with him, and to become blessed with him eternally in the glory of the contemplation of the holy Trinity.[77]

---

laudantes et benedicentes pro victoria qua victores suos honestavit, regem et suos sublimavit, super omnia majestatis suae Deus nomen glorificavit, ecclesiamque suam ab inquinatoribus in parte mundavit, et gloriosum illum martyrem suum consulemque bonorum tunc primum deflendum pia veneratione et oratione fidelium suorum circumfultum donavit" (Galbert, [63], 61/70, my emphasis). On this remarkable sentence, see Rider, *God's Scribe,* 93–94.

77. "Quod igitur prius non licuit tunc tandem Fromoldo juniori licuit, ex longo desiderio et ardenti animo vota Deo pro salute domini sui consulis offerre, lachrimis et cordis contritione sacrificium mactare, et gaudio gaudere pro inspectatione loci in quo dominus suus humatus quiescebat. Et tunc primum exequias praeparabat domino suo quem per tot dies sepultum, id est quadraginta quatuor, videre non poterat, neque enim corpus ejus, sed solum vidit a foris sepulchrum. Optabat quidem et oris et cordis oratione deprecabatur ut Deus in die resurrectionis communis inter rectores fideles et summos suae praesentis ecclesiae principes concederet sibi tandem dominum suum Karolum principem duplici gloria sublimatum videre et cum ipso manere et gloria contemplationis Trinitatis sanctae cum illo perenniter beatificari" (Galbert, [64], 1/14). According to Pirenne, chapter 64 was written several days after April 14 (*Histoire du meurtre de Charles le Bon, comte de Flandre par Galbert de Bruges, suivie de poésies latines contemporaines,* ed. Henri Pirenne [Paris, 1891], vii); according to J. M. De Smet this chapter cannot have been written before May 7 ("Bij de latijnsche gedichten over den moord op den Glz. Karel den Goede, Graaf van Vlaanderen," in *Miscellanea historica in honorem Alberti De Meyer,* 2 vols., Recueil de Travaux d'histoire et de philologie, ser. 3, 22–23 [Louvain, 1946], 440n3). Neither author is very explicit in his argumentation.

Fromold wants to experience the pleasure of Charles's physical appearance. His "lord and prince" was not only an immaterial soul, but a body too, and he longs to see him again in double glory, as a blessed soul and, after the common resurrection, in a glorified body. Fromold's longing fits with the central Christian mystery, celebrated on Easter: the resurrection of Christ as the guarantee of the resurrection of the body.

Fromold's repeatedly mentioned wish to see the tomb evokes, as J. M. De Smet pointed out, the biblical story of the women who went to Jesus's grave to embalm his hastily buried body.[78] Moreover, it evokes the "disciple whom Jesus loved": in the Gospel according to St. John, we read that, hearing from Mary Magdalene that Jesus's tomb was empty, this disciple hastened to the tomb together with the apostle Peter and could find only the shroud.[79] Soon the women, and later on the other disciples, saw their Lord, risen from the dead in bodily form. Fromold, however, would have to wait for the day of the common resurrection to see Charles in his bodily form, but his heart's long-fostered desire was nevertheless fulfilled. Galbert continues: "He considered it a great boon to be able to mourn the death of his lord at his tomb, to lament the ruin of the fatherland, and to perform with the greatest love the last rites for one whom he cherished in life and who was now betrayed by his serfs. He did so indeed, and not without tears!"[80] Galbert could not have heard Fromold's prayer at that moment, and Fromold would not have expressed himself in such elevated and sonorous words during a friendly conversation with Galbert! J. M. De Smet presumes that Galbert was paraphrasing a lost mourning poem composed by Fromold, which, because the passage contains a quotation from the Easter office and references to the events on Easter morning, was probably written around April 3, the date of Easter that year.[81]

Among the surviving poems written about Charles's death, one attracts attention by its uncommonly personal and affective tone. The author addresses himself to Charles in fourteen strophes of four metric verses. Each

78. De Smet, "Bij de latijnsche gedichten," 442n4. References given to Mk 16:1 and 16:6; Lk 23:56 and 24:1; Mt 28:1 and 28:6.

79. Jn 20:1–8.

80. "Reputaverat igitur pro grandi dono quod juxta tumbam domini sui liceret sibi mortem deflere, casum totius patriae conqueri, et quem viventem dilexerat, jam traditum a servis, summa dilectione exequi. Non sine lachrimis quidem hoc faciebat" (Galbert, [64], 14/18).

81. De Smet, "Bij de latijnsche gedichten," 441–43. Rider suggests, however, that "the poetic aspects of the passage, as well as its insight into the psychology of devotion, may well be due to Galbert himself" (*God's Scribe,* 122).

strophe begins with the vocative "Karole," as does each verse of the first strophe:

Charles, my care you still remain.
Charles, oh you, my glowing flame,
Charles, my tongue reveres your name.
Charles, my muse will chant your fame.[82]

This poem was undoubtedly written by a Fleming before May 6, 1127, perhaps even before March 20, 1127.[83] It must have been written by someone who knew and loved Charles very much, probably, as J. M. De Smet argued, by Fromold the Younger. He was Charles's most intimate friend and he took care of the comital house, and of Charles. Addressing himself to his deceased friend, the poet says: "Charles, my care you still remain" or, more prosaically, "you remain the object of my 'care,'" referring not only to the dutiful performance of a task, but to the loving care of a friend. "My care" in this verse means the same as "my love" or the "my glowing flame" of the second verse.[84]

After the murder of his lord and friend, Fromold did not feel any affection for the murderers. He did not want to be reconciled with them on any account because, as Galbert writes in one of his rare philosophical moments, "it is a most grievous thing for a man to be in accord with his enemy, and it is against nature, for every creature flees, if possible, what is inimical to it."[85] What kind of relations did Fromold have with his Erembald in-laws before the murder? Isaac, at least, did not really like his sister's husband. He suspected that Fromold spoke ill of him and other Erembalds to the count.[86]

Was the love between Charles and Fromold tinged with eroticism? "Eroticism" is often linked to, or even identified with, sexual lust, but

82. "Karole, tu mea cura manes. / Karole, tu mea flamma calens, / Karole, te mea lingua colit. / Karole, te mea musa canit" ("Karole, tu mea cura manes," ed. J. Rider, in Walter, 187).

83. See De Smet, "Bij de latijnsche gedichten," 431. The poet feels implicated in the shame that Charles's murder has brought on the *Flandrica gens,* the Flemish people, but this people will, according to the poet, blot out this shame by persecuting and killing the guilty (strophe 12). As the murderers and their henchmen were already dead on May 6, the poem had to have been written before that date. On March 20, 1127, De Smet argues, the king of France took the lead of their persecution; and as the poet is ignorant of this fact (or rather does not mention it), he guesses that the poem was written before that date.

84. Cf. De Smet, "Bij de latijnsche gedichten," 431–32.

85. "Gravissimum enim est viro cum inimico concordem esse et contra naturam, cum omnis creatura sibi inimica, si possit, effugiat" (Galbert, [24], 17/19).

86. Galbert, [18], 26/36.

there is a kind of eroticism that does not necessarily induce a tendency to sexual behavior and that springs from the desire for a person's appealing and enchanting bodily presence. We can presume, and not without reason, that the love between Charles and Fromold was of an erotic character in the latter sense, but did their friendship have a sexual component as well? We cannot know. It was said that homosexuality flourished in the circle around Charles's second cousin, William, son of King Henry I and grandchild of William the Conqueror and Mathilda, Charles's great-aunt. The White Ship disaster, which sent William and his noble companions to their deaths, was, so it was said, a divine punishment for the sodomy in which they were all, or nearly all, ensnared.[87] Such rumors are of course not a reliable basis on which to judge Charles's sexual behavior, which remains a mystery.

The intimate love, be it sexual or not, between Charles the Good and Fromold the Younger appears to be a strong motive for Charles's controversial plans that led to tensions and discord within the Erembald clan, to Charles's murder, to the ruin of the Erembalds, and to anarchy in Flanders. This love at least offers us a more satisfying, more encompassing explanation for the disastrous turn of the events than Charles's somewhat strange pursuit of justice.

Charles's Strange Pursuit of "Justice"

According to Galbert, Charles "fell dead in the cause of justice betrayed and slain by his own people, or, rather, by his most vicious serfs."[88] But for what kind of justice was he killed? Galbert writes that the pious count, "wishing to restore the realm to its former honor,"[89] sought to find out who in the realm belonged to him as comital serf, who was free or servile. He called for an inquiry into the status of the population, and if he found out that someone was a comital serf, he endeavored to lay hands on him. And so the truth concerning the status of the Erembalds came to light in

87. "All of them, or nearly all, were said to be tainted with sodomy and they were snared and caught. Behold the glittering vengeance of God!" (Qui omnes, vel fere omnes, sodomitica labe dicebantur, et erant irretiti. Ecce coruscabilis Dei vindicta!; Henry, Archdeacon of Huntingdon, *Historia Anglorum/The History of the English People* 7.32, ed. and trans. Diana Greenway [Oxford, 1996], 466, 467).

88. "a suis, immo nefandissimis servis, traditus et occisus, pro justitia occubuit" (Galbert, [Prol.], 13/14).

89. "Volens itaque comes pius iterum revocare honestatem regni" (Galbert, [7], 6/7); [7], 6/13.

the course of a supposedly general effort to reestablish honor in the realm. They appeared to be comital serfs. When the count learned of this, he tried to claim them.[90] In their haughtiness, however, they would not accept servitude and tried to hold on to their usurped liberty. Seeing no other means, they decided to kill their lord, who died in the cause of "justice."

"Justice" here is slightly ambiguous. Was Charles just because he was striving to restore "the rightness" of a situation, trying to put and to keep all men in their supposedly "right" place? Or was he just because he was striving to exercise "a right" that he supposedly had: the right to subdue the Erembalds. Galbert tends to equate rightfulness with righteousness, "justice" in the sense of having a right and fighting for it with "justice" in the sense of being right. This mixed notion of justice appears clearly in his final apology for count Thierry: Thierry was acting justly in trying to acquire the countship because he had a title, a hereditary right, and when he did so, divine justice was realized.[91]

Charles claimed the right to subdue the Erembalds, the so-called serfs. Was it a valid claim? Charles's predecessors and he himself, during the first years of his reign, never raised the question of the servile status of the provost and his kin.[92] According to the men of Bruges, "the provost and his brothers together with his nephews were among the most powerful and most noble men in the county."[93] Guy of Steenvoorde, "who was one of the chief counselors of the counts of Flanders," was married to a niece of Bertulf, the sister of Isaac.[94] And Guy of Steenvoorde was not the only prominent man who had married an Erembald woman! Why would members of the Flemish nobility, who were so proud of their noble ancestry, marry a servile woman and associate their kin with the Erembalds? Did the power and the wealth of the Erembalds compensate for their servile status? Or was this servile status only a malicious concoction invented to defame the Erembalds?

According to Galbert, Robert of Crecques, the husband of one of Bertulf's nieces, challenged a noble knight to a judicial duel in the presence of the count. The knight answered venomously that it was beneath

90. Galbert, [7], 36/39.

91. Galbert, [121], 1/25. On the ambiguity of the concept of a "right," see Robert van Es, *Negotiating Ethics: On Ethics in Negotiation and Negotiating in Ethics* (Delft, 1996), 15–19.

92. Galbert, [7], 39/44.

93. "praepositum et fratres simulque ejus nepotes, potentiores et nobiliores in comitatu" (Galbert, [45], 38/40).

94. "qui de consilio comitum Flandriae praecipuus erat" (Galbert, [58], 1/2).

his dignity to fight a serf. For, Galbert says, according to a comital law, a free man who had been married to a servile woman for more than a year lost his freedom.[95] If Robert's wife was indeed of servile origin, and if there really was, as we believe, such a law, Robert was no longer free. The noble knight's refusal to duel thus becomes understandable, since such combats were preserved for free men. Galbert tells us that the Erembalds' servile status—a status that had "so to speak, been slumbering and ignored for long time"[96]—was rescued from oblivion thanks to this event. After hearing this refusal, the count started an inquiry as if he had suddenly become aware of the Erembalds' possible servile origin. This inquiry led to the conclusion "that they belonged to him beyond doubt,"[97] and he endeavored to claim them as his serfs.

The people of Bruges were not the only ones who must have been surprised by Charles's pursuit of "justice." Elsewhere too, notwithstanding the comital claim, people saw the Erembalds, even after the murder of Charles, as free men. After Charles's murder, Isaac's brother Didier did not dare to appear openly at the court of Charles's successor because, as Galbert writes, "there were many in our countship who were ready to prove, by challenging him to a judicial duel, that he was guilty of treachery."[98] If they were convinced of Didier's servile status, they would not have deigned to fight him. The highborn Guy of Steenvoorde, who ought ostensibly to have lost his liberty on account of his wife, Isaac's sister, was actually challenged to a judicial duel at Ypres on April 11, 1127.[99]

A Selective Prosecution

Was the reply of the knight who was challenged by Robert of Crecques prepared ahead of time in collusion with Charles? Was the objective to discredit the Erembalds publicly in order to open the way for the inquisition and their degradation? Walter of Thérouanne, relating the same event, writes:

> A noble knight, however, happened to accuse another nobleman in the count's court of violating truces, but the latter confronted him with the stigma of his

95. Galbert, [7], 22/32; [25], 44/52.

96. "quasi sopitum et multis temporibus neglectum" (Galbert, [7], 41/42).

97. "quod sibi sine cunctatione pertinuissent" (Galbert, [7], 38); [7], 36/39; [10], 21/22.

98. "Nam plures fuerant in comitatu nostro qui illum appellassent ad bellum et reum traditionis convicissent" (Galbert, [92], 6/8).

99. Galbert, [58], 1/10. Lambert of Aardenburg purged himself from guilt in the treachery

servile status (because the woman his accuser had married was a relative of the provost and was said to be a serf of the count) and refused to defend himself against his accuser as if he were a free man. Therefore the whole family of the provost flew into an uncontrollable rage against Count Charles and the knight on account of the defaming imputation [*calumnia*], which indeed seemed to implicate them all. The case was discussed animatedly at great length, but finally settled in the following way. With the count's permission, the discredited matron could prove her liberty by a personal oath with that of eleven compurgators, but the count's suit against the rest of the clan would remain unaffected. *The fact that this defaming imputation was pending in this way was apparently the main reason for Charles's murder for they conceived a bitter hatred for him because of this.*[100]

The poor Robert of Creques was undoubtedly startled when the proceedings took such an unexpected turn. His social status was suddenly at stake, not the violation of peace, but his honor and that of his wife and her family. Charles apparently accepted the defense of Robert's opponent, and this started a long, exciting debate concerning the servile status of Robert's wife that enflamed the Erembalds with rage against the knight and Charles. The discussion was bad enough, but the solution was even worse. The woman and her husband would be saved—if enough compurgators were found and proof succeeded—but the rest of the family would still be stained with dishonor. And according to Walter of Thérouanne, at least, this was the main source of Erembalds' mortal hatred of Charles, a hatred that led finally to murder.

It was shocking that a member of a family could prove her freeborn status without that proof having any implication for the status of her relatives. The suspension of a judgment with respect to the status of the other members of the family prolonged their awkward situation and gave defamatory rumors a chance to grow and spread![101] Perhaps Charles did have a right,

---

by the proof of hot iron (Galbert, [105], 1/3), but we do not know how he was related to the Erembalds.

100. "Accidit autem ut quidam miles nobilis aduersus alium nobilem in curia comitis de treugarum infractione placitaret et ille, nota ei seruilis conditionis obiecta, eo quod consanguineam illius prepositi, quę comitis ancilla esse diceretur, uxorem duxisset, respondere ut libero refutaret. Quamobrem omnis illa prepositi cognatio in intolerabilem aduersus comitem Karolum et militem illum exarsit iram. In omnes enim hęc uidebatur redundare calumpnia. Causa ergo hęc quidem diu uentilata, sed tandem est tali ratione terminata, ut quę notata fuerat matrona duodecima nobilium manu libertatem suam personaliter assensu comitis euendicaret, et querela comitis in reliquam illam parentelam salua maneret. *Huius igitur calumpnię talis suspensio domno Karolo prima fuisse uisa est interfectionis occasio. Hinc namque grauissima contra eum ceperunt exercere odia*" (Walter, [16 (15)], 2/17, my emphasis).

101. In the early forties of the twelfth century Herman of Tournai (c. 1091–c. 1147) tells us

but was he right to rake up the past and to use his right? One may well suspect that he was not trying to restore the "honor of the realm," but that he was looking for a stick with which to beat the Erembalds, or at least some of them, and that he intended to use this stick at his own discretion.

On February 27, 1127, a crowd of peasants appeared before the comital court at Ypres. They came from the region southwest of Bruges and were there to complain about the suffering and the pillaging they had endured in the course of the private war between Borsiard, the brazen nephew of Bertulf, and Thancmar of Straten. They apparently named Borsiard and his armed following as the culprits. According to Walter of Thérouanne, the innocent Thancmar, believing that Borsiard would respect the truce imposed on them by Charles, was totally surprised by the attack by Borsiard and his henchmen.[102] Perhaps it was the truth. However, we cannot exclude the possibility that the peasants' complaint before the court at Ypres was organized and paid for by the men of Straten who "by deceit, strife and payment"[103] channeled all suspicions in the direction of Borsiard and his henchmen, thus offering the count a marvelous opportunity to lash out at some of the Erembalds.

In any case, Charles was not an impartial judge in the eyes of Borsiard and his supporters. Galbert writes: "Then Borsiard, the provost and their accomplices felt exceedingly hurt, both because the count seemed to have given his approval and aid to their enemies by doing this, and because he harassed them, day after day, with their servile status and made every effort to subjugate them as his serfs."[104] According to Galbert, the count, a paragon of impartiality, asked the convoked advisers, among whom there were many kinsmen of the provost, by what punishment the crime of Borsiard should be avenged. They advised him to burn down Borsiard's house with-

---

a doubtful story that was perhaps invented to explain Charles's selective pursuit of "justice," putting him in a favorable light at the expense of Bertulf and his nephews. Shortly before he was murdered, so the story goes, the count set a day for a hearing at Kassel, where the Erembalds could prove that they were not his serfs. Bertulf appeared before the court with an armed band of three thousand knights(!), and the count, fearing that so many people might cause a tumult, postponed the case (Herman, 29, p. 286). Neither Galbert nor Walter mentions an aborted hearing at Kassel, and, if there was such a hearing, it is impossible to know what really happened there.

102. Walter, [18 (17)], 11/18.

103. "fraude, seditione, coemptione facta" (Galbert, [45], 40).

104. "Tunc ille Borsiardus et praepositus et ipsorum complices ultra modum indoluerunt, tum quia comes in hoc facto videbatur consensum et auxilium praestitisse inimicis eorum, tum quia comes quotidie ipsos de servili conditione pulsaret et ad sibi mancipandos omni modo laboraret" (Galbert, [10], 18/22).

out delay, and so Charles did.[105] Walter of Thérouanne was present at the court at Ypres, and his version of what took place there is slightly different: the count explained what had happened and, wanting to avoid the impression that he was seeking personal vengeance, urged all his counselors to give advice one by one. They had different opinions, but finally agreed to let the count judge by himself and to determine a punishment fitting the nature of the crime.[106]

On March 1, 1127, the aforementioned intercessors came, through the agency of Bertulf, to Charles, pleading for reconciliation between him and Borsiard. According to Walter, however, as we have seen, their plea was more an invective accusation of the count. The latter riposted: "What do you mean by asserting that I let myself be overwhelmed by my passions and have undeservedly afflicted your Borsiard with abusive wrongs? . . . Well then, let him justly restore what he stole unjustly, *and let him recognize the status of his family* and find in this way the mercy he is looking for!"[107] Charles lays down two conditions for the reconciliation between him and Borsiard. The latter had to restore the seized goods and to recognize publicly the status of his family or, in other words, to recognize that he was a comital serf.

The reconciliation failed. The intercessors reported the count's proposition to Bertulf and his henchmen. Walter writes:

> And although nothing could be said to be more just than the count's proposition insofar as it was congruous with the law and the precepts of the Gospel, nevertheless he [Bertulf], . . . blind in heart, began to rage more. . . . The fury of the raging and the rage of the furious was also roused because the messengers did not act sincerely. *They gave the words of the count a false twist—embittering the hearts of the young men even further—by saying that they would never obtain mercy from the count unless they all declared publicly that they were his serfs.*[108]

105. Galbert, [10], 8/18.

106. Walter, [21 (20)], 2/19.

107. "Quid est quod me motibus meis tantopere asseritis indulsisse, et Burchardo uestro immerito iniurias contumeliosas intulisse? . . . Quę ergo iniuste rapuit iuste restituat *et conditionem sui generis agnoscat* et sic misericordiam quam querit inueniat" (Walter, [23 (22)], 20/28, my emphasis).

108. "quamuis hac comitis allegatione nichil iustius dici ualeret, utpote quę et legis et euangelii mandatis congrueret, ille tamen . . . cęcate mente magis cepit insanire . . . . Auxit quoque furorem dementium et dementiam furentium quod prefati legati non sinceriter egerunt, *sed, uerba comitis deprauantes et superbos iuuenum animos deterius exacerbantes, dixerunt quod numquam misericordiam a comite consequerentur, nisi seruos eius se esse omnes profiterentur*" (Walter, [24 (23)], 3/16, my emphasis).

The direct object of the count's action was undoubtedly Borsiard, whom the count wanted to humiliate himself publicly, recognizing "the status of his family." The other Erembalds would seemingly not have been required to debase themselves in this way, as if Borsiard's public humiliation would not have embarrassed the whole family! According to his devotees, Charles could not be blamed for the failed attempt at reconciliation. But how was Bertulf—the head of the family and the person who was primarily responsible for its honor, the uncle of Borsiard and the initiator of the attempt at reconciliation—to interpret the count's proposition, even if we believe that it was wrongly transmitted by the "impertinent" intercessors?

Tension and Discord within the Erembald Clan

Although Charles's actions were not aimed directly at the Erembalds as a whole, the stigma of servitude tended to affect the whole family. Conversely, although not all the Erembalds were involved in the murder of Charles or approved of it, the murder seemed to tarnish all of them. Charles's selective persecution of the Erembalds, provoking them to murder, was a source of tension and discord within the Erembald clan.

On March 2, 1127, the day of the great slaughter, Didier Hacket, brother of Bertulf and castellan of Bruges, took two of Borsiard's enemies under his protection in the count's house and saved them from the bloodthirsty murderers.[109] Two weeks later, on March 17, he appeared together with Bertulf on the ramparts of the beleaguered castle at Bruges. As the spokesman for Bertulf and all the besieged, he pleaded for mercy in words that clearly reveal a tension between his commitment to his kin and his abhorrence of the treacherous murderers: "[T]ogether with you we bewail and deplore the death of the count, we condemn the guilty and we would cast them out from us totally if we were not, albeit reluctantly, bound to help them out of blood-kinship." He begged that his guilty nephews be allowed to leave the castle and, safe in life and limb, be condemned to perpetual exile, and he asked—at least according to his speech as rendered by Galbert—that he himself, Bertulf, and Robert the Boy, together with their men, be given the opportunity to prove their innocence according to any kind of trial that was decided on. Finally Didier said: "If you disdain our offer, we would rather remain besieged with the guilty than come out

109. Galbert, [16], 10/16.

to you and die dishonorably."[110] The offer was refused. Bertulf and Didier Hacket retreated to stay, be it temporarily, with the guilty.

On April 1, Didier Hacket escaped and went to Lissewege, where he hid, waiting to see what would happen and what he could do.[111] The following day he was dismissed as castellan of Bruges in favor of Gervaise, but after 1130 he again became castellan of Bruges, even if only for a short time.[112] There is no reason to believe that Didier Hacket was not really torn between his sense of family loyalty and his condemnation of the murder. Bertulf had escaped on the night of Thursday, March 17, but for him, as we know, things went very badly. On April 11, he was lynched in the marketplace at Ypres.[113] As head of the family, he could not easily run away from his responsibility and break with his kin, but maybe, despite the bad things that were said about him, he did not in fact approve of the treacherous murder.

Didier, brother of Isaac, did not take an active part in the conspiracy. On the contrary, on March 9, 1127, he appeared together with Gervaise as the first in Bruges to avenge the murder of the count. He hunted for the henchmen of the traitors outside the castle and participated in the siege of the Erembalds, his kinsmen, who holed up in the castle.[114] The following day, at least according to Walter of Thérouanne, he burned down the fortified house of his brother Isaac with his own hands.[115] On March 19, the day that the besiegers rushed into the castle and the besieged retreated into the church, Gervaise planted his banners on top of the count's house, while Didier, together with the men of Bruges, occupied the lower part of the house, fixing his banners on the balcony. From the church Robert the Boy saw Didier crossing the courtyard and shouted: "'Hey Didier, do you not remember that in former days you advised us to betray the lord count? You have betrayed your faith and loyalty in this, and now, seeing our misfortune, you are glad and you persecute us. Ah, if I could only get out! I would challenge you to a duel! As God is my witness, you are more of a traitor than we are, for first you betrayed your lord and now you have

110. "mortem domini comitis vobiscum conquerimur, deflemus, reos damnamus et prorsus expelleremus a nobis nisi quod nostri sanguinis propinquitatem inviti quidem servamus in ipsis. . . . Quod si fieri abominaveritis, volumus melius sic obsessi simul cum reis vivere quam ad vos exire et turpiter mori" (Galbert, [38], 12/15, 33/35).

111. Galbert, [54], 1/5.

112. See Warlop, 1:210.

113. Galbert, [46], 1/17; [57], 1/93.

114. Galbert, [29], 1/9; Walter, [37 (36)], 2/3.

115. Walter, [35 (34)], 9/12.

betrayed us!' This reproach was not made without everyone's noticing," Galbert says.[116] It was undoubtedly Robert's purpose to impugn the good name of his cousin, and to make him suspect in everyone's eyes, and Galbert was of course impressed by the words of his favorite, the noble young Robert! After the death of Didier on December 17, 1127, he wrote: "As an accomplice in the treachery, he did not deserve to taste the joy of life any longer."[117]

It is very doubtful that Didier knew anything about the conspiracy before the murder of Charles, and it is certain that Fromold the Younger, the husband of his sister, was not involved in it at all. But Fromold probably did have a hand in Charles's controversial plans and also, consequently, in the creation of tensions and discord within the Erembald clan. When it was announced to Isaac on that bloody Wednesday, March 2, 1127, that Fromold had been found hiding, Isaac "was seized by an access of wild fury against Fromold the Younger, so fiercely that he swore by God and the saints that Fromold's life could not be redeemed by a pile of gold as big as the church itself! He turned everyone's fury against Fromold, shouting that no one had done more to slander the provost and his nephews to the count." Galbert presents Fromold as candid innocence itself. In the confrontation with Isaac that immediately follows, Fromold, thinking that his brother-in-law is going to save him, says: "'Isaac, my friend, I adjure you by that friendship that has till now existed between us, save my life, and by saving me take care of my sons, your nephews, who will be without a protector if I am killed.' But he [Isaac] replied: 'Mercy you will receive, that mercy you have deserved for having slandered us to the count.'"[118]

Apparently the friendship between Charles and Fromold had caused some resentment and suspicion, but had Fromold indeed said slanderous

116. "'O Desideri, non es memor quod tu hactenus nobis consuluisti tradere dominum consulem? Fidem super hoc et securitatem tradidisti et nunc, viso infortunio nostro, gaudes et persequeris nos. O utinam liceret mihi exire! ad singulare bellum te evocarem. Deum testor quod tu magis sis traditor quam nos eo quod olim dominum, modo nos tradidisti.' Quod improperium non sine omnium nota tulit" (Galbert, [44], 21/28).

117. "traditionis conscius, non promeruit ulterius vitae felicitate perfrui" (Galbert, [92], 4/5).

118. "commotus est Isaac vehementissime in Fromoldum juniorem furore repentino et gravi ita ut juraret Deum et sanctos vitam ejus non posse redimi auro tantae quantitatis quantae ipsum templum fuisset. Omnium quoque furorem in Fromoldum illum convertit, clamando neminem magis praeposito et nepotibus suis apud comitem detraxisse. . . . 'Amice mi Isaac, te obsecro per eandem quae hactenus fuit inter nos amicitiam, observa vitam meam, et liberis meis, scilicet tuis nepotibus, per me conservatum consule, ne forte, me occiso, ipsi fiant sine tutore.' At ille respondit: 'Illam habiturus es veniam quam detrahendo apud comitem nobis promeruisti'" (Galbert, [18], 23/36).

things about Isaac and other Erembalds to the count? Galbert gives no explicit information on this point, but it is unthinkable that the two friends had never discussed Charles's scheme.

Charles's Project, His Love for Fromold, and the Disaster

What did Charles have in mind? The Erembalds were of obscure, maybe even servile, origin, but they had achieved an elevated social status. They were associated by marriage with free and highborn families, and they lived as nobles with substantial households, including knights and servants. Didier Hacket was castellan of Bruges, and the rich and mighty Erembalds were held in high esteem, especially in Bruges. Didier's brother Bertulf, the head of the big clan, had held the highest position in the political bureaucracy of Flanders for thirty-six years at the time of the murder. Opulent and awe inspiring, used to wielding power, supported by his kin, his friends and his men, Bertulf, Walter says, had "a large multitude obeying him, reached the highest summit of power."[119] He was, in the words of Galbert, "the mightiest man in the realm after the count."[120]

Of course, one could dream of a world without Erembalds, or a world in which they were simple, obedient serfs, lacking power, political offices, wealth, and mighty connections. Such a world could not, however, be realized as if by magic. Impugning the Erembalds would undoubtedly tarnish their reputation. By bringing to light their allegedly lowborn origin and by claiming them as his serfs, Charles could deal them a blow; by validating his claim before the court, he could bring down those Erembalds who impeded the realization of his own plans. He threatened Bertulf's authority, the solidarity within the Erembald clan, and their prestige within society.

But how could he imagine that he could dishonor the mighty clan without unleashing almost infernal storms, and risking his and other people's lives? What urgent motives pushed him to this action, which looks very much like a suicide attempt? Were the problems he faced truly insoluble, every apparent solution resulting inevitably in disaster? Was the pressure applied by the nobles who did not want to see the newcomers penetrate the nobility that strong? Was Charles frustrated and anxious, perceiving the immense power of the old Bertulf? Was he fighting reck-

119. "turba magna sibi obediente, culmen adeptus est maximę potestatis" (Walter, [15], 10/11).

120. "post comitem in regno potentior" (Galbert, [8], 1/2).

lessly for "justice," convinced that he was right in claiming a right and enflamed like a zealous crusader with the ardent desire for martyrdom, a desire that, according to Walter of Thérouanne, he nursed?[121] Or was it his passionate love for Fromold—along, perhaps, with other motives—that slightly muddled his mind?

On bloody Wednesday, when Fromold and other faithful men of the count fell into the hands of the murderers, they were, the reader will remember, placed in the custody of Bertulf, who had interceded for them at the request of the clergy. He led those under his charge into the hall of his house. He looked at them warily and, descrying Fromold, he spoke to him: "Oh Fromold, bear in mind that you will not get my provostship by next Easter as you were hoping. No, I did not deserve your having intrigued against me in this way." What could Fromold do except plead his innocence? Galbert, however, without explicitly affirming it, does not deny that there was indeed a plan to pass the provostship from Bertulf to Fromold. To him it seemed very plausible, if not certain. He continues:

> But Fromold swore that he was innocent! Yet it was true that no one in the comital court was so intimate with the count in his lifetime, or so beloved as the named Fromold. For after his house, a regal building, had been completely destroyed by fire, the count rebuilt it for him, better and finer than it had been before. In comparison to it, no house in the world could be considered better or more comfortable.[122]

We assume that Bertulf was well informed and that a change of power was indeed planned. A date was already set: April 3, 1127, Easter Sunday. A cozy office for Fromold was in the offing: the highest post in Flanders, generating power, prestige, and wealth. Bertulf, a so-called serf, would be robbed of his office in favor of Fromold, another "serf" since he had been married to one of Bertulf's nieces for many years. Such a shift in power was not unknown, especially not to Bertulf: thirty-six years before, with the approval of the count, he obtained the position previously held by Ledbert, the respectable man "who bore everything for the sake of God."[123]

121. Walter, [28 (27)], 21/37.

122. "'Scias, Fromolde, te in proximo Pascha praepposituram meam non possessurum, sicut sperabas. Neque hoc apud te promerueram ut sic detraheres mihi.' Et ille se innocenter egisse jurabat. Verum tamen fuit quod nullus de curia comiti ita familiaris esset, cum viveret, neque ita carus sicut praefatus Fromoldus. Nam domum regali aedificio funditus post combustionem sui reaedificavit meliori et decentiori compositione quam unquam constitisset prius. Comparatione quoque illius, nulla aestimabatur in mundo melior vel utilior" (Galbert, [19], 21/30).

123. "propter Deum omnia patienti" (Galbert, [57], 34).

In the first years of his government Charles, like his predecessors, had bestowed large gifts on Bertulf. The provost's alleged objectionable practices were apparently not so important to him then. At some point, however, Charles decided to strive for "justice." New plans began to come together! Charles wanted to get rid of a nuisance, the old and powerful Bertulf, and to put in his place a man with whom he was on very close terms. The friends, Charles and Fromold, trusted and loved each other. It seems likely that they often discussed the Erembalds' position and made plans for the future. They were the pioneers of a "new political culture," but first the "Old Guard," especially the old string puller, had to leave the field. Wild, but vain, dreams, as the course of events was to prove. The friendship and solidarity within the Erembald clan was fractured, Charles was assassinated, Flanders fell into dramatic anarchy, and Fromold was left alone in deep distress, full of hatred for the murderers, and longing for the reunion with his friend after the resurrection of the body.

The Tears of Fromold

A number of Flemish literary works of the nineteenth and twentieth centuries were based partly on Galbert's narrative.[124] In an apparent attempt to make their works more dramatic and sensational, the authors include some prominent female characters who are involved in the world of men through heterosexual love affairs. In doing so, the authors depend almost totally on their fanciful imagination. The cinematic aspects of Galbert's story cry out for a film adaptation, and if it comes to this, we can only hope that such imaginings will not be included, that Charles and Fromold the Younger will be the main dramatis personae, and that dramatic effects will be sought through the portrayal of same-sex relations. The film's title is already available: *The Tears of Fromold.*

124. See Hendrik Conscience, *De Kerels van Vlaanderen* (Antwerp, 1871); Hektor Plancquaert, *De dood van Karel den Goede, Graaf van Vlaanderen. Drama in vijf bedrijven* (Ghent, 1889), 24; Vic De Donder, *Zonsverduistering boven Brugge* (Leuven, 2000).

PART FOUR

THE MEANINGS OF HISTORY

8

The Devil in Flanders

Galbert of Bruges and the Eschatology of Political Crisis

ALAN V. MURRAY

The murder of Charles "the Good," count of Flanders, resulted from a struggle between the count himself and one of the most powerful and well-connected families in Flanders, a kin group at whose head stood Bertulf, provost of the church of Saint Donatian in Bruges and chancellor of the county.[1] The actual origins of this clan are difficult to establish with certainty; Galbert of Bruges relates that its members were descended from one Erembald of Veurne, a steward to a castellan of Bruges living at an unspecified time during the second half of the eleventh century. According to Galbert, this Erembald murdered his master and proceeded to marry his widow, thereby establishing the foundations for the future wealth and power of their offspring.[2]

Irrespective of the accuracy of Galbert's story, it is certain that by the reign of Count Charles (1119–27), the descendants of Erembald, castellan of Bruges from around 1067 to 1089, had achieved an unrivalled position of power within the county of Flanders. The senior member of the house at this time was Erembald's son Bertulf, who had effectively become head of the comital administration based at Bruges. Bertulf's brother Desid-

1. This essay develops ideas originally presented in two papers, "The Divine and the Diabolic in Twelfth-Century Historiography: The Chronicle of Galbert of Bruges" (University of Leeds, Centre for Medieval Studies Research Association, July 1, 1997), and "The Erembalds Revisited: The Political and Literary Destruction of a Twelfth-Century Clan" (International Medieval Congress, Leeds, July 9–12, 2001). I am also grateful for comments from participants of a research seminar on Galbert of Bruges at Wesleyan University (Middletown, Conn.) on March 26, 2003, organized by Prof. Jeff Rider.

2. Galbert, [71].

erius Hacket was castellan of Bruges. Their nephew Isaac held the office of chamberlain to the count. Other family members had made important marriage connections within the Flemish nobility, and together they held extensive properties in and around Bruges and along the coast of northwestern Flanders. The immediate cause of the murder of Charles was his attempt at the end of the winter of 1126–27 to prove by judicial means that Bertulf's family was of servile origin; any legal decision that established that the family were serfs would have swept away the power, wealth, and privileges they had painstakingly built up.[3]

In order to forestall the completion of the legal process against them, Bertulf and his kinsmen resorted to drastic action: on the morning of March 2, 1127, a group of knights and retainers led by Isaac the Chamberlain and his cousin Borsiard burst into the church of Saint Donatian and murdered Charles along with various advisors, officials, and clerics who were present.

The family of the provost Bertulf was thus central to the political crisis that engulfed the county of Flanders in 1127 as well as to the several narrative sources that recorded it, particularly our principal source, Galbert of Bruges. Whether or not the family was of actual servile origin, as claimed by the count, argued by Galbert, and accepted by most modern scholarship, it may well be impossible to establish with any certainty, and this essay will be less concerned with the historical truth of the rise and fall of Erembald and his descendants than with the manner in which these events are depicted by Galbert; its aim is rather to discuss what the portrayal of the provost Bertulf and his kin reveals about the historical understanding and historiographical art of Galbert of Bruges.[4]

As Galbert originally composed the *De multro* in the form of a journal and never completed a fully revised version of his work, he was long regarded as a relatively unskilled and unsophisticated writer. The great Belgian historian Henri Pirenne accepted that his account had a certain liveliness and charm, but saw Galbert as someone who was fundamentally naive and disorganized, and who did not reflect upon the significance

3. Jan Dhondt, "Medieval Solidarities: Flemish Society in Transition, 1127–28," in *Lordship and Community in Medieval Europe,* ed. Frederic L. Cheyette (New York, 1968), 268–96; James B. Ross, "Rise and Fall of a Twelfth-Century Clan: The Erembalds and the Murder of Count Charles of Flanders, 1127–1128," *Speculum* 34 (1959): 367–90; Warlop, 185–95; and van Caenegem, "Galbert of Bruges on Serfdom," 89–112.

4. Cf. Rider, *God's Scribe,* 66.

of the events he was recording.[5] Pirenne's views prevailed until the 1950s, when, particularly as a result of the work of Heinrich Sproemberg and Jan Dhondt, a picture began to emerge of Galbert as a learned, reflective, and sophisticated observer, an evaluation that has by and large been developed and elaborated by subsequent scholarship.[6]

The nature of earthly authority was a particular subject of Galbert's constant reflection and concern. In the prologue to the *De multro,* in which Galbert sets out the matter and purpose of his work, he gives the admonition that no one should betray earthly rulers who have been placed over their subjects by God: "Let every soul be subject to every power, either to the king as supreme or to governors as sent by God."[7] This passage was identified by Ross as a reference to 1 Peter 2:13.[8] However, Galbert's formulation indicates just as much, if not greater, correspondence with Romans 13:1; Galbert's citation does not correspond to either passage precisely.[9] It is difficult to explain the discrepancy, even allowing for the fact that the Vulgate text known to Galbert may have differed from the modern one. Galbert may have been citing from memory; yet given medieval scholars' facility with memorizing as a process of learning, that explanation is no reason for assuming that citations from memory should have necessarily been defective. It is possible that Galbert's biblical allusion in the prologue derived from an exegetical commentary that cited both biblical passages.

Galbert subsequently cites a similar passage at the point where he is de-

5. *Histoire du meurtre de Charles le Bon comte de Flandre (1127–1128) par Galbert de Bruges,* ed. Henri Pirenne (Paris, 1891).

6. Heinrich Sproemberg, "Das Erwachen des Staatsgefühls in den Niederlanden. Galbert von Brügge," in *L'Organisation corporative du Moyen Age à la fin de l'Ancien Régime. Etudes présentées à la Commission Internationale pour l'histoire des Assemblées d'etats* 3 (Louvain, 1939), 31–89; Sproemberg, "Galbert von Brügge—Stellung und Bedeutung. Die Anfänge demokratischer Geschichtsschreibung im Mittelalter," in Sproemberg, *Mittelalter und demokratische Geschichtsschreibung,* ed. Manfred Unger, Lily Sproemberg, and Wolfgang Eggert, Forschungen zur mittelalterlichen Geschichte 18 (Berlin, 1971), 319–24; Dhondt, "Une mentalité du douzième siècle," 101–9. For a comprehensive conspectus of scholarship on Galbert, see most recently Rider, *God's Scribe,* 1–10.

7. *"Omnis anima omni potestati subjecta sit, sive regi tamquam praecellenti sive ducibus tamquam a Deo missis"* (Galbert, [Prologue], 41/43; trans., 80).

8. Ross, trans., 80n13.

9. Pt 2:13–14: "Be subject for the Lord's sake to every human institution, whether it be to the emperor as supreme, or to the governors as sent by him to punish those who do wrong and to praise those who do right" (subiecti estote omni humanae creaturae propter Dominum sive regi quasi praecellenti sive ducibus tamquam ab eo missis ad vindictam malefactorum laudem vero bonorum); Rom 13:1: "Let every person be subject to the governing authorities. For there is no authority except from God, and those that exist have been instituted by God" (omnis anima potestatibus sublimioribus subdita sit non est enim potestas nisi a Deo quae autem sunt a Deo ordinatae sunt).

scribing how the people of Flanders revolted against their new count, William Clito, who had been installed by King Louis VI of France acting as overlord of the county, and acclaimed by the nobility and urban communities of Flanders.[10] In the same context he further cites other biblical passages from John 19:11, "You would not have any power over me, if it had not been given to you from above by my Father,"[11] and the famous observation on authority, "Render unto God the things that are God's and unto Caesar the things that are Caesar's."[12] The importance of the reference to Romans 13:1 / 1 Peter 2:13 is that its message is established at the beginning of the *De multro* as a fundamental lesson of the work, as it explains the great evil that befalls Flanders as a result of the overthrow of divinely ordained authority. Galbert proceeds to give an exegesis of this passage, but he then chooses to conclude his prologue with a much broader theological pronouncement: "When the Devil saw the progress of the church and the Christian faith, as you are about to hear, he undermined the stability of the land, that is, of the Church of God, and threw it into confusion by guile and treachery and the shedding of innocent blood."[13] It has long been argued that Galbert, like other authors who gave an account of the Flemish Crisis of 1127–28, interpreted the murder of Charles the Good according to a model ultimately based on Saint Augustine's *De Civitate Dei,* which viewed the progress of history as a continual conflict between the City of God, that is the community of the good, and the City of the Devil, the community of evil.[14] The influence of Augustine, carried on and reinforced by the works of Gregory the Great, Gregory of Tours, Bede, the school of Laon, and others, meant that theologians could and frequently did interpret disasters and calamities in earthly society as the result of diabolic intervention, a tendency that was commonplace until well into the thirteenth century.[15]

10. Galbert, [118], 30/31.

11. *"non haberes . . . potestatem in me nisi tibi datum fuisset desuper a patre meo"* (Galbert, [118], 33/34; trans., 306).

12. *"quae sunt Dei Deo reddite et quae sunt Cesaris Cesari"* (Galbert, [118], 35; trans., 306); cf. Mt 22:21; Mk 12:17; Lk 20:25.

13. "Videns ergo diabolus ecclesiae et fidei christianae profectum, sicut subsequenter audituri estis, commovit terrae, hoc est ecclesiae Dei, stabilitatem et conturbavit eam dolis, traditionibus et effusione innocentium sanguinis" (Galbert, [Prol.], 51/55; trans., 81).

14. For Galbert, see Mohr, "Geschichtstheologische Aspekte," 246–62. For Walter of Thérouanne and other authors, see David C. Van Meter, "Eschatology and the Sanctification of the Prince in Twelfth-Century Flanders: The Case of Walter of Thérouanne's *Vita Karoli comitis Flandriae,*" *Sacris Erudiri: Jaarboek voor Godsdienstwetenschappen* 35 (1995): 115–31. Rider, *God's Scribe,* 164–65, 249–50, while admitting Augustinian influence, argues that Orosius had a far greater influence on Galbert's thinking.

15. Brian P. McGuire, "God, Man and the Devil in Medieval Theology and Culture," *Ca-*

Galbert's exposition of his purpose evidently locates the theme of divinely ordained authority within a wider, Augustinian frame of reference, namely the perennial attempts of the Devil to subvert the divine order. As the source of good government in Flanders, Count Charles figures as God's faithful servant by guaranteeing the order that enabled the church to prosper. In a section consisting of six chapters (1–6) placed subsequent to the prologue and before his introduction of the alleged servile origins of Bertulf's kinsmen, Galbert describes Charles's accession and the boons of his rule; he then develops the theme of how the peace and stability of Flanders are threatened by evil intent, directed primarily at the person of the count himself. Firstly, Galbert enumerates various portents that he interprets as divinely ordained omens whose purpose is to enjoin penitence on "those whom He had foreseen as prone to evil."[16] At the beginning of the following chapter we are told that the impious were not dissuaded by these portents, but that even at that time they were plotting the death of Charles.[17] Thus, by the beginning of chapter 3, Galbert has identified a constituency of "the impious" (*impii*) whom he places in—quite literal—opposition to the "most pious" (*piissimus*) count.[18] Although characterized as determined to carry out the work of the Devil, they are not yet explicitly identified. However, greater precision is provided in the course of the following two chapters, which describe offers of the succession to the thrones of Germany and the kingdom of Jerusalem supposedly made to Charles by the leading men of those countries.

The first of these two parallel episodes, telling how Charles was offered the throne of Germany on the death of the Emperor (Henry V) in 1125, can be traced back to an actual but ultimately unsuccessful candidature of Charles that was mounted on the initiative of the archbishop of Cologne and his allies in the Rhineland.[19] What is important about this episode is less its actual historical significance than its role in Galbert's unfolding narrative. The candidature of Charles is not portrayed as one among several, but rather as an offer made to Charles unanimously by the leading princes

hiers de l'Institut du Moyen Age Grec et Latin 18 (1976): 18–82. McGuire cites Galbert's prologue as evidence of his Augustinian attitudes, but does not investigate this theme further with regard to the *De multro.*

16. "quos pronos praeviderat ad malum" (Galbert, [2], 3/4; trans., 84–85).

17. Galbert, [3], 1/2.

18. Galbert, [3], 1/2; trans., 87.

19. Galbert, [4], 1/32; Heinrich Sproemberg, "Eine rheinische Königskandidatur im Jahre 1125," in *Aus Geschichte und Landeskunde: Forschungen und Darstellungen. Franz Steinbach zum 65. Geburtstag gewidmet,* ed. Max Braubach et al. (Bonn, 1960), 50–70.

and prelates of Germany after discussion of the merits of several potential candidates. While Charles's loyal subjects fear that the country will be ruined if he leaves it, his enemies, by contrast, extol how much glory and fame will come to him as king of the Romans; their purpose is, however, a nefarious one, since they hope, by means of this trickery, to remove Charles from Flanders.[20] Charles, however, follows the counsel of those who loved him, and remains in Flanders, thus guaranteeing its peace and security, and frustrating the schemes of the "evil traitors."

The themes of evil and treachery also figure in the second parallel passage, which tells of an attempt in 1123 or 1124 by the disenchanted nobility of the kingdom of Jerusalem to place Charles on the throne in place of King Baldwin II (1118–31). Baldwin had come to the throne in 1118 as the first representative of a new dynasty. After he was taken prisoner while campaigning against the Turks of northern Syria in 1123, the forces of opposition to his policies seized the opportunity presented by his enforced absence by attempting to replace him on the throne.[21] It is likely that some kind of offer or appeal to Charles was made, but according to Galbert, he was once again unwilling to desert his fatherland, "which in his lifetime he was to govern well, and would have ruled even better if those evil traitors, full of the demon, had not slain their lord and father, who was imbued with the spirit of piety and wisdom and courage."[22] The characterization of the traitors as being "full of the demon" is repeated in the next chapter (*pleni demonio . . . demonio pleni*), which provides a laudatory summation

20. "But those who had rightly cherished and loved him, and who venerated him as a father, began to grieve and to lament his departure, predicting that it would prove the ruin of the fatherland if he should desert it. Those evil traitors, however, who were threatening his life, advised him to assume the German kingship and its dignities, pointing out to him how much glory and fame would be his as king of the Romans. Those wretches were trying by this guile and trickery to get rid of him; later when they had been unable to remove him while he was alive, they betrayed him while he was contending with them on behalf of the law of God and men" (At illi, qui ipsum justo amore et dilectionis virtute dilexerant et ut patrem venerabantur, ceperunt dolere et discessum ejus deflere et ruinam patriae gravem fore, si forte eam desereret. Tandem illi traditores pessimi qui vitae ipsius insidiabantur consuluerunt ei ut regnum et ejus honores praeriperet inter Teutonicos, persuadentes ei quantae gloriae et quantae famae sibi foret regem Romanorum esse. Laborabant miseri illi qua astutia, quibus dolis carerent eo, quem postmodum, dum amovere non poterant, viventem tradiderunt pro lege Dei et hominum cum ipsis decertatem; Galbert, [4], 22/32; trans., 91).

21. Alan V. Murray, *The Crusader Kingdom of Jerusalem: A Dynastic History, 1099–1125* (Oxford, 2000), 136–46.

22. "Noluit igitur, super hoc fidelium suorum accepto consilio, deserere patriam Flandriarum, quam vita comite bene recturus foret et satis melius quam adhuc rexisset, nisi traditores illi pessimi, pleni demonio, dominum et patrem plenum spiritu pietatis et consilii et fortitudinis enecassent" (Galbert, [5], 10/14; trans., 93).

of Charles's virtues.[23] The characterization of the enemies of Charles as "those traitors" (*illi traditores . . . traditores illi*) in chapters 4–5 anticipates the treachery that brings about the murder of Charles, which will be described at chapter 15. Not only is this a clear indication that the initial section was either composed or revised well after the assassination, but it also constitutes an accusation that Bertulf and his kinsmen had attempted to remove the count before their strike against him on March 2, 1127, and in doing so were attempting to pervert the divine order.

It can thus be seen that in a preliminary section of the *De multro* (from the prologue to the end of chapter 6), placed before the day-by-day narrative of the course of the conspiracy against Charles, Galbert constructs an exegetical exposition in which those who will betray Charles are not only characterized as being inspired by the demon, but explicitly identified as *instruments* of the Devil in his perennial attempts to overthrow the divine order. It is noteworthy that up to this point the traitors are not distinguished by name, either as a group or as individuals; only in the following chapter does Galbert identify the provost Bertulf and various named kinsmen as the family against whom the accusation of servile origin is raised. From this time he is able to develop the characterizations of the principal members of the family. To a large extent these are dependent on the actual or presumed roles played by individuals in the plotting and execution of the conspiracy against Charles and the subsequent struggle against their enemies, as Ross has shown.[24] The distinctive characterizations are exemplified in Galbert's account of how the leading conspirators gather at the provost's house in Bruges on the evening of March 1 to swear a compact against Charles. A select group including Bertulf, his nephews Isaac and Borsiard, and other family members and allies, such as Ingran of Esen and William of Wervik, withdraw into an inner room to pledge themselves to carry out the murder of the count. Robert *Puer* (the Boy), son of Bertulf's deceased brother the Castellan Robert, is then brought in and inveigled into pledging himself, without being told what he has promised. Only then do the others reveal to him that in doing so he has unwittingly agreed to betray the count. Robert's horrified response is to threaten to reveal the plot, whereupon the others restrain him, passing off the treachery as a joke: "Listen, friend, we were only pretending to you that we were in

23. Galbert, [6], 18; trans., 95.

24. For individual characterizations in general, see Ross, "Rise and Fall of a Twelfth-Century Clan."

earnest about that treachery so that we could try out whether you want to stay by us in a certain serious matter; for there is something we have concealed from you up to this point, in which you are bound to us by faith and compact, which we shall tell you about in good time."[25] The gathering breaks up, but while Robert supposedly goes to bed with a clear conscience, Isaac merely pretends to retire, and in the middle of the night collects a select band from whom the assassins are chosen. Recent commentaries have stressed how much Galbert's account of the swearing of the plot is a literary construction, with quite detailed description—including purported speeches—of a gathering at which he had undoubtedly not been present.[26] It serves several purposes. The main conspirators—Bertulf, Isaac, and Borsiard—are identified as treacherous to their lord and even duplicitous toward one of their own kinsmen. Their supposed dupe, Robert *Puer,* presented a particular problem for Galbert in the aftermath of the murder of the count. Robert joined his relatives in seizing the castle of Bruges, where they were besieged by forces consisting of knights of King Louis VI of France, much of the Flemish nobility and their retinues, and the urban militias of Bruges and Ghent.[27] Yet right up to the ending of the siege, many of the burgesses of Bruges refused to accept that Robert was a traitor, and tried to intercede with King Louis to save him after the surrender of the traitors. Galbert's account of a credulous but fundamentally innocent Robert strains belief; but it serves less as an exoneration of Robert than as a retrospective justification of the burgesses' stubborn support of him in the face of his evident complicity.

The roles outlined in the depiction of the conspiracy are reinforced subsequently. Isaac the Chamberlain is "the head of the treachery" (*caput traditionis*);[28] he functions as the leader of the assassination attempt, giving directions and encouragement to his fellow conspirators. Borsiard, the actual killer of the count, is portrayed as a raging psychopath, who cannot stop killing even after all the victims agreed on by his fellow conspirators have been cut down, and who has to be calmed down by his kins-

25. "Audi, amice, quasi serio facturi essemus praefatam traditionem tibi eam intimavimus ut per hoc probaremus utrum in aliquo gravi facto nobiscum velis permanere. Est quidem aliud quidam quod adhuc tibi celavimus, causa cujus obligatus es nobis fide et taxatione, quod in futuro dicemus" (Galbert, [11], 36/41; trans., 110).

26. Murray, "Voices of Flanders," 111–12; Marc Carnier, "De Goede en de heel erg slechten. De moord op Karel graaf van Vlaanderen (1127)," in *Koningsmoorden,* ed. Tom Verschaffel (Louvain, 2000), 127–41 (here 135).

27. On the course of the siege, see Marvin, "'Men Famous in Combat and Battle,'" 243–58.

28. Galbert, [28], 16; trans., 151.

men.[29] However, it is Bertulf who is the evil genius who first conceives and plots the murder of the count. He is willing to leave the actual direction of the assassination attempt to his nephew Isaac, but after the murder, it is Bertulf who arrives at the castle of Bruges to take charge of operations there and to look for support beyond Bruges.[30]

Despite the much more distinctive and multi-faceted depiction of Bertulf's kindred evident from the account of the conspiracy onward, the themes of evil, treachery, and eschatological struggle continue to be developed. One piece of evidence that is particularly illuminating in this respect is the historical excursus that makes up chapter 71 of Galbert's narrative and provides an account of the origin of the family of the provost Bertulf:

There was once a castellan in Bruges named Boldran, whose wife was called Dedda or Duva. This Boldran had a vassal and knight called Erembald, who had been born in Veurne. It happened that the Flemings were ordered to join an expedition, and in defence of their country they travelled on horseback and by ship to that dangerous place where the country was under attack. As they were sailing along the River Schelde—Boldran the castellan and Erembald, his knight whom he trusted more than anyone, as well as many others who were armoured ready for combat—night fell; they cast anchor in the middle of the water to wait for day. Now Erembald had often committed adultery with the wife of his lord, the castellan. That adulteress, so it is said, had promised her husband's office of castellan to the adulterer, if her husband should happen to die soon. From that time onward the adulterer was constantly plotting the death of his lord. And so, during the silence of the night, while the castellan was standing at the side of the ship in order to relieve himself, Erembald ran up from behind and pushed his lord into the depths of the current, far away from the ship. This happened while the others were asleep, and no-one except the adulterer knew the fate of the castellan, who had died by drowning, leaving no heirs. On his return Erembald married the adulteress, and used the wealth of his lord to purchase the office of castellan.[31]

29. Ross, "Rise and Fall of a Twelfth-Century Clan," 373–75.

30. Galbert, [8], [11], [19], [21].

31. "Boldrannus castellanus fuit in Brugis, cujus uxor erat nomine Dedda vel Duva. Hujus Boldranni homo et miles fuit Erembaldus de Furnis natus. Imperata fuit quaedam expeditio Flandrensibus, et itum est equis et navibus pro defensione patriae usque ad locum periculi et insultus terrae. Cum vero navibus prolaberent Scaldim fluvium, Boldrannus castellanus et Erembaldus miles suus, cui prae ceteris confidebat, ceterique plures omnes loricas induti et ad pugnam praeparati, venit nox et fixerant anchoram in medio amne ut diem expectarent. At praefatus ille Erembaldus adulterio abutebatur saepe uxore domini sui castellani. Illa quoque adultera, sicut aiunt, promiserat adultero suo vicecomitatum si forte vir ejus cito moreretur. Unde adulter domino suo semper machinabatur mortem. Facto quoque noctis silentio, dum castellanus ad mingendum in ora stetisset navis, ille Erembaldus retro accurrens, longe a navi

This story of adultery, betrayal, and murder is Galbert's explanation for the rise of Bertulf's family, since it enabled the traitor Erembald of Veurne to exploit the fruits of his treachery by allowing him to obtain the office of castellany of Bruges. From the marriage of Erembald and Dedda were born Bertulf and his brothers Robert (castellan of Bruges), Desiderius Hacket, Wulfric Cnop, and Lambert Nappin, all of whom except Robert were still alive in 1127.[32]

Galbert's account of Erembald raises several problems. It is placed much later than the section in which Galbert has introduced Bertulf and his nephews, and sketched their characters and their hold on power in the county.[33] Erembald is described as a "vassal and knight" (*homo et miles*) of Boldran, and is again referred to as Boldran's knight shortly afterward. Nowhere in this entire excursus is Erembald (or any of his descendants) referred to as a serf. If Erembald had indeed been of servile origin, as Galbert has previously claimed, then this would be an obvious place to reinforce this point. The story of the clandestine murder of Boldran raises even greater doubts about the accuracy of this story. The historical Erembald was in possession of the office of castellan of Bruges by 1067 at the latest, and so, if Galbert is to be believed, his treachery must have taken place at least fifty years before the murder of Charles.[34] Yet the circumstances of the murder of Boldran, on Galbert's own evidence, were hardly conducive to being known five decades later. It supposedly occurred on board ship and at dead of night, and Galbert concludes that "no-one but the adulterer knew what had become of that castellan, who had died by drowning, leaving no heirs." One must therefore ask how Galbert knows of these events: by his own testimony, the only surviving witness to the murder had no incentive to reveal his treachery.

Galbert is not the only source to give an account of the origins of Erembald of Veurne. His version of events can be compared with that given in an anonymous early twelfth-century narrative of the murder of Charles the Good, the "Passio Karoli comitis":

---

projectum dominum in profundum torrentis aquosi praecepitavit. Hoc vero dormientibus ceteris factum est et nemo praeter adulterum illum sciebat quo devinisset castellanus ille, qui absque liberis submersus erat. Reversus ergo Erembaldus, adulteram suam duxit uxorem et facultatibus opum domini sui emit vicecomitatum" (Galbert, [71], 2/22; my translation).

32. Lambert Nappin is not to be identified with Lambert, lord of Aardenburg, as much earlier scholarship believed. See Penelope Adair, "Lambert Nappin and Lambert of Aardenburg: One Fleming or Two?" *Medieval Prosopography* 11 (1990), 17–34.

33. Galbert, [7]–[13].

34. Warlop, 721.

At the time of Count Robert the Elder, the Frisian, who was also called Robert the Bearded, and who had a son called Count Robert the Younger, there was a certain castellan of Bruges named Holdran [*sic*], who had a steward by the name of Erembald, a man competent in his duties, but unfaithful to his lord, defiling his marriage-bed. This Erembald was so sunk in perversity that once, while his lord was fighting with the townspeople on one of the bridges at Bruges, he stabbed him with his sword, and in the confusion pushed him down to his death. Holdran's wife married the adulterer, the betrayer of her husband, from which it became evident that the evil deed had been caused by the counsel of the treacherous wife.[35]

There are considerable similarities between the two accounts. However, it is striking that they do not agree as to the location or circumstances of the treachery. For Galbert, the murder occurred at night, on board ship, and involved only the murderer and his victim; in the anonymous "Passio," it happened on one of the bridges of the town of Bruges, in the tumult of battle; intriguingly, both sources agree that the death of the castellan involved being pushed or cast down to his death, for which they use the same verb (*praecipitare*). This comparison does suggest, however, that by the 1120s there was at least hearsay evidence that the castellan Boldran had been betrayed, although there was less than certain knowledge about the manner in which he had met his death.

The final sentence of the above citation from the considerably less sophisticated "Passio" may well give an indication of how such stories may have arisen. If the wife of a deceased castellan went on to marry his competent steward, who then stepped into the dead man's shoes, and particularly if this had happened soon after the death, it would be an entirely natural reaction for suspicious-minded human nature to conclude—rightly or wrongly—that the two surviving parties must have been in league to do away with the deceased, and had probably been lovers into the bargain.[36] Galbert appears to signal that he is repeating hearsay; he reports that "the adulteress,

35. "Tempore Roberti Fresonis comitis seniori, qui et Robertus barbatus dictus est, habens filium Robertum comitem iuniorem, fuit Bruggis quidam pretor nomine Holdranus, habens dapiferum nomine Ermboldum, virum quidem officui gnarum, sed infidelium in dominum et ipsius domini maculantem thorum. Qui Eremboldus in tantum perversitatis deiectus est, ut ipsum dominum suum, in quodam ponte Bruggis cum populo dimicantem, interceteros mucrone confoderet, et perfossum inter tumultum in mortem precipitaret. Uxor vero Holdranni adulterum suum, mariti proditorem, accepit inmaritum, unde innotuit, quod consilio perfidae coniugis Eremboldus tam grande piaculum subiit" ("Passio Karoli comitis auctore anonymo," 620; my translation).

36. One could compare such an inference with the frequent suspicions of poisoning raised by chroniclers in the cases of many deaths of monarchs as a result of illness.

so it is said, had promised her husband's office of castellan to the adulterer," using the phrase *ut aiunt,* literally, "so they say," while his admitted uncertainty about the precise form of the name of Boldran's wife (*nomine Dedda vel Duva*) also suggests that his knowledge of this episode is sketchy.

The story of the murder of Boldran in both of these accounts has all the hallmarks of a calumny repeated to discredit the descendants of Erembald *after* their treachery toward Charles. Although Erembald figures as the ancestor of a family of traitors in the *De multro,* the story of his rise to power is not told until long after the provost Bertulf and the members of the second and third generations have been introduced. The delayed placing of this chapter within Galbert's narrative indicates that its primary purpose is a teleological one, the key to which is the use of the word "precipitation" (*praecipitatio*) to describe the casting down of Boldran from the ship. On April 19 the surviving traitors holding the castle of Bruges finally surrendered to the besieging forces, and on May 5 the majority were executed by being thrown off one of the castle towers.[37] This unusual punishment is referred to both in this context and earlier in chapter 71 by the noun *praecipitatio* and related verbal forms. Galbert is thus able to demonstrate how the evil "ancient precipitation" (*antiqua praecipitatio*) by which Erembald murdered his lord was punished by the "new precipitation" (*nova . . . praecipitatione*) of Erembald's descendants from the tower, thus proving the truth of the biblical prophecy of Exodus 20:5, that God will punish iniquities even unto the third and fourth generations.[38] However, the placing of the story suggests that the origins of Erembald of Veurne were not prominent in Galbert's mind when he began writing, and that it was only *after* the punishment of the traitors that he remembered, sought out, or was confronted with sketchy, hearsay accounts of an earlier treachery. This is further supported by his previous reference, in connection with the death of Bertulf, to "the adulterous origin of the family of the provost and his kin."[39] This phrasing indicates that at that stage the principal sin that Galbert associated with the family's origins was adultery. After the punishment of the traitors, he shifted the emphasis of the sinful origins away from the adultery of Erembald and Dedda toward the killing of Boldran, probably as a result of the influence of the precipitation.

37. Galbert, [74], 1/19; [81], 15/52.

38. Galbert, [71], 28/36.

39. "adulterinum exordium generationis praepositi et suorum" (Galbert, [57], 53/54; trans., 210).

The story of Erembald of Veurne is interesting in one further respect, although this is, in Sherlock Holmes's phrase, a dog that did not bark in the night: the designation of the family. Terms such as "the Erembald family," "the Erembald clan," or simply "the Erembalds" have long been a commonplace of scholarship on eleventh- and twelfth-century Flanders. The acute reader may have noticed that such formulations have been avoided in this essay up to this point. The reason is that there are no corresponding Latin terms in the *De multro;* this is in itself tells us something about Galbert's perceptions. When referring to the family as a whole, he tends to use the words *cognatio* and *genus.* However, the name Erembald is not used as an appellative in connection with these. In fact, the family or clan is usually designated explicitly or implicitly as a kin-group centered on the provost Bertulf, who is clearly depicted as the head of the family (*caput sui generis*).[40]

These usages are a clear indication that Galbert regards Bertulf as head of his family and the true founder of its fortunes. Provost of the church of Saint Donatian and chancellor of Flanders since 1091, he must have been at least in his sixties by the year 1127.[41] One of the earliest chapters to be composed by Galbert gives an extended account of his career:

> It was ordained by God that bold and arrogant descendants of Bertulf's ancestors should be left behind to carry out the crime of treachery. The others, prevented by death, were influential men in the fatherland in their lifetime, persons of eminence and of great wealth, but the provost passed his life among the clergy, extremely severe and not a little proud. For it was his habit when someone whom he knew perfectly well came into his presence, to dissemble, in his pride, and to ask disdainfully of those sitting near him, who that could be, and then only, if it pleased him, would he greet the newcomer. When he had sold a canonical prebend to someone he would invest him with it not by canonical election but rather by force, for not one of his canons dared to oppose him either openly or secretly. In the house of the brothers in the church of Saint Donatian the canons had formerly been deeply religious men and perfectly educated, that is, at the beginning of the provostship of this most arrogant prelate. Restraining his pride,

40. Galbert, [7], 15/16: "de illa cognatione"; [7], 39: "praepositus et cognati ejus"; [8], 10: "toto genere meo" (speech of Bertulf); [10], 10: "de cognatione praepositi"; [13], 21: "caput sui generis"; [17], 14: "illam cognationem praepositi"; [57], 48: "sui generis"; [71], 1/2: "principium generis praepositi et nepotum suorum." Users of Rider's edition should be aware that the index entries *genus (cognatio) Erembaldi* (205) are extrapolated forms rather than terms that actually occur in the text itself.

41. Warlop, 722.

they held him in check by advice and by Catholic doctrine so that he could not undertake anything unseemly in the church. But after they went to sleep in the Lord, the provost, left to himself, set in motion anything that pleased him and toward which the force of his pride impelled him. And so when he became head of his family, he tried to advance beyond everyone in the fatherland his nephews who were well brought up and finally girded with the sword of knighthood. Trying to make their reputation known everywhere, he armed his kinsmen for strife and discord; and he found enemies for them to fight in order to make it known to everyone that he and his nephews were so powerful and strong that no one in the realm could resist them or prevail against them.[42]

The opening allusion to the "audaces et praesumptuosi de sanguine praedecessorum praepositi Bertulfi" is quite strange: "bold and arrogant descendants of Bertulf's ancestors," as Ross translates it, or more literally, "bold and presumptuous men of the blood of the predecessors of the provost Bertulf." The identity of these predecessors is not specified, so that one must ask why they are mentioned at all. Galbert implies that they died before they could carry out the crime of treachery, and thus distinguishes them from the generations of Bertulf and his nephews. Galbert's formulation focuses attention on Bertulf, rather than his ancestors. This is a further indication of the relatively late subsequent insertion of the passage concerning Erembald of Veurne, since he offered a case of an ancestor who *had* committed treachery.

Galbert's unusual formulation, however, is apposite in one important respect: in a sense Bertulf is "his own ancestor," since it was he above all

42. "Ad hoc quoque traditionis facinus peragendum dispensatum est a Deo ut audaces et praesumptuosi de sanguine praedecessorum praepositi Bertulfi relinqueretur, ceteris morte praeventis, qui potentes in patria, dum viverent, fuerunt personae graves et divitiis affluebant. Sed praedictus praepositus in clero severitate gravissima degebat et non modice superbus. Nam sui moris erat quando in praesentiam ejus aliquis accessisset quem optime novisset, ut, superbia animi sui dissimulante, ex indignatione juxta se sedentes interrogaret quisnam esset ac tunc primum si placuisset ei accitum salutaret. Cum vero alicui praebendulam vendidisset canonicam, nulla electione canonica immo violenter illi investituram dedit. Non enim aliquis canonicorum suorum audebat vel tacite ipsum redarguere vel aperte. In praedicto fratrum loco ecclesiae beati Donatiani canonici valde religiosi et perfecte litterati olim, scilicet in principio praepositurae hujus arrogantissimi praelati, fuerunt qui, ejus superbiam reprimentes, consilio et doctrina catholica constrictum tenebant ne quid inhonestum in ecclesia praesumeret. Postquam vero in Domino obdormierunt, relictus sibi ille praepositus ad quidquid sibi videbatur et quo eum impetus arrogantiae impulit ferebatur. Siquidem, cum esset caput sui generis, nepotes suos admodum enutritos et tandem militia praecinctos omnibus in patria praeferre studuit et ut fama eorumdem ubicumque innotesceret laboravit, unde ad lites et seditiones cognatos suos armavit, hostes eis quos impugnarent opposuit ut sic fama per universos volaret, scilicet quantae potentiae ac virium ipse et nepotes ejus fuissent, cui nullus in regno resisteret vel praevaleret" (Galbert, [13], 1/28; trans., 114–16).

others who had brought his family to power by arranging advantageous marriages for his younger kinsmen and kinswomen and corruptly exploiting the church through the sale of offices once he was free from the restraining influence of the truly religious. Galbert later returns to the charge of traffic in church offices, which he this time explicitly refers to as simony, and it may be significant that Bertulf was married.[43] He has the main attributes of a worldly, unreconstructed pre-Gregorian cleric.

The descriptive vocabulary applied to Bertulf is also revealing. He is characterized as having "arrogance" (*arrogantia*) and being "most arrogant" (*arrogantissimus*).[44] An equally, if not more, important characteristic is pride; in the extract cited above, he is three times referred to by the words *superbus* and *superbia.*[45] From the time of Augustine, *superbia* was a sin particularly associated with Satan, whose overweening pride had led him to aspire to become like God and to rebel against him. Pride caused Satan to be cast out of Heaven, and thereafter he became the continual seducer, determined to subvert man, God's own favored creation.[46] This association seems to be crucial in Galbert's portrayal of Bertulf. His essential characteristics are pride and arrogance, which lead him to challenge and ultimately betray his master, and in doing so, to execute the work of the Devil in attempting to subvert divinely ordained authority. What is striking, however, is that Bertulf not only is shown as a tool of the Devil in the perennial struggle between good and evil, but in his characterization as full of *superbia,* is portrayed as a kind of surrogate Satan himself.

The theme of pride comes to a climax in the final depiction of Bertulf, that is, of his torture and death on April 11, 1127, which forms one of most extended pieces of dramatic writing in the *De multro.* After secretly escaping from the siege of the castle of Bruges, Bertulf had fallen into the hands of William of Ypres, the illegitimate son of Charles's half-brother. Ironically, Bertulf may have intended or hoped to install William as count after the death of Charles. However, when the struggle began to go against the conspirators, William began to distance himself from them, so much so that Galbert remarks during this chapter that William had largely succeeded in covering up his complicity, but that God ensured that the be-

43. Galbert, [57], 35/36. Chapter [46], 5/6, relates how, when Bertulf escaped from the siege of the castle of Bruges, he fled to his wife at Veurne.

44. Galbert, [8], 4; [13], 16, 20/21.

45. Galbert, [13], 6, 8, 17.

46. Cinzia Bianchi and Christof Müller, "Diabolus," in *Augustinus-Lexikon,* ed. Cornelius Mayer et al., vol. 2, fasc. 3/4 (Basel, 1999), 381–95.

trayers of Charles would be revealed and cast down. When Bertulf was apprehended, William had him tortured and executed in the market place at Ypres. In his account of the execution, Galbert rehearses the provost's vices and crimes, and enumerates all the benefits that had been bestowed upon him by God, but that had not satisfied him. Once Bertulf has been brought to the gallows, he looks to the heavens, a gesture that Galbert interprets as an invocation to God. At this point one of his torturers strikes him on the head with a stick, saying, "'Oh, you proudest of men, why do you scorn to look at us and to speak to the barons and us who have the power of destroying you?'"[47] This is a moment of high dramatic climax. At the precise instant that Bertulf seems to invoke divine mercy on the human condition, he is condemned as "the proudest of men." In Galbert's account this condemnation is spoken not by William of Ypres, Bertulf's accuser, but by a nameless member of the crowd. Throughout his work, some of Galbert's most profound oral statements are pronounced not by important, highly placed individuals, but by anonymous members of the commonality.[48] It is this common voice that damns Bertulf as the proudest of men, the perpetrator of the diabolic sin par excellence.

Bertulf is then strung up on a gibbet, at which point William of Ypres calls for silence, and in the midst of the assembled crowd calls on Bertulf to name those who were guilty of the murder of his lord. Bertulf replies only, "'You know as well as I!'" a retort that only enrages William, who orders that Bertulf should be stoned and stabbed to death.[49] This dramatic moment may well be a reflection of historical reality. In such a case Bertulf's terse but ingenious answer would have given nothing away that might be used against his kinsmen and allies, but at the same time implicated his accomplice turned accuser for all to hear. However, at the level of Galbert's eschatological understanding of unfolding events, Bertulf's last words reveal a providential working by which one of the traitors reveals the complicity of another who had almost succeeded in covering it up.

Bertulf's reply also marks him out from his other kinsmen. During the extended account of the provost's torture and execution, Galbert speculates on his thoughts as he goes to his death, giving a detailed catalogue of the many sins and crimes that Bertulf had committed during the thirty-six

47. "'O superbissime hominum, cur indignaris respicere et loqui principibus et nobis qui habent potestatem perdendi te?'" (Galbert, [57], 61/62; trans., 210).

48. On this, see Murray, "Voices of Flanders."

49. "'Aeque tu, sicut et ego, nosti'" (Galbert, [57], 79/80; trans., 211).

years in which he had held high secular and clerical office and that "he could indeed have remembered, if he had wished."[50] We have already seen the importance of the theme of penitence in the eschatological framework set out at the very beginning of the *De multro.* There Galbert records how the agents of the Devil refuse to heed God's admonitions, and in his discussion of the aftermath of the conspiracy the question of the penitence of those complicit in it is such an important one that he devotes a complete chapter to it, a comparative account that brings together events that had occurred at different places and times. Galbert sets great stress on the fact that while Isaac, Borsiard, and even Robert *Puer* all confess their guilt and even express penitence, Bertulf alone fails to do this.[51]

It is largely because of the testimony of Galbert that subsequent ages have viewed the clan of Bertulf as scheming traitors, bent on overthrowing authority, rather than as desperate men forced into violence as a last resort in the face of an implacable enemy determined to consign them to servility. We need therefore to be deeply suspicious of judgments on the family that rely on his evidence; rather, we should ask why Galbert chose to portray the clan of Bertulf in such diabolic terms. After all, by the time that he completed his account, its power had been smashed; most of its members and allies had been punished or fled from Flanders. In Galbert's understanding, the members of Bertulf's clan had attempted to overthrow divine-ordained order on earth by murdering their lord. Furthermore—at least for a time—they had successfully duped Galbert's fellow citizens, the burgesses of Bruges, into lending them comfort and support. Undoubtedly he had an interest in their exoneration, but to him the fact that the citizenry had been deceived may have only constituted further proof of diabolic intervention. The *De multro, traditione, et occisione gloriosi Karoli comitis Flandriarum* shows us Galbert of Bruges attempting to make sense of God's purpose and to impose order and meaning on the terrible events he was witnessing. He responded to political crisis, as many of his contemporaries and predecessors had done, with an Augustinian interpretation of history, which reveals how his gradual understanding of the events he was witnessing was built by him into a sophisticated eschatological narrative in which Bertulf's kin are unmasked as agents of the Devil: deceivers, betrayers, and destroyers of God's creation.

50. "Poterat quidem reminisci, si debuit" (Galbert, [57], 32; trans., 209).
51. Galbert, [84].

9

Death from a Trivial Cause

Events and Their Meanings in Galbert of Bruges's *Chronicle*

ROBERT M. STEIN

This essay reconsiders the very large problem of historical explanation in Galbert of Bruges's chronicle by looking at some moments where Galbert reports events that have obvious symbolic significance, in fact, symbolic significance intended by their makers as part of the urban spectacle.[1] In reporting these events Galbert necessarily has to take a position regarding them since the events themselves often have a polemical purpose. At times he reads the events as their makers intend them to be read; at other times he either deflects or even omits any suggestion of significance. I will argue that these omissions constitute a direct, conscious, and legible refusal to read the signs. And let me underline "legible" here, because I think the conclusion is inescapable that Galbert's audience would recognize Galbert's refusal of meaning, and know what to make of it.[2] I realize that this is going to be a difficult argument to make, for I will ultimately need to draw attention to a silence. And not even a total silence, but rather the silence of an implication, a process of silencing, of deflection of signification away from a strongly anticipated direction, a direction that Galbert's text

1. A version of this paper was read at the annual meeting of the Medieval Academy of America, New York, March 5, 2002. I want to thank the participants in the session for their comments and questions. My preliminary research on Galbert of Bruges was made possible by a grant from the National Endowment for the Humanities.

2. Just whom Galbert thought he was writing for has vexed scholarship since the time of Pirenne. For a survey of the literature addressed to this question see Rider, *God's Scribe,* 74–76. Rider sensibly concludes that Galbert anticipated an audience of mixed status comprising the aristocrats who frequented the comital court, his fellow clerical intellectuals, and the urban bourgeoisie.

simultaneously indicates and disavows. I will therefore spend the first part of this essay discussing places where Galbert's operations with symbolic material are fairly obvious before concluding with the more difficult, but of course also more interesting, possibilities.

Let me start therefore with the most direct evidence that I can find, however small and incidental to the larger question that I want to pursue: Galbert's notice of the fire at Isaac's house. For regarding this passage we possess the direct testimony of a medieval reader, the fifteenth-century French translator of Galbert's chronicle, part of whose translation survives.[3] In the vernacular rendition of the scene the translator supplies precisely what I am calling the "missing" implication from Galbert. Isaac, a party to the assassination, flees with his whole household. An armed band goes to his abandoned house, plunders it, and now I quote Galbert:

> Finally, by placing burning torches under the roofs they set fire to the house and farm buildings, and whatever they found there that could be destroyed by fire. Everyone who saw it marveled at how exceedingly quickly everything was destroyed by the fanning and fomenting of the winds and the mad fury of the fire, for such a big building and such a large amount of wood had never before been so quickly consumed.[4]

And here is the vernacular translation:

> a la fin bouté le fu dedans et gasté tout ce que le feu povoit consummer. Laquelle maison incrediblement tost a esté gastee par le grand vent, et disoient pour vray les presentz que la soubite destruction estoit en vengeance du grand mesfaict du possesseur.[5]

This little example concerns the reading of what medieval commentators from Augustine on called a natural sign.[6] In the French translation, the speed and vehemence of the fire makes legible the moral dimension of the act and

3. Hannover, Niedersächsisische Landesbibliothek, 1499.

4. "Tandem faculis igneis tectis suppositis incenderunt domus et curtes et quaecumque igne consumi poterant ibidem reperta, quae quam citissime omnia conflatione et ventorum fomentis et insania tempestatis ignis destructa sunt, omnium admiratione testificatum est, scilicet nihil tanti aedificii et lignorum tam celerem passum fuisse adnihilationem" (Galbert, [30], 13/19; trans., 157).

5. The surviving portion of this translation can be found on the pages facing the corresponding Latin text in Rider's edition of Galbert. This passage is found on Galbert, 40.

6. For the definition of natural signs as things of nature that nevertheless signify other things, see Saint Augustine, *On Christian Doctrine,* trans. D. W. Robertson (Indianapolis, 1958), 8. On the significance of natural signs for historiography in the age of the Gregorian Reform see my "Signs and Things: The Vita Heinrici IV Imperatoris and the Crisis of Interpretation in Twelfth Century History," *Traditio* 43 (1987): 105–19.

of the actors involved, a leap from the visible to an invisible significance, from the force of "the great wind" and "incredible speed" of the destruction, that is, to the moral realm of vengeance enacted for the "great misdeed" that had been committed. It is precisely this leap that Galbert's narrative refuses at this point to make; it remains rather at the level of natural description—the marvel is not the manifestation of justice but simply how fast the house is consumed. Remaining at this level is an important part of the effect of transparency in Galbert's narrative, the sense that we readers are in the presence of a consummate observer who will not go beyond the evidence in what he reports. I will return to the question of narrative transparency and its relation to the particular concerns and operations of Galbert's historiography in a moment.

To be sure, although Galbert's chronicle is for the most part organized annalistically, reporting one thing after another from day to day as they seem to have happened, he is nevertheless throughout the chronicle concerned with finding a significance to the day-to-day accumulation of events. Jeff Rider has drawn attention to the providential pattern that Galbert shapes his events to demonstrate, a pattern based on the combination of the Petrine injunction to obey all secular authority, and Exodus 20:5, "I am a jealous god who punishes iniquity even to the third and fourth generation."[7] Galbert's particular deployment of these texts is unusual in the twelfth century, where forms of biblical exegesis, and especially among them typology, are typically used to construct the signifying structure of the historian's narrative.[8] Thus, for example, Orderic Vitalis treats the victorious Normans of 1066 as God's new Israel, thus making the significance of the spread of Norman hegemony in England and southern Italy arise

7. "ego sum Dominus Deus tuus fortis zelotes visitans iniquitatem patrum in filiis in tertiam et quartam generationem." In his prologue, 41/43 (trans., 80), Galbert quotes a version of 1 Pt 2:13–14: "Let every soul be subject to every power, either to the king as supreme or to governors as sent by God" (*Omnis anima omni poetestati subjecta sit, sive regi tamquam praecellenti sive ducibus tamquam a Deo missis*). The vulgate text reads: "Be subject for the Lord's sake to every human institution, whether it be to the emperor as supreme, or to the governors as sent by him" (subiecti estote omni humanae creaturae propter Dominum sive regi quasi praecellenti sive ducibus tamquam ab eo missis). This text is always connected to Rom 13:1: "Let every person be subject to the governing authorities. For there is no authority except from God, and those that exist have been instituted by God" (omnis anima potestatibus sublimioribus subdita sit non est enim potestas nisi a Deo quae autem sunt a Deo ordinatae sunt).

8. See Robert W. Hanning, *The Vision of History in Early Britain* (New York, 1966), and my "Making History English: Cultural Identity and Historical Explanation in William of Malmesbury and Laȝamon's *Brut*," in *Text and Territory: Geographical Imagination in the European Middle Ages*, ed. Sealy Gilles and Sylvia Tomasch (Philadelphia, 1998), 97–115, and "Signs and Things."

from a secret but legible relation between present circumstance and biblical precedent. I note in passing that the meditation on legitimate power and tyranny through the use of the particular biblical texts that Galbert uses, unusual if not unprecedented in twelfth-century historiography, will reemerge in exactly the same combination of texts as an important explanatory device among writers in Elizabethan England, a historical reemergence that may not be precisely a coincidence.[9]

In this essay, I am particularly interested not in such uses of sacred history or even of the presence in historical narrative of natural occurrences read as moral signifiers or portents, but rather in Galbert's treatment of the kind of deliberate symbolic activity that the city itself invites.[10] Throughout the events following the assassination of Count Charles, people hang banners, toll bells, sound trumpets. They exact spectacular vengeance—legal, quasi-legal, and illegal—all in public display. The city becomes a theater where scenes of public activity directly intended by its participants to be meaningful are staged. Among these are, for example, the elaborately staged public rituals of homage, fealty, and investiture and Galbert's wonderful descriptions of "defiance" (*exfestucatio*) that balance them, from which we all have learned so much about legal forms and public ritual in the twelfth century.[11] Galbert is generous, too, in his representations of festive scenes such as the arrival of William in Saint-Omer. The new count, we remember, is met outside the town by a band of boys "pretending they were going to resist, girded and ready with drawn bows." They demand the "fief" that boys had formerly obtained from his predecessors: "It is our right to acquire this privilege from you, that is, on feast days of the saints and in the summer time to wander freely about the woodland glades, to snare small birds, to shoot arrows at squirrels and foxes, and spend our time in boyish play of this kind."[12] In these descriptions the content of

9. See Josephine Waters Bennett, *Studies in the English Renaissance Drama* (London, 1961).

10. Urban spectacle in the later middle ages has been much studied. A useful starting point is Barbara Hanawalt and Kathryn Reyerson, *City and Spectacle in Medieval Europe* (Minneapolis, 1994). See also Bailey K. Young, "The Lively and the Dead in Medieval European Towns," *Journal of Urban History* 25 (1998): 144–49; Louise O. Aranye Fradenburg, *City, Marriage, Tournament: Arts of Rule in Late Medieval Scotland* (Madison, 1991).

11. See especially the researches of R. C. Van Caenegem. They are surveyed and listed in Rider, *God's Scribe,* 7.

12. "quasi per pugnam resistere simulantes, succincti et praeparati arcubus intensis . . . 'Quatenus feodum quod a praedecessoribus tuis semper pueri nostri obtinuerant, hoc a te obtinere juris erat nostris, circa nemorum saltus in festis sanctorum et aestatis tempore licenter vagari, aviculas capere, spiriolos et vulpes sagittare et hujusmodi puerilia recreando satagere'" (Galbert, [66], 6/7, 10/15; trans., 228).

scenes of ritual performance is contributory to the signifying form of Galbert's own chronicle. The ethical significances of the performance of social bonds and their violent disruptions that the rituals enact themselves serve the historiographical pattern by which Galbert intends to signify the meaning of the assassination and its aftermath.

These are so far examples of behavior whose meanings are public, explicit, and uncontested. Galbert's narrative is also shaped by the implicit significance of things—landscapes, interiors, architecture among them. Consider for example the descriptions of the conspirators' meetings in closed rooms, or of Bertulf's wandering, betrayed, in a wilderness.[13] Or this, the description of the rebuilt church of Saint Donatian with its tuile roof: "From this place it dominated the scene in the splendor of its beauty like the throne of the realm; in the midst of the fatherland it called for safety and justice everywhere in the land through security and peace, right and laws."[14] In this passage concrete physical description is left far behind, as Galbert moves into the register of secular homily: the besieged church becomes a sign embodying in its very materiality the breach in the social world that the count's assassination has created. Galbert's ability to wed moral evaluation so closely to description—and most often, this means to supply a conventionalized moral evaluation—makes in large part for the absolutely transparent appearance of his narrative: generations of readers, both ordinary readers and professionally skeptical historians, feel that his text provides a clear window through which we can see the world of 1127 in action. In contrast, Walter of Therouanne's contemporary *Vita Karoli comitis Flandrię* is marked by exactly the sort of rhetorical interjections that Galbert avoids. In these interjections, Walter directly instructs his audience about the meaning of events (along the lines of "you can behold in this how . . .").[15] What such rhetorical interjection does is place the moral

13. In *Medieval French Literature and the Law* (Berkeley and Los Angeles, 1977), R. Howard Bloch has drawn attention to the significance in the custumals of Beauvais of interiors and wilderness, the places of secrecy, for the legal definition of *meurtre.*

14. "Unde honestatis suae fulgore praeeminebat velut regni sedes, et in medio patriae securitate et pace, jure et legibus undique terrae partibus salutem et justitiam demandans" (Galbert, [37], 11/14; trans., 167).

15. For one example of Walter's rhetorical interventions in the narrative among many, see Walter, [27], 3/6: "But now it is right that the pen stray a bit from the events of the narration and to consider however briefly the enormity of such a great crime and the most cruel inhumanity of these criminals" (Sed iam libet stilum a narrationis serie parumper declinare et enormitatem tanti facinoris ac facinorosorum illorum crudelissimam inmanitatem pro modo nostro uel tenuiter considerare; my translation). Walter proceeds from here to address the characters in the narrative directly, asking the five questions that famously gave James Bruce Ross

evaluation directly in the mouth of the writer, who provides a reading lesson for his audience. Galbert's avoidance of such well-marked moralizing does not mean that he is not interested in communicating the moral significance—indeed, what he would no doubt call the truth—as he sees it, of the events of his narrative, but it is a way of making this truth seem to arise from the things themselves without the mediating, directive intervention of the writer. This narrative practice, recommended throughout the classical rhetoricians' discussions of the *narratio* in forensic oratory, is thus an important key to the rich texture of Galbert's historiography.[16]

So far, the acts I have spoken about have had relatively uncontested symbolic meanings: everyone present at a defiance agrees about the meaning of breaking the bonds of homage and fealty; however, most of the symbolic activity that fills Galbert's chronicle is in fact not of this unequivocal sort but rather is performed in a highly contested field, often intended to win over a divided company of spectators, and performed as well in a state of emergency. And it is performed above all not by Galbert but by the characters of his narrative. That is to say, the meaning of Count Charles's assassination is neither given at the outset nor understood once for all but rather continuously created by the assassins and their avengers throughout their interactions with one another, and this continuous creation is often the result of deliberate activity intended to sway the sympathies of urban onlookers, interested parties, and perhaps sometimes even a certain posterity. In this process, Galbert—and here I name something that we come to know only as a textual function, a trace present in the language and structure of the chronicle and yet one who had real existence during the unfolding of the events—Galbert is never a static, all-knowing source of meaning as he narrates the events taking place around him, but he is rather engaged in a continuous, dynamic acceptance and rejection of meanings that others are constantly in the process of making and he of reporting. The operation of

the organization of her magisterial introduction. In the course of the address Walter compares their behavior, as he has already done in [14], 15/20, "to the crime of your ancestors, the detestable Jews" (facinori patrum uestrorum detestabilium Iudeorum; [27], 13/14). I do not think it clearly out of the question that Walter might mean these remarks to imply that the Erembald family is itself literally of Jewish ancestry.

16. Galbert's familiarity with the techniques of forensic oratory was stressed by Heinrich Sproemberg, one of Galbert's best readers. See the four essays reprinted in Heinrich Sproemberg, "Galbert von Brügge—Die Geschichtsschreibung des Flandrischen Bürgertums," in Sproemberg, *Mittelalter und demokratische Geschichtsschreibung,* ed. Manfred Unger, Lily Sproemberg, and Wolfgang Eggert, Forschungen zur mittelalterlichen Geschichte 18 (Berlin, 1971) 223–272, especially the posthumously published essay from 1961, "Galbert von Brügge—Persönlichkeit und Werk," 239–77.

the reality effect of Galbert's chronicle is inseparable in this case from what we can call, following Foucault, the "truth effects" of his narrative.[17] And these effects arise, I am suggesting, from both what Galbert assents to and what he refuses to understand, what meanings, or more correctly operations of meaningfulness, in the social world he directly resists even as he reports their performance. Perhaps here we can understand the profound significance of Galbert's departure from the procedures of meaning-making that we come to expect in twelfth-century historiographical practice. The discovery of typological patterns and the explication of events as miraculous signs all have the effect of installing the historian as the sole source of historical meaning: he is the ultimate reader of divine signification, the voice of the divine judgment, and he reports this judgment as the truth of the events. Galbert presents himself as a historical authority not by means of his access to typological understanding but by actively intervening in a continuous process of meaning-making by the historical agents themselves. For he is himself, as an eyewitness, part of the audience that the historical actors intend to influence. The pattern of history that Galbert will ultimately assert as the truth of what has taken place is guaranteed by seeming to arise in his narrative directly from the events and their consequences, whereas it in effect arises from a continual transaction between the events and their contested self-representation. That this appearance is the result of careful and deliberate narrative construction can never be overstated.

* * *

Let me begin again with a place where Galbert's assent to meaning is clear. A week after the assassination, Galbert describes a series of acts of vengeance in open battle:

> The knight Didier, brother of Isaac the traitor hurled him [a knight named George who was in league with Charles's assassins] from his horse and cut off both his hands. (This Didier, although he was the brother of the traitor, was not, however, an accessory to the plot.) That most wretched George, his hands cut off, fled to a place where he hoped to hide but he was immediately denounced to a certain Walter . . . and dragged out. The knight, sitting on his horse, ordered a fierce young swordsman to kill him. The latter rushed at George, struck him with his sword and knocked him to the ground; then, dragging him by his feet into a sewer, he saw to it that he drowned for his evil deserts.[18]

17. See Michel Foucault, "Truth and Power," in *Power/Knowledge: Selected Interviews and Other Writings, 1972–1977,* ed. Colin Gordon (New York, 1980), 109–33.

18. "Quem Desiderius miles, frater Isaac traditoris, equo dejecit et ei utrasque manus trun-

And slightly later in the same chapter:

Another one taken was the most evil of Borsiard's serfs, Fromold by name, who in his flight had hidden between two mattresses, dressed in a woman's cloak as a disguise. Pulled out, he was taken to the middle of the market and, in the sight of all, hanged with a stick thrust through his shanks and shins, and his head bent down so that his shameful parts, his behind and buttocks, were turned toward the castle to the disgrace and ignominy of the traitors who were standing attentively on the balcony of the count's house and on the towers watching this done to dishonor them.[19]

Here Galbert aligns himself directly with the avengers. The first passage sketches a process of revelation. Twice it traces a movement from inside to outside, from a hiding place into the light of public witness, where the truth of criminality is made known, acknowledged, and avenged: the conspirator George emerges from the interior of the castle, is pursued, and has his hands cut off, a manifest sign because a legal sanction of his treason.[20] The action is then repeated with only a slight variation: dragged out of a second hiding place, he is knocked down, and then drowned in a sewer. The significance of his second punishment as a sign of treason is proclaimed in free indirect discourse ("he saw to it that he drowned for his evil deserts"). In the second passage, the avengers themselves rewrite Fromold's implicit sexual transgression—he had dressed as a woman to make a getaway—as a scene of explicit sexual degradation. The whole scene is performed before the conspirators, who like an audience in the upper gallery, view a performance aimed directly at them.

There are many such similar scenes of symbolic activity—often involving spectacular punishment—in which Galbert's own positioning is clear. More difficult are those places where Galbert resists meanings implied by

cavit. Hic Desiderius, quamvis frater traditoris fuisset, non tamen conscius traditionis fuerat. Fugerat truncatis manibus in locum ille miserrimus Georgius in quo se sperabat latere, sed statim accusatus cuidam Waltero . . . extrahitur. Nam sedens in equo miles ille praecepit cuidam juveni gladiatori ferocissimo ut occideret. At ille irruens in Georgium, percussit gladio et dejecit eum in terram. Deinde per pedes in cloacarium projectum submergi ex malo merito suo gladiator ille coegit" (Galbert, [29], 7/16; trans., 154).

19. "Interceptus est quoque quidam nefandissimus servorum Borsiardi, Fromoldus nomine, qui fugiens latuerat inter duas culcitras, indutus superpellicium mulieris quo se dissimularet. At inde retractus, ductus est in medium fori et, inspectantibus universis, suspensus est, fuste transfixo per suffragines et crura, capite dejecto deorsum, ita ut verecundiora, scilicet culus et nates, adverterentur versus castrum ad dedecus et ignominiam illorum traditorum qui obsessi stabant ad lobium comitis et ad propugnacula, inspectantes hoc fieri sibi ipsis in opprobrium" (Galbert, [29], 18/27; trans., 154–55).

20. Cf. Walter, [43], 8/12, for cutting off hands as a punishment for treason.

the makers of the scene. Among these I would include the famous and troublesome description of the exile, capture, and death of the provost Bertulf. Bertulf, whom Galbert considers one of the most guilty of the assassins, attracts to himself narrative motifs of pathos, betrayal, torture, suffering, and penitence that force inescapably christological significances on his death, significances that Galbert seems to toy with, and to assert even as he denies them.[21] The execution is presided over by William of Ypres, an unjust judge, and takes place in the midst of the marketplace, among a violent crowd, out of control and clamoring for Bertulf's death. It is in this light that I think we may consider the difficult climax of the scene: "Then the people of Ypres, thirsting for the death of the provost, twisted the viscera of a dog around his neck, and placed the muzzle of a dog next to his mouth, now drawing its last breath, thus likening him and his deeds to a dog."[22] James Bruce Ross suggests that Galbert may be unaware of "the persistence here of elements of old Germanic ritual."[23] I think it is equally likely that Galbert may be pretending ignorance, resisting the legal legitimacy of the whole execution. For evil as he considers Bertulf, he also resists any claims to the authority of William of Ypres, who, he even implies in this scene, may himself have been instrumental in the conspiracy.

Similar is Galbert's very equivocal discussions of the conspirators' treatment of Charles's body. Galbert reports their keeping a continuously burning candle at the head of his tomb, "although they scarcely called to mind the lord whom they had betrayed," and in the same place mentions that "they had laid out around the tomb of the count the flour and legumes which they consumed daily to sustain life."[24] Later, in a less revised portion of the text, Galbert writes:

It should be noted that after Count Charles was killed, Borsiard and his accomplices in the crime, on the night when Count Charles was first buried, followed the custom of pagans and sorcerers. Taking a vessel full of beer, and bread, they

21. See Galbert [46] and [57]; the preceding essay in this volume by Alan V. Murray; and Rider, *God's Scribe,* 108–11.

22. "Iprensium igitur turba, furens in mortem praepositi, canis viscera contorserat circa collum ejus et os canis ad os ejus jam vitalem spiritum expirantis opposuerunt aequiparantes cani ipsum et facta ipsius" (Galbert, [57], 90/93; trans., 211–12). In his *Vita Ludovici,* Suger transforms this into a scene of unequivocal torture, saying that the citizens hung a live dog face to face with Bertulf and that it continually bit him as they both were dying (Suger, 30, p. 248).

23. See Ross, trans., 212n11.

24. "quod vix dominum suum recognoscentes quem tradiderant . . . . farinam et legumina circa tumbam comitis reposuerant, quibus quotidie in usus suos assumptis vitam continuabant" (Galbert, [60], 22/23, 26/28; trans., 217–18).

sat around the tomb and placed that drink and bread on the top of the tomb as if it were a table, eating and drinking over the body of the dead count in the belief that no one could in any way avenge him.[25]

Some scholars have explained this behavior as a ritual of reparation to appease the soul of the dead;[26] Galbert may be dissimulating here, too. The first time he mentions food in connection with the tomb he merely comments on its physical location and is silent about any possibility that the food might be there for a ritual purpose. The candle is mentioned again after the besiegers break through a wall of the church with the battering ram, and the besieged conspirators abandon the gallery and flee to the tower. Here the text moves through a variety of genres—starting with the description of the siege in heroic language and passing through a passage attributing base motives to the besiegers (a passage to which we will return shortly) to culminate in a lament, a formal *planctus* for the dead count Charles, modeled in its language very closely on parts of the Easter Office.[27] Here again, the conspirators are said to have placed a candle at the head of the tomb, "in honor and veneration of their lord."[28] What pulls Galbert in this direction, a direction that otherwise contradicts the whole sense of the conspiracy as he presents it in the text, is the force of a complex and contradictory desire provoked directly by the situation that gave rise to the assassination and the political events following it, not least the rise to power in Flanders of the Norman prince William Clito and the opposition to him on the part of several of the most important towns in the territory.[29]

As he narrates the events following the assassination of Charles, the

25. "Notandum quod, occiso comite Karolo, Borsiardus et sui sceleris participes more paganorum et incantatorum, nocte qua primo sepultus erat comes Karolus, accepterunt cyphum plenum cervisiae et panem, considentes circa sepulchrum, posuerunt potum illum et panem in mensa sepulchri, edentes et bibentes super beati comitis corpus ea fide ut nullo modo illum quis vindicaret" (Galbert, [90], 5/11; trans., 263).

26. See Ross, trans., 263n4.

27. Ross, trans., 224–225n1. On the *planctus* see Carolyn Cohen, "Les éléments constitutifs de quelques *Planctus* des Xe et XIe siècles," *Cahiers de Civilisation Médiévale, X^e–XIIe Siècles* 1 (1958): 83–86.

28. "in honorem et venerationem domini sui" (Galbert, [64], 23; trans., 225).

29. Sproemberg notes the important alliance between the Flemish cloth makers and England, the source of their wool. While never analyzing the international significance of the assassination of Charles the Good, Galbert rather consistently places himself in opposition to the anti-English political maneuvers of the king of France that had the effect of enhancing the power of the Flemish aristocracy to the detriment of the urban bourgeoisie. See Sproemberg, "Galbert von Brügge—Die Geschichtsschreibung des flandrischen Bürgertums."

providential pattern of vengeance is shadowed by an alternative, secular version of vengeance that Galbert both evokes and disavows, the aristocratic self-celebration of its own power in chivalry and heroism.[30] I suggest that we understand this shadowing as a kind of intertextuality, a strong relation between Galbert's chronicle and the *chanson de geste,* particularly the texts of the so-called cycle of revolt. Several of these texts are set in the very territory in question in Galbert's chronicle, urbanized Flanders and its neighboring territories—the Artois, the Vexin, the Cambresis—and they turn on some of the same questions of power that are at stake in the assassination and the difficult succession after the death of Charles—contested election, the relation between the king and his vassals, contradictions between election and hereditary right, the strained relations between the traditions of local power and the state-making intentions of distant authority.[31]

Again the French translator provides us with a way to open this question. By translating Galbert's characterization of Baldwin VII as an *adolescens fortissimus* ("extraordinarily brave youth") by *qui estoit encore jeusne homme tres vaillant* ("who was still a most valiant young man"), he thoroughly reinscribes Galbert's classical republican terms of praise into exactly the register of aristocratic value that Galbert evokes and resists.[32] Galbert's

30. Jeff Rider points out that "the aristocracy is the most individuated group in the *De Multro,*" strong evidence for Rider that Galbert, as a notary in the comital administration, "spent a great deal of time in secular administrative circles" (*God's Scribe,* 19), and, I would add, strong evidence that Galbert was well aware of aristocratic behavior and modes of self-presentation.

31. Most to my point is, of course, *Raoul de Cambrai,* but examples are too numerous to cite. See Robert M. Stein, *Reality Fictions: Romance, History, and Governmental Authority 1025–1180* (Notre Dame, 2006), 161–206; see also Sarah Kay, *The Chansons de Geste in the Age of Romance: Political Fictions* (Oxford, 1995).

32. Galbert, [1], 9; trans., 82. The translator's reinscription into chivalric praise of what in Galbert is either neutral or carried by the range of reference of his classical Latinity is fairly widespread in the text. Galbert's comment about the death of Charles, for example—"Now it should be known what a noble man and distinguished ruler those impious and inhuman serfs betrayed" (Et sciendum quam nobilem virum et egregium consularem tradiderunt servi impiissimi et inhumani; [12], 22/23; trans., 112)—provokes what appears to be a long *amplificatio* that contains a paraphrase of the Latin original, saturated with the language of chivalric value: "Similarly, having heard about the nobility, goodness and prudence of the good Count Charles, and, on the contrary, of the falseness, malice and pride of the evil traitors, you will understand easily the indignity of what occurred and why the whole world was troubled, for good reason, when his evil and inhuman serfs, the enemies of God and men, betrayed so vilely such a noble man, an altogether excellent and paternal governor" (Pareillement, ouy la noblesse, bonté et prudence du bon conte Charles et, ou contraire, la faulseté, malice et orgueil des meschants treistres, entenderés facilement la indignité du cas advenu et que non pas sans cause le

narration of the siege of the castle, into which the conspirators and their allies have been driven, constantly oscillates between evoking aristocratic heroism—often enacted by non-noble participants—and denying it. Conflicts characteristic of the *chanson de geste* between the king and his barons, between the barons and the lesser nobility, and above all between the demands of feudal obligation and kin loyalty are played out continually. Finally, all such matter is written out of the story, as Galbert changes register completely to conclude the episode. Let me remind you of the moment when the battering ram has finally broken through the wall of the church:

> But when the drivers of the ram, and other knights of the king, and the young men of our place, armed and avid for conflict, finally saw the besieged opposite them, they summoned all their courage. They may have been picturing in their mind's eye how noble it would be to die for father and fatherland, and what an honorable victory was set before the conquerors, and how infamous and criminal those traitors had been who had made a den for themselves out of the church of Christ, but in fact it seems more likely that they were intent on rushing against the besieged because they were avid and greedy to seize the treasure and money of the lord count, and that for this reason alone they were hastening forward.[33]

Aristocratic heroic motives are evoked only to be immediately rejected out of hand in favor of greed.[34] Galbert's treatment of the scene of trial by combat between Guy of Steenvoorde and Herman the Iron provides us with a similar example. Here the aristocratic legal process is emptied of legal meaning. Galbert, who probably creates the scene out of whole cloth, narrates it as a messy and bloody affair where the exhausted participants throw away their weapons and wrestle. In the process Guy of Steenvoorde, we remember, is defeated not by strength but by cleverness. To narrate the defeat Galbert employs one of the only self-conscious classical allusions in the narrative:

---

monde en estoit tourblé quant tel noble, homme tout excellent et paternel gouverneur, ses serfz meschantz et inhhumains, ennemis a Dieu et aux hommes, tant vilainement ont trahy). See also Galbert, [15], 27/30.

33. "At quidem illi exactores arietis et ceteri milites regis et loci nostri juvenes armati et audaces avidique pugnae, cum ex adverso inspexissent obsessos, jam animos revocaverant suos, prae oculis cordis habentes quam egregie pro patre et patria moriendum foret et quam honesta victoria vincentibus praeposita esset, quamque scelesti et facinorosi fuissent traditores illi qui de templo Christi speluncam sibi fecissent, et, quod magis videbatur, quam avide et cupide propter thesauri et pecuniae domini consulis rapinam irruerent super obsessos ipsi et idcirco solummodo festinabant" (Galbert, [63], 42/52; trans., 223–24).

34. On this passage, see also Rider, *God's Scribe,* 126–27.

Herman the Iron fell prostrate on the ground, and Guy was lying on top of him smashing the knight's face and eyes with his iron gauntlets. But Herman, prostrate, little by little regained his strength from the coolness of the earth, as we read of Antaeus, and by cleverly lying quiet made Guy believe he was certain of victory. Meanwhile, gently moving his hand down to the lower edge of the cuirass where Guy was not protected, Herman seized him by the testicles, and summoning all his strength for the brief space of one moment he hurled Guy from him; by this tearing motion all the lower parts of the body were broken so that Guy, now prostrate, gave up, crying out that he was conquered and dying.[35]

The allusion to Antaeus, as well as the victory through *ingenium,* provides a serious alternative to the world where aristocratic heroism can be read legally as divine judgment. In the similar scene of trial by combat that closes the *Chanson de Roland,* Charlemagne's Thierry, although remarkably overmatched, defeats the huge and powerful Pinabel, and does so cleanly with a powerful single blow that kills Pinabel outright.[36] Justice in this famous text is made manifest precisely by heroic strength, and it is all the more manifestly just because unanticipated and otherwise unexplainable. In the chronicle, something entirely other than justice is made manifest. Indeed, when William of Ypres has Guy's defeated body hung on the same gallows with Bertulf, "bending their arms around each other's necks as if in mutual embrace," Galbert reports this public proclamation of guilt as a disculpating gesture on William's part—William, he says, wished "above all to look after his own reputation in this fight."[37] Galbert contests the meaning of the sign.

The mention of the *Chanson de Roland* brings me to my final example, which has provided me with the title of my essay. The count's assassination took place on March 2, and Galbert's chronicle continues from that point to May and then breaks off, resuming in mid-September with the capture of William of Ypres and the report of the new count's inquest into the assassination. As the legal proceedings begin, Galbert inserts two chapters

35. "Et cecidit ille Hermannus Ferreus in terram prostratus, cui Wido incumbebat maniculis ferreis ora et oculos contundens militis. At ille prostratus, sicut legitur de Antheo, a frigiditate terrae vires paulatim resumpsit et callide dum quiesceret Widonem de victoria securum reddidit. Interim manum suavius subducens usque ad inferiores loricae oras, in qua parte non fuerat Wido praemunitus, per testiculos raptum, collectis viribus ad puncti unius momentum a se propulit, in quo rapticio pulsu tota de subtus natura corporis rupta, ita prostratus defecit Wido ut victum et mortuum se fore exclamaret" (Galbert, [58], 20/30; trans., 212–13).

36. See *La Chanson de Roland,* laisse 286, ed. and French trans. Ian Short (Paris, 1990), 272.

37. "per omnia famae suae in hoc bello consulere . . . brachiaque mutuis quasi amplexibus ad colla flectentes" (Galbert, [58], 30/31, 36/37; trans., 213).

reporting divine justice taking place at the same time against some of the most powerful lords in Flanders. Among them are Walter of Vladslo, who was thrown from his horse "while he was on a certain knightly expedition" and died a lingering and painful death,[38] and Baldwin of Aalst, who, "in the full strength of life, . . . died from a trivial cause, that is, while he was blowing a horn." After a paragraph of physiological description, explaining how "the inner parts which had lain in the brain boiled up" as a result of the pressure from blowing the horn and burst from an old wound, Galbert proceeds to a description of extreme political and moral complexity: "they were remembered and discussed by the inhabitants of the land; they talked about the sudden death of those whom God had deprived of life after the death of lord Charles by such a swift sentence and had ordained that they should die from such trivial causes." Their guilt is compounded by their treatment of their own allies in the conspiracy, for these men also took money from the provost to help him and his family escape, and then abandoned them in the wilderness "destitute and solitary . . . until they were seized" and died "the most wretched kind of death."[39] In these deaths, Roland's horn and the whole world of aristocratic praise and memorialization is evoked precisely in order to be read out of the story. Whatever scale of value is being employed here, and there are several of them simultaneously in operation, heroism is not among them. Throughout the chronicle Galbert presents aristocratic self-signifying, dramatizes it, and strictly refuses to say that it means what aristocratic self-consciousness says it means.

The meanings that Galbert resists are those precisely in the service of aristocratic power—the very thing that Charles himself was trying to control by prohibitions on "private war" and to limit by his attempt to disenfranchise non-noble families such as the Erembalds, and the very same thing that families not noble by origin were attempting by various strategies, especially by strategic marriage and the appropriation of aristocratic public rituals of homage and fealty, to claim for themselves.[40] Galbert as

38. "in quadam militiae expeditione" (Galbert, [89], 2/3; trans., 262).

39. "hac vita potitus exspiravit leviori occasione mortis, dum scilicet cornu flaret . . . ebullierant medullae quae in cerebro jacuerant . . . omnibus terrae incolis in ore et memoria fuerant ita ut de subita morte eorum tractarent, quos post mortem domini Karoli Deus tam veloci sententia a vita privaverat et tam levis causae moriendi ipsis occasionem ordinemque disposuerat . . . nudos et solos . . . quousque . . . capti sunt et miserrimae mortis exterminio" (Galbert, [91], 4/5, 9/10, 15/19, 23/25; trans., 264).

40. These processes, and especially the tension between the growing power of princely authority and the traditional nobility, have been much studied for the period in question in Flanders, often using Galbert's chronicle as evidence. Among others, see especially Geoffrey

an active authorial presence in the chronicle is simultaneously on two sides of a growing and irreconcilable conflict, as status hierarchy in the emergent market capitalism of Flanders was rapidly transforming itself into class antagonism and producing a marked triangulation of claims to political authority among the traditional aristocracy, the count, and the urban population.[41] Galbert sees the assassination of Charles as an unequivocal violation of sacred order and natural authority, a violation that the Epistle of Peter unequivocally condemned and that would be providentially avenged "even to the third and fourth generation." Yet, Galbert's historiography aligns him at the very same time, and as if behind his own back, with exactly those new social formations that were beginning to undermine the conditions to which the sense of natural hierarchy and the divine authorization of rule correspond—social formations with which Galbert identifies as completely as he does with the count's "natural" authority, and which he evokes over and over again in language antithetical to aristocratic formulas of chivalric worth, language such as "our merchants," "our young men," and "our citizens of Bruges."

Koziol, *Begging Pardon and Favor: Ritual and Political Order in Early Medieval France* (Ithaca, N.Y., 1992), 140–45, who argues that Charles's immediate predecessors used the rituals and emblems of the Peace of God movements precisely for gaining supremacy over the nobility. Similarly, David C. Van Meter, "Eschatology and the Sanctification of the Prince in Twelfth-Century Flanders," demonstrates the continuing importance of Peace iconography for Walter's representation of Count Charles. As a notary in the collegiate church of Saint Donatian intimately involved in the comital administration, Galbert can be presumed to understand this tension from inside. For an excellent discussion of the process of status enhancement in this period, see among others Jean-François Lemarignier, *Le gouvernement royal aux premiers temps capétiens 987–1108* (Paris, 1965).

41. See Sproemberg's analysis of urban discontent and the growing sentiment for communal forms of urban governance, forms that guarantee the hegemony of merchant traders ("Galbert von Brügge—Die Geschichtsschreibung des flandrischen Bürgertums," 226–28).

10

History as Fabliau and Fabliau as History

The Murder of Charles the Good and *Du provost a l'aumuche*

LISA H. COOPER & MARY AGNES EDSALL

When Charles the Good was murdered in his own chapel on the second day of March in 1127, his death sparked turbulent times in the city of Bruges and the surrounding land of Flanders, gripping the popular imagination. In his *De multro, traditione, et occisione gloriosi Karoli comitis Flandriarum,* Galbert of Bruges expresses astonishment over how fast the story spread from Bruges to England and France. "No one," he writes of the quickly moving news, "could have spanned these intervals of time or space so quickly either by horse or by ship."[1] The reports of the count's assassination not only spread quickly by word of mouth, but also rapidly inspired a variety of written texts. These ranged from verse encomia of Charles's life to poetic lamentations upon his death, and from brief accounts of the event in historical record to Galbert's own extended daily record, itself a narrative that deploys a wide range of genres—chronicle, encomium, martyrology, even a gesture toward epic—in its presentation of what Galbert insists is "the truth of things," the *rerum veritas* of unfolding events.[2]

This essay makes two different but related arguments, both of which seek to broaden awareness of the discursive field created by those unfold-

1. "Intervalla ergo vel temporum vel locorum nec equo nec navigo quisquam transisse tam velociter poterat" (Galbert, [12], 53/55; trans., 114).

2. Galbert, [Prologue], 16; trans., 80. For a description of martyrological themes in Galbert's book, see chapter 3 of Jeff Rider, *God's Scribe,* 50–76. Galbert's description of the death of Baldwin of Aalst by "a trivial cause, that is, while blowing a horn" (leviori occasione mortis, dum scilicet cornu flaret; Galbert [91], 4/5; trans., 263–64) is almost certainly an ironic allusion to the *Chanson de Roland* (see the preceding essay in this volume by Robert M. Stein).

ing events and particularly by the perceived villainy of the Erembalds, the family widely deemed responsible for Count Charles's murder. We show that while what happened in Bruges was clearly no laughing matter, Galbert's narrative of the Erembald family's social trajectory, their crime, and their subsequent punishment makes use at key points of a satirical mode strikingly similar to the discourse of the fabliaux, a genre that more often than not concerns itself with trickery and unwarranted (or unmerited) social aspiration. We then argue that while the treachery of the Erembalds led Galbert to briefly explore the comic mode, it also seems to have led another (anonymous) author to create a comic text, the fabliau *Du provost a l'aumuche,* which we believe belongs to the family of works composed in reaction to the events at Bruges in 1127–28.

Both Galbert's account of what James Bruce Ross calls the Erembald family's "rise and fall"[3] and this little-studied fabliau share a number of crucial details that suggest that the two texts arose in response to the same set of historical circumstances; both also negotiate the telling of their respective tales in remarkably similar ways. Galbert's chronicle repeatedly and emphatically depicts the transgression of class boundaries as the origin of the strife that led directly to Charles's murder and all that followed from that catastrophic act. Devoting an entire section of his chronicle to an account of how the Erembalds were revealed to be of servile origin, Galbert also goes out of his way to explain how this family had aspired to, illegally and violently acquired, and then continued to grasp at social and political positions well beyond their station, thus bringing Bruges to and then over the brink of disaster; he then depicts in grisly detail the violent punishment meted out to them in return. The fabliau *Du provost a l'aumuche,* like many other narratives of its kind, also concerns itself with social transgression and deception. But where the central characters of most fabliaux are nameless, in this case both transgression and deception are performed by a provost with the family name of Erembald—a provost, moreover, of apparently servile origins—who is then punished for his crimes with what is, even for a fabliau, an unusually unamusing degree of violence.

This essay, we hasten to make clear, argues neither for the contemporaneity of chronicle and fabliau nor for the direct influence of the one upon the other, appealing as such speculation might be.[4] Rather—to borrow a

3. Ross, "The Rise and Fall of a Twelfth-Century Clan," 367–90.

4. While it is indisputable that the fabliaux did not flourish as a written genre until perhaps a century after Galbert's chronicle was written, critics agree that they are essentially undatable.

phrase from Paul Strohm's analysis of the relationship between chronicle accounts of the English Rising of 1381 and Chaucer's *Cook's Tale*—it stakes a claim for the two works' "mutual participation in [the] larger representational environment" that grew from the political and social tragedy at Bruges.[5] It points as well to the way they share what Gabrielle Spiegel has called a "social logic," a term that usefully encompasses a text's formal characteristics as well as its historical circumstances.[6] Not only do chronicle and fabliau seem to respond to the same events, but they also speak with similar voices as they confront historically pressing and highly vexed questions of wealth, power, and social status, not to mention the physical aggression to which such questions could, and often did, give rise. To make these points most clearly, we first briefly review some examples of the way the fabliaux often use comedy to respond to class tensions and to issues of social mobility. Then, turning to Galbert's chronicle, we consider how Galbert occasionally adopts a comic mode to depict the crimes of the Erembalds. Finally, we argue that when its peculiar details are scrutinized, the violence that the fabliau *Du provost a l'aumuche* enacts against a greedy provost can almost certainly be connected to the vicious backlash against the Erembald clan in the wake of the murder of Charles the Good.

Indeed, Galbert's Flanders was almost as socially mobile a world as the world that gave rise to and that was depicted in the fabliaux, and it is not difficult to imagine that the comic tale related in *Du provost a l'aumuche* might have circulated, orally if not in writing, much earlier than is suggested by the one 13th-century manuscript in which it survives. On the other hand, the memory of the crisis of 1127 seems to have lived long enough in the imagination of the people of Flanders to inspire the creation of new texts long after the fact. For example, around a third of a French translation of Galbert (it breaks off in chapter 37) survives in a sixteenth-century manuscript, and a "brief resumé" drawn from the French translation is found in the late fifteenth-century register of the De Baensts, a "noble family prominent in both Bruges and Ghent" (Rider, "Introduction," in Galbert, xxix and xxvi–xxvii; Rider, *God's Scribe,* 138). Jeff Rider's edition of Galbert's Latin text includes the French translation (facing page) and the De Baenst resumé (Appendix I, 173–75).

5. Paul Strohm, "'Lad with Revel to Newegate': Chaucerian Narrative and Historical Meta-Narrative," in *Art and Context in Late Medieval English Narrative: Essays in Honor of Robert Worth Frank, Jr.,* ed. Robert R. Edwards (Cambridge, 1994), 167; rpt. in Paul Strohm, *Theory and the Premodern Text* (Minneapolis, 2000), 55. See also Strohm's introduction to *Hochon's Arrow: The Social Imagination of Fourteenth-Century Texts* (Princeton, 1992), which argues for the way that texts can be read within a "larger field or 'environment' of previous and contemporary texts, visual representations, pageants, social dramas, and political acts" (6).

6. Gabrielle Spiegel, *Romancing the Past: The Rise of Vernacular Prose Historiography in Thirteenth-Century France* (Berkeley, 1993). For Spiegel, the "social logic" of texts includes both their "relation to the site of articulation—the social place they occupy, both as products of a particular social world and as agents at work in that world—and . . . their discursive character as articulated 'logos,' that is, as literary artifacts composed of language and thus requiring literary (formal) analysis" (9). See also Spiegel's earlier articulation of this idea in her "History, Historicism, and the Social Logic of the Text in the Middle Ages," *Speculum* 65 (1990): 59–86.

Class, Social Tension, and the World of the Fabliaux

The humor of the fabliaux, like that of other forms of Old French comic literature, frequently derives from situations in which the categories of class and gender are transgressed by one or more characters.[7] The fabliaux are filled with knights, provosts, clerks, bourgeois, peasants, prostitutes, vavasors, priests, and the ubiquitous wives, all characters who are often shown striving to position themselves in ways that will enable them to take advantage of opportunities both social and sexual. There are (among others) the putatively celibate priests and clerks who usurp the sexual roles of laymen, the women whose tricks allow them sexual and social agency, the nouveaux-riche peasants and bourgeois who marry up the social ladder, the knights who seduce, the peasants whose simple wit unwittingly wins the day, and the peasants who are put in their place.[8] Despite Charles Muscatine's caveat against taking "social issues" as the "central topic of these poems," the very pages of his book that lead up to his warning show that class is undoubtedly an important aspect of fabliaux humor.[9]

The heightened class-consciousness in these texts appears to have been a response to a social system that was mobile in reality while rigid in theory. Muscatine links "the flourishing of the fabliaux, the rise of the cities, and the emergence of an urban middle class," noting that the genre came into its own in the commercial regions of northeastern France.[10] By the end of the thirteenth century, the expansion of arable territory in this area had created a flourishing market economy.[11] The same phenomenon had taken place even earlier in Flanders, which already possessed a strong market economy in Galbert's time.[12] In both city and countryside the ability

7. Kathryn Gravdal, *Vilain and Courtois: Transgressive Parody in French Literature of the Twelfth and Thirteenth Centuries* (Lincoln, Neb., 1989), 19. See also Carol Parrish Jamison, "The Social Satire of the Fabliaux: A Literary/Historical Approach to the Genre" (diss., University of Georgia, Athens, 1993). Jamison's fourth chapter highlights the real social mobility of the 13th–14th centuries and shows how the fabliaux reflect "tensions between social reality and class consciousness" (99).

8. As Nykrog has demonstrated, the fabliaux do not deal with individuals as much as they deal with types, and they essentially define their characters by social rank. See Per Nykrog, *Les Fabliaux: Etudes de littérature populaire et de stylistique médiévale* (Copenhagen, 1957), 107 and 109.

9. Charles Muscatine, *The Old French Fabliaux* (New Haven, 1986), 45.

10. Ibid., 29.

11. Mary Jane Stearns Schenck, *The Fabliaux: Tales of Wit and Deception* (Amsterdam/ Philadelphia, 1987), 111–12. In this section of her book, Schenck draws heavily on Fossier's research on Picardy.

12. See David Nicholas, *Medieval Flanders* (London, 1992), chapter 5: "The Social and Economic Transformation of Flanders in the Eleventh and Twelfth Centuries," 97–123.

to amass wealth and rise in standing became available across class lines, even—if not especially often—to the peasantry. As Mary Jane Stearns Schenck puts it, "[t]he love of profit seems naturally coupled with a desire to move up socially, and in all areas touched by the economic revival, the conventional division among classes was seriously threatened."[13] Schenck sees the spirit of the fabliaux as "an ironic casting aside of the idealism and class-consciousness of the official culture by large groups of newly enriched, socially mobile country dwellers," and relates their exaltation of "the value of cunning and aggression" to "the fusion of a peasant mentality with the ethos of a money economy."[14]

If the fabliaux are to some degree reflective of the social possibilities generated by a new market economy in which class boundaries were becoming more permeable and established hierarchies were beginning to break down, they are also symptomatic of the social anxieties generated by the same phenomenon: conservatism speaks through them along with aspiration. Thus we find fabliaux that celebrate the intelligence and double-dealing that allowed those from the middling and lower classes to take advantage of new opportunities alongside fabliaux that reinforce the system of the three estates or that center on plots where the duper is duped and put back in his or her place. There are, moreover, tales that express an acute awareness of social mobility at the same time that they try to repress it.[15]

De Berengier au lonc cul, in which a noble lady is given in marriage to a would-be knight of wealthy peasant stock, provides a prime example of fabliau conservatism. One version of this tale emphasizes the generally catastrophic social results of class misalliance: "Thus a good lineage is abased and everything declines and goes to shame when castellans and counts marry low for gain. Thus they deserve great shame, and thus they will have great harm. Bad, dishonorable, and cowardly knights issue from such people who love gold and silver more than chivalry. Thus largesse has per-

13. Schenck, *The Fabliaux,* 116.

14. Ibid., 120. Paul Freedman also notes that in a range of literary texts the "peasant could be credited with a degree of cleverness, not that of literate erudition but a certain practical shrewdness" (*Images of the Medieval Peasant* [Stanford, 1999], 205).

15. As Howard Bloch notes, "the comic tale works not . . . only to subvert the social, but to reinforce it as well"; useful also to our argument about both Galbert's chronicle and *Du provost a l'aumuche* is Bloch's connection of the "essentially conservative impulse" of the fabliaux to their frequent physical violence, for he observes that "[b]ehind every beating is a lesson to be learned; and behind every castration, a reimposition of the law." Furthermore, he argues that in this way "storytelling" is inscribed within "a symbolic exercise of power" (*The Scandal of the Fabliaux* [Chicago, 1986], 120).

ished. Thus declines honor and worth."[16] Here, the erosion of social values follows immediately from genealogical debasement. The type of behavior that the fabliau predicts will be true of the offspring of such an ill-advised marriage is exemplified in advance by the actions of the pseudo-knightly husband, who goes out pretending to seek adventure but spends the day mutilating his own armor to create the appearance of having engaged in combat. Aware of this subterfuge, his wife arms herself, challenges, and then humiliates him, for out of cowardice he agrees to kiss her rear end rather than fight. The wife is ultimately permitted to entertain her lover, a real knight, with impunity, since her husband will accept anything as long as his base background is not revealed. In this tale, the illusion of upward mobility is ultimately preserved, but it is also depicted as a fiction supported by the higher estates for their own ends.

Another tale that deals with transgression of class boundaries is *Du vilain asnier,* in which a peasant who comes to town each day to gather manure strays onto a street of spice shops. Sickened by the unfamiliar odors, he passes out cold and is taken for dead until a quick-thinking bourgeois waves some manure under his nose. The peasant revives, swearing never to go down that street again. The tale concludes with the moral, "From this I want to show you that he who goes against his nature out of pride has no sense and no judgment: No one should change his nature."[17] Here the social and the biological collapse into one immutable category that renders transgression physically impossible. Although Paul Freedman has significantly qualified Georges Duby's assertion that "noble" and "serf" were understood as "genetic categories. . . . [that] constituted two species, two 'races,'" in the end this fabliau accords with Duby's claim.[18] At least

16. "Ensi lo bon lignage auille / Et dechiet tot et ua a'honte / Que li chastelain et li conte / Se marient bas por auoir / Si doivent grant honte auoir / Et grant domage si ont il / Li cheualier mauuais et uil / Et coart issent de tel gent / Qui miauz aiment or et argent / Que il ne font cheualerie / Ensi est largesce perie / Ensi dechiet enor et pris . . ." (Willem Noomen and Nico van den Boogard, eds., *Nouveau Recueil Complet des Fabliaux* [NRCF], 10 vols. [Assen/Maastricht, 1983–], 4:252). The quotation is from the B manuscript, l.24–35; the translation is ours.

17. "Et por ce vos vueil ge monstrer / Que cil fait ne sens ne mesure / Qui d'orgueil se desennature: / Ne se doit nus desnaturer" (NRCF 7:214, l.48–51; our translation).

18. Georges Duby, *The Three Orders: Feudal Society Imagined,* trans. Arthur Goldhammer (Chicago, 1980), 51; Freedman, *Images of the Medieval Peasant,* chapter 5, "National Myths, Origins of Serfdom," 105–30. Freedman reveals that some nations, including France, developed a genealogy of serfdom based not on a long-cursed bloodline but on a more recent act of military cowardice, the shame of which was passed on to descendants through the potentially reversible social and economic penalty of serfdom. Freedman argues that "the medieval period did not share the tendencies of modern racism to posit literal biological distinction," as Duby suggests it did, but he does also note that often "it placed the moment of division far enough

according to *Du vilain asnier,* a person who strays from one social sphere to another *se desnature*; he goes against his own inborn nature or, at the very least, his inherited and thus "natural" social status.

The moral of *Du vilain asnier,* with its warnings of the danger of transgressing the natural boundaries of social class, could easily apply to what Jeff Rider calls the "central narrative" of Galbert of Bruges's story of the murder of Charles the Good: that is, the "narrative of the good prince and the wicked *servi* [serfs]."[19] This is certainly how a fifteenth-century member of the prominent and noble De Baenst family of Flanders chose to represent the story after reading a French translation of Galbert's chronicle. Inserted into the De Baenst record book we find a summary of the events of 1127 that focuses almost exclusively on the ignoble origins, transgressive rise, and ultimate fall of the Erembalds.[20] In the record book, this section is preceded by the biblical phrase "Vanity of vanities! All is vanity"[21]—an opening quotation perhaps meant to indicate the futility of the Erembalds' attempt to rise above their station and then stay risen.

Like the socially turbulent world in which the fabliaux circulated, Flanders in Galbert's time had its fair share of experiencing what it meant to be "a society in flux," what with, as James Bruce Ross puts it, "[t]he rapid increase in population, the reclamation of land . . . the quickening tempo of Flemish mercantile activity at home and abroad, the multiplication of fairs and towns"—all of which, she notes, resulted in a "mobile and restless society."[22] Galbert's narrative serves as a witness to this changing world not only in recounting the story of a lord murdered by men who had risen in power and prestige (if not in actual estate), but also in representing this rise as having been facilitated by trickery, adultery, and deceit.

Narrative and Class in Galbert

In order to understand why the Erembalds, and Bertulf in particular, were willing to kill their lord, the count of Flanders, in order to protect

back in the historical past to account for the marked, physical difference of the servile population" (113). On that "genealogical paradigm," developed from the biblical story of Noah's curse upon his son Ham, see Freedman, *Images of the Medieval Peasant,* chapter 4, "The Curse of Noah," 86–104; the phrase is from 86.

19. Rider, *God's Scribe,* 67 and passim.

20. Rider, *God's Scribe,* 138.

21. "Vanitas vanitatum et omnia vanitas" (cf. Ec 1:2).

22. Ross, "Rise and Fall," 387–88.

their own interests, it is important to recall just how powerful the family had become by 1127. Two brothers, Didier Hacket and Bertulf, stood at the family's head. Didier was the castellan of Bruges, a position that had been held by the Erembalds since 1067 and that carried with it a substantial amount of military, judicial, and fiscal power. Even more prominent and powerful than Didier was his brother Bertulf, who as provost of Saint Donatian, the collegiate church of Bruges, held a position remarkable in its scope and in its multiple responsibilities.[23] In 1089, Count Robert II of Flanders had granted a charter appointing the provost of the church of Saint Donatian to be "chancellor and *susceptorum et exactorem de omnibus reditibus principatis Flandrie* [receiver and collector of all the revenues of the principality of Flanders]."[24] Therefore, only slightly before Bertulf's accession to the post in 1091, the provost of Saint Donatian had become the central figure in a far-flung system of castellanies and smaller centers that collected and, with the help of the local colleges of canons, accounted for taxes and other revenues that were then funneled into the treasury of the count.[25] In their study of medieval financial institutions, Bryce Lyon and A. E. Verhulst summarize the way this once exclusively clerical position had grown to include secular power:

> the provost of the chapter of St. Donatian of Bruges would be chancellor and . . . in addition to guarding the comital seal and supervising the clerical staff, he would assume control of finances. To him were to be accountable the local collectors of revenue from the comital domain. Control of finance, while still remaining in the household, shifted to the chancellor whose responsibility for auditing the accounts placed him above the chamberlain who, in the thirteenth century, was relegated to the more pedestrian duty of receiving, guarding, and disbursing money from the chamber treasury.[26]

Such was the immensely powerful office that Bertulf held from 1091 to 1127. For thirty-six years, twenty-seven of which had preceded the accession of Charles, Bertulf practically stood at the head of Bruges and at the center of the government of Flanders. Furthermore, in addition to his father (Erembald), two brothers (Robert and Didier), and a nephew (Walter),

23. Ross notes that Bertulf's position was "unique in its multiple functions" ("Rise and Fall," 372).

24. Bryce Lyon and A. E. Verhulst, *Medieval Finance: A Comparison of Financial Institutions in Northwestern Europe* (Providence, 1967), 12.

25. Ibid., 12–19.

26. Ibid, 61–62; cf. Rider, *God's Scribe,* 16–18.

who had served in their turns as castellan of Bruges, and another nephew, Isaac, who was one of the count's chamberlains, Bertulf had a number of nieces who married into the knightly class.[27] As Karl Leyser puts it, the Erembalds "had become [part of] . . . a new caste of princes' agents with immense opportunities to rise in the world under the patronage of their employers and to shuffle off their modest beginnings."[28]

For quite a time, the best of two generations, the power and prestige gained by the Erembalds seems to have overshadowed any awareness of their servile origin. Hence the troubled reaction of the clan when Robert of Crecques, husband to one of Bertulf's nieces, was refused equal combat with another knight who publicly claimed that Robert had become a serf as a result of his marriage into the Erembald family.[29] Galbert's account of this event is prefaced in the same chapter by Charles's announcement that he intended to survey the county to determine the free from the servile in order (according to Galbert) "to reestablish proper order in his realm."[30] Whether by fortuitous accident or by design,[31] Charles had found a legal way to check the rise of the Erembald clan and of their leader, who wielded a power almost equal to his own.[32] In the attempt, however, his relationship with the family reached its breaking point. Galbert depicts this double crisis for the Erembalds—Charles's general inquiry and the unnamed knight's specific accusation—as the source of their increasing panic and their quickly growing impulse to murder. Here he introduces Bertulf, a "certain provost" whom he shows first "striving by every device of craft and guile to find a way by which they [the Erembalds] could slip out of

27. On Didier, see Ross, trans., 9/116; on the marriages of Bertulf's nieces, see Ross, "Rise and Fall," 377–79.

28. Karl Leyser, review of Ross's trans., *Medium Aevum* 32 (1963): 53; cited by Ross, trans., 1. Leyser compares the Erembalds to two other early twelfth-century families that rose in class through government posts, the family of Roger of Salisbury in England under Henry I and the Garlandes in France under Louis VI.

29. Ironically, according to Galbert, Robert of Crecques had contracted the marriage in the belief that it would improve his status: "And so that knight mourned who had lost his liberty on account of his wife, through whom he had believed he could become freer when he married her" (Indoluit ergo miles ille qui propter uxorem suam libertatem amiserat, per quam liberiorem se fore crediderat cum eam accepisset; [7], 33/35; trans., 100). See also Rider, Galbert, viii.

30. "iterum revocare honestatem regni, perquisivit qui fuissent de pertinentia sua proprii, qui servi, qui liberi in regno" ([7], 8; trans., 96).

31. Ross notes that "The sequence of events is not entirely clear, nor is their relationship" (trans., 100n17).

32. Walter of Thérouanne describes Bertulf as "after the count alone, the most powerful man in the land" (post comitem solum fere totius terrę huius potentissimum; Walter, [40], 36/37; our translation).

servitude and cease belonging to the count."[33] In the next chapter, Galbert represents Bertulf as defying Charles outright: "'But let him try as much as he wants, we shall be free and we are free, and there is no man on earth who can make us into serfs!'"[34] According to Galbert, words soon turned to deeds as the Erembalds, "in the guile of abominable deliberation . . . began secretly to plot the death of the most pious count, and finally to fix on a place and an opportunity for killing him."[35]

It was clearly the growing legal threat to the Erembalds' position, more than any previously harbored malice, that led them to plot and carry out the assassination of Count Charles; even Galbert admits that the matter might "have been consigned to oblivion . . . if it had not been brought to the attention of the courts by the challenge to combat."[36] And yet for

33. "praepositus . . . ille . . . elaborabat omni astutia et ingenio, quomodo a servitute et pertinencia comitis sese absentaret et subterfugeret" ([7], 13/18; trans., 98).

34. "'Sed querat quantum velit, nos semper erimus et sumus liberi, et non est homo super terram qui possit nos constituere servos'" ([8], 11/12; trans., 101). On Galbert's invention of this speech to characterize the provost, see Rider, *God's Scribe,* 119–20. Galbert clearly states his view of the Erembalds' status: the family, he writes, "belonged to him [Charles], being of servile status" (ipsi de comitis pertinentia erant conditione servili; [7], 18/19; trans., 98).

35. "Perverso tandem et nefandi consilii dolo ceperunt de morte piissimi consulis seorsum tractare, tandem locum et oportunitatem occidendi illum pretendere" ([8], 19/22; trans., 102). In the sixteenth chapter of his life of Charles (entitled "The Accusation of Servility"), Walter of Thérouanne also describes the anger of the Erembalds over the threat of being exposed as servile and sees this as the direct cause of the plot against Charles's life: "A certain noble knight happened, however, to accuse another noble in the count's court of having broken the peace, and the latter refused to respond to the accusation as he would have if the former had been a free man, casting the stigma of servile status in his accuser's teeth because the woman he had married, a blood relative of the provost, was reputed to be the count's serf. The provost's whole family burned with unbearable rage against Count Charles and that knight because of this accusation of servility, which seemed to implicate them all. The case was discussed for a long time, therefore, but was finally concluded by an agreement whereby the woman who had been stigmatized would, with the count's assent, maintain her own freedom in the company of twelve nobles, and the count's suit against the rest of that family would remain unaffected. The failure to resolve this accusation thus seems to have been the first cause of the murder of the lord Charles, for they began subsequently to cultivate a most intense hatred for him" ("De calumpnia seruilitatis": "Accidit autem ut quidam miles nobilis aduersus alium nobilem in curia comitis de treugarum infractione placitaret, et ille, nota ei seruilis conditionis obiecta, eo quod consanguineam illius prepositi, quae comitis ancilla esse diceretur, uxorem duxisset, respondere ut libero refutaret. Quamobrem omnis illa prepositi cognatio in intolerabilem aduersus comitem Karolum et militem illum exarsit iram. In omnes enim haec uidebatur redundare calumpnia. Causa ergo haec quidem diu uentilata sed tandem tali est ratione terminata: ut, quae notata fuerat, matrona duodecima nobilium manu libertatem suam personaliter assensu comitis euendicaret et querela comitis in reliquam illam parentelam salua maneret. Huius igitur calumpniae talis suspensio domno Karolo prima fuisse uisa est interfectionis occasio. Hinc namque grauissima contra eum ceperunt exercere odia"; Walter, [16], 1/17; trans. Jeff Rider).

36. "omnium oblivioni tradebatur, nisi in praedicta belli appellatione ad recordationis veritatem revocatum fuisset" ([7], 42/43; trans., 100). This is noted by Rider, *God's Scribe,* 66. Rider also examines other potential motives for and suspects in Charles's murder on 63–66.

Galbert as for other chroniclers, the newly revealed servile background of the Erembalds came to account not only for the clan's immediate motives for murder but for its murderous character as a whole.[37] Even if Charles's murder had been instigated by the Devil, who (Galbert claims) sought the count's death in order to throw the peaceful land of Flanders into "confusion by guile and treachery and the shedding of innocent blood," a further explanation for the involvement of the Erembalds in the murder of a good lord like Count Charles was apparently a narrative necessity, and this explanation could be found in the family's tainted bloodline.[38] In his prefatory chapters, for example, Galbert excoriates the Erembalds, calling them "iniquitous serfs" and "foul dogs, full of the demon," who performed "unheard of treachery" when they "did away with their lord."[39] In later chapters, Galbert refers to the Erembalds as "impious and inhuman serfs" and as "wretched serfs."[40] Like the authors of other texts about these calamitous events, Galbert traces Bertulf's malignant actions back to his base heritage and to his blatant attempts at social advancement.

Yet Galbert goes further than his contemporaries when he interpolates into his daily record a tale that he may have drawn from popular legend: the story of how Erembald of Veurne, the first of the clan to rise to power, purportedly murdered his lord, the castellan Boldran, in order to marry his wife, Dedda or Duva, and gain his position as castellan of Bruges.[41] Galbert even

37. Whether or not the Erembalds were actually serfs is unclear; at the very least, as Rider observes, "their servility was perhaps not as evident as Galbert and some other contemporary sources make it out to be" (*God's Scribe,* 66 and 278n58).

38. "conturbavit eam dolis, traditionibus et effusione innocentium sanguinis" ([Prol.], 54/55; trans., 81). On Galbert's need for this double explanation—"the envy of the devil and the ire of the Erembalds"—see Rider, *God's Scribe,* 61–63, quotation from 63.

39. "nefandissimus servis" ([Prol.], 13; trans., 79); "canes immundi, demonio pleni" ([6], 18; trans., 95); "inaudita traditione dominum suum, ipsi servi . . . disperdiderunt" ([6], 21; trans., 95). All of these references occur in what is commonly referred to as the preface of *De multro,* which consists of the prologue and first fourteen chapters of the modern edition. This preface was almost certainly written at least three months after Charles's death, sometime during May to September of 1127. The order in which Galbert appears to have composed and revised his work is complex; Rider provides a suggested chronology in his introduction to *De multro,* xx–xxviii, and analyzes Galbert's working methods in chapter 2 of *God's Scribe,* 29–49 and in appendices V and VI, 226–30.

40. "servi impiisimi et inhumani" ([12], 23; trans., 112); "pessimi servi" ([26], 9; trans., 148).

41. The story is recounted in [71]. Rider dates the writing of this chapter to the summer and fall of 1127, when Galbert revised his first draft (*God's Scribe,* 250n61); see also Ross, trans., 65. Ross cites conjectures regarding the potentially legendary nature of this story in "Rise and Fall," 371n17, and trans., 239n2. Rider speculates that this "ribald and otherwise unknown history . . . . was made up and seems to have been shaped at the rumor mill to titillate a popular palate" (*God's Scribe,* 250–251n61). In her essay in this volume, Nancy Partner discusses the figure of Erembald's wife within the larger context of female agency in Galbert's narrative, and

presents this crime as a foreshadowing of the events of 1127. Introducing Erembald as an "adulterer [who] was always plotting the death of his lord,"[42] Galbert recounts a river expedition during which a dastardly deed was done under the cover of night: "When . . . the castellan had gone to the rim of the ship to urinate, Erembald, running up from behind, precipitated his lord into the depths of the rushing water."[43] For Galbert, this is the first evidence of an inbred evil that generated both this initial treason and the Erembalds' later treachery, a malignancy that he sees finally recognized and punished by the fall of the clan in 1127: "by the dispensation of God," he writes, "they [the Erembalds] were punished for the sins of their parents."[44] In Galbert's narrative as a whole both the inherent evil of the Erembalds and its eruption into action in 1127 take on a tragic significance. But with its love triangle, its emphasis on lower physical functions, and Erembald's comic and quick-minded response to finding his lord in a rather awkward position at the ship's edge, Galbert's tale of the first evil genius of the Erembald family slips, if only for a moment, into the world of trickery and physicality that is usually associated with the fabliaux. Strikingly, the later De Baenst version increases the slippage between chronicle and comedy when it reorders the narrative, listing the full cast of characters up front and emphasizing their relationship to one another in stereotypical terms that resemble the stock openings of many a fabliau:[45] Boldran's wife becomes little more than a whore, while Erembald

she too observes the fictional quality of the episode. It is worth noting that Galbert clearly deliberated upon the proper place for this narrative within his chronicle, for he mentions his decision to defer the Erembald genealogy as a whole in [57]; on a possible reason for that decision see Rider, *God's Scribe,* 40–41.

42. "adulter domino suo semper machinabatur mortem" ([71], 14/15; trans., 239).

43. "dum castellanus ad mingendum in ora stetisset navis, ille Erembaldus retro accurens, longe a navi projectum dominum in profundum torrentis aquosi praecipitavit" ([71], 15/18; trans., 239).

44. "dispensante Deo, punitum est in eis peccatum parentum" ([71], 31/32; trans., 240). Galbert goes on to paraphrase the Bible (Ex 20:5) to further strengthen his hypothesis: "I, the lord your God, am a jealous God, visiting the iniquities of the fathers upon the sons, even unto the third and fourth generation of those who hate me" (Ego sum dominus Deus tuus fortis zelotes, visitans iniquitatem patrum in filiis, in tertiam et quartam generationem eorum, qui oderunt me; [71], 34/36; trans., 240). For Rider's discussion of Galbert's turn to this explanatory model, which he applied to both the murder of the count and subsequent execution of the traitors, see *God's Scribe,* 71–72.

45. See for example the opening of the BN MS. 837 version of *De Berengier au lonc cul,* which tells of "a knight who had a wife. In all the country there was none more beautiful or courteous or wise, and she was of high lineage as well. But her husband was of peasant stock and was thus both lazy and vain" (un chevalier qui avoit fame / N'ot el pais plus bele dame / Ne plus cortoise ne plus sage / Et si estoit de haut parage / Mes son mari ert des vilains / Et si ert pereceus et vains (NRCF 4:252, l.5–10; trans. Jeff Rider).

is depicted as a disloyal and above all a lascivious servant eager to join Duva/Dedda in bed and participate in her machinations.[46]

But this tale of murder on board ship is not the only place in Galbert's narrative in which scenes of deception and class tension involving Erembalds recall the comic plots of fabliaux. Later in the *De multro,* Galbert condemns the knight Walter of Vladslo, a "peer of the realm," for his part in the plot against the count, seeing Walter's fatal fall from a horse as part of the "judgment of God."[47] Yet in this chapter Galbert's real scorn is reserved for Bertulf's attempt to enhance his family's station by marrying his niece into Walter's noble family. Thus he tells with evident relish a tale of deception in which he claims that Walter's son, whom one of Bertulf's nieces married, was "actually the son of a cobbler," a boy switched at birth with the knight Walter's real son, who was born dead.[48]

The furtive exchange of a dead baby for a living one from a lower social class, an exchange hidden from the father and revealed by the mother only following that father's death for reasons of inheritance, may read to our modern eyes less like historical fact than fable, particularly when we note that the trope appears in other historical records. For example, a similar story was told before 1117 by Florence of Worcester regarding Harold, son of Cnut, who was rumored to be the child of a cobbler.[49] Galbert, too,

46. "In former days there was in Bruges a hereditary castellan who was most prominent in the town and region of Bruges, whose name was Boldran. He had a wife named Duva or Dedda, who was an evil and dishonest ribald. Her husband the castellan had a servant whom he trusted greatly, named Erembald, who came from Veurne, a disloyal and evil man who often took his pleasure with his master's wife, who encouraged him in this lechery" (Ou temps passé y eust a Bruges ung chastelain heritable ayant grandt preminence en la ville et ou terroir de Bruges, lequel avoit nom Boldrannus. Lequel eust une femme nommé Duva ou Dedda, laquelle fut meschante et deshoneste rybaulde. Monsieur son mary le chastelain avoit ung serviteur en quel il se fioyt fort, nommé Erembaldus, natif de Furnes, lequel desloyal et meschant s'abusoit souvent aveque la femme de son maistre, laquelle l'entretenoit en ces luxures; Galbert, Appendix I, 173; trans. Jeff Rider). For a very similar revision of a specific historical event into a more generalized "scandalized anecdote," see Paul Strohm, "Treason in the Household," in *Hochon's Arrow,* 121–44, 135–36; phrase from 135.

47. "It came about by the severe and horrible judgment of God that Walter of Vladslo, one of the peers of the land, was hurled from his horse by its motion while he was on a certain knightly expedition and died after languishing for a few days in a shattered condition" (Factum est igitur Deo districto et horribile examine quod Walterus es Florerdeslo, unus parium terrae, in quadam militiae expeditione, ex proprio cursu suo ab equo praecipitatus, totus confractus langueret et postmodum in paucis diem obierit; [89], 1/4; trans., 262).

48. Her child having died at birth, Walter's wife "substituted the cobbler's son, who had been born about the same time, and secretly sent the dead child, whom she had borne, to the wife of the cobbler" (Supposuit ergo filium sutoris, qui circa idem tempus genitus fuerat, et emortuum quem peperat uxori sutoris clanculo submisit ([89], 12/14; trans., 262.)

49. "Harold also said that he was the son of king Canute and Elfgiva of Northampton,

presents the story of Walter's son not as rumor but as a revealed truth; however, he also uses it as a narratological device to further develop a running theme in his tale—that is, as yet more evidence of the provost Bertulf's attempts to raise his family above its proper station. Here, in true fabliau fashion, the duper ends up duped himself: "God's stratagem," Galbert writes, "foiled the stratagem of the provost, who, when he wanted to exalt his family proudly and arrogantly by that marriage, joined it to the son of a cobbler."[50] Where in the semi-comic tale of the provost's murderous ancestor Galbert finds a genealogical explanation for Bertulf's treachery, here Galbert seems pleased to turn to a rather shocking tale to further highlight the provost's social pretensions as well as their ultimate futility.

The fabliaux tend to celebrate the quick-witted underdog who gains the upper hand in a sexual and/or social situation. On the other hand, quite a number of fabliaux work in just the opposite direction, cruelly mocking those who fail in their efforts at social pretension.[51] It is to just this end that Galbert uses the tale of Walter of Vladso's wife's substitution of the cobbler's son. And it is also to this end that the class-conscious humor of the fabliau *Du provost a l'aumuche* operates. This tale seems to participate in exorcising the anxieties raised by the rapacious nature and devious schemes of the Erembalds, for numerous details suggest that it is meant to wreak comic revenge on the supposed authors of the urban disaster at Bruges in 1127.

---

although that is far from certain; for some say that he was the son of a cobbler, and that Elfgiva had acted with regard to him as she had done in the case of Sweyn: for our part, as there are doubts on the subject, we cannot settle with any certainty the parentage of either" (Haroldus vero dixit se filium esse Canuti regis et Northamtunensis Alfgivae, licet id verum est minime; dicunt enim nonnulli filium cujusdam sutoris illum fuisse, sed Alfgivam eodem modo de illo fecisse, quo de Suano fertur egisse: nos vero, quia res in dubito agitur, de neutrorum genitura quid certi scivimus definire; Florence of Worcester, *Chronicon ex chronicis,* ed. Benjamin Thorpe, Publications of the English Historical Society 13, 2 vols. [London, 1848], 13.1: 190; *The Chronicle of Florence of Worcester,* trans. Thomas Forester [London, 1854], 140). Florence's reluctance here to acknowledge the truth of the rumor suggests that such tales may also have circulated as a popular form of slander against those in high places. For example, Freedman notes the rumor that the early Capetian kings were descended from a butcher (*Images of the Medieval Peasant,* 64). Rider, however, notes two other references to apparently factual occurrences of this sort, which clearly provoked a good deal of anxiety; one is recorded in a charter and another in Adam of Eynsham's *The Life of St. Hugh of Lincoln,* in which a sterile woman fakes a pregnancy and acquires a baby from a townswoman. See Rider, *God's Scribe,* 291n57.

50. "Sicque arte Dei delusa est ars praepositi qui cum vellet superbe et gloriose per illus conjugium cognationem suam extollere, filio sutoris, Dei arte deceptus, eam copulavit" ([89], 25/27; trans., 262–63). Rider reads this event as an example of tragic irony in the chronicle (*God's Scribe,* 132).

51. Among examples of these one could include *Du Berengier au lonc cul, Du chevalier a la robe vermeille, Sire Hain et Dame Anieuse, De la dame escoillée,* and *Aloul.*

Du Provost a l'aumuche and the Murder of Charles the Good

This fabliau, a tale of only 132 lines, is easily summarized. A rich knight, a wise and peaceful ruler, goes on pilgrimage to Santiago de Compostela, leaving his land in the care of his provost. The provost wears a big fur-lined *aumuche*—a type of headgear that we examine in more detail below—and is a crude man of dubious background who has managed to become wealthy. The text describes him in insulting terms: he is a "low fellow and a rascal."[52] As we will also discuss below, it further intimates that he comes from a family of servile origin. The tale proper, however, begins not with this provost's stewardship in his lord's absence, but rather with the knight's return from his pilgrimage.

As the knight nears home, he sends ahead to have a feast prepared. The provost, feigning pleasure at his lord's return, is the first to arrive. He is seated well, next to a knight with whom he is to share the meal, but his despicable nature surfaces when the first dish, a bowl of peas and salt pork, is served. The slab of meat in the shared dish is irresistible to the provost, and he steals it while the knight turns to talk with a friend, sneaking it into his *aumuche* while he pretends to mop his nose behind his table-neighbor's back. He then slips the *aumuche* back onto his head. The theft goes unnoticed until a servant builds up a fire near the provost's seat. The hidden piece of pork begins to melt, and rivulets of fat start running down his face. A passing server, annoyed by the *aumuche,* knocks it off. The pork falls out of the hat, and the provost jumps up and dashes through the fire to escape. But instead he is caught, beaten, and thrown out in a scene of great violence.

Several pieces of evidence link this fabliau to Galbert's story of the historical Bertulf. First is the fact that although the given name of the fabliau's anti-hero is not Bertulf but Gervais, the fabliau identifies him as the son of one "Erembaut Brache-huche" (l. 19). The relevance of "Erembaut" (or Erembald) is of course clear, but the term *brache-huche,* while enigmatic, is also suggestive. The English translation renders the phrase as "Howlbitch," which, as will become clear from our discussion of the tale's conclusion, may not be far from the mark, since *brache* (also *brachet* or *bracet*) signifies

52. "vilains et pautoniers" (l. 13). We have used the critical text of the fabliau in the NRCF 4: 37–44; the translation, with modifications as noted, is taken from Raymond Eichmann and John DuVal, eds. and trans., *The French Fabliau: B.N. MS. 837,* Garland Library of Medieval Literature, Series A, 16–17, 2 vols. (New York, 1984–85), 2:56–61.

a type of hunting dog and *huche* comes from *huchier,* meaning to cry out or announce in a loud voice.[53] However, the phrase may also allude to the roles played by the Erembalds in the governing of Flanders, as well as to popular sentiment regarding the grasping nature of the family. *Brache,* the Picard form of *brace,* literally means "arm"; however, it specifically refers to "spread arms" and thus, by extension, to "the space arms can encircle," or "an armful."[54] *Huche,* however, poses more difficulty. This noun has a range of meanings, including (from the verb *huchier*) a crier or a hawker of wares; a trunk or coffer; a shop for the display of merchandise; or a market tax paid by merchants.[55] Thus *brache-huche* can be construed variously, but it might bring to mind the phrases "tax-arm"—as in exactor of taxes—or "coffer-arm"—as in one whose arms can receive a large amount. The potential for this name to suggest financial matters is intriguing, since members of the Erembald clan held offices supervising taxation and the accounting of the comital revenues.

But the precise meaning of *brache-huche* aside, many other details indicate that the story may be a semi-comic indictment of the historical provost Bertulf and, by extension, the whole Erembald family. First, there is the provost's *aumuche,* to which the fabliau insistently draws our attention. An *aumuche* was, most simply, a type of short, hooded cape that could also be rolled up into a cap; it was a common part of the lay medieval wardrobe. But it was also a defining part of the garb of canons, whose hoods were characteristically lined with fur.[56] The attention drawn to Gervais's well-furred

53. See Algirdas Julien Griemas, *Dictionnaire de l'ancien français, le Moyen Age* (Paris, 1992), s.v. *Brache,* 75; for *huchier* see note 55 below.

54. See Frédéric Godefroy, *Dictionnaire de l'ancienne langue Française et de tous ses dialectes du IXe au XVe siècle,* 10 vols. (Paris, 1880–1902), s.v. *Brace:* "bras, et surtout le bras étendu, l'espace que les bras étendus peuvent entourer, la brassée. . . . Par métonymie, force, valeur, carrure. . . . La forme *brace, brache,* est restée dans le rouchi et dans le picard" (1:175).

55. See Adolf Tobler and Erhard Lommatzsch, *Altfranzösisches Wörterbuch* (Stuttgart, 1925–), s.v. *Huche:* "Trueh, Lade, Trog; Arche; Sarg" as well as "Marktabgabe der Tuchhändler." Godefroy (s.v. 3. *huche*) says that a *huche* can in one sense be a "crieur, qui huche" (4:518), from the verb *huchier:* "crier, publier à haute voix" (4: 519). In another sense (s.v. 1. *huche*), it is a "boutique où sont étalées des marchandises," or a "droit payé par les marchands" (4:518). A related term supplied by Godefroy is *huchage:* "revenu provenant du ban ou encan" (4:517).

56. Françoise Pipponier and Perrine Mane define the *almuce* [*sic*] as a "headdress in the shape of a long hood, lined with fur; worn originally by the laity of both sexes, and later exclusively by clerics" (*Dress in the Middle Ages,* trans. Caroline Beamish [New Haven, 1997], 166). Millia Davenport gives a more complete description: "*Almuce* (O.Fr., O.Engl. *Aumuce*): Fur lined, hooded choir vestment worn from the XII c. by church canons over the surplices, against cold; by the XVI c. hung over left arm as a badge of office. Certain academic and monastic bodies were also granted its use, and by the XII c. the laity also wore it" (*The Book of Costume,* 2 vols. [New York, 1948], 1:95). Godefroy has no entry for the word, but mentions it in his definition of *aumure:*

(*bien forree* [l. 21]; *forree* [l. 101]) hood and the fabliau's repeated references to his office as provost (ll. 13, 18, 55, 61, 67, 78, and 106), a title also given to the heads of cathedral and collegiate chapters,[57] reinforce the probable connection of the two provosts Gervais and Bertulf. Furthermore, although the provost Gervais appears to hold only a secular position, the possible double meaning of his defining garment—the *aumuche* that can serve as both secular and canonical garb—is analogous to Bertulf's double political position. For Bertulf, as we noted above, served two roles for Charles the Good, acting both as provost of the collegiate chapter of Saint Donatian and as a secular provost managing the central administration of the county.

Gervais's hood, however, does not simply signify a double political role; it also mixes the high and the low. The text is careful to tell us that the hood is made of *burel,* a common, coarse, low-cost wool fabric.[58] But its fur lining, by contrast, is a mark of some status, and the hood is a garment of which the provost seems quite proud—after all, he chooses to wear it to the great feast for his lord's return. The oddly double *burel*-and-fur *aumuche* weds humble beginnings to signs of new-found success, melding Gervais's *put aire* or "stinking heritage" (l. 23) with the riches that have "overtaken"

"fourrure de peau de lapin, qu'on employait pour doubler les aumusses que les chanoines portaient en hiver, afin de tenir chaudement la tête et les épaules" (1:499). Iris Brooke provides us with details of the variety of ways that the hood could be worn. She writes that "when they were not employed purely for protection against wind and weather, they could be pushed back and worn as a shoulder cape or taken off the head and shoulders and hung safely by the long liripipe attached to some button or buckle on the gown. They were in fact often taken off and rolled into a hat, the face opening serving as the opening that was put on to the head. . . . the liripipe was . . . used to tie around the head in order to keep the hood in the shape of a hat" (*Medieval Theatre Costume: A Practical Guide to the Construction of Garments* [London, 1967], 71–72). Hence, probably, the Töbler-Lommatzsch definition of *aumuce* as *mütze,* or cap (1:674).

57. See the entry for *prevost* in Godefroy, vol. 10 (the supplement to his dictionary).

58. G. de Poerck defines *burel* as: "Tissu de laine grossière, médiocrement estimé, ayant un comte et un mode de tissage particuliers" (*La Draperie médiévale en Flandre et en Artois: Technique et terminologie,* 3 vols. [Bruges, 1951], 2:30). He also gives us an idea of the market for this cloth: "Cette grossièreté a fait des bures des tissus pour pauvres, que l'auteur du *Roman de la Rose* oppose symboliquement aux brunettes: 'car ausinc bien sont amouretes—Sous bureaus com souz brunettes'" (1:207). Chaucer uses the word *burel/borel* as an adjective meaning "lay" or "unlearned" in the tales of both Summoner and Franklin (*The Riverside Chaucer,* 3rd ed., ed. Larry D. Benson [Boston, 1987], III.1872, 1874, and V.716), and the Wife of Bath uses it to ridicule a jealous husband who thinks that she is out flaunting her finery. She retorts, "'This is to seye, if I be gay, sire shrewe, / I wol renne out my borel for to shewe'" (III.355–56), implying that the best clothing that he has furnished her with is made out of cheap, coarse cloth. A tantalizing detail, given Bertulf's bureaucratic career, is that the word *bureau* derives from *burel. Burel* was the cloth used to cover desks and the term came to connote desks and, by extension, offices in general as well as government agencies. See the entry for *bureau* in *Le Petit Robert 1, Dictionnaire alphabétique et analogique de la langue française* (Paris, 1989).

him and given him a station that he does not actually deserve: "his reputation," the fabliau declares, has "been improved" by his money, "[j]ust as wealth always does to wicked hands."[59] This is strikingly similar to what Bertulf's *aumuche,* his garment of office, did for him; the position signified by the garment served to gloss over his servile origins. Furthermore, in both of these narratives the *aumuche* also masks villainy of another sort. In Gervais's case, it conceals the theft of the bacon, an act that is itself a sign of his congenitally base nature. In the case of Bertulf, as we have seen, it masked the potential for congenital treachery of the "like father, like son" variety: just as his father Erembald of Veurne had murdered his lord to gain office, so did he participate in a murderous plot to retain that office.

The provost of Galbert's history and the provost of the fabliau both hold positions of great power and responsibility; they also share a name, a low-class background, and a base nature. So, too, do their lords have much in common. Where Galbert's preface tells us that Charles's subjects "rightly cherished and loved him, and . . . venerated him as a father,"[60] the fabliau begins in praise of a knight, "considered as good as a count," who "was loved in his land by his men and by other people."[61] Where Charles the Good spent his time of rule "seeking and establishing . . . the peace and well-being of the fatherland," achieving such success that he could not find any "enemies around his land,"[62] the fabliau's knight "[l]ived without war and without contention" for "twenty years and more."[63] Finally, both men make pilgrimages to distant lands. Galbert makes much of the fact that Count Charles "took the road of holy pilgrimage to Jerusalem,"[64] while the writer of the fabliau juxtaposes the good knight's journey to "the noble Saint James" with his provost's rascality.[65] In the chronicle, Charles's pilgrimage provides Galbert with a place from which to begin his lament for a fallen hero; in the fabliau, the knight's return from Santiago de Compostela

59. "richece l'avoit seurpris, / Si en ert amendez ses pris, / Si comme il fet a mains mauvais" (l. 15–17).

60. "justo amore et dilectionis virtute dilexerant et ut patrem venerabantur" ([4], 23/24; trans., 91).

61. "par samblant *valoit un conte*" (l. 2; our emphasis); "Molt fu amez en sa contree / de ses homes et d'autre gent" (l. 9), a point the fabliau repeats when the knight returns from his journey and is greeted with "great joy" by "those who loved him" (grant joie . . . celes qui l'amerent; l. 48–49).

62. "pacem et salutem patriae . . . demandans et constituens . . . hostes circa terram suam" ([4], 33/35, 37; trans., 91).

63. "vint anz . . . et plus / vesqui sanz gerre et sanz meslee" (l. 6–7).

64. "arripuit sanctae peregrinationis viam Hierosolimitanorum" ([12], 30/31; trans., 113).

65. "baron saint Jaque" (l. 11; cf. l. 14–17).

provides both a rationale and a setting for the remainder of its narrative: the revelation of the provost's grasping nature at the knight's welcome-home feast. Both the triumphant march of Count Charles's life and the triumphal feast marking the fictional knight's return are spoiled when the historical Bertulf and the fictional Gervais attempt to reach out from their already established positions of power and influence for more, be it status or food—and fall from grace in their greed.

"Greed" is certainly the operative word, for another similarity between chronicle and fabliau is the way that both texts make alimentary plenitude an image of good governance and alimentary transgression a symbol of treachery. Where Galbert praises Count Charles for his peaceful rule, for his piety, and particularly for his prompt and charitable response to the famine that struck Flanders before his death, the fabliau emphasizes the generosity of the peace-keeping and God-fearing knight who wanted to be sure that there would be plenty of food and drink for all at his homecoming feast.[66] Furthermore, Galbert accentuates the horror of Charles's betrayal by comparing it to the breaking of the bond established between people at a common table. "His intimates betrayed him, increasing trickeries against him," he writes, adding, "as it is said in the Psalm [40.10]: 'For my intimate friend, who ate my bread, increased trickery against me.'"[67] The fabliau, as we have noted, situates its central moment of betrayal at the table. There the provost Gervais, "the son of Erembault Brace-Huche,"[68] shares in a feast with his lord but, true to one connotation of his surname, grasps more meat than is his due in a bold-faced theft, an act against the common good that leads directly to his punishment at the tale's conclusion.

66. For Galbert's description of Charles's actions during the famine, see [2] and [3]; trans., 84–89. In the fabliau, as the knight approaches home, he sends ahead for his wife and friends to come to meet him and also to be sure that enough food will be ready for the homecoming feast: "And so he made sure there was more than enough meat and fish to eat in the house, that they had plenty of wine there, so that they had plenty of everything" (Et si feïst appareillier / A l'ostel assez a mengier, / De char, de poisson sanz devin, / Qu'a plenté i eüssent vin, / Si qu'a plenté aient trestout; l. 41–45).

67. "Quem homines suae pacis super illum magnificantes supplantationes tradiderunt, ut in psalmo: Etenim homo pacis meae, qui edebat panes meos, magnificavit super me supplantationem" ([6], 36/38; our translation). In a quotation that is otherwise verbatim from the Gallican Psalter, Galbert chooses to omit part of the opening phrase. Jerome's translation has: "Even my bosom friend in whom I trusted" (Etenim homo pacis meae in quo speravi; Ps 40:10; Ps 41:9 in the Revised Standard Version). Perhaps the omission of this phrase—"in quo speravi"—signaling hope or trust was meant to signal Charles's misgivings regarding the Erembalds, for the very next chapter turns to the topic of the discovery of the Erembalds' servitude and their use of "craft" and "guile" to retain their positions of freedom and power.

68. "fils Erembault Brace-Huche" (l. 19).

The shared narrative territory of fabliau and chronicle is, finally, also suggested by the similarities between the violent ends of both provosts. In his account of Bertulf's death, Galbert writes that Bertulf

> was pulled along nude except for breeches, the target of mud and stones. Except for the clergy and a few who had formerly known him as a religious man, no one took pity on him. Exhausted by so many insults and wounded by so many taunts and blows, he saw the punishment of death approaching him. . . . [H]e was hanged on a gallows in the middle of the market place at Ypres, like a thief or robber. They took off his breeches so that his shameful parts could be seen, and there was nothing vile or shameful he did not undergo in his punishment.[69]

Once his "arms were stretched out like a cross on the gibbet, and his head thrust through the hole on the gibbet," placing him in a physical position that mimicked a crucifixion, Bertulf was assailed by a huge, vindictive crowd.[70] According to Galbert, "those who had come to the market to buy fish set about destroying the body of the man with iron hooks, clubs, and stakes."[71] And as Bertulf was expiring, "hanging in the shadow of the most bitter death," the people of Ypres performed a striking symbolic act that allows us to draw another connection between chronicle and fabliau. In *De multro,* the mob at Ypres is said to have "twisted the viscera of a dog around his [the provost's] neck, and placed the muzzle of a dog next to his mouth, now drawing its last breath, thus likening him and his deeds to a dog."[72]

In the fabliau, Gervais, provost and son of an Erembald, suffers a simi-

69. "Nudus prorsus praeter braccas, luto et lapidibus obrutus, trahebatur. Praeter clerum et paucos qui dudum religiosum virum cognoverant, nemo miseratus est illum. At ille tot injuriis fatigatus totque opprobriis et tunsionibus lesus, mortis suae supplicium eminus expectabat . . . et suspensus est in medio fori Iprensium juxta supplicia furum et latronum in patibulo, et braccas detraxerunt ei ut illa verecundiora corporis apparerent. Nihil turpe vel ignominiosum erat quod in ejus supplicium non inferrent" ([57], 25/29 and 63/67; trans., 209–10).

70. "In quo patibulo brachia in crucem extensa et manus insertae sunt et caput transjectum per foramen ejusdem patibuli" ([57], 67/68; trans., 210). On Galbert's dramatic account of Bertulf's execution, which clearly alludes to the crucifixion of Christ, see Rider, *God's Scribe,* 108–11, and Lisa H. Cooper, "Making Space for History: Galbert of Bruges and the Murder of Charles the Good," in *Place, Space, and Landscape in Medieval Narrative,* ed. Laura L. Howes, Tennessee Studies in Literature 43 (Knoxville, 2007), 3–26.

71. "qui pro piscibus emendis in foro convenerant, uncis ferreis, fustibus et sudibus corpus viri dissipabant" ([57], 82/83; trans., 211).

72. "suspendium . . . sub acerrimae mortis tenebris . . . canis viscera contorserat circa collum ejus et os canis ad os ejus jam vitalem spiritum expirantis opposuerunt aequiparantes cani ipsum et facta ipsius" ([57], 86, 91/93; trans., 211–12). Van Caenegem has connected this act to Germanic ritual and other popular traditions. Ross cites Van Caenegem, *Geschiedenis van het Strafrecht,* 173 and n3 (Ross, trans., 212n11), and Rider directs us to R. C. Van Caenegem, "Misdaad en Straf bij Galbert van Brugge," in *Liber Amicorum Jules d'Haenens* (Ghent, 1993), 321–31 (Rider, *God's Scribe,* 283n45).

larly symbolic and shameful punishment, one preceded by what is, even for a fabliau, an astounding degree of vindictive and not very amusing violence.[73] The provost is knocked down with "a big whack" from the squires, pelted with coals by the cooks, and beaten without mercy. In the words of the fabliau:

> [T]he squires serving the party,
> Who had seen this scene quite clearly
> Struck him such a mighty smack
> That they laid him right out flat,
> Beating his head, beating his back.
> The cooks ran in through the kitchen door.
> Without even questioning the uproar,
> From the fireplace they grabbed hot coals.
> They hurled these—blow after blow after blow,
> Striking so hard, both high and low,
> That they broke his back.
> With sticks and feet and hands
> They gave him more than thirty wounds
> And even made him shit his pants.
> Finally, after all these harms,
> They dragged him roughly by the arms.
> Then out of the door, and with a pitch,
> They threw him with a dead dog in a ditch.
> The flesh really brought him great shame.[74]

73. Schenck observes that "[s]ince few tales end with a just settlement and since retaliations, especially brutal ones, are more common than resolutions, the world of the fabliau is not one where problems are actually worked out and resolved. On the contrary, these tales reflect a world of immediate retributory justice administered by the injured party, who, if he is the most clever person, will prevail" (Schenck, *The Fabliaux,* 60). Note that in *Du provost a l'aumuche,* the violent punishment is administered not by the injured party, but by a mob of servants. It is tempting to see that mob as corresponding to the crowd that attacks Bertulf.

74. [L]it escuier qui servoient,
qui l'afere veü avoient,
li donerent grant hatiplat,
si qu'il firent cheoir plat;
fierent en teste et en l'eschine.
Li keu saillent de la cuisine;
ne demanderent que ce fu,
ainz traient les tisons du fu
si fierent lor lui a un tas.
Tant le fierent et haut et bas,
que brisiés li ont les rains.
Aus bastons, aus piez et aus mains,
li ont fet plus de .XXX. plaies,
et l'ont fet chier en ses braies.
A la parfin tant le menerent,
que par les bras le traïnerent
fors de la porte en un fossé
ou l'en avoit un chien tué:
molt li fist grant honte la chars.
(*l. 118–27*)

Our translation, with reference to that of Eichmann and DuVal.

The use of animals, and particularly dogs, as part of medieval executions was not at all uncommon.[75] But the excessive violence of this scene, which, like that of Bertulf's execution, closes by—to use Galbert's phrase—"likening [the provost] and his deeds to a dog," does not quite seem to fit the fabliau provost's crime. This radical shift in tone—from fabliau humor to vengeful retaliation—signifies something beyond the provost's foolish theft and, given the other connections between the two texts that we have noted above, suggests that the link between the provosts of chronicle and fabliau may go beyond mere coincidence.

Without the evidence provided us by Galbert's narrative, we might find an explanation for the fabliau's violent conclusion in the fact that the tale introduces the provost to us using the stock insults "vilains" and "pautonier" (l. 13).[76] Gervais is of low birth and base nature, and the fabliau can be read at face value as a moral exemplum demonstrating what happens when a member of the lower class is allowed to mingle too freely with his superiors. But the fabliau is extremely concerned, well beyond most tales of its kind, to name this particular provost and thus to locate him within a specific lin-

75. On the judicial practice of hanging with dogs, see Mitchell B. Merback, *The Thief, the Cross and the Wheel: Pain and the Spectacle of Punishment in Medieval and Renaissance Europe* (Chicago, 1999), 187; on its connection to hanging with animals in what was known as "Jewish execution," although it was not reserved for Jews alone, see Esther Cohen, "Symbols of Culpability and the Universal Language of Justice: The Ritual of Public Executions in Late Medieval Europe," *History of European Ideas* 11 (1989): 407–16, esp. 411–12, and her *The Crossroads of Justice: Law and Culture in Late Medieval France* (Leiden, 1993), 88–94 (both cited by Merback). The shameful connotation of dogs and ditches also appears in another much later vernacular text; the English poem *Cleanness* ends with the deadly beating of King Baltazar, who is compared to a "dogge . . . that in a dych lygges" (*The Poems of the Pearl Manuscript,* rev. ed. Malcolm Andrew and Ronald Waldron [Exeter, 2002], l. 1792). We thank Brenna Mead for bringing this line to our attention.

76. Gravdal notes that while the term *vilain* "was not initially pejorative . . . its homonymic confusion with 'vil' (from the Latin 'vilem' 'of little worth,' 'of low price')" led to its "negative expansion . . . [by which] the meaning 'low born' comes to include the meaning 'ugly,' then 'unrefined,' then 'stingy.'" The vilain, she concludes, is generally to be understood as "morally ugly, of ignoble ideas and base instincts" (*Vilain and Courtois,* 12). For *pautonier,* Töbler-Lommatzch gives us "Troßknecht; Landstreicher, Lumpenkerl" and the insulting adjectives *lumpig, lumpenhaft* (7:508–11). Godefroy defines *pautonier* as "valet" and as "coquin, scélérat, homme dur, méchant, prêt a tout faire; homme sans profession et sans aveu; souteneur de tripot, de taverne, et de mauvais lieu; enfin, homme ignoble par ses moeurs, par ses manières, par son extérieure; adj. dur, méchant, insolent, drôle, lâche" (6:48–49). It should be noted that for the most part these types of derogatory terms, originating in class bias, became general insults or "descriptive labels" "rather than . . . identification of class origins" (Schenck, *The Fabliaux,* 71; see also Nykrog, *Les Fabliaux,* 127). Nevertheless this does not eliminate the possibility that at times the terms are used with their class connotations, and the other evidence in *Du provost* makes it clear that in this case the class connotations are meant to be noticed.

eage of dubious quality.[77] The fabliau, as we have seen, not only provides us with the name of Gervais's father, Erembaut Brache-huche (l. 19), but adds that the provost "molt ert cuivert et de put aire" (l. 23). This insult, which means that Gervais is crude and has a foul disposition, is a loaded phrase whose etymology suggests both disreputable family origins and low social class. The noun *cuivert* originally designated a category of unfree persons legally and socially almost indistinguishable from serfs. From it comes the pejorative adjective meaning "weak, pusillanimous, base, vile, traitorous."[78] *Aire,* in the simplest sense, means "place"; by extension, however, it connotes a person's origin, descent, race, or family—and only by further extension from the latter does it mean a person's disposition or nature.[79] The fundamental meaning of "molt ert cuivert et de put aire" is thus, "he was very low class and from a rotten family." This single but telling phrase both condemns the provost's evil character and alludes to his corrupt bloodline. Furthermore, as we observed above, the fabliau emphasizes that wealth has allowed this man of disreputable background to rise higher than he should (ll. 15–17). Gervais's ham-fisted theft of the piece of pork is thus another symptom of his *put aire* in all senses of the phrase.

Galbert's several stories of Bertulf's family ties and the fabliau *Du provost a l'aumuche* not only operate in the same generic register, they also perform the same social task: by undermining the status of the Erembalds, they attempt to put this upstart family back in its place. For Galbert, as for the writer of the fabliau, psychological causality and historical explanation are to be found in the long-established but newly revealed *put aire* of a provost and his family. Galbert's tale of the vassal who pushes his pissing lord overboard in the dead of night, while funny, has highly serious consequences, including the murder of a much-beloved leader many years later. For Galbert, at least a partial explanation of Bertulf's treachery is to be found in the tale he tells of the provost's rotten lineage, his *put aire.* Galbert's second fabliau-like tale, that of the cobbler's child, allows him to turn the joke on the Erembalds. The chronicler clearly sees poetic justice

77. Schenck notes that "very few characters [in fabliaux] are named" (*The Fabliaux,* 71).

78. See Marc Bloch, "The *Colliberti:* A Study on the Formation of the Servile Class," in *Slavery and Serfdom in the Middle Ages: Selected Essays by Marc Bloch,* trans. William R. Beer (Berkeley, 1975), 93–121.

79. Godefroy defines *aire* as "Lieu, place, salle, [sp. Xxx non-cultivé]. Aire, par extension, a signifié la race, l'extraction, et par suite les qualités, les dispositions bonnes ou mauvais" (1:194). See also Töbler-Lommatzch (1:252–54).

in the fact that the overreaching provost's niece should be tied by marriage to a "false son" of the aristocracy[80]—a son whose real father, a worker in the leather trades, would clearly have been considered of *put aire*—if not by his fellow burghers, then at least by the aristocracy.[81]

The death of Charles the Good inspired a great deal of writing in the tragic and elegiac modes, and the *De multro* certainly contains a good deal of both. But getting at what Galbert calls the *rerum veritas* can call for more than two voices, particularly when the "thing" in question is as complex as the crisis of 1127–28. "All texts," observes Gabrielle Spiegel, "occupy determinate social spaces, both as products of the social world of authors and as textual agents at work in that world, with which they entertain often complex and contestatory relations. Texts both mirror and generate social realities, are constituted by and constitute social and discursive formations, which they may sustain, resist, contest, or seek to transform depending on the individual case."[82] These are useful terms for approaching the chronicle *De multro,* the fabliau *Du provost,* and their relationship not only to one another but also to the events that they depict or to which they allude. In working to mirror what happened in Bruges and so provide an accurate picture of the "truth of things," Galbert's *De multro* also generates a family history for the Erembalds—a genealogy that the fabliau, in turn, appears to take for granted. Galbert turns to a particular discursive formation, a semi-comic morality tale, in order to solidify the case against the Erembalds, making their guilt more explicit while providing a satisfactory explanation for its origin. His narrative, however, simultaneously enacts a rhetorical punishment perhaps not quite as brutal as execution but certainly of much longer duration; while Bertulf died in an afternoon, his family's *put aire* is revealed in perpetuity to each new reader of Galbert's text. Like Galbert, the writer of the fabliau appears to have been highly aware that rhetoric can be a very powerful weapon.[83] As we hope we have shown, the same tensions that provoked the murder of Count

80. "furtivo filio" ([89], 19; trans., 262).

81. See Jacques Le Goff, "Licit and Illicit Trades in the Medieval West," in *Time, Work, and Culture in the Middle Ages,* trans. Arthur Goldhammer (Chicago, 1980), 58–70, esp. 59–60.

82. Spiegel, *Romancing the Past,* 10.

83. Galbert concludes the opening chapter of his record with a reflection on the increasing use of rhetoric in the courts for the purposes of both attack and self defense ([1], 22/36; trans., 84). See Nancy F. Partner, "The New Cornificius: Medieval Historiography and the Artifice of Words," in *Classical Rhetoric and Medieval Historiography,* ed. Ernst Breisach, Studies in Medieval Culture 19 (Kalamazoo, Mich., 1985), 5–59, esp. 40–41 and 49.

Charles in historical Flanders seem also to rankle beneath the surface of a fictional text, one that enacts its own form of physical and social revenge upon those it finds guilty of both physical and social violence. Not only does the fabliau *Du provost a l'aumuche* nearly kill off the provost Gervais by its end, but it also—like sections of Galbert's *De multro*—renders an overreaching Erembald ridiculous for as long and as far as its tale of his wrongdoings might spread.

11

Chronicles of Revolt

Galbert of Bruges's *De multro* and Jean Froissart's *Chronique de Flandre*

GODFRIED CROENEN

Galbert of Bruges and Jean Froissart feature among the Low Countries' best-known medieval historiographers, popular with the modern undergraduate student and general reader alike, although only partly for the same reasons. Both chroniclers are generally seen as key witnesses or principal sources for important historical events—the murder of the Flemish count in Galbert's case; the Hundred Years' War in the case of Jean Froissart. Both use direct speech and other rhetorical devices to recreate a sense of dramatic space, thereby achieving an intense effect of directness, as if the reader were personally present at the battlefield or in the count's hall, witnessing for himself the events described.[1] Modern critics and historians—to an extent deceived by this directness of style—have often ignored, misunderstood, or played down the literary aspects of both authors' writings.[2] As a result, Galbert and Froissart have frequently been

I should like to thank Jeff Rider warmly for inviting me to widen my current research on Froissart by comparing his historiographical work to Galbert's *De multro.* Jeff's stimulating remarks have helped me greatly in developing further some parts of the paper given at the Leeds 2001 conference. Peter Ainsworth has given much-valued feedback on an earlier version of this essay.

1. For Galbert, see Rider, *God's Scribe,* 77–111; for Froissart, see P. F. Ainsworth, "Style direct et peinture des personnages chez Froissart," *Romania* 93 (1972): 498–522; idem, "Froissardian Perspectives on Late-Fourteenth-Century Society," in Jeffrey Denton, ed., *Orders and Hierarchies in Late Medieval and Renaissance Europe* (Basingstoke/London, 1999), 61; and George T. Diller, *Attitudes chevaleresques et réalités politiques chez Froissart. Microlectures du premier livre des* Chroniques (Geneva, 1984), 162.

2. Compare Rider, *God's Scribe,* 3–8; and Diller, *Attitudes chevaleresques,* 2–4, 75. The re-

seen as naive and rather uncomplicated or uncritical history-writers. But because of their supposedly uncomplicated character, they have also been singled out as excellent mirrors of the medieval mind-set or *mentalités*—of twelfth-century Flemish burghers and fourteenth-century aristocracy of Western Europe respectively.[3]

The similarities between the two historiographers, however, go beyond the modern reception of their work, as a closer inspection will show, in particular a comparison of Galbert's narrative of the events of 1127–28 with one of Froissart's lesser known writings, the so-called *Chronique de Flandre.*[4] This latter text records the urban revolt in Flanders against the count in the years 1379–85, also known as the "Ghent War." The *Chronique de Flandre* is best known as part of Book II of Froissart's general *Chroniques,* but it was in origin probably a separate work, written around 1385–86, after Froissart had finished Book I of his *Chroniques,* but before he began work on the continuation of this text, what scholars now refer to as Book II; when he extended his historical narrative to 1386, Froissart must have decided to incorporate his *Chronique de Flandre* as one of the narrative threads in the general *Chroniques.*[5]

Like the events recorded by Galbert, the Flemish revolt of 1379–85 and Froissart's narrative of it are closely linked with the question of good government and legitimate rulership; with the political power struggles between the large Flemish cities—Bruges, Ghent, and Ypres—and between cities and countryside; and with the issue of princely taxation versus urban privileges and liberties. The direct cause of the conflict in 1379 lay in the undertaking of the citizens of Bruges to try, with the consent of Count

habilitation of Froissart's reputation as a literary author is mainly due to Diller (*Attitudes chevaleresques*), Ainsworth (*Jean Froissart and the Fabric of History: Truth, Myth, and Fiction in the* Chroniques [Oxford, 1990]), and Michel Zink (*Froissart et le temps* [Paris, 1998]). For Galbert's literary artistry, see Rider, *God's Scribe,* 77–111.

3. Hervé Martin, *Mentalités médiévales XIe–XVe siècle* (Paris, 1996), 57–58, 172–73, 392–393.

4. The *Chronique de Flandre* survives in three 15th-century manuscripts, BnF Paris, MS français 5004, BM Cambrai, MS 746 and MS 792. A scholarly edition of this text is not available but is currently being prepared by the present author. BnF Paris, MS français 5004 is the only complete manuscript, and all references in this essay will be to that manuscript.

5. Book II of Froissart's *Chroniques* will be referred to in the scholarly edition by G. Raynaud (Jean Froissart, *Chroniques,* ed. S. Luce, et al., 15 vols. [Paris, 1869–1975]). Short extracts concerning Flanders can be found in Jean Froissart, *Chronicles,* selected, trans., and ed. Geoffrey Brereton (Harmondsworth/Baltimore/Victoria, 1968), 231–51. A translation into modern French of a large selection of relevant passages can be found in Jean Froissart, *Chroniques de Flandre, de Hainaut et d'Artois au temps de la Guerre de Cent Ans (1328–1390),* trans. D. Poulet, with a historical introduction by M. Sommé (Troesnes/La Ferté-Milon, 1986), 107–71.

Louis of Male, to circumvent the Ghent staple monopoly by constructing a canal that would link Bruges to the river Leie (Lys), thereby providing it with direct access to the grain-producing areas of Northern France.[6] When construction workers entered the Ghent area in 1379, dissatisfaction amongst the Ghent shippers, already fuelled by recent new duties levied on behalf of the count, reached boiling point and led to a military expedition against the Bruges workmen. The situation quickly worsened as the result of the arrest of a Ghent burgher in the city of Eeklo by the comital *bailli* Roger of Atrive, which was perceived as an infringement of the city's privileges. This affair eventually came to a head with the attack on the person of the *bailli* himself inside the city of Ghent, which left the *bailli* dead and the county in disarray.

The killing of Roger of Atrive and the expedition against the Bruges canal builders were both the work of the so-called White Hoods, an urban paramilitary band led by Jan Yoens, the former dean of the Ghent shippers' guild. During the civil war that ensued, this gang was seen terrorizing the Ghent hinterland and organizing military expeditions further afield. As a result of these military operations, weaver-dominated magistracies were installed at Bruges and Ypres; smaller cities and towns, such as Oudenaarde, Damme, Dendermonde, and Kortrijk, were all forced into the coalition led by Ghent. The Ghent rebellion entered a new phase in January 1382, when Philip of Artevelde, son of James of Artevelde, the popular Ghent leader of the 1340s, became one of the captains of Ghent and effective leader of the opposition against the Flemish count. At the instigation of Artevelde, the Ghent forces marched on Bruges, where the count was preparing an attack, and defeated the troops of Bruges at Beverhoutsveld (May 3, 1382), thereby forcing the count to seek refuge in France. Artevelde claimed the regency over the whole county of Flanders and quickly implemented a personal rule based on a combination of brutal force and intimidation of political enemies. By the summer and autumn of 1382, however, a military expedition led by the French king was under way that ended in the battle at Westrozebeke (November 27, 1382), where Philip of Artevelde was killed and the Ghent militia humiliatingly defeated.

6. For the historical context of the Ghent War of 1379–85, see David Nicholas, *The Van Arteveldes of Ghent: The Varieties of Vendetta and the Hero in History* (Ithaca, NY, 1988); idem, "The Scheldt Trade and the 'Ghent War' of 1379–1385," in *Trade, Urbanisation and the Family: Studies in the History of Medieval Flanders,* ed. David Nicholas (Aldershot, 1996), 1–9; idem, *Medieval Flanders* (London/New York, 1992), 227–31; and J. Van Herwaarden, "The War in the Low Countries," in *Froissart: Historian,* ed. J. J. N. Palmer (Woodbridge/Totowa, 1981), 101–17.

Despite this defeat and despite the recapture or re-submission of most cities in Flanders, including Bruges and Ypres, the Ghent rebels continued to hold out against the allied forces of the French king and the Flemish count. Supported by the English, who sent a—largely ineffective—military expedition to Flanders, Francis Ackerman, the new Ghent captain and regent of Flanders, achieved some measure of military success by taking Oudenaarde and holding Damme, but he failed in his attempt to capture the town of Aardenburg. Efforts to reestablish peace led to nothing as Ghent hardened in its refusal to accept Louis of Male as legitimate count. Only after the count's death, in January 1384, and after further military defeats of the Ghent militia, could the city be forced into submission. Ghent agreed to a relatively favorable peace treaty with Philip of Burgundy, son-in-law and successor of Louis of Male, which marked the end of the Ghent War.

* * *

Although the events recorded by Froissart in his *Chronique de Flandre* took place almost exactly two and a half centuries after those in Galbert's *De multro,* the two narratives, by and large, share the same geographical setting and important aspects of the socioeconomic and cultural context. The general themes, of uprising against the count, of military clashes, and of acts of violence, are also common to both works. It should, then, come as no surprise that they share a number of recurring motifs and themes.

Both Galbert and Froissart refer repeatedly to the practice of burning down houses as a thoroughly effective and highly symbolic means of punishment. In the opening chapters of his work, Galbert recounts how the count was advised to burn down Borsiard's house as punishment for his plundering of the peasants, an action that was the direct cause for the murderous attack on Count Charles.[7] On April 7 the citizens of Saint-Omer burned down the house to which Eustace of Steenvoorde had fled, and on July 9, 1128, Count William Clito burned down the houses of the knight Ansbold and his brothers and sisters in Oostkamp when he realized that he was not able to take the stronghold of the local *praeco.*[8] Froissart refers to the same practice early on in his narrative, when the Ghent people, after killing the count's *bailli,* went to the houses of the Mayhuus brothers, Jan Yoens's personal enemies. When they found nobody there, "all their houses were demolished so that nothing remained, immediately knocked

7. Galbert, [10], 11/12, 17/18; trans., 105–6.
8. Galbert, [56], 14/15; trans., 207; [116], 35/36; trans., 303.

and thrown to the ground as if they [the Mayhuus brothers] were traitors to the whole city."[9]

Another parallel between the two works is the references to disguise as a means of escaping. Galbert mentions Fromold, "the most evil of Borsiard's serfs," who tried but did not succeed in escaping "dressed in a woman's cloak as disguise."[10] Alger, the chamberlain of Bertulf, was more successful and made his escape disguised as a priest.[11] In Froissart's *Chronique de Flandre,* the motif of disguise is used elaborately in the chapters recounting the humiliation of Count Louis of Male fleeing after Artevelde's victory at Beverhoutsveld.[12] Upon hearing the news of the Ghent victory and warnings about the Ghent militia heading for the market place, the count swapped his harness and military attire for the *houppelande* (a tunic with a long skirt) of his squire.[13] Louis was then forced to seek refuge in a poor woman's house, sharing a humble bed with her children in order to mislead the men of Ghent who were in hot pursuit. The next day, the count finally managed to escape the city, on his own, without being recognized or having the normal honors being paid to him, forced to go on foot and dressed like a servant.[14]

Another way of escaping immediate danger or a violent death was to seek refuge in a church, but from Galbert's and Froissart's works the reader learns that in the heat of the battle the protection offered by such sacred

9. "La furent touttes leurs maisons fustees ne riens n'y demoura, et tantost abattues par terre et jectees tout ainsi comme se ilz fussent trahitour a tous le corps de la ville" (MS fr. 5004, fol. 16r; compare Froissart, *Chroniques,* 9:178). The following year the Ghent troops destroyed houses in the countryside around Ghent belonging to noblemen who supported the count (MS fr. 5004, fol. 44r–v; compare Froissart, *Chroniques,* 9:226–27).

10. "nefandissimus servorum Borsiardi . . . indutus superpellicium mulieris quo se dissimularet" (Galbert, [29], 19/21; trans., 154).

11. Galbert, [35], 26/29; trans., 163–64.

12. The episode starts with Philip of Artevelde's dramatic speech at the Ghent market place, inciting the people to a final stand, and ends with the pillaging and partial destruction of the castle of Male after the defeat of the Bruges militia (MS fr. 5004, fol. 91v–116r; compare Froissart, *Chroniques,* 10:212–41). On this whole episode and its literary value, see the detailed analysis in P. F. Ainsworth, "Du Berceau à la bière: Louis de Male dans le deuxième livre des *Chroniques* de Froissart," in *Dies Illa: Death in the Middle Ages. Proceedings of the 1983 Manchester Colloquium,* ed. Jane H. M. Taylor (Liverpool, 1984), 125–52.

13. MS fr. 5004, fol. 105r–v; compare Froissart, *Chroniques,* 10:230.

14. "Sunday night, the count of Flanders left the town of Bruges, alone and disguised in the robe of one of his servants" (Le dimence de nuyt, le conte de Flandres yssy de la ville de Bruges, tous seulz et descongneuz, de la robbe de l'un de ses varletz; MS fr. 5004, fol. 112v). In the later version that was inserted into his *Chroniques,* Froissart specifies that the count was dressed in a "poor and simple *houppelande*" (povre et simple hoppelande; Froissart, *Chroniques,* 10:237).

buildings was often only theoretical. Hence the repeated accounts in both works of people seeking refuge in churches only to find that the church is set alight and that they will be burned alive. This happened for example during the siege of Oudenaarde by Count William Clito on May 5, 1127.[15] The next year the same William tried to burn alive one of his rivals, Arnold, in the church of Saint Bertin, and on May 15, 1128, William attacked Oostkamp and set fire to the church after the *praeco* had fled inside.[16]

Froissart recounts with verve the defeat of the Ghent militia in Nevele, where the count ordered fire to be set to the church into which one of the Ghent captains, Jean de Launnoy, and his men had fled. In a scene reminiscent of the siege of Count Charles's murderers in the castle in Bruges in Galbert's narrative, Jean de Launnoy, who had barricaded himself in the church tower, asked the besiegers to be ransomed but was taunted to take the "nice jump." Feeling the heat of the flames, Jean decided he would rather be killed than burnt alive, but in the end—as Froissart notes with a macabre sense of irony—he suffered both fates: after jumping onto the drawn weapons of the besiegers he was cut into pieces and thrown back into the fire.[17]

* * *

15. Galbert, [80], 15/17; trans., 250.

16. Galbert, [97], 21/22; trans., 272; [111], 7/14; trans., 292–93.

17. "When the count of Flanders had come to the square in front of the abbey and he saw that the men of Ghent were seeking sanctuary inside it and were being taken in, he ordered that the abbey be set on fire and that the whole place be burned. His order was carried out immediately and fire was brought and a great deal of straw and small pieces of wood that were strewn around the abbey and then set on fire. The fire immediately burned high and set alight the roof of the abbey. The men of Ghent who were inside died there in great suffering, for they were burned alive, and if they came out, they were rushed upon and thrown back into the fire. Jehan de Launoy, who was in the bell tower, saw that he was about to die and be burned, because the bell tower was beginning to burn. He thus cried out 'Ransom!' to those below and showed them his purse, which was full of florins. But they only laughed at his words and made fun of him and said: 'Jehan de Launoy, come out here through those windows and talk to us and we will take care of you. Make a nice jump, like you made our men jump. You'll have to make this jump.' Jehan de Launay, who saw that there was no way out and that the fire was so close to him that he was about to be burned, grew afraid and decided it was better to be killed than burned. But he suffered both, for he jumped from the window down among them and was received with lances and pikes and was there cut into pieces and then thrown in the fire. Such was the end of Jehan de Launoy" (Quant le conte de Flandres fu venus en la plache devant le moustier et il vey que les Gantois se recueilloient la dedens et estoient recueilliet, il commanda a boutter le feu ou moustier et tout ardoir. Son commandement fu tantost fait et le f[e]u aporté et grant foison d'estrain et de menus bois que on mist et appoya tout autour du moustier et puis boutta on le f[e]u dedens. Ce f[e]u monta tantost amont qui se prist es couvretures du moustier. La mouroient les Gantois qui estoient dedens, a grant martire, car ilz estoient ars et se ilz yssoient hors, ilz estoient emboulez et regectez ou f[e]u. Jehan de Launoy,

Although it seems highly unlikely that Galbert's work had any direct textual influence on Froissart's *Chronique de Flandre,* it is striking that some scenes in Froissart's narrative seem to echo Galbert's quite closely.[18] One such passage concerns the Ghent militia marching on Bruges. Galbert describes how the men of Ghent arrived on March 14 and 15, 1127, to assist with the siege of the count's murderer: "[W]hen they heard that they could make their own attack in the siege, they assembled all the bowmen and skilful makers of military equipment, and also bold plunderers, murderers, thieves, and anyone ready to take advantage of the evils of war, and they loaded thirty wagons with arms."[19]

Froissart tells us of a similar endeavor when in 1379, after the initial hostilities that marked the beginning of the Ghent War, Jan Yoens suggested taking the Ghent militiamen to Bruges to test whether that city would side with the count or with rebel Ghent: "Then those who were going on this mission were ordered per parish: and so they took provisions

qui estoit en la tour du clocquier, se veoit ou point de la mort et estre tous ars, car le clocquier s'esprendoit a ardoir. Si cryoit a ceulx qui estoient bas: 'Raenchon!' et offroit sa taisse qui estoit toutte plainne de flourins. Mais on ne faisoit de ses parolles que rire et galler et disoit on: 'Jean de Launoy, venez ycy par ces fenestres parler a nous et nous vous recueillerons. Faictes le beau sault, ainsi que vous advez fait saillir les nostres. Il vous convient faire ce sault.' Jehan de Launay, qui se veoit en tel party que c'estoit sans remede et que le f[e]u le costoioit de si prez que ilz couvenoit que il fust ars, entra en paour et eult plus chier a estre occhis que ars. Et il fu l'un et l'auttre, car il sailly hors par les fenestres enmy eulx et fu recueilliés des lanches et picques et la fu decoppez et depechiés et puis jetté ou f[e]u. Ainsi fina Jehan de Launoy; MS fr. 5004, fol. 60v–61r; compare Froissart, *Chroniques,* 10:69–70).

18. It seems indeed very unlikely that Froissart had any knowledge of Galbert's work, given the manuscript tradition of the *De multro,* which lay virtually buried and unknown to most people until it was edited in the 17th century by Henschen and Van Papenbroeck, cf. Rider, *God's Scribe,* 2, and Galbert, xxix–xl. One further striking textual parallel between Galbert and Book II of Froissart's *Chroniques,* however, should be mentioned here. Galbert describes how Boldran, castellan of Bruges, was murdered by Erembald when Boldran and his men were taking part in a military expedition on the river Scheldt. They were fully prepared for the fight and were wearing their cuirasses, when night fell. During the night, when the castellan went "to the rim of the ship to urinate, Erembald, running up from behind, precipitated his lord into the depths of the rushing water, far from the ship" (ad mingendum in ora . . . navis, ille Erembaldus retro accurrens, longe a navi projectum dominum inprofundum torrentis aquosi praecipitavit; Galbert, [71], 16/18; trans., 239). The danger of wearing armor close to deep water is echoed by Froissart when he tells us about the fate of Albert of Hangest (Godfried Croenen, "Heroes and Anti-Heroes in Book II of Jean Froissart's *Chroniques,*" in *Le Héros bourguignon: histoire et épopée,* ed. Jean-Marie Cauchies, Graeme Small and Andrew Brown, Publications du Centre européen d'études bourguignonnes 41 [Neuchâtel, 2001], 14n32).

19. "Cumque sese singulariter in obsidione insultum facturos audissent, associaverunt sibi universos sagittarios et ingeniosos operum artifices et audaces raptores, homicidas, latrones et quoscumque praesumptores in omne belli nefas, atque triginta plaustra oneraverunt armis" (Galbert, [33], 10/14; trans., 160).

and were mustered appropriately and then they left Ghent, between nine and ten thousand troops, and took with them plenty of wagons loaded with provisions."[20] Although Froissart does not refer explicitly here to the spoils of war as an incentive for the Ghent expedition, the behavior of the militiamen in later expeditions shows that this must have been a factor in the eagerness with which Yoens's proposal was met.[21]

Galbert, in his description of the arrival of the Ghent militias outside the city walls of Bruges, stresses the initial tense situation and the danger of enmity and aggression on both sides, but then goes on to describe how talks between the leaders of the parties quickly led to a compromise, whereby the Ghent troops were allowed inside the city:

> When they had reached the gates of the town, they dared to enter forcibly, but all the men of the siege, who ran up from the inside, resisted them face to face, and there would have been a general struggle if the wiser ones in both ranks had not come to terms. For, after giving and receiving hands, the men of Ghent pledged themselves by faith and swore an oath that they would join them in the siege and share fully their efforts and arms and counsels, while respecting the place and the property of our [Bruges's] citizens. . . . Then the men of Ghent came in with a great crowd and filled up the area around the castle.[22]

The arrival of the Ghent militias outside the city walls of Bruges in Froissart's *Chronique de Flandre* in 1379 is very reminiscent of the scene in Galbert's work. Here Jan Yoens also finds the city gates closed; the request to open the gates is met with what Yoens sees as a delaying tactic, which prompts him to launch an attack immediately to force his entry.

> And the men of Ghent arrived at the palisades and the moat surrounding Bruges, headed by Jan Yoens on a black horse. There Yoens dismounted and took his battle axe in his hand. When those who were defending the gate saw that they

20. "Adont furent ordonnez par paroiches tous ceuls qui yroient en celle legation. Si se pourveirent et ordonnerent et tout par moustre, ainsi comme a eulx appartenoit. Et se partirent de Gand entre IX a X mille hommes et emmenerent grant charroy et grant pourveanches" (MS fr. 5004, fol. 21v; compare Froissart, *Chroniques,* 9:187).

21. Galbert also repeatedly mentions the treasure of the count as one of the reasons why the murderers were besieged. See, e.g., [63], 42/52; trans., 224.

22. "Qui cum juxta portas suburbii accessissent, violenter ingredi ausi sunt sed in faciem restitit eis omnis obsidionis quae intro occurrebat multitudo. Et pene pugnatum fuisset undique, nisi quod sapientiores sese composuissent in utraque acie. Nam datis dextris et acceptis, fide et sacramento juramenti sese taxabant, quatenus eadem intentione eisdemque armis et eodem consilio in obsidione cum ipsis jungerentur, salvo loco et rebus nostrorum civium. . . . Ingressi sunt ergo cum maxima multitudine Gendenses illi et compleverunt locum circa castrum" (Galbert, [33], 17/27; trans., 161).

were no match and that the Ghent troops were ready to attack them, they were all afraid. And some went through the high street to the market, shouting "Here! Here! The Ghentenars are here! Quickly, quickly, to the city walls! They are already at the gates!" Those of Bruges who ran up to the market to take counsel were all afraid and the masters of the great guilds were in no mood to have long talks about our or their business. And the majority of the community wanted the gates to be opened at once.[23]

Under pressure from the townspeople, the burgomaster, and others from the urban government go to the gates to talk with Jan Yoens; an agreement is quickly reached after which the Ghent troops enter the city; a treaty is then sealed.

In this parley they came to such a satisfactory agreement that they opened the defenses and the gate to them out of friendship, and all then entered the city. . . . And it was a most beautiful thing to see them enter the city in orderly fashion. They then went to the market place. . . . . A sworn and covenanted alliance was made there between those of Ghent and those of Bruges by which it was agreed that they would always stand shoulder to shoulder, like good friends and neighbors.[24]

Galbert's and Froissart's historiographical works thus share a number of motifs, some of which have been briefly discussed above. More importantly, some of the central themes are also common to both narratives. Of crucial importance in both works are the interconnected themes of excessive pride and revenge. Feuds, as chains of attack, counterattack, and revenge, play an important role as the initial cause of larger historical developments and as almost inexhaustible reservoirs of uncontrollable energy that move the action and the narratives forward. In Galbert's *De multro,* it is the vi-

23. "Vindrent les Gantois jusques aux barieres de Bruges et aux fossez, Jehan Lyon tout devant, monté sur ung noir morel et mist tantost se piet a terre et prist sa hache en sa main. Quant ceulx qui gardoient la porte, veïrent que point n'estoient si fort et veïrent les Gantois en belle ordonnance pour eulx assailir, si furent tous effraez. Et s'en alerent les aucuns parmy la grant rue jusques au marchié en criant: 'Veez les cy ! veez les cy, les Gantois ! Or tost ! or tost aux deffenses ! Ilz sont ja devant nos portes !' Ceulx de Bruges qui s'assambloient ou marchié pour eulx conseillier, furent tous effraez et n'orent les grans maistres loisir de parler ensamble ne de ordonner nulles de nos besoingnes ne des leurs. Et voulloient la plus grant partie de la communaulté que tantost on leur alast ouvrir les portes" (MS fr. 5004, fol. 22r–v; compare Froissart, *Chroniques,* 9:188).

24. "En ce parlement ilz furent si bien d'accort que par grant amour on leur ouvry les bailles et la porte, et entrerent tous dedens . . . . Et fu adont tres belle chose d'eux veoir entrer en la ville par ordonnance. Et s'en vinrent ens ou marchié. . . . Entre ceulx de Gand et ceulx de Bruges furent la faictes alyances jurees et convenenchees que ilz devoient demourer a tousjours les ungz dalez les aultres, ainsi comme bons amis et voisins" (MS fr. 5004, fol. 22v–23r; compare Froissart, *Chroniques,* 9:189).

olent feud between the nephews of provost Bertulf and the nephews of Thancmar of Straten that triggers the murder of Count Charles.[25] The attack on the count is immediately followed by a killing spree in which Borsiard and his men take revenge on a number of people against whom they had been harboring grievances, including a certain Henry "whom Borsiard suspected of the death of his brother Robert."[26] The murders of Walter of Loker and the castellan of Bourbourg were also obviously the result of intense hatred directed at the people close to the murdered count.[27]

Once Count Charles was murdered, revenge for this deed was sought by his kinsmen and vassals. Gervaise the chamberlain was the first to set the vengeance on foot,[28] but he was soon joined by other vassals of the count. Among the kinsmen were the different candidates for the office of count,[29] but also the French king Louis VI, who was at the same time feudal lord and first cousin of the murdered count.[30] In the letters he sent to the Flemings the king stated explicitly that he had come "to carry out vengeance" and he sent them his "thanks for avenging Charles, his kinsman."[31]

In Froissart's *Chronique de Flandre* it is a complex web of feuds, hatred, and enmity that sparks off the machinations to oust Jan Yoens from the office of dean of the shippers' guild, which in turn leads to Yoens's burning desire for revenge on the Mayhuus family.[32] Froissart tells us that Yoens had long enjoyed Count Louis of Male's favor and that he had, in the past, carried out a contract-killing for him. Because of this murder, Yoens had

25. [9]; trans., 102–4.

26. "quem suspectum habebat Borsiardus de mortis fratre sui nomine Roberti" (Galbert, [16], 11/12; trans., 121).

27. Galbert, [16], 1/6; [17], 8/54; trans., 120–21, 125–27.

28. Galbert, [26]; [54], 19/21; trans., 147–49, 200.

29. The execution of Bertulf by William of Ypres was characterized as a "harsh vengeance" (vindictam . . . gravem; Galbert, [57], 5/6; trans., 208), indicating that William was acting not just as the presumptive ruler but also as kinsman of the murdered count.

30. Gertrude of Saxony, who was first married to count Florent I of Holland and then to count Robert I of Flanders, was the maternal grandmother of both Count Charles and King Louis VI of France, see Galbert, 184–85. This fact escaped J. B. Ross, see trans., 187n4. Galbert refers three times to the kinship ties between King Louis VI and Count Charles, twice calling Charles the king's "nepos," which here must be understood as cousin or kinsman (Galbert, [47], 5; trans., 187; [64], 32; trans., 226). In their defiance of the king and of his choice of William Clito as count, the burghers of Bruges claim that the Flemings had exceptionally allowed the king to intervene in the election of a new count because of his close family relationship to the deceased count (Galbert, [106], 48/49; trans., 285).

31. "ad faciendam vindictam" (Galbert, [52], 9/10; trans., 195); "gratiam pro vindicando nepote suo" (Galbert, [47], 4/5; trans., 187).

32. MS fr. 5004, fol. 3v–7r; compare Froissart, *Chroniques,* 9:158–67.

been banned from the city of Ghent, but the count had been able to get this punishment reversed. Yoens had been reinstated in his possessions and appointed to the office of dean of the Ghent shippers' guild. The favor enjoyed by Yoens, however, had awakened the jealousy of the Mayhuus brothers, a family of Ghent shippers. The Mayhuuses, furthermore, were related to one of the parties in a long-running blood-feud in the city of Damme, in which Yoens was also involved because of his kinship ties with the other party.

Although the details of the Damme feud are fairly vague and although Yoens did not seem to care too much about it at all,[33] by the time he lost the office of dean of the shippers' guild as well as his livelihood, the desire for revenge had become all-consuming and unstoppable. Outwardly, Yoens placidly accepted falling out of the count's grace, but inside there burned a violent energy as he promised himself to take revenge: "'I have slept a while, but it is clear that at the slightest opportunity I will wake up and cause such trouble between the city and the count, that it will cost 100,000 lives.'"[34] Soon enough, the incident with the Bruges canal builders provided him with that opportunity, and this set into motion a cycle of violence that ac-

33. "There was at this time another family in Ghent named the Mayhuus, and these seven brothers were the greatest of the shippers. Among these seven brothers, there was one named Ghiselbrecht who hated Jan Yoens greatly but secretly since he saw that Jan was in the count's favor, and he plotted night and day for a way to make him fall from grace. Several times, he thought to have him killed by his brothers, but he didn't dare do so for fear of the count. But he continued to plot, watch and imagine until at last he found a way. And I'll tell you the main reason they hated each other so much. Some time ago, there had been a deadly feud in the city of Damme between two rich shippers and their families, one of whom was named Jan Piet and the other Jan Bar. Eighteen of their friends and family had died in this feud. Ghiselbrecht Mayhuus and his brothers were related to one of these families and Jan Yoens to the other. So a hidden hatred was nourished for a long time between these two even though they sometimes spoke, drank or ate together" (En ce temps avoit ung aultre lignaige a Gand, que on appelloit les Mahieu [Mayhuus], et estoient iceulx VII freres les plus grans de tous les navieurs. Entre ces VII freres y avoit ung que on appelloit Ghiselbrecht, lequel avoit grant envie sur Jehan Lyon [Yoens]. Couvertement de ce que il le veoit si bien du conte, et soubtilloit nuit et jour comment il le pourroit hoster de sa grace, pluiseurs fois ot empensé que il le feroit occhire par ses freres, mais il ne ousoit pour la doubtance du conte. Tant subtilla, visa et ymagina que il trouva le chemin. Et la cause principalment pourquoy il s'entrehayoient, je le vous diray. Anchiennement avoit en la ville du Dam eu une guerre mortelle de deux riches hommes navieurs et de leurs lignaiges, qui s'appelloient l'ung messire Jehan Piet et l'autre sire Jehan Bar. De celle guerre d'amis estoient mors eulx XVIII. Ghiselbrecht Mahieu et ses freres estoient du lignaige de l'un et Jehan Lyon de l'autre. Ces haynnes couvertes estoient ainsi de longtemps nourries entres ces deux, quoy que ilz parlaissent, beussent ou mengassent aucunes fois ensamble; MS fr. 5004, fol. 3v–4r; compare Froissart, *Chroniques,* 9:160–61).

34. "'J'ay dormy ung temps, mais il appert que a petit d'affaire je me resveilleray et metteray ung tel trouble entre ceste ville et le conte qu'il coustera cent milles vies'" (MS fr. 5004, fol. 7v; compare Froissart, *Chroniques,* 9:166).

quired its own logic and quickly became virtually unstoppable. Yoens's manipulation of the Ghent people fuelled the initial action against the Bruges workmen and the attack on Roger of Atrive, and it led to the destruction of the count's castle at Wondelgem and finally to the military expedition against Bruges, after which Yoens died of a sudden illness.[35]

Much more than in Galbert's narrative, revenge and counter-revenge are the prime motives for many of the actions taken in Froissart's *Chronique de Flandre.* Count Louis of Male by no means stands outside this logic of violence, as he is involved with the violent and manipulative ways of Yoens and the Mayhuus brothers right from the beginning. He also falls into all the traps set for him by Yoens, who realizes that he will not escape the count's wrath if peace is ever reestablished between Ghent and the count.[36] Yoens, therefore, keeps manipulating the people of Ghent into actions that will further incense the count and make any chance of peace impossible, a tactic that later in the *Chronique de Flandre* will also be wholeheartedly adopted by Yoens's successors as leaders of the Ghent rebellion, Philip of Artevelde and Pieter van den Bossche.

The deliberate destruction of the count's favorite castle of Wondelgem, presented by Yoens as an accident, prompts the count to summon his noblemen and vassals to his court at Lille "to take counsel as to how they could further their interests and avenge themselves on the men of Ghent."[37] The result, however, is a more general rising of the Flemish cities and the siege of the city of Oudenaarde by the rebellious urban troops, which is ended only after peace talks organized at the initiative of the

35. MS fr. 5004, fol. 7r–24r; compare Froissart, *Chroniques,* 9:166–90.

36. Yoens deliberately sets fire to the castle at Wondelgem, pretending that it was an accident, at the very moment a Ghent delegation is holdings talks with the count: "And Jan Yoens did it because he did not want any peace, for he knew well that if there were any peace treaty, he would lose his life" (Et pour ce le fist Jehan Lyon que il ne voulloit venir a nulle paix, car bien savoit que quelque traictié que il y auroit de paix, si y mettroit il la vie; MS fr. 5004, f. 19v; compare Froissart, *Chroniques,* 9:184). When the count hears the news, he immediately sends the Ghent delegation home, refusing any further talks, which was exactly what Yoens wanted: "Jan Yoens was delighted when he saw that the count of Flanders clearly wanted to do something and that he was burning with such anger that the men of Ghent could not arrange a peace and that he, Jan, had by his subtle arts pushed the city of Ghent so far down the road to war that they would have to fight—whether they wanted to or not" (Or fu Jehan Lyon trop grandement resjoys quant il vit que le conte de Flandres volloit ouvrer adcertes et que il estoit si enflambés en felonnie que ceulx de Gand ne pouoient venir a paix et que il avoit par ses soubtilz ars boutté la ville de Gand si avant en la guerre que il convenoit—voulsissent ou non—que ilz guerroyaissent; MS fr. 5004, fol. 21r; compare Froissart, *Chroniques,* 9:186).

37. "pour avoir conseil comment ilz se pourroient cheuir de ces besoingnes et contrevengier de ceulx de Gand" (MS fr. 5004, fol. 21r; compare Froissart, *Chroniques,* 9:186).

count's son-in-law, Philip of Burgundy. Louis of Male accepts the peace deal, but continues secretly to seek vengeance on Bruges and Ghent, especially for the destruction of his much-loved castle at Wondelgem.[38]

The struggle reignites in early 1380 when some noblemen, relatives of the murdered *bailli* Roger of Atrive, avenge him with a vicious attack on forty Ghent shippers. This attack eventually leads the White Hoods to destroy part of the fortifications around Oudenaarde, an action explicitly characterized as *contrevengance* in the accusation addressed to the city of Ghent by the count's councilors.[39] As a result, the captain of the White Hoods, Jan Pruneel, is banished and peace with the count is again established. But the count, again, takes advantage of the temporary reestablishment of law and order to have Pruneel executed and Ypres purged of his enemies, contrary to the peace deal that had been brokered.[40] The White Hoods react to this defiantly by destroying castles of the nobility in the vicinity of the city. "The count then let the knights and squires wage war against the Ghentenars and avenge their losses."[41]

The logic of the feud—hatred fuelled by violent actions, in turn leading to new actions which themselves cry out for revenge—does not stop there but keeps moving forward in the *Chronique de Flandre* until, finally, in 1385, the more sensible and peace-loving members of the Ghent patriciate, tired of years of violence and of being dominated by an easily manipulated mob, succeed in brokering a peace deal with the duke of Burgundy.

* * *

Revenge, in Galbert's and Froissart's works, is an important theme, a catalyst for the actions and reactions of individual characters and thus a structuring principle for the dramatic action. Furthermore, it is also at the heart of an eschatological conception of history and historiography that is clearly predominant in the whole of Galbert's work and to an extent also in Froissart's *Chronique de Flandre.* In the *De multro,* to be sure, vengeance operates not only on the level of the human individual, but also on a second, higher level. For Galbert sees history as directly planned and arranged by God, and divine punishment as one of the principal ways in which God intervenes directly in this world.[42]

38. MS fr. 5004, fol. 34r–v; compare Froissart, *Chroniques,* 9:211–12.
39. MS fr. 5004, fol. 41r; compare Froissart, *Chroniques,* 9:222.
40. MS fr. 5004, fol. 43v–44r; compare Froissart, *Chroniques,* 9:226.
41. "Adont habandonna le conte aux chevaliers et escuyers a faire guerre aux Gantois et a contrevengier leurs dommaiges" (MS fr. 5004, fol. 45r; compare Froissart, *Chroniques,* 9:226).
42. Galbert, [14], 19/25; trans., 117–18.

Although the immediate causes for the murder of Count Charles are to be sought in the feud between the nephews of Bertulf and those of Thancmar of Straten, the underlying logic is a divine retribution for events that had taken place generations earlier, that is, the betrayal of Arnold of Flanders by his uncle Robert the Frisian and the murder of castellan Boldran by Erembald.[43] Galbert explains a number of unusual deaths in 1127 and 1128 from the same eschatological point of view as divine punishments and thus as clear signs of the guilt of the persons concerned. Galbert sees God's hand in the deaths of Walter of Vladslo, Baldwin of Aalst, and Didier, who died from apparently natural causes, and of Lambert of Aardenburg, who died in battle.[44]

God's wrath is released to punish deeds that are, in Galbert's eyes, contrary to important moral values and principles, as is the case with Walter of Vladslo and Baldwin of Aalst, who in Galbert's words, "had . . . acted contrary to Christian conduct."[45] When looked at more closely, however, most of the crimes punished in Galbert's *De multro* can be classed primarily in three general categories: a breach of kinship solidarity, a breach of loyalty between feudal lord and vassal, or a refusal to accept the God-given social order. The first two are represented by the betrayals of Arnold of Flanders, the castellan Boldran, and Count Charles by their vassals and kinsmen; the last by the failure of the Flemish people to accept William Clito as count, even though he acted as a tyrant.[46]

The crimes committed by Bertulf and his family members are exacerbated by their being unrepentant and overproud, something Galbert stresses time and again.[47] This attitude is most clear in the hardening position of the conspirators, who would rather die than give up and admit guilt.[48] *Superbia,* or excessive pride, is ultimately the refusal to accept the divine truth as signified to humans by the events of history, by supernatural signs of the kind mentioned several times in Galbert's narrative,[49] or in ordeals.[50]

Excessive pride in itself can also be seen as a crime that should be pun-

43. Rider, *God's Scribe,* 70–73.

44. Galbert, [89], [91], [92] and [108]; trans., 262–65 and 287–89; compare Rider, *God's Scribe,* 175–76.

45. "contra morem christianum . . . egerant" (Galbert, [91], 19/20; trans., 264).

46. Rider, *God's Scribe,* 142–83.

47. Galbert, [8], [13], [26], 40/43; trans., 101–2, 114–15, 149.

48. Galbert, [8] 16/19; [38], 34/35; trans., 102, 170.

49. Galbert, [12], 1/6; [59], 5/14; [84], 43/58; trans., 111–12, 214, 256.

50. Galbert, [105], 2; trans., 282.

ished, just as repentance makes it possible for those who have sinned to avoid divine punishment. So, when William Clito repents before the battle of Axspoele, he is victorious against the obstinate Flemings, who refuse to accept him; and when subsequently the Flemings and Count Thierry finally repent, God intervenes again and William Clito dies in an accident.[51]

Although Froissart shares Galbert's eschatological view of history in general, he is too much imbued with the complex reality of history to try to explain every event he narrates in terms of God's intervention. He may, like Galbert, point a condemning finger at the Devil as the originator of the conflict in Flanders and as instigator of sin and *superbia,*[52] but this seems little more than a literary commonplace, for he is acutely aware of the social and economic circumstances and the personal frictions that contributed to the beginnings of the Ghent War. Unlike Galbert's, Froissart's historiography also has a place for contingency in history, for accidental and random events, a worldview that he undoubtedly shared with his contemporaries.[53] Because of this, God intervenes only intermittently and not systematically in the *Chronique de Flandre.*

51. Galbert, [114], 18/24, 68/76; [120]; trans., 297, 299–300, 308–10. See also Rider, *God's Scribe,* 176–82.

52. In the opening chapter of his description of the Ghent War in the *Chroniques,* Froissart remarks that some of his readers would say "that it was the Devil's work; because you know and have heard the wise say that the Devil works night and day to instigate war and hatred wherever he sees peace" (que ce fut <oe>uvre du deable, car vous savez et avez ouï dire aux sages que le deable subtile et attire nuit et jour à bouter guerre et haine là où il voit paix). This remark does not appear in the original and was, in my opinion, inserted when the *Chronique de Flandre* was incorporated into the general *Chroniques* (Froissart, *Chroniques,* 9:159; compare MS fr. 5004, fol. 1r–2v). Other references to the Devil's work in the *Chroniques* were also inserted when, as I believe, the *Chronique de Flandre* was reworked (compare, for example, Froissart, *Chroniques,* 9:165 and MS fr. 5004, fol. 7r). Froissart does mention the Devil in the *Chronique de Flandre,* but only when reporting direct speech (compare, for example, MS fr. 5004, fol. 40v, and Froissart, *Chroniques,* 9:221), and in his description of ominous signs before the battle at Westrozebeke, he reports on loud noise and light heard and seen by Artevelde: "Now some say that it was devils from Hell who were playing or holding a tournament there where the battle was to take place on account of the large number of prey they were expecting there" (Or dient aucuns que c'estoient les deabbles d'enffer qui la jouoient et tournoyoient ou la battaille devoit estre pour la grant proie que ilz y atendoient; MS fr. 5004, fol. 184v; compare Froissart, *Chroniques,* 11:41–42).

53. Ainsworth, *Jean Froissart and the Fabric of History,* 88. To give but one example of this: in Book I ("première rédaction proprement dite") of his *Chroniques,* Froissart blames the disastrous outcome for the French of the Battle of Crécy not on divine punishment but simply on bad fortune: "You have heard about the battle of Crécy earlier in this history and how Fortune surprised the French" (Vous avés ci dessus en ceste hystore bien oy parler de le bataille de Creci, et comment fortune fu moult mervilleuse pour les François; Froissart, *Chroniques,* 5:42). In the margin of one of the manuscripts, a 15th-century reader noddingly noted: "Fortune, not divine sanction" (Fortune, non mies permission divinne; BM Arras, MS 1063, fol. 229v).

Froissart refrains from seeing God's hand in most deaths, as becomes clear, for example, from his narration of the death of Yoens. The first major episode in the *Chronique de Flandre* tells how Yoens is driven out of office by the Mayhuus brothers and shows the lengths to which he goes to take revenge on them and their patron, the count. This first episode ends shortly after the Bruges expedition, discussed above, when the Ghent troops march on Damme. The people of Damme open the city gates and entertain Yoens and his men for two days. On the second night, Yoens suddenly becomes ill, and he dies the following day. Because of the suddenness of his death, Froissart reports a rumor that Yoens may have been poisoned, but completely forgoes the opportunity here to explain this death as divine punishment.[54] The same is true for the death of another Ghent captain, Francis Ackerman, which concludes the final major episode.

The case is less clear for the death of Count Louis of Male, who died in 1384, toward the end of the *Chronique de Flandre.* Although Froissart, like Galbert, was essentially conservative in social outlook, believing in a divinely sanctioned social order, he voices fairly implicit but still fairly strong criticism of the count throughout the *Chronique de Flandre.*[55] The Ghent vic-

54. "Jan Yoens was stricken very suddenly while he was staying there by an illness that made him swell up all over, and the very night that the illness attacked him, he had supped pleasurably with young women of the city, which is why some would say and allege that he was poisoned there. I don't know anything certain about this. But the next day he was placed in a litter and carried to Aardenburg. He could go no further and died there, which made the men of Ghent very angry and discouraged" (En ce sejour et moult soubdainement prist une maladie a Jehan Lyon, dont il fu tout enflez et la proppre nuyt que la maladie lui prist, il avoit souppé en revel avec damoiselles de la ville, pourquoy les aucuns vouldrent dire et maintenir que il fu la empoisonnez. De ce ne sçay je riens de certain. Mais l'endemain que la maladie lui prist, il fu mis en une littiere et aportez a Ardembourch. Il ne peult aler plus avant et la morut, dont ceulx de Gand furent moult courouchiés et desbaretez; MS fr. 5004, fol. 23v–24r; compare Froissart, *Chroniques,* 9:190).

55. See Ainsworth, "Froissardian Perspectives," 67–72, and idem, "Du Berceau à la bière," who shows many of the literary means used by Froissart to construct this negative judgment on Louis of Male. Ainsworth, however, ultimately hesitates to embrace this negative interpretation of the character of Louis of Male in the *Chronique de Flandre.* The context of the present essay does not permit me to discuss this important issue at full length. It is, however, interesting to pause for a moment over the opening passage dealing with the causes of the Ghent War, which was heavily expanded when Froissart reworked his text for inclusion into the general *Chroniques.* In the reworked version, the author presents the envy between the main Flemish cities as the prime cause of the war. He then praises the "wise and subtle" (sage et subtil) count, who "did more than any lord ever had to avoid war and friction between his people and himself" (ressoignoit si la guerre et le mautalent entre ses gens et lui que oncques seigneur ne fit plus de lui), because "no war could break out between them [Bruges and Ghent] unless their lord, the count, agreed to it" (que nulle guerre entre elles principaument ne se pouvoit mouvoir ni élever, si leur sire le comte ne le consentoit; Froissart, *Chroniques,* 9:159–60). This statement is in stark contrast to the immediately following narration, in which Froissart shows how it was in fact the count who allowed

tory at Beverhoutsveld, represented explicitly by Froissart as an ordeal, is in this respect very similar to the battle of Axspoele in Galbert's narrative. But in 1382 it is the Ghent militia who are victorious over the count. God teaches the count a lesson, by giving victory to Philip of Artevelde and the Ghent troops after their public and honest act of penitence. Louis is utterly humiliated in the chase after the defeat, just as he will have to humiliate himself again later on in the narrative by asking the French king for mercy on behalf of the cities of Bruges and Kortrijk after the battle at Westrozebeke.

Froissart repeatedly represents the victory at Beverhoutsveld as the outcome of God's intervention.[56] But fortunes for Ghent change quickly as Artevelde forgets humility and penitence and instead shows an overweening pride: he behaves like a prince and governs as if he were the count. No wonder, then, that God looks favorably on the French expedition, because he "wanted these overproud Flemings to be beaten."[57] The battle at Westrozebeke a few months later, like that at Beverhoutsveld, is represented as an ordeal. Again, Artevelde requests God's help, but various supernatural signs clearly point already to an imminent defeat. Artevelde, who anticipates the outcome, makes cowardly arrangements to flee the battlefield at the slightest bad sign, but eventually dies a dishonorable death, from asphyxiation rather than from battle wounds.

* * *

The theme of divine or supernatural punishment for pride puts the *Chronique de Flandre* firmly in an epic tradition.[58] It also shows interesting differences between Galbert and Froissarts moral value systems and our own time. For *orgueil* (pride) seems to be the only serious sin for which divine punishment is unleashed in Froissart's work.[59] Other types of behavior, such as cunning, duplicity, and cruelty, that would be seen as morally wrong and unfitting for a ruler today, are tolerated or even reported positively by Froissart, who is much more Machiavellian and far less a naive admirer of chivalry than often claimed.[60] Time and again Froissart stresses

---

the conflict to develop and continue over several years. In my view, this should be read as a sharp oxymoron that sums up Froissart's judgment of Louis of Male's qualities as a ruler.

56. MS fr. 5004, fol. 109r, 112r, 114r; compare Froissart, *Chroniques,* 10:234,236, 238. See also Ainsworth's important discussion of Froissart's conflation of scriptural references, which brings out the count's hubris (Ainsworth, "Du Berceau à la bière").

57. "Mais Dieu y fu pour eulx qui voulloit consentir que l'orgueil de Flandres fust abbatus" (MS fr. 5004, fol. 165v; compare Froissart, *Chroniques,* 11:14).

58. See Croenen, "Heroes and Anti-Heroes."

59. Ainsworth, *Jean Froissart and the Fabric of History,* 76.

60. See the percipient discussion of this general feature of the *Chroniques* in George T.

the pride and presumption of characters such as Artevelde, whom the people of Ghent see "as their God" after the victory at Beverhoutsveld,[61] or the bishop of Norwich, who led the disastrous English expedition to the Continent and who "thought he could fly as if he had wings."[62] It is these mental states and their effects that warrant divine intervention and the ultimate failure of the characters' endeavors. This is summed up succinctly by Pieter van den Bossche when he comments on Artevelde's demise: "If Philip of Artevelde is dead, it is because of his pride."[63]

The question of punishment of course also raises the question of guilt and in particular of who is to blame for the disastrous effects on the county of the uprisings of 1127–28 and 1379–85. In this respect, Galbert and Froissart both seem to conceive of guilt as something fairly mechanical that is in important respects different from a modern, individualistic concept reliant upon the idea of responsibility. In terms of narrative technique, Froissart's work is structured as long chains of events, often developed in parallel.[64] Through these chains the author contrasts, juxtaposes, and links specific episodes, especially the opening events of a chain, with their eventual outcome as he sees them. The instigators of the initial events are held responsible, in the final analysis, for all that is eventually caused by their actions, whether or not they could foresee the effects of their deeds. That is why Froissart lays a good deal of blame on the people of Bruges, because they wanted to build a canal, and returns in his conclusion to the fairly trivial Damme feud as one of the main contributing factors to the Ghent War. While Galbert's narrative technique is in this respect different from Froissart's, he passes a similar judgment on Borsiard and the nephews of Thancmar, who, because of their feud, are seen as equally guilty of the murder of the count and hence responsible for all subsequent events.[65]

Diller, "Froissart: Patrons and Texts," in *Froissart: Historian,* ed. Palmer, 145–60. See also Gerald Nachtweg, "The Murder of Pierre Arnaut: Jean Froissart, William Morris and the Changing Image of Chivalric Violence," *Medieval Perspectives* 20 (2005): 57–78.

61. "Ainsi comme leur dieu" (MS fr. 5004, fol. 117v; compare Froissart, *Chroniques,* 10:242).

62. "Qui cuidoit voller avant [*read* ançois] que il eust elles" (MS fr. 5004, fol. 238v; compare Froissart, *Chroniques,* 11:132).

63. "Se Phelippe d'Artevelle est mors, ce a esté par son oultrage" (MS fr. 5004, fol. 201v; compare Froissart, *Chroniques,* 11:67).

64. See William Calin, "Narrative Technique in Fourteenth-Century France: Froissart and his *Chroniques,*" in *Studies in Honor of Hans-Erich Keller: Medieval French and Occitan Literature and Romance Linguistics,* ed. Rupert T. Pickens (Kalamazoo, 1993), 227–36; and George T. Diller, "Romanesque Construct in Froissart's *Chroniques:* The Case of Pierre de Craon and Louis d'Orléans," *Fifteenth-Century Studies* 26 (2001): 66–74.

65. Galbert, [45], 1/2; [113], 29/32; trans., 182, 295.

Galbert's and Froissart's narratives of the uprisings in Flanders in the twelfth and fourteenth centuries are both intelligent, complex, and interesting works, for their value as historical sources as well as for their literary qualities. In several respects they are quite different. Jean Froissart wrote in Middle French, which was his mother tongue. Galbert wrote in Latin, a language he mastered because he used it extensively in his professional capacity as comital notary.

As far as known, the *De multro* was Galbert's first and only work as an author, and he probably decided to write it following the traumatic events of 1127–28, which he witnessed at first hand and which must have had a profound impact on him, both professionally and personally. Froissart, on the other hand, was an accomplished author by the time he wrote his *Chronique de Flandre* in the mid-1380s. He had already written a verse chronicle, now lost, and part of his poetic *oeuvre,* which at this stage included the Arthurian romance *Meliador* and a number of shorter pieces of narrative and lyric poetry. He had furthermore completed a version of the first book of his general *Chroniques.* Froissart's reasons for writing the *Chronique de Flandre* were probably less personal than Galbert's. Unlike Galbert, Froissart was not an eyewitness to the events he described, although he was clearly very familiar with them—he must have had access to inside information—and with the regional and urban politics in the southern Low Countries in general. The occasion for writing this text may have been Froissart's search for a new patron after the death of Wenceslas of Luxemburg, duke of Brabant, in 1383. The *Chronique de Flandre* could also have been a first offering for his new patron Guy de Blois. Guy, as well as some of the other potential patrons Froissart may have been pursuing in this period—Enguerrand de Coucy, Albert of Bavaria, count of Holland and Hainaut, and Philip of Burgundy—had been involved in the French king's military expedition to quell the Ghent revolt, and had an obvious interest in the subject matter of Froissart's work.[66]

Despite these and other differences, Galbert and Froissart also have a number of similarities, some of which I have addressed in this essay and which—when compared—serve to highlight the specificities of each. Both authors wrote on very similar subject matter, within the same geographical setting, and they shared important aspects of the socioeconomic and

66. On Froissart's patrons in this period see Godfried Croenen, "Froissart et ses mécènes: quelques problèmes biographiques," in *Froissart dans sa forge,* ed. Michel Zink (Paris, 2006), 9–32.

cultural context. This partly explains why they used similar literary motifs and explored similar moral and political motives. They share also some of their main themes, especially the theme of feud and revenge, which not only was particularly relevant to the historical events recorded by each author, but—as I have shown—also has an important narrative function in their texts. Feuds played a significant part in social relations and in politics in the medieval Low Countries in general, and both Galbert and Froissart, who lived and worked in this context, must have been fully familiar with them.[67]

In Galbert's and Froissart's work revenge also operates at a higher level, in the form of divine retribution. In this respect both authors' works seem to be grounded in a similar philosophy of history. They seek to establish an understanding of current events by tracing back causal chains of events whose initial impetus explains the eventual outcomes. In so doing they are able to identify who—in the final analysis—is to receive the blame. For Galbert the question of guilt is formulated in rather traditional feudal and social terms. For Froissart excessive pride is the cardinal sin, both morally and politically. Whether or not their conclusions are correct, their works show that both authors were ultimately deeply committed to developing a real understanding of the events about which they wrote and were not satisfied by simply and naively recording them.

67. Godfried Croenen, *Familie en macht: de familie Berthout en de Brabantse adel* (Louvain, 2003), 246–64.

SELECTED BIBLIOGRAPHY OF EDITIONS, TRANSLATIONS, AND STUDIES

EDITIONS OF THE CHRONICLE OF GALBERT OF BRUGES

"Alia vita [B. Caroli boni comitis Flandriae], auctore Galberto notario," edited by Godefroid Henschen and Daniel Van Papenbroeck. In *Acta Sanctorum,* 1 March, 179–219. Antwerp, 1668. [Based on four unidentified manuscripts.]

De multro, traditione, et occisione gloriosi Karoli comitis Flandriarum. Edited by Jeff Rider. CC CM 131. Turnhout, 1994. [Based on all the surviving manuscripts and early editions.]

Histoire du meurtre de Charles le Bon comte de Flandre (1127–1128) par Galbert de Bruges. Edited by Henri Pirenne. Collection de textes pour servir à l'étude et à l'enseignement de l'histoire 10. Paris, 1891. [Based on two surviving manuscripts and the edition by Henschen and Van Papenbroeck.]

"Historia vitae et passionis S. Caroli Com. Flandr. Auctore Galberto notario," edited by Jacob Langebek. In *Scriptores rerum Danicorum medii aevi* 4, 110–92. 1776; rpt. Nendeln, 1969. [Reprint of the edition by Henschen and Van Papenbroeck.]

"Passio Karoli comitis auctore Galberto." Edited by Rudolf Köpke. MGH SS 12, 561–619. Hanover, 1856. [Reprint of Langebek's reprint of the edition by Henschen and Van Papenbroeck.]

TRANSLATIONS OF THE CHRONICLE OF GALBERT OF BRUGES

Dutch

De Moord op Karel de Goede. Dagboek van de gebeurtenissen in de jaren 1127–28. Translated by Bert Demyttenaere, general editor R. C. Van Caenegem. Antwerp, 1978.

De Moord op Karel de Goede. Translated by Bert Demyttenaere. Louvain, 1999.

English

The Murder of Charles the Good, Count of Flanders. Translated by James Bruce Ross. Records of Civilization, Sources and Studies 61. 1959; rev. ed., 1967;

rpt. Medieval Academy Reprints for Teaching 12, Toronto, 1982; rpt. New York, 2005.

French

Histoire du règne de Charles le Bon, précédée d'un résumé de l'histoire des Flandres. Translated by Joseph-Octave Delepierre and Jean Perneel. Brussels, 1830; rpt. 1831, 1844.

La Légende du bienheureux Charles le Bon, Comte de Flandre: Récit du XIIe siècle. Bibliothèque des chemins de fer, 2 sér., Histoire et Voyages. Paris, 1853.

Le Meurtre de Charles le Bon. Translated by J. Gengoux, general editor R. C. Van Caenegem. Antwerp, 1978.

"Vie de Charles le Bon, comte de Flandre." Translated by François P. G. Guizot. In *Collection des mémoires relatifs à l'histoire de France depuis la fondation de la monarchie française jusqu'au XIIIe siècle,* 8, 237–433. Paris, 1825.

STUDIES ON GALBERT OF BRUGES AND HIS CHRONICLE

Carton, Charles-Louis. "Galbert." In *Biographie des hommes remarquables de la Flandre occidentale.* 4 vols., 3:122. Bruges, 1843–49.

Cheyette, Frederic L. "A Case in Point: Galbert of Bruges." In *1983 NEH Institute Resource Book for the Teaching of Medieval Civilization,* edited by Howell Chickering, 193–95. Amherst, 1984.

Cooper, Lisa H. "Making Space for History: Galbert of Bruges and the Murder of Charles the Good." In *Place, Space, and Landscape in Medieval Narrative,* edited by Laura L. Howes. Tennessee Studies in Literature 43, 3–26. Knoxville, Tenn., 2007.

Coué, Stephanie. "Der Mord an Karl dem Guten (1127) und die Werke Galberts von Brügge und Walters von Thérouanne." In *Pragmatische Schriftlichkeit im Mittelalter: Erscheinungsformen und Entwicklungsstufen,* edited by Hagen Keller, Klaus Grubmüller, and Nikolaus Staubach, 108–29. Münstersche Mittelalter-Schriften 65. Munich, 1992.

Czock, Miriam. "Gott schenkte ihm die Märtyrerpalme: Einige Überlegungen zur Funktion der Heiligkeit Karls des Guten bei Galbert von Brügge." In *Recht, Religion, Gesellschaft und Kultur im Wandel der Geschichte: Ferculum de cibis spiritualibus—Festschrift fur Dieter Scheler,* edited by Iris Kwiatkowski and Michael Oberweis. Studien zur Geschichtsforschung des Mittelalters 23, 121–32. Hamburg, 2008.

Declercq, Georges. "Galbert van Brugge en de verraderlijke moord op Karel de Goede." *Handelingen der Maatschappij voor Geschiedenis en Oudheidkunde te Gent* n.s. 49 (1995): 71–119.

Demyttenaere, Bert. "Mentaliteit in de twaalfde eeuw en de benauwenis van

Galbert van Brugge." In *Middeleeuwse cultuur: Verscheidenheid, spanning en verandering,* edited by Marco Mostert, R. E. Künzel, and A. Demyttenaere, 77–129. Hilversum, 1994.

———. "Galbert of Bruges on Political Meeting Culture: Palavers and Fights in Flanders during the Years 1127 and 1128." In *Political Assemblies in the Earlier Middle Ages,* edited by Paul S. Barnwell and Marco Mostert. Studies in the Early Middle Ages 7, 151–92. Turnhout, 2003.

Deploige, Jeroen. "Political Assassination and Sanctification: Transforming Discursive Customs after the Murder of the Flemish Count Charles the Good (1127)." In *Mystifying the Monarch: Studies on Discourse, Power, and History,* edited by Jeroen Deploige and Gita Deneckere, 35–45. Amsterdam, 2006.

Devliegher, Luc. "Galbert et la topographie de Bruges." In *Galbert de Bruges, secrétaire comtal, Le Meurtre de Charles le Bon,* translated by J. Gengoux, general editor R. C. Van Caenegem, 254–64. Antwerp, 1978.

Doehaerd, Renée. "*Flandrenses* dans la *Passio Karoli* de Galbert de Bruges (1127)." *Revue belge de philologie et d'histoire / Belgisch tijdschrift voor filologie en geschiedenis* 71 (1993): 841–49.

Dhondt, Jan. "Une mentalité du douzième siècle: Galbert de Bruges." *Revue du Nord* 39 (1957): 101–9.

Elias, Lorraine. "Augustinian Elements in the Record of Galbert of Bruges." In *Proceedings of the PMR Conference* 18, edited by Karl A. Gersbach, Frederick Van Fleteren, and Joseph C. Schnaubelt, 35–48. Villanova, Pa., 1996.

Groten, Manfred. "In tanto tumultu rerum. Die Bürger von Brügge in Galberts Bericht über die Ermordung Graf Karls von Flandern 1127." In *Vielfalt der Geschichte: Lernen, Lehren und Erforschen vergangener Zeiten. Festschrift für Ingrid Heidrich zum 65. Geburtstag,* edited by Sabine Happ and Ulrich Nonn, 126–40. Berlin, 2004.

Ganshof, François-Louis. "*Armatura* (Galbert de Bruges, c. 106, éd. Pirenne, p. 152)." *Bulletin Du Cange: Archivium Latinitatis Medii Aevi* 15 for 1940 (1941): 179–93.

———. "*Coemptio gravissima mansionum* (Galbert de Bruges, c. 55)." *Bulletin Du Cange: Archivium Latinitatis Medii Aevi* 17 for 1942 (1943): 149–61.

Goeminne, Luc. "Het verhaal van Galbertus over de moord op Karel de Goede en de grafelijke watergraanmolen te Brugge in 1127." *Molenecho's* 10 (1982): 96–97.

Groote, Wolfgang von. "Die Angaben Galberts über Personen und Gremien des 'Öffentlichen Rechts' in Flandern 1127." *Handelingen der Maatschappij voor Geschiedenis en Oudheidkunde te Gent* n.s. 34 (1980): 109–23.

Häcker, Martina. "Mothers, Wives and Witches: The Depiction of Women in Galbert of Bruges' Account of the Murder of Charles the Good." *Bulletin of International Medieval Research* 2–3 for 1996–97 (1997): 10–26.

Heirbaut, Dirk. "Galbert van Brugge: Een bron voor de Vlaamse feodaliteit in de XIIde eeuw." *Tijdschrift voor Rechtsgeschiedenis / Revue d'histoire du droit / The Legal History Review* 60 (1992): 49–62.

Huyghebaert, Nicolas. "Galbert de Bruges." In *Dictionnaire d'histoire et de géographie ecclésiastiques* 19, 737–39. Paris, 1981.

Le Goff, Jacques. "Les gestes symboliques dans la vie sociale. Les gestes de la vassalité." In *Simboli e simbologia nell'alto Medioevo.* 2 vols., 2:689–788. *Settimane di studio del Centro italiano di studi sull'alto Medioevo* 23. Spoleto, 1976.

Marotta, J. "Teaching Medieval Narrative." In *1983 NEH Institute Resource Book for the Teaching of Medieval Civilization,* edited by Howell Chickering, 13–35. Amherst, 1984.

Messyne, M. "Galbert van Brugge en de vroegste geschiedenis van de stad Ieper." *Iepers Kwartier: Driemaandelijks Tijdschrift voor Heemkunde* 27 (1991): 116–19.

Mohr, Walter. "Geschichtstheologische Aspekte im Werk Galberts von Brugge." In *Pascua Mediaevalia: Studies voor Prof. Dr. Jozef-Maria De Smet,* edited by R. Lievens, E. Van Mingroot, and W. Verbeke, 246–62. Mediaevalia Lovaniensia, ser. 1, Studia 10. Louvain, 1983.

Murray, Alan V. "Voices of Flanders: Orality and Constructed Orality in the Chronicle of Galbert of Bruges." *Handelingen der Maatschappij voor Geschiedenis en Oudheidkunde te Gent* n.s. 48 (1994): 103–19.

Nip, Renée. "Gendered Memories from Flanders." In *Medieval Memories: Men, Women and the Past, 700–1300,* edited by Elisabeth Van Houts, 113–31. Harlow, 2001.

Noterdaeme, Jérome. "Galbert en de ridders van Straten." *Het Brugs Ommeland* 2 (1962): 12–21.

Partner, Nancy F. "The New Cornificius: Medieval History and the Artifice of Words." In *Classical Rhetoric and Medieval Historiography,* edited by Ernst Breisach, Studies in Medieval Culture 19, 5–59. Kalamazoo, Mich., 1985.

Rider, Jeff. "Galbert of Bruges' 'Journal': From Medieval Flop to Modern Bestseller." In *Verhalende Bronnen: Repertoriering, Editie en Commercialisiering,* edited by Ludo Milis, Véronique Lambert, and A. Kelders, 67–93. Studia Historica Gandensia: Publicaties van de Opleiding Geschiedenis van de Universiteit Gent 283. Ghent, 1996.

———. *God's Scribe: The Historiographical Art of Galbert of Bruges.* Washington, D.C., 2001.

———. "The God of History: The Concept of God in the Works of Galbert of Bruges and Walter of Thérouanne (1127–1130)." In *"In Principio erat verbum." Mélanges offerts en homage à Paul Tombeur par des anciens étudiants à l'occasion de son éméritat,* edited by Benoît-Michel Tock, 357–78. Textes et Etudes du Moyen Age 25. Turnhout, 2005.

Spiegel, Gabrielle. *The Past as Text: The Theory and Practice of Medieval Historiography.* Baltimore, Md., 1997.

Sproemberg, Heinrich. "Das Erwachen des Staatsgefühls in den Niederlanden: Galbert von Brügge." In *L'Organisation corporative du Moyen Age à la fin de l'Ancien Régime: Etudes présentées à la Commission Internationale pour l'histoire des assemblées d'états* 3, 31–89. Université de Louvain, Recueil de Travaux publiés par les Membres des Conférences d'Histoire et de Philologie, 2 série, 50. Louvain, 1939.

———. "Galbert von Brügge—Die Geschichtsschreibung des flandrischen Bürgertums." In Sproemberg, *Mittelalter und demokratische Geschichtsschreibung,* edited by Manfred Unger, Lily Sproemberg, and Wolfgang Eggert, 223–372. Forschungen zur mittelalterlichen Geschichte 18. Berlin, 1971.

———. "Galbert von Brügge—Persönlichkeit und Werke." In Sproemberg, *Mittelalter und demokratische Geschichtsschreibung,* edited by Manfred Unger, Lily Sproemberg, and Wolfgang Eggert, 239–77. Forschungen zur mittelalterlichen Geschichte 18. Berlin, 1971.

———. "Galbert von Brügge—Stellung und Bedeutung. Die Anfänge demokratisches Geschichtsschreibung im Mittelalter." In Sproemberg, *Mittelalter und demokratische Geschichtsschreibung,* edited by Manfred Unger, Lily Sproemberg, and Wolfgang Eggert, 319–24. Forschungen zur mittelalterlichen Geschichte 18. Berlin, 1971.

Thomas, P. "Notes sur Galbert de Bruges." In *Mélanges d'histoire offerts à Henri Pirenne.* 2 vols., 2:515–17. Brussels, 1926.

Van Caenegem, R. C. *Galbert van Brugge en het Recht,* Mededelingen van de Koninklijke Academie voor Wetenschappen, Letteren en Schone Kunsten van België, Klasse der Letteren 40/1. Brussels, 1978.

———. "Galbert of Bruges on Serfdom, Prosecution of Crime, and Constitutionalism." In *Law, Custom and the Social Fabric in Medieval Europe: Essays in Honor of Bryce Lyon,* edited by Bernard S. Bachrach and David Nicholas, 89–112. Studies in Medieval Culture 28. Kalamazoo, Mich., 1990.

———. "Misdaad en Straf bij Galbert van Brugge." In *Liber Amicorum Jules D'Haenens,* 321–31. Ghent, 1993.

———. "Notes on Galbert of Bruges and His Translators." In *Peasants and Townsmen in Medieval Europe: Studia in honorem Adriaan Verhulst,* edited by Jean-Marie Duvosquel and Erik Thoen, 619–29. Ghent, 1995.

Viaene, Antoon. "Galbert van Brugge in eerste moderne vertaling: Een Vlaams initiatief van archivaris Delepierre." *Biekorf* 78 (1978): 193–99.

Ward, John O. "Some Principles of Rhetorical Historiography in the Twelfth Century." In *Classical Rhetoric and Medieval Historiography,* edited by Ernst Breisach, 103–65. Studies in Medieval Culture 19. Kalamazoo, Mich., 1985.

Wauters, Alphonse "Gualbert." In *Biographie nationale.* 34 vols., 8:392–94. Brussels, 1866–1968.

OTHER PRIMARY SOURCES

Actes des comtes de Flandre 1071–1128. Edited by Fernand Vercauteren. Actes des princes belges. Brussels, 1938.

Cartulaire de l'abbaye de Saint-Bertin. Edited by Benjamin Guérard. Paris, 1840.

Cartulaire de l'abbaye de Saint-Vaast d'Arras rédigé au XIIe siècle par Guimann. Edited by Eugène-François Van Drival. Arras, 1875.

De Oorkonden der graven van Vlaanderen (1191–aanvang 1206). Edited by Walter Prevenier. 3 vols. Brussels, 1964–71.

De Oorkonden der graven van Vlaanderen (juli 1128–september 1191), 2/1: *Regering van Diederik van de Elzas (juli 1128–17 januari 1168).* Edited by Thérèse De Hemptinne and Adriaan Verhulst. Verzameling van de akten der belgischen vorsten 6. Brussels, 1988.

"Enqueste et jugement de chiaus qui le Conte Charlon avoient ochis." In *Walteri archidiaconi Tervanensis, Vita Karoli comitis Flandrię et Vita domni Ioannis Morinensis Episcopi,* edited by Jeff Rider, 199–209. CC CM 217. Turnhout, 2006.

Gesta episcoporum Cameracensium continuata. Edited by Georg Waitz. MGH SS 14, 183–253. Hanover, 1883.

Gesta Stephani, edited and translated by K. R. Potter. Oxford, 1976.

Gilbert of Mons. *La Chronique de Gislebert de Mons.* Edited by Léon Vanderkindere. Brussels, 1904.

———. *Chronicle of Hainaut.* Translated by Laura Napran. Woodbridge, Suffolk, 2005.

Guibert of Nogent. *Autobiographie.* Edited by Edmond-Réné Labande. Paris, 1981.

———. *A Monk's Confession: The Memoirs of Guibert of Nogent.* Translated by Paul J. Archambault. University Park, Pa., 1996.

Hariulf of Oudenburg. *Vita Arnulfi episcopi Suessionensis.* Edited by Oswald Holder-Egger. MGH SS 15.2, 872–904. Hanover, 1888.

Herman of Tournai. "Herimanni liber de restauratione monasterii Sancti Martini Tornacensis." Edited by Georg Heinrich Waitz. MGH SS 14, 274–317. Hanover, 1883.

———. *The Restoration of the Monastery of Saint Martin of Tournai.* Translated by Lynn H. Nelson. Washington, D.C., 1996.

Istore et croniques de Flandres. Edited by J. Kervyn de Lettenhove. 2 vols. Brussels, 1879–80.

Koch, A. C. F. "Actes des comtes de Flandre de la période de 1071 à 1128." *Bul-*

letin de la Commission royale d'histoire / Handelingen van de Koniklijke Commissie van Geschiedenis 122 (1957): 261–78.

Lambert of Ardres. *Historia comitum Ghisnensium.* Edited by Johann Heller. MGH SS 24, 550–642. Hanover 1879.

———. *The History of the Counts of Guines and Lords of Ardres.* Translated by Leah Shopkow. Philadelphia, 2001.

Lambert of Wattrelos. *Annales Cameracenses.* Edited by Georg Heinrich Pertz. MGH SS 16, 509–54. Hanover, 1859.

L'Histoire-polyptique de l'abbaye de Marchiennes (1116–1121). Edited by Bernard Delmaire. Louvain-la-Neuve, 1985.

Lisiardus of Soissons. *Vita Arnulfi episcopi Suessionensis.* Edited by Renée Nip. In Nip, *Arnulfus van Oudenburg, Bisschop van Soisssons (†1087),* 321–46. Louvain, 2004.

Oorkondenboek van Holland en Zeeland tot 1299. Edited by A. C. F. Koch. 5 vols. The Hague, 1970–2005.

Orderic Vitalis. *The Ecclesiastical History.* Edited and translated by Marjorie Chibnall. 6 vols. Oxford, 1969–80.

"Passio Karoli comitis auctore anonymo." Edited by Rudolf Köpke. MGH SS 12, 619–23. Hanover, 1856.

"Poemata de morte Karoli comitis Flandrie conscripta." In *Walteri archidiaconi Tervanensis, Vita Karoli comitis Flandrię et Vita domni Ioannis Morinensis Episcopi,* edited by Jeff Rider, 157–97. CC CM 217. Turnhout, 2006.

Recueil des actes de Louis VI, roi de France (1108–1137) . Edited by Jean Dufour. Chartes et diplômes relatifs à l'histoire de France publiés par les soins de l'Académie des Inscriptions et Belles-Lettres. 3 vols. Paris, 1992–.

Recueil des Chroniques de Flandre / Corpus Chronicorum Flandriae. Edited by Joseph Jean De Smet. 4 vols. Brussels, 1837–65.

Suger. *Vie de Louis VI le Gros.* Edited and translated by Henri Waquet. Les Classiques de l'histoire de France au Moyen Age. 11. is. 1929.

———. *The Deeds of Louis the Fat.* Translated by Richard Cusimano and John Moorhead. Washington, D.C., 1992.

Walter of Thérouanne. "Vita domni Ioannis Morinensis episcopi." In *Walteri archidiaconi Tervanensis, Vita Karoli comitis Flandrię et Vita domni Ioannis Morinensis Episcopi,* edited by Jeff Rider, 81–155. CC CM 217. Turnhout, 2006.

———. "Vita Karoli comitis Flandriae." In *Walteri archidiaconi Tervanensis, Vita Karoli comitis Flandrię et Vita domni Ioannis Morinensis Episcopi,* edited by Jeff Rider, 1–79. CC CM 217. Turnhout, 2006.

William of Andres. *Chronica Andrensis.* Edited by Johann Heller. MGH SS 24, 684–773. Hanover, 1879.

GOVERNMENT AND INSTITUTIONS OF FLANDERS IN THE AGE OF GALBERT OF BRUGES

Barthélemy, Dominique. *Les Deux âges de la seigneurie banale: Pouvoir et Société dans la terre des Sires de Coucy (milieu XIe–milieu XIIIe siècle).* Paris, 1984.

Bisson, Thomas. "Lordship and Tenurial Dependence in Flanders, Provence and Occitania (1050–1200)." In *Il feudalesimo nell'alto medioevo.* 2 vols., 1:389–446. *Settimane di studio del Centro italiano di studi sull'alto medioevo* 47. Spoleto, 2000.

Bloch, Marc. "Les formes de la rupture de l'hommage dans l'ancien droit féodal." *Revue historique de droit français et étranger* 36 (1912): 141–77.

Bonenfant, Paul. "La dépendance du château d'Alost au XIIe siècle." In *Album Dr Jan Lindemans,* edited by Robert Foncke et al., 169–73. Brussels, 1951.

Burgers, J. W. J. "Het ontstaan van de twaalfde-eeuwse Vlaamse stadskeuren." In *Van vader- naar moedertaal: Latijn, Frans en Nederlands in de dertiende-eeuwse Nederlanden,* edited by Rita Beyers, 81–99. Brussels, 2000.

De Hemptinne, Thérèse. "De gravinnen van Vlaanderen in de 12de eeuw." *Spiegel Historiael: Maandblad voor Geschiedenis en Archeologie* 15 (1980): 450–55.

———. "Clementia van Bourgondië, gravin van Vlaanderen." In *Nationaal Biografisch Woordenboek* 9, 148–50. Brussels, 1981.

———. "Les Epouses des croisés et pèlerins flamands aux XIe et XIIe siècles: L'Exemple des comtesses de Flandre Clémence et Sibylle." In *Autour de la première croisade: Actes du Colloque de la Society for the Study of the Crusades and the Latin East (Clermont-Ferrand, 22–25 juin 1995),* edited by Michel Balard, 83–95. Paris, 1996.

De Hemptinne, Thérèse, Walter Prevenier, and Maurice Vandermaesen. "La Chancellerie des comtes de Flandre (12e–14e siècle)." In *Landesherrliche Kanzleien im Spätmittelalter: Referate zum VI. Internationalen Kongreß für Diplomatik, München 1983,* edited by Gabriel Silagi. 2 vols., 1:433–54. Münchener Beiträge zur Mediävistik und Renaissance-Forschung 35. Munich, 1984.

De Hemptinne, Thérèse, and Maurice Vandermaesen. "De ambtenaren van de centrale administratie van het graafschap Vlaanderen van de 12e tot de 14e eeuw." *Tijdschrift voor Geschiedenis* 93 (1980): 177–209.

Declercq, Georges. "De dekens van het Sint-Donaaskapittel in Brugge voor 1200." *Handelingen van het Genootschap voor Geschiedenis Gesticht onder de Benaming "Société d'émulation" te Brugge* 125 (1988): 39–54.

Dhondt, Jan. "Vlaanderen van Arnulf de Grote tot Willem Clito, 918–1128." In *Algemene Geschiedenis der Nederlanden,* 2, 66–93. Utrecht, 1950.

———. "Le Droit urbain en Flandre au début de la première phase de son histoire (1127)." *Tijdschrift voor Rechtsgeschiedenis / Revue d'histoire du droit / The Legal History Review* 19 (1951): 387–416.

Ganshof, François-Louis. *Etude sur les ministeriales en Flandre et en Lotharingie,* Mémoires de l'Académie royale de Belgique, Classe des Lettres et des sciences morales et politiques, 20/1. Brussels, 1926.

———. "Les Transformations de l'organisation judiciaire dans le comté de Flandre jus'qu'à l'avènement de la maison de Bourgogne." *Revue belge de philologie et d'histoire / Belgisch Tijdschrift voor Filologie en Geschiedenis* 18 (1939): 43–61.

———. *La Flandre sous les premiers comtes.* Brussels, 1943.

———. "Les origines du concept de souveraineté nationale en Flandre." *Tijdschrift voor Rechtsgeschiedenis / Revue d'histoire du droit / The Legal History Review* 18 (1950): 135–58.

———. "Le Droit urbain en Flandre au début de la première phase de son histoire (1127)." *Tijdschrift voor Rechtsgeschiedenis / Revue d'histoire du droit / The Legal History Review* 19 (1951): 387–416.

———. "Einwohnergenossenschaft und Graf in den flandrischen Städten während des 12. Jahrhunderts." *Zeitschrift der Savigny-Stiftung für Rechtsgeschichte, Germanische Abteilung* 74 (1957): 98–118.

———. "La Flandre." In *Histoire des institutions française au Moyen Age, 1: Institutions seigneuriales,* edited by Ferdinand Lot and Robert Fawtier, 343–426. Paris, 1957.

Ganshof, François-Louis, R. Van Caenegem, and Adriaan Verhulst. "Note sur le premier traité anglo-flamand de Douvres." *Revue du Nord* 40 (1958): 245–57.

Groote, Wolfgang von. "Der 'Magnus Praeco' und sein Amtsnachfolger in Flandern im 12. Jahrhundert." *Handelingen der Maatschappij voor Geschiedenis en Oudheidkunde te Gent* n.s. 29 (1975): 39–48.

Heirbaut, Dirk. "De militaire rol van de feodaliteit in het graafschap Vlaanderen gedurende de 11de en 12de eeuw." *Revue belge d'histoire militaire* 29 (1992): 311–17.

———. *Over heren, vazallen en graven: Het persoonlijk leenrecht in Vlaanderen, ca. 1000–1305.* Studia, Algemeen Rijksarchief en Rijksarchief in de Provinciën 69. Brussels, 1997.

———. *Over lenen en families: Een studie over de vroegste geschiedenis van het zakelijke leenrecht in het graafschap Vlaanderen (ca. 1000–1305).* Verhandelingen Koninklijke Vlaamse Academie van België voor Wetenschappen en Kunsten, nieuwe reeks 2. Brussels, 2000.

———. "Flanders: A Pioneer of State-Oriented Feudalism? Feudalism as an Instrument of Comital Power in Flanders during the High Middle Ages (1000–1300)." In *Expectations of the Law in the Middle Ages,* edited by Anthony Musson, 23–34. Woodbridge, Suffolk, 2001.

———. "On and Over the Edge of the Empire: The Counts of Flanders and Hainault and the Election of the Kings of the Romans (1000–1314)." In

Königliche Tochterstämme, Königswähler und Kurfürsten, edited by Armin Wolf, 419–55. Frankfurt am Main, 2002.

Koziol, Geoffrey. *Begging Pardon and Favor: Ritual and Political Order in Early Medieval France.* Ithaca, N.Y., 1992.

Lambert, Véronique. "Methodologische beschouwingen bij het onderzoek naar de concepten 'natie', 'nationalisme' en 'nationale identiteit' in de Middeleeuwen." *Jaarboek voor middeleeuwse geschiedenis* 4 (2001): 66–85.

Lambrecht, Daniel, and Jan Van Rompaey. "De staatsinstellingen in het Zuiden van de 11de tot de 14de eeuw." In *Algemene geschiedenis der Nederlanden* 3, 77–134. Haarlem, 1982.

Lestocquoy, J. *Histoire de la Flandre et de l'Artois.* Paris, 1949.

Lyon, Bryce, and A. E. Verhulst. *Medieval Finance: A Comparison of Financial Institutions in Northwestern Europe.* Providence, Rhode Island, 1967.

Monier, Raymond. *Les Institutions centrales du Comté de Flandre de la fin du IXe siècle à 1384.* Paris, 1943.

———. *Les Institutions financières du comté de Flandre du IXe siècle à 1384.* Paris, 1948.

Nicholas, David. "Of Poverty and Primacy: Demand, Liquidity and the Flemish Economic Miracle, 1050–1200." *American Historical Review* 96 (1991): 17–41.

———. *Medieval Flanders.* London, 1992.

Nicholas, Karen S. "Countesses as Rulers in Flanders." In *Aristocratic Women in Medieval France,* edited by Theodore Evergates, 111–37, 220–25. Philadelphia, Pa., 1990.

———. "The Role of Feudal Relationships in the Consolidation of Power in the Principalities of the Low Countries, 1000–1300." In *Law, Custom and the Social Fabric in Medieval Europe: Essays in Honor of Bryce Lyon,* edited by Bernard Bachrach and David Nicholas, 113–30. Studies in Medieval Culture 28. Kalamazoo, Mich., 1990.

Prevenier, Walter. "La chancellerie des comtes de Flandre dans le cadre européen à la fin du XIIe siècle." *Bibliothèque de l'Ecole des Chartes* 125 (1967): 34–93.

Pycke, Jacques. *Le Chapitre cathédral Notre-Dame de Tournai de la fin du XIe à la fin du XIIIe siècle: Son organisation, sa vie, ses membres.* Université de Louvain: Recueil de travaux d'histoire et de philologie 6/30. Louvain-la-Neuve, 1986.

Reusens, E. "Les chancelleries inférieures en Belgique depuis leur origine jusqu'au commencement du XIIIe siècle." *Analectes pour servir à l'histoire ecclésiastique de la Belgique* 26 (1896): 57–133.

Reynolds, Susan. *Fiefs and Vassals: The Medieval Evidence Reinterpreted.* Oxford, 1994.

———. "Afterthoughts on *Fiefs and Vassals*." *Haskins Society Journal* 9 (1997): 7–12.

Sproemberg, Heinrich. "Clementia, Gräfin von Flandern." *Revue belge de philologie et d'histoire / Belgisch Tijdschrift voor Filologie en Geschiedenis* 42 (1964): 1203–41, reprinted in Sproemberg, *Mittelalter und demokratische Geschichtsschreibung*, edited by Manfred Unger, Lily Sproemberg, and Wolfgang Eggert, 192–220. Forschungen zur mittelalterlichen Geschichte 18. Berlin, 1971.

Van Caenegem, R. C. *Geschiedenis van het strafrecht in Vlaanderen van de XIe tot de XIVe eeuw.* Verhandelingen van de Koninklijke Vlaamse Academie voor Wetenschappen, Letteren en Schone Kunsten van België, Klasse der Letteren 19. Brussels, 1954.

———. *Geschiedenis van het strafprocesrecht in Vlaanderen van de XIe to de XIVe eeuw.* Verhandelingen van de Koninklijke Vlaamse Academie voor Wetenschappen, Letteren en Schone Kunsten van België, Klasse der Letteren 24. Brussels, 1956.

———. *Coutumes et législation en Flandre au XIe et XIIe siècles.* Brussels, 1968.

———. *Law, History, the Low Countries and Europe.* London, 1994.

———. "Democratie en rechtsstaat in het twaalfde-eeuwse graafschap Vlaanderen." *Tijdschrift voor Rechtsgeschiedenis / Revue d'histoire du droit / The Legal History Review* 61 (1993): 205–15.

———. "Law and Power in Twelfth-Century Flanders." In *Cultures of Power: Lordship, Status, and Process in Twelfth-Century Europe*, edited by Thomas N. Bisson, 149–71. Philadelphia, 1995.

Vanderkindere, Léon. *La formation territoriale des principautés belges au Moyen Age.* 2 vols. Brussels, 1902.

Verbruggen, Jan Frans. *Het leger en de vloot van de graven van Vlaanderen vanaf het ontstaan tot in 1305.* Brussels, 1960.

Verhulst, Adriaan. "The Origins of Towns in the Low Countries and the Pirenne Thesis." *Past and Present* 122 (1989): 3–35.

Verhulst, Adriaan E., and Thérèse De Hemptinne. "Le Chancelier de Flandre sous les comtes de la maison d'Alsace (1128–1191)." *Bulletin de la Commission royale d'histoire / Handelingen van de Koniklijke Commissie van Geschiedenis* 141 (1975): 267–311.

Warlop, Ernest. *De Vlaamse adel vóór 1300.* 3 vols. Handzame, 1968.

———. *The Flemish Nobility before 1300.* Translated by James Bruce Ross and H. Vandermoere. 2 vols. in 4 parts. Kortrijk, 1975–76.

Warnkönig, Leopold August, *Flandrische Staats- und Rechtsgeschichte,* 3 vols. in 5 parts. Tübingen, 1835–42.

THE REIGN OF CHARLES THE GOOD AND THE FLEMISH CRISIS OF 1127–28

Adair, Penelope. "Lambert Nappin and Lambert of Aardenburg: One Fleming or Two?" *Medieval Prosopography* 11 (1990): 17–34.

Carnier, Marc. "De Goede en de heel erg slechten. De moord op Karel graaf van Vlaanderen (1127)." In *Koningsmoorden,* edited by Tom Verschaffel, 127–42. Louvain, 2000.

Carton, Charles-Louis. "Bertulf." In *Biographie des hommes remarquables de la Flandre occidentale.* 4 vols., 3:45. Bruges, 1843–49.

———. "Charles." In *Biographie des hommes remarquables de la Flandre occidentale.* 4 vols., 3:122. Bruges, 1843–49.

———. "Erembald." In *Biographie des hommes remarquables de la Flandre occidentale.* 4 vols., 3:167. Bruges, 1843–49.

De Hemptinne, Thérèse, and Michel Parisse. "Thierry d'Alsace, comte de Flandre: Biographie et actes." *Annales de l'Est* 43 (1991): 83–113.

De Smet, J.-M. "Bij de latijnsche gedichten over den moord op den Glz. Karel den Goede Graaf van Vlaanderen." In *Miscellanea historica in honorem Alberti de Meyer.* 2 vols., 1:418–43. Université de Louvain, Recueil de Travaux d'histoire et de philologie, ser. 3, 22–23. Louvain, 1946.

———. "Le vexilla regis prodeunt du cod. brux. 6837–40, composé pour l'expédition de Louis le Gros contre les meurtiers de Charles I le Bon (1127)." *Revue d'histoire ecclésiastique* 46 (1951): 165–69.

———. "Bijdrage tot de iconographie van de Glz. Karel de Goede, Graaf van Vlaanderen." In *Studies over de Kerkelijke en Kunstgeschiedenis van West-Vlaanderen opgedragen aan Z. E. H. Michiel English,* edited by A. Hodüm, N. Huyghebaert, and E. Strubbe, 117–57. Bruges, 1952.

———. "Charles le Bon." In *Dictionnaire d'histoire et de géographie ecclésiastiques* 12, 483–86. Paris, 1953.

Declercq, Georges. "Bertulf, kanselier van Vlaanderen." *Nationaal Biografisch Woordenboek* 13, cols. 73–80. Brussels, 1990.

Derville, Alain. *Saint-Omer des origines au début du XIVe siècle.* Lille, 1995.

Dhondt, Jan. "Note sur les événements de 1127 en Flandre." *Handelingen van het Genootschap voor Geschiedenis Gesticht onder de Benaming "Société d'émulation" te Brugge* 67 (1924): 97–107.

———. "Le Roi de France en Flandre en 1127 et 1128." *Revue historique de droit français et étranger* 4th ser., 27 (1949): 204–28.

———. "Trois mandements perdus du roi de France, Louis VI, intéressant la Flandre." *Handelingen van het Genootschap voor Geschiedenis Gesticht onder de Benaming "Société d'émulation" te Brugge* 87 (1950): 117–33.

———. "Les 'Solidarités' médiévales. Une société en transition: La Flandre en 1127–28." *Annales ESC* 12 (1957): 529–60.

———. "Medieval 'Solidarities': Flemish Society in Transition, 1127–28." In *Lordship and Community in Medieval Europe,* edited by Frederic L. Cheyette, 268–96. New York, 1968.

Espinas, Georges. "Le privilège de Saint-Omer de 1127." *Revue du Nord* 29 (1947): 43–48.

Ganshof, François-Louis. "Note sur les événements de 1127 en Flandre." *Handelingen van het Genootschap voor Geschiedenis Gesticht onder de Benaming "Société d'émulation" te Brugge* 67 (1924): 97–107.

———. "Le roi de France en Flandre en 1127 et 1128." *Revue historique de droit français et étranger* 27 (1949): 204–28.

———. "Trois mandements perdus du roi de France Louis VI intéressant la Flandre." *Handelingen van het Genootschap voor Geschiedenis Gesticht onder de Benaming "Société d'émulation" te Brugge* 87 (1950): 117–33.

———. "Einwohnergenossenschaft und Graf in den flandrischen Städten während des 12. Jahrhunderts." *Zeitschrift der Savigny-Stiftung für Rechtsgeschichte, Germanische Abteilung* 74 (1957): 98–118.

———. "Note sur le premier traité anglo-normand de Douvres." *Revue du Nord* 40 (1958): 245–57.

Ghent: In Defence of a Rebellious City. Edited by Johan Decavele. Antwerp, 1989.

Goetinck, Marc, and Jean Luc Meulemeester. *Karel de Goede, 1127–1977: Tentoonstelling, Brugge, van 13 augustus tot 2 oktober 1977.* 2 vols. Bruges, 1977.

Hicks, Sandy Burton. "The Impact of William Clito on the Continental Policies of Henry I of England." *Viator* 10 (1979): 1–22.

———. "England's King Henry I and the Flemish Succession Crisis of 1127–1128." *Journal of the Rocky Mountain Medieval and Renaissance Association* 2 (1981): 41–49.

Hollister, C. Warren. "The Anglo-Norman Succession Debate of 1126: Prelude to Stephen's Anarchy." *Journal of Medieval History* 1 (1975): 19–35.

Huyghebaert, Nicolas. "Abt Giselbrecht van Eename en de Gelukzelige Karel de Goede: Nota over Herman van Doornik." *Sacris Erudiri* 1 (1948): 225–31.

Lambert, Véronique. "Middeleeuwse historiografie en nationale identiteit. Een vergelijking van het graafschap Vlaanderen en het hertogdom Normandië." 2 vols. Unpublished doctoral thesis, University of Ghent, 2000.

Luchaire, Achille. *Louis VI le Gros. Annales de sa vie et de son règne (1081–1137.* Paris, 1890.

Marvin, Laurence W. "'Men Famous in Combat and Battle . . .': Common Soldiers and the Siege of Bruges, 1127." *Journal of Medieval History* 24 (1998): 243–58.

Meulemeester, Jean Luc. "Twee minderbekende afbeeldingen van Karel de Goede." *Het Brugs Ommeland* 20 (1980): 106–24.

Mohr, Walter. *Die Entwicklung des flämischen Eigenständigkeitsgefühls bis zum Beginn des 13. Jahrhunderts.* Saarbrücken, 1977.

———. "Richilde vom Hennegau und Robert der Friese. Thesen zu einer Neubewertung der Quellen." *Revue belge de philologie et d'histoire / Belgisch Tijdschrift voor Filologie en Geschiedenis* 58 (1980): 777–796.

———. "Richilde vom Hennegau und Robert der Friese. Thesen zu einer Neubewertung der Quellen (2. Teil)." *Revue belge de philologie et d'histoire / Belgisch Tijdschrift voor Filologie en Geschiedenis* 59 (1981): 265–291.

Murray, Alan V. "The Judicial Inquest into the Death of Count Charles of Flanders (1127): Location and Chronology." *Tijdschrift voor Rechtsgeschiedenis / Revue d'histoire du droit / The Legal History Review* 68 (2000): 47–61.

Murray, James M. "The Liturgy of the Count's Advent in Bruges, from Galbert to Van Eyck." In *City and Spectacle in Medieval Europe,* edited by Barbara A. Hanawalt and Kathryn Reyerson, 137–52. Medieval Cultures 6. Minneapolis, Minn., 1994.

Nicholas, Karen. "When Feudal Ideals Failed: Conflicts between Lords and Vassals in the Low Countries, 1127–1296." In *The Rusted Hauberk: Feudal Ideals of Order and Their Decline,* edited by Liam O. Purdon and Cindy L. Vitto, 201–26. Gainesville, Fla., 1994.

Nieus, Jean-François. "Aux marges de la principauté: les 'comtés vassaux' de la Flandre, fin Xe–fin XIIe siècle." In *VIe Congrès de l'association des Cercles francophones d'histoire et d'archéologie de Belgique,* 309–32. Mons, 2002.

———. *Un pouvoir comtal entre Flandre et France: Saint-Pol, 1000–1300.* Brussels, 2005.

———. "Du donjon au tribunal. Les deux âges de la paire châtellaine en France du Nord, Flandre et Lotharingie (fin XIe–XIIIe s.)." *Le Moyen Age* 112 (2006): 9–41, 307–36.

Nip, Renée. "The Political Relations between England and Flanders (1066–1128)." In *Anglo-Norman Studies, XXI: Proceedings of the Battle Conference, 1998,* edited by Christopher Harper-Bill, 145–67. Woodbridge, Suffolk, 1999.

Noterdaeme, Jérome. "De ridders van Straten." *Het Brugs Ommeland* 1 (1961): 23–30.

Ross, James Bruce. "Rise and Fall of a Twelfth-Century Clan: The Erembalds and the Murder of Count Charles of Flanders, 1127–28." *Speculum* 34 (1959): 367–90.

Sigmund, Pia. "Far og søn. Knud den Hellige og Karl den Gode." *Fynske Årbøger* for 2003: 19–26.

Sproemberg, Heinrich. "Eine rheinische Königskandidatur im Jahre 1125." In *Aus Geschichte und Landeskunde: Forschungen und Darstellungen. Franz Steinbach zum 65. Geburtstag gewidmet,* edited by Max Braubach et al., 50–70. Bonn, 1960.

———. *Mittelalter und demokratische Geschichtsschreibung.* Edited by Manfred

Unger, Lily Sproemberg, and Wolfgang Eggert. Forschungen zur mittelalterlichen Geschichte 18. Berlin, 1971.
Tanner, Heather J. *Families, Friends and Allies: Boulogne and Politics in Northern France and England, c. 879–1160*. Leiden, 2004.
Van Acker, Karel Gerard. "Een jachtpartij met rivalen: intriges en gevolgen (1140)." *Appeltjes van het Meetjesland* 40 (1989): 193–197.
Van Caenegem, R. C. "De Gentse februari-opstand van het jaar 1128." *Spiegel Historiael: Maandblad voor Geschiedenis en Archeologie* 13 (1978): 478–83.
———. "De Keure van Sint-Omaars van 1127." *Tijdschrift voor Rechtsgeschiedenis / Revue d'histoire du droit / The Legal History Review* 50 (1982): 253–62.
———. "The Ghent Revolt of February 1128." In R. C. Van Caenegem, *Law, History, the Low Countries and Europe,* edited by Ludo Milis et al., 107–12. London, 1994.
———. "Law and Power in Twelfth-Century Flanders." In *Cultures of Power: Lordship, Status, and Process in Twelfth-Century Europe,* edited by Thomas N. Bisson, 149–71. Philadelphia, 1995.
———. "Mediaeval Flanders and the Seeds of Modern Democracy." In *Foundations of Democracy in the European Union: From the Genesis of Parliamentary Democracy to the European Parliament,* edited by John Pinder, 4–17. New York, 1999.
Van Meter, David. "Eschatology and the Sanctification of the Prince in Twelfth-Century Flanders: The Case of Walter of Thérouanne's *Vita Karoli comitis Flandriae.*" *Sacris Erudiri* 35 (1995): 115–31.
Warlop, Ernest. "Willem van Ieper, een Vlaams condottiere (vóór 1104–1164)." *De Leiegouw* 6 (1964): 167–92; 7 (1965): 197–218.
Wauters, Alphonse. *Thierry d'Alsace: Etude sur le règne de ce prince.* Ghent, 1863.

TOPOGRAPHY AND HISTORY OF BRUGES

De Brugse Burg. Edited by Hubert De Witte. Bruges, 1991.
Coornaert, M. "Over de hydrografie van Brugge." In *Album Albert Schouteet,* 23–25.Bruges, 1973.
De Poorter, Alphonse. *Catalogue des manuscrits de la Bibliothèque publique de la ville de Bruges.* Catalogue général des manuscrits des bibliothèques de Belgique 2. Gembloux, 1934.
De Smet, J.-M. "De oude hydrografie van de stad Brugge." *Handelingen van het Genootschap voor Geschiedenis Gesticht onder de Benaming "Société d'émulation" te Brugge* 86 (1949): 5–22.
De Sturler, Jean. "Note sur l'emploi de poteries creuses dans les édifices du Moyen Age. A propos de la première église de Saint-Donatien à Bruges." *Le Moyen Age* 63 (1957): 241–65.
Declercq, Georges. "De dekens van het Sint-Donaaskapittel in Brugge voor

1200." *Handelingen van het Genootschap voor Geschiedenis Gesticht onder de Benaming "Société d'émulation" te Brugge* 125 (1988): 39–54.

Dhondt, Jan. "Iets over Brugge gedurende de preconstitutionele periode van haar geschiedenis." *Nederlandsche Historiebladen* 1 (1938): 218–303.

———. "De vroege topografie van Brugge." *Handelingen der Maatschappij voor Geschiedenis en Oudheidkunde te Gent* n.s. 11 (1957): 3–30.

Koch, A. C. F. "Brugge's topografische ontwikkeling tot in de 12e eeuw." *Handelingen van het Genootschap voor Geschiedenis Gesticht onder de Benaming "Société d'émulation" te Brugge* 99 (1962): 5–67.

Laude, Pierre-Joseph. *Catalogue méthodique, descriptif et analytique des manuscrits de la Bibliothèque publique de Bruges.* Bruges, 1859.

Mansion, H. "A propos de l'ancienne église Saint-Donatien à Bruges." *Revue belge d'archéologie et d'histoire de l'art* 8 (1938): 99–112.

Noterdaeme, Jérome. "De vroegste geschiedenis van Brugge, I: Ouderdom en herkomst van de Sint-Salvatorskerk." *Handelingen van het Genootschap voor Geschiedenis Gesticht onder de Benaming "Société d'émulation" te Brugge* 112 (1975): 5–30.

———. "De vroegste geschiedenis van Brugge, II: Ouderdom en herkomst van de O.L.-Vrouwekerk te Brugge." *Handelingen van het Genootschap voor Geschiedenis Gesticht onder de Benaming "Société d'émulation" te Brugge* 112 (1975): 31–59.

———. "De vroegste geschiedenis van Brugge, III: De burcht van Brugge." *Handelingen van het Genootschap voor Geschiedenis Gesticht onder de Benaming "Société d'émulation" te Brugge* 112 (1975): 171–89.

———. "De vroegste geschiedenis van Brugge, IV: Het problem van de twee marktpleinen." *Handelingen van het Genootschap voor Geschiedenis Gesticht onder de Benaming "Société d'émulation" te Brugge* 112 (1975): 190–204.

———. "De vroegste geschiedenis van Brugge, V: De Oudburg." *Handelingen van het Genootschap voor Geschiedenis Gesticht onder de Benaming "Société d'émulation" te Brugge* 113 (1976): 87–137.

———. "De vroegste geschiedenis van Brugge, VI: Ein ander 'Oudburg' te Brugge?" *Handelingen van het Genootschap voor Geschiedenis Gesticht onder de Benaming "Société d'émulation" te Brugge* 114 (1977): 211–48.

———. "De vroegste geschiedenis van Brugge, VII: Burg en Oudeburg." *Handelingen van het Genootschap voor Geschiedenis Gesticht onder de Benaming "Société d'émulation" te Brugge* 114 (1977): 249–310.

———. "De vroegste geschiedenis van Brugge, VIII: De eerste omwalling van Brugge." *Handelingen van het Genootschap voor Geschiedenis Gesticht onder de Benaming "Société d'émulation" te Brugge* 114 (1977): 311–38.

Rolland, Paul. "La Première église de Saint-Donatien à Bruges (quelques remarques)." *Revue belge d'archéologie et d'histoire et de l'art* 14 (1944): 101–11.

Ryckaert, Marc. "De Oudeburg te Brugge." In *Album Albert Schouteet,* 155–68. Bruges, 1973.

———. "Die Topographie der flandrischen Hafenstädte bis 1300: Das Beispiel von Brügge." *Lübecker Schriften zur Archäologie und Kulturgeschichte* 7 (1983): 47–55.

Strubbe, Egied I. "Van de eerste naar de tweede omwalling van Brugge." *Handelingen van het Genootschap voor Geschiedenis Gesticht onder de Benaming "Société d'émulation" te Brugge* 100 (1963): 271–300.

Verhulst, Adriaan. "Les origines et l'histoire ancienne de la ville de Bruges (IXe–XIIe siècle)." *Le Moyen Age* 66 (1960): 37–63.

———. "Les biens et revenus du chapitre Saint-Donatien de Bruges en 1089." In *Campagnes médiévales: L'homme et son espace. Etudes offertes à Robert Fossier,* edited by Elisabeth Mornet, 513–31. Histoire ancienne et médiévale 31. Paris, 1995.

Vincent, Jacques. "Au sujet de la tour et du 'solarium' de l'ancienne église Saint-Donatien à Bruges." *Revue belge d'archéologie et d'histoire de l'art* 14 (1944): 47–55.

CONTRIBUTORS

LISA H. COOPER is Assistant Professor in the Department of English of the University of Wisconsin-Madison. With the exception of her ongoing fascination with Galbert of Bruges, her work focuses primarily on the intersection of late-medieval literature and material culture. She is co-editor of *Lydgate Matters: Poetry and Material Culture in the Fifteenth Century* (New York: Palgrave Macmillan, 2008) and has recently completed a monograph on the literary representation of artisanal labor in the later Middle Ages.

GODFRIED CROENEN teaches at the University of Liverpool, where he is Director of the Liverpool Centre for Medieval and Renaissance Studies. He received his Ph.D. in medieval history from the University of Ghent for a study of the medieval nobility of Brabant, which was the subject of his first book (Leuven University Press, 2003). He has also published an innovative source edition connected to the same project: a reconstruction of the medieval archives of the Berthout family (Académie Royale de Belgique, 2007). His current research is concerned with vernacular historiography and the growing market for manuscripts in late medieval northwest Europe. He has recently co-edited a volume on manuscript culture in Paris (Peeters, 2006) and has published articles on the biography and the manuscripts of Jean Froissart's work in *Viator* (2002), in the *Journal of the Early Book Society* (2008), and in the conference volume *Froissart dans sa forge* (Collège de France, 2006). He is Associate Director of the Online Froissart Project (Sheffield and Liverpool).

BERT DEMYTTENAERE studied philosophy and history at the University of Ghent, taught medieval history and the theory of history for more than thirty years at the University of Amsterdam, translated the *De multro, traditione et occisione gloriosi Karoli comitis Flandriarum* of Galbert of Bruges into Dutch (last revised edition 2000), and has published a number of articles about Galbert and his world. In cooperation with Louk C. Meijer he is preparing a Dutch translation of Walter of Thérouanne's "Vita Karoli comitis Flandrię."

MARY AGNES EDSALL received her Ph.D. in English from Columbia University and is Assistant Professor of English at Bowdoin College, Maine. Her work focuses on reading practices and religious formation, lay, clerical, and monastic. Her long-standing interest in the fabliaux, however, keeps her aware of the lighter side of medieval life. Recent publications include articles on *Ancrene Wisse* and on *The Wanderer.* She is currently working on monastic anthologies and vernacular devotional collections, on the *Arma Christi,* and on Anselm's *Prayers and Meditations* as charismatic text.

MARTINA HÄCKER received her doctorate from the University of Freiburg, Germany, where she studied English language, medieval history, and medieval Latin, and gained her *Habilitation* in 2008. She currently teaches the history of the English language and linguistics at the University of Paderborn. She combines her diverse research interests in studies of the depiction of women in medieval literary and non-literary texts.

DIRK HEIRBAUT studied both law and history and is currently Professor of legal history and Roman law at the University of Ghent. His Ph.D. thesis was on feudal law in the county of Flanders from 1000 to 1305, and he has written or co-edited fifteen books on medieval legal history, the history of private law in Belgium after 1804, and legal history in general. His current work is on the spokesmen of the courts of customary law in Northern France. He is a Korrespondierender Mitglied der Zentraldirektion der Monumenta Germaniae Historica, secretary of the legal history committee of the Royal Flemish Academy of Belgium for Science and Arts, and a member of the board of editors of the *Tijdschrift voor Rechtsgeschiedenis/Legal History Review.*

STEVEN ISAAC earned his Ph.D. in medieval history from Louisiana State University and is now an Associate Professor of history at Longwood University in Virginia. Isaac's work looks most often at military culture, especially at the places before/after/around battles. To that end, his primary research has been on the mercenaries of the twelfth century: their origins, their motivations, the biases held against them, and their effect on both warfare and the societal institutions around them. Several book chapters and encyclopedia articles have resulted from this research. An interest in the emotional pressures of battle led to the current work on Galbert as well as a recent article, "Cowardice and Fear Management: the 1173–74 Conflict as a Case Study," in the *Journal of Medieval Military History* (2006).

ALAN V. MURRAY studied history, German language and literature, and folk studies at the universities of St. Andrews, Salzburg, and Freiburg and received his Ph.D. for a dissertation on the origins of the nobility of the kingdom of Jerusalem. He is currently Senior Lecturer in medieval studies at the University of Leeds and Editor of the *International Medieval Bibliography*. He has written numerous studies on the history of Germany and the Low Countries, the crusades and the Latin states of Outremer, medieval chronicles, and Middle High

German literature, and is particularly interested in reflexes of orality in medieval written narratives. His publications include two articles dealing with Galbert of Bruges and the Flemish Crisis of 1127–28: "Voices of Flanders: Orality and Constructed Orality in the Chronicle of Galbert of Bruges," *Handelingen der Maatschappij voor Geschiedenis en Oudheidkunde te Gent* n.s. 48 (1994): 103–19, and "The Judicial Inquest into the Death of Count Charles of Flanders (1127): Location and Chronology," *Revue de l'histoire du droit* 68 (2000): 47–61.

NANCY F. PARTNER is Professor of history at McGill University. Her research fields are medieval historical writing, applications of psychoanalysis for historical interpretation, and historical theory with special emphasis on narrative theory and epistemology. Recent publications include her edited book, *Writing Medieval History* (London: Hodder Arnold, 2005) to which she contributed the chapter, "The Hidden Self: Psychoanalysis and the Textual Unconscious." Forthcoming articles include: "The Linguistic Turn along Post-Postmodern Borders: Israeli/Palestinian Narrative Conflict," *New Literary History* (2009); and "Narrative Persistence: The Post-Postmodern Life of Narrative Theory," in *Refiguring Hayden White,* edited by Frank Ankersmit et al. (Stanford University Press). She is currently co-editing (with Sarah Foot, Oxford University) *The Handbook of Historical Theory* for Sage Publications.

JEFF RIDER received his Ph.D. in comparative literature from the University of Chicago and is a Professor of Romance languages and literatures and medieval studies at Wesleyan University. His work focuses on the history and literature of northern Europe from the eleventh through the thirteenth centuries. His recent publications include *God's Scribe: The Historiographical Art of Galbert of Bruges* (Washington, D.C.: The Catholic University of America Press, 2001) and Walter of Thérouanne, *Walteri archidiaconi Tervanensis, Vita Karoli comitis Flandrię et Vita domni Ioannis Morinensis Episcopi,* ed. Jeff Rider, Corpus Christianorum, Continuatio Medieualis 217 (Turnhout, Belgium: Brepols, 2006). He is currently at work on English translations of Galbert of Bruges's *De multro, traditione et occisione gloriosi Karoli comitis Flandriarum* and Walter of Thérouanne's *Vita Karoli comitis Flandrię.* He has received grants from the National Endowment for the Humanities, the Fulbright Commission, the American Philosophical Society, and the Rotary Foundation.

ROBERT M. STEIN is Doris and Carl Kempner Distinguished Professor in the Humanities at Purchase College, SUNY, and Adjunct Professor of English and comparative literature at Columbia University. He has written on contemporary critical theory as well as on medieval historiography and romance. His recent publications include *Reading Medieval Culture,* a festschrift for Robert Hanning, which he edited with Sandra Pierson Prior (2005), and *Reality Fictions: Romance, History, and Governmental Authority, 1025–1180* (Notre Dame, 2006). He is currently at work on an English translation, with introduction and commentary, of Gaimar's *Estoire des Engleis* (ca. 1150) for the French of England project.

R. C. VAN CAENEGEM is a medievalist and legal historian, who taught in the Faculty of Letters and the Faculty of Law in Ghent University from 1955 till 1992. He has written several books and articles on the general and legal history of England and the continent of Europe, as well as on introduction to the sources of medieval history. His collected articles were published in 1991 and 1994 by the Hambledon Press. His books have been translated into Chinese, Japanese, French, German, Italian, Portuguese, Spanish, Hungarian, and Macedonian.

INDEX

Galbert of Bruges and the Historiography of Medieval Flanders was designed and typeset in Adobe Garamond Premier Pro by Kachergis Book Design of Pittsboro, North Carolina. It was printed on 60-pound House Natural Smooth and bound by Sheridan Books of Ann Arbor, Michigan.